OWN ᴛʜᴇ DAY,
OWN YOUR LIFE

OWN THE DAY,
OWN YOUR LIFE

Optimized practices for

WAKING
WORKING
LEARNING
EATING
TRAINING
PLAYING
SLEEPING
and SEX

AUBREY MARCUS

Founder and CEO of Onnit

Thorsons

Thorsons
An imprint of HarperCollins*Publishers*
1 London Bridge Street
London SE1 9GF

www.harpercollins.co.uk

First published by in the USA by HarperWave,
an imprint of HarperCollins*Publishers* 2018

First published in the UK by Thorsons,
an imprint of HarperColllins*Publishers* 2018

9 10

A catalogue record of this book is
available from the British Library

ISBN 978-0-00-828641-5

Printed and bound in Great Britain by
CPI Group (UK) Ltd, Croydon, CR0 4YY

MIX
Paper from
responsible sources
FSC™ C007454

This book is produced from independently certified FSC™ paper
to ensure responsible forest management.

For more information visit: www.harpercollins.co.uk/green

Dedicated to your future self

CONTENTS

OWN THE DAY,
OWN YOUR LIFE

INTRODUCTION

Nothing is worth more than this day.

–JOHANN WOLFGANG VON GOETHE

Nutrition, mind-set, productivity, performance, fitness, sex, sleep—when we look through a keyhole at these areas of focus, we forget that they are interconnected and interdependent. They are spokes on the wheel of the day, every one of them necessary to ride the twenty-four-hour cycle into a life worth living. Because a day isn't just about what you put into your body, how you look in the mirror, or how much production you can squeeze from eight hours of work. It's about how you feel, whose lives you connect with, and how much fun you have along the way.

We have to transcend the tendency to place all of our effort on one thing at a time, instead of one day at a time. Just look at the flood of transformational programs out there: twelve days to detox, twenty-eight days to skinny, forty days to enlightenment, ninety days to astronaut. What do they give you? A diet that statistically fails 95 percent of all people or some email batching tips that are magically supposed to make you more productive. If you're lucky you'll leave with one or two takeaways that you actually implement in your life for a week or two. But real transformation? Unlikely. What is more likely is that everything else falls out of balance while you doggedly pursue your eight-pack abs.

So we are going to flip the script and recalibrate. We are going to focus on that single indivisible unit. That twenty-four hours. Just one day. You gotta walk before you run, and a day is the first step. To own your life, you gotta own the day. You're going to read this book, and then prepare to live one single day completely optimally.

Mark it on your calendar, get your head right, get your food right, and do it. You won't live every day like this right away. You may never live another day exactly like this again. But owning just one of them will be the catalyst to meaningful, demonstrable change. Maybe it's your morning routine, maybe it's how you prepare for sleep, or how you spend your drive to work. Maybe it's how you work out, or how you eat. Maybe it's everything! But one of those things is going to click first, and when it does, every day after that will be different. I dare you to read this book and not find things that substantially change how you live, and how you look at life. Maybe that will seem small at first. But small things, when compounded over time, tend to have big consequences. That, after all, is the essence of evolution.

Tipping Points and the Process

How many choices in your daily life are essentially toss-ups? Pizza or home cooking? Soda or sparkling water? Netflix or a night out? Should I go to the gym or not? Every day, nearly all of these choices are a fifty-fifty call. You could just as easily land in one place as the other. If you changed one thing you do within the first twenty minutes of waking up (I am going to give you three), however, or you had just a little bit more energy from a high-fat, low-sugar breakfast, maybe you'd choose differently. Maybe it would cease to be a question at all. *Of course you're going to the gym*. Then, because you went to the gym, you find yourself less stressed that night. So you have sex. Then you sleep better. Then you wake up more vibrant and with more energy. And you have set in motion a positive cascade of choices. The tipping point was one small change in breakfast. You exchanged your Apple Jacks for an avocado, and all of a sudden your day was different, your week was different, maybe your whole month was different.

Nick Saban, possibly the greatest coach in the history of college football, tells his players to follow what he calls "the Process." He tells them that the average down in football lasts about seven seconds. If they want to win an SEC championship, or a national title, they should focus on that smallest unit of measurement. Seven seconds. Don't get lost in the big picture, he says, and risk taking your eye off the prize. Focus on what's in front of you, focus on something you can chew and swallow. Focus on the micro, in other words, and the macro takes care of itself.

That's the approach we're going to take: The way to own your life is to own your day. *Today*. Because that's all you have.

The samurai master Miyamoto Musashi told students in his *Book of Five Rings*, "When you freely beat one man, you beat any man in the world. The spirit of defeating a man is the same for ten million men. The strategist makes small things into big things, like building a great Buddha from a one-foot model. The principle of strategy is having one thing, to know ten thousand things."

To live one day well is the same as to live ten thousand days well. To master twenty-four hours is to master your life.

Everyone Has Room to Improve

All human beings, every single one of us, have in some way taken a detour off the blueprint of optimal living. We can't help it, it's the world we live in. So we have to take measures as strong as the forces opposing us, or else we struggle.

I know from experience. Before I built Onnit into a movement that touches the lives of millions of people, I was stressed, depressed, and suffering as a consequence. Wild blood sugar swings from poor diet choices were exhausting me. I hurt my body with all sorts of toxic substances. I was sick . . . a lot. Then one day near my thirtieth birthday I made a commitment to be better. It was so significant that I decided to adopt my middle name as my first name, Aubrey, and to strike out from that moment as a better human being. I didn't have a perfect plan yet, like the one contained in this book. I wish I did. But I had choices, and I started making them. *Good* ones. I chose to take responsibility for my life. To own it. I chose to accept that whatever happened was on me. I would not hide behind the cozy blankets of relinquished responsibility any longer. I researched furiously, talked to everyone I could, and experimented tirelessly until I found the tools and practices that could bring me total human optimization. These hard-won understandings formed the nexus of a company with the mission to help bring these tools and techniques to the world.

This company, Onnit, has been as great a success as I dared to dream. Based in Austin, Texas, we've been honored to be of assistance to some of the most impressive people in the world: my partner from the word go, quintuple threat Joe Rogan; drummer Travis Barker; platinum rapper and actor Ludacris; Olympic gold medal downhill skier Bode Miller; three-time NHL Stanley Cup winners

Duncan Keith and Jonathan Toews; US women's soccer team member Lori "Lightning" Lindsey; Allison Holker of *Dancing with the Stars*; and mixed martial arts champions Cody Garbrandt, Tyron Woodley, and Michelle Waterson, among many others. You'll meet some of them in the book.

You know what we find when we sit down with them? They're not perfect either. They have the same struggles as you and I do. Maybe it's not getting enough sleep. Maybe their nutrition is off. Maybe they've got a bad habit, or they feel foggy all morning. Maybe they have some nagging injury that bothers them through the day. They are almost always dealing with stress, and they too sometimes doubt themselves.

The first thing we do with them is the first thing I'm going to do with you: examine your day. What do you do when you wake up? What do you eat? Are you getting enough of this vitamin or that one? Are you seeking good stress and avoiding the bad? Are you taking advantage of dead time when you travel? How do you wind down after a long day? Are you having enough sex? These little things add up. The little things *are* the big things—even for some of the most accomplished people on earth. If you fight in a cage for a living or dance live on television in front of millions of people, those smallest details can be the difference between success and failure. If you are the everyday kind of superhero, the one who works hard to support a family or build your career, these details are the tipping point between a life of passion and zeal and a life of gray monotony.

A Guide to the Book

To help guide you through the process of owning the day, we repeat the same formula in every chapter. We begin with a section we call "Getting Owned." We've all been there, getting pummeled by the waves of life, never seeming to catch our breath. Then we move on to "Owning It." Owning it is a matter of having the knowledge and the specific prescription needed to create positive, repeatable habits. We've tried to make this process as affordable as possible, but in the case where there are cool biohacking or performance techniques that cost a little more out of pocket, we have broken them into sections called "Pro Tips." Those are nonessential additions to owning the day. When we geek out on the science, you might see a section called "Deep Dive." Like the hundreds of citations at the end of the book, those are purely educational pieces for those of us with an inquiring mind. A section called "Caveat" will warn you about any non-obvious risks associated with a particular practice. All of this leads up to the section called "Prescription," which is the detailed specifics of how to accomplish what we are telling you to do. This leads to the most important section: "Now Do It." If we did a fraction of what we already knew we should, we would be in pretty good shape. Sometimes you just need a reminder and a kick in the ass to get it done. Finally, as a nod to my years spent on the basketball court, we end with a section called "Three Pointers," three important take-aways you need to remember from each chapter.

Ultimately, we are building toward one single day for you to plan, in advance, to completely own. It could be next week or next month or next fiscal quarter, but as you read, feel free to employ any of the techniques you find in these pages as you go along. That will only help you troubleshoot and be fully ready for that very first fully owned day. But make no mistake about it, your goal is to prepare and own one full day, like a total boss.

Are you ready? Then let's go hero, go!

1

WATER. LIGHT. MOVEMENT.

Well begun is half done.

—ARISTOTLE

How you wake up sets the tone for your day. Do you slide out of bed and slink through your social media, or do you have purpose in your actions? You want to take control of your day from the word go. So hydrate immediately (not with coffee!), then seek light and get moving to reset your internal clock. That's three simple things to do within twenty minutes of waking—and your day will be primed for perfection.

Getting Owned

In the days before fuel-injected engines, if you lived in a cold-weather city in the wintertime, you couldn't just hop in your car first thing in the morning, turn over the engine, throw it in gear, hammer the accelerator, and speed off into the rest of your day. If you tried, the car would be sluggish and perform haltingly at first, because the fluids that make the critical components of the engine function were not properly primed. If you persisted in speeding out of the driveway before the fluids were warm, you'd start to damage internal components, throwing off the engine's timing, resulting in a hefty mechanic's bill.

Even today, with fancy onboard computers, high-tech fuel injection, and all sorts of automotive bells and whistles, most experts will tell you that it's not a bad idea to let your car warm up for thirty to sixty seconds and then take it easy for the first few miles, especially if you're concerned with maximum performance and long-term durability.

Do you want to guess what proportion of people follow those fairly simple guidelines for warming up their vehicles? It's about the same as those who properly warm up their bodies upon waking. As a society, we tend to be as rough on our bodies as we are on our cars, which is unfortunate, since, unlike cars, we can't trade in our bodies for a newer model with lower mileage after twenty years of steady abuse. Instead of paying the mechanic, we pay the doctor—neither of which is a fun check to write.

A brief walk through the first hour of the average day should give you a good sense of what we're talking about here. The first sensation most of us register when we wake up is thirst. If you've managed to sleep well, you've just gone seven-plus hours without drinking a drop of water. If you're in a dry climate, worked out the previous afternoon, or partied hard the night before, you likely hit the pillow at a fluid deficit out of the gate. Depending on the temperature of your room and how many blankets you sleep under, you may have even accelerated the dehydration process through sweat. In combination, the vapor from respiration and perspiration can often amount to a pound of water lost overnight. As a result, we regularly wake up feeling like we've been nursing on a cotton ball.

You would think that the logical response to this condition would be to get up and drink some water, to lubricate all those critical internal components we need to fire correctly for our bodies to be most effective today and for the long haul. Instead, what most of us do is hide under the covers, hitting the snooze button like a snare drum until the last possible moment, at which point we hurry out of bed, strip our clothes off, step into the shower and pour an average of twenty scalding-hot gallons of water over our body, then dump three more quarts through a drip coffee maker. We rarely think to actually *drink* any of this water before it goes down the drain or through the filter, which is insane; if the physical sensations we experience when we wake up happened to us in the middle of our day, we'd say "Damn, I'm thirsty" and then crush a glass of water. Starting the day, though, it always ends with us holding a cup of coffee.

I have news for you: the best part of waking up is *not* coffee in your cup. *But, Aubrey, I'm not myself without a cup of coffee in the mornings. I need it.* No, you don't. Waking up your body with coffee is like setting off a fire alarm as an alarm clock. When you're dehydrated and have nothing in your stomach, the caffeine enters your bloodstream incredibly fast, releasing a flood of stress hormones from your adrenal glands that your body reads as a fight-or-flight trigger. Like you've been woken up being chased by a predatory cat. While this is effective in the short term, it's generally a good rule of thumb to keep aggressive caffeine and feline doses to a minimum first thing in the morning. Drinking caffeine when you are dehydrated may feel good for the mouth, but you aren't exactly digging out of the hole. The hydrating water in the coffee is somewhat offset by the dehydrating nature of caffeine. Yet we still reach for coffee in the morning, in large part because these adrenal effects are so damn good at dealing with the other problem we face when we wake up: *we're still tired*.

Only one in seven people report waking up feeling refreshed after sleeping. Almost half of all Americans report feeling fatigued at least three times during the week. As a nation, Americans are owned and controlled by fatigue and the tools used to fight it. We are chronically tired because we are constantly screwing up our sleep. Sleepiness and energy levels are regulated by something called circadian rhythm, which tells your body when it's time to wake up and when to sleep. You may have heard it referred to as your body clock or your internal clock. And contrary to popular practice, the hands of that internal clock are not powered by Starbucks. They are powered by sunlight and movement. So when you shuffle your feet around a dimly lit house with your comfy robe on, your body can't tell if you are awake, asleep, or skinwalking as a cave bear. By restricting those important cues that signal the start of a circadian cycle on a regular basis, your entire body gets thrown out of whack. When you add dehydration to the equation, things only get worse. That's why, despite our best intentions, we so often don't feel like working out, our brains are in a fog, we suffer from headaches, and we're generally on edge and just plain tired. Really tired. Except when it comes time to go to sleep, of course, because then, miraculously, despite being tired all day, we can't sleep. Sound like anyone you know? If not, you need more friends, because the CDC estimates that between 50 and 70 million Americans have a sleep disorder. You *have* to know at least one of those people!

There are studies on both men and women showing that even

mild dehydration resulting from fluid loss equaling roughly 1 percent of your body weight can cause headaches, moodiness, irritability, anxiety, and fatigue. Decreases in mental performance and short-term memory loss can start at as little as a 2 percent loss in water. You ever find yourself being 1 or 2 percent lighter in the morning than before bed? That is enough. And for reference, mixed martial arts fighters commonly cut up to 10 percent of their body weight before a fight. No wonder they are always yelling and pointing at each other in their underwear on weigh-in day! When you consider that 78 percent of Americans are chronically dehydrated, based on their water intake, that does not paint a pretty picture of the start of the average day. It paints a picture of us getting royally owned.

But it isn't just the water itself that is the problem. We lose electrolytes and minerals over the course of our sleep as well. Minerals are key to modulating and supporting numerous body processes, from the muscles to the organs and even the brain. Without adequate minerals, many of the body's normal functions start to diminish. Well, guess what, we are just as bad at replacing our minerals on a regular basis as we are at getting ourselves moving and into the sunlight to start our days.

There is a solution to all that: a three-part formula that involves a simple morning mineral cocktail for hydration and adds a little bit of sunlight and a little bit of movement to reset your internal clock, taking you from getting owned to owning it within the first twenty minutes of your day. I've tested it, the athletes and high performers I work with have confirmed it, and clinical research has proven it: hydration and circadian balance are the essential ingredients to the consistent perfect wake-up. The formula I am going to walk you through now, then, is about mastering the levels of these essential ingredients so that the morning sets you up for owning the day every time.

Owning It

On an ordinary day a thousand years ago, Emperor Marcus Aurelius had trouble getting out of bed. We know this because he wrote about it in his journal, a remarkable document never intended for publication that somehow managed to survive through the eons. What's most remarkable is how modern Marcus's struggle reads to us.

A notorious insomniac but a dedicated public servant, Marcus writes: "At dawn, when you have trouble getting out of bed, tell yourself: 'I have to go to work—as a human being. What do I have to complain of, if I'm going to do what I was born for—the things which I was brought into the world to do? Or is this what I was created for? To huddle under the blankets and stay warm?'"

Of course, no matter how much we love our life, getting out of bed is no easy task. As a Stoic, Marcus suggested one remedy for getting over this hump: discipline. His sense of duty was what propelled him through the morning and into the world.

You can have all the stoic discipline you want, but if you don't handle the first twenty minutes after you get out of bed correctly, you are going to be fighting an uphill battle all day. Tough mornings aren't tough because of insufficient willpower. They're tough because no one teaches us how to make them easy, let alone perfect, even though the perfect start to your day is perfectly within reach.

It's about building momentum. You know this because you've had one of these mornings before. When there isn't a rushed second, when you feel like you're a step ahead of everything and the whole day feels like it's at your leisure. Most of us have these days completely by accident, but the reality is, we can have them on purpose, and we can have them regularly.

Hydration

The first step is proper hydration. Sixty percent of the average adult human body is made up of water. About the same percentage of Earth's surface is covered by water. The world is water, we are water, yet here we are, every morning, essentially starving for it. And we wonder why we wake up feeling miserable so often.

A glass of water from the bathroom tap or tipping your head back in the shower is not going to cut it, however. This isn't just about curing cottonmouth. Health coach and sleep expert Shawn Stevenson calls that first glass of water in the morning "a cool bath for your organs." Another way of putting it: it's priming your internal fluids before hitting the road.

All I am asking is that you swap your first-thing-in-the-morning coffee for some water and minerals, in a drink I call the morning mineral cocktail. I'm not asking you to eliminate coffee—God forbid, coffee is delicious—just hold off on it until you've hydrated properly and can mix it with some fats like butter or coconut oil to slow it down. (You'll learn more about the importance of fats in the coming chapters.) The components of my morning mineral cocktail are water, sea salt, and a splash of lemon. I'm not saying that the cocktail is magic, but . . . it's basically magic. (Drink it and thank me.)

Morning Mineral Cocktail

350ml filtered water   ¼ lemon, squeezed
3g sea salt

▮ WATER: DO IT RIGHT

Despite the proliferation of fitness magazine listicles and online hydration calculators, there is no magic formula for the amount of water you should be drinking. Depending on habituation, diet, workload, toxicity, and a number of other fluctuating factors, every individual's water needs will vary. As a general rule of thumb, err on the side of more water than not enough. Make a good glass or aluminum water bottle your favorite accessory so you have water available to you at all times. If it's in another room and you're like me, you'll probably wait until you are dying of thirst to get up and go chug some water like a toddler who just found his sippy cup after a long day on the playground. Keep your water close, and sip often.

Just as important as drinking enough water is drinking the right kind of water. Water is one of nature's best solvents, which means that most of the solids it comes in contact with eventually dissolve into it. That's great when it comes to absorbing minerals, but problematic when it comes to certain solids like plastics that contain harmful chemicals like BPA that can throw your hormone balance out of whack and set you up for a host of associated issues. As such, it's important to choose your water sources wisely.

In a perfect world, you'd be able to suckle from the teat of Mother Nature and drink spring water exclusively. Spring water has the right balance of what you want (useful minerals), with little to none of what you don't (chlorine, heavy metals, contaminants). When I switched to spring water, I stayed more hydrated through the night, which meant a better quality of sleep all around. The reason is that my body wasn't just thirsty for water; it was thirsty for the minerals called electrolytes that are present in spring water but absent in most filtered waters.

I recognize that buying several liters of spring water in glass bottles every day can get expensive, but many of us still have access to free spring water. Before you go buying anything, check findaspring .com to see if there is any clean, free spring water next to where you live. For those of us not quite that lucky and who also do not have a line item for water in our grocery budgets, the next best thing is filtered water—either through a Brita pitcher you fill and stick in the refrigerator, a Pur filter you attach straight to your kitchen tap, or whatever high-quality filter is available near you. This takes care of the problem of things floating in your water that you don't want. But then you have to make sure you get enough of the stuff you do want. Specifically, you need to add mineral electrolytes, like those found in sea salt, to get you properly hydrated and mineralized. A small pinch of sea salt into distilled or filtered water should help reset the balance. Add a wedge of lemon juice for some additional refreshing nutrients (a lighter version of the morning mineral cocktail) and you've optimized your water. It's what the pro fighters do when they are recovering from cutting weight, and if it's good enough for the best in the world on their most important day, it should be good enough for us too. (We'll cover the effects of inadequate mineralization in chapter 4.)

SALT: THE ORIGINAL MINERAL SUPPLEMENT

Sea salt contains upward of sixty trace minerals above and beyond the sodium, chloride, and iodine in regular table salt, including phosphorus, magnesium, calcium, potassium, bromine, boron, zinc, iron, manganese, and copper. Together they are essential for healthy bodily function and contribute meaningfully to optimal performance. Sodium binds to water in the body to maintain the proper level of hydration inside and outside our cells. Along with potassium, it also helps maintain electrical gradients across cell membranes, which are critical for nerve transmission, muscle contraction, and various other functions. Without it, needless to say, we would be toast.

Unfortunately, salt has become a dirty word over the past few decades—for two reasons: (1) it causes water retention (really just another way to say "makes us more hydrated"), and (2) it increases blood pressure. Both of these claims are technically true. When there are higher concentrations of salt in the body, it is able to hold more water, and your blood will be a little bit thicker. Thicker blood raises your blood pressure slightly because it takes more force to pump.

But is this a problem? While high blood pressure is correlated to cardiovascular disease, an analysis of eight randomized controlled trials showed insufficient evidence that the reduction of salt in one's diet prevented cardiovascular death or disease. Two further epidemiological studies on populations of 11,346 and 3,681 subjects confirm those findings. There is no conclusively proven benefit to sodium restriction when it comes to preventing heart disease or death—especially for those with a healthy heart. What likely happened here was a classic case of correlation, rather than causation. High blood pressure is correlated to obesity. Obesity is correlated to heart disease. But the increase in high blood pressure caused by salt has not been shown to cause heart disease. As we'll learn throughout this book, this isn't the first time that the authorities got their nutrition advice wrong. They should have looked to the history books for some commonsense guidance.

Salt has been a part of our diet for millennia. Roman soldiers of antiquity were "paid" with an allotment of salt. The words *salt* and *salary* are derived from the same Latin root word: *sal*. When we describe people's worth or utility, we refer to whether they are "worth their salt." So why was salt such a big deal? Well, if you were a Roman soldier marching around the empire, swinging swords everywhere you went, you had to hydrate and replenish the minerals you lost through sweat, and salt was the surest way to do that.

Can you overdo salt consumption? Of course you can. All medicine becomes poison at a certain dose, but the point of all this is that salt, particularly in its most mineral-rich form, is not the demon it has been made out to be. As for which sea salt to choose, pink Himalayan salt comes from ancient oceanic deposits—long before oil tankers and Jet Skis were crisscrossing Earth's waters—and also has the benefit of additional iron, which gives it its pink hue. For women who tend to be lower in iron, cooking, seasoning, and mineralizing with pink salt is a great option. But any regular old sea salt will do, as long as it comes from a good source. Kosher salt means nothing nutritionally; it is purely a religious distinction, so don't get confused. Shalom!

Get Lit

You can give a plant all the water it will ever need, but if it isn't exposed to enough light, it just won't grow. It'll only drown. The same is true for human beings. You can hydrate until you have mineral cocktail coming out of your ears, but that's only one of the variables in this morning math problem we're trying to solve. A lack of sufficient or timely exposure to light will short-circuit every attempt you make to start your mornings off with the kind of energy necessary to own the day. This is a problem that everyone faces, from students to self-employed moms to workaholic dads to professional athletes. Biologically we are supposed to wake up with the sun and go to sleep with the stars. This is the timing that our body patterned for millennia, and the essence of circadian rhythm.

To the average person, circadian balance might not seem all that important until you realize that, as your circadian rhythms go, so goes the rest of your life. Women with atypical circadian rhythm, for example, have unusual eating and hormone patterns. This physiological and behavioral cycle follows the typical twenty-four-hour day, and controls a huge variety of biological processes, from the sleep-wake cycle to body temperature, metabolism, and even the life of the cell. The timing of these rhythms can easily become altered by the environment or choices we make, which can cause internal desynchronization. Sometimes this desynchronization manifests as jet lag, sometimes as sleep problems. There is even an association with increased incidence of cancer. Not to mention waking up extremely freaking early, even though all you really want to do is sleep in a little bit. What this means, very simply, is that the more synchronized your circadian rhythms are, the better your life becomes.

The strongest synchronizing agent for the circadian system? You guessed it: light. Specifically, blue light. Even more specifically, environmental light, aka sunlight, which is the most natural and abundant source of blue light. None of this should be too much of a surprise. The natural life-giving, regulating force of the sun—whether we understood it as a source of blue light or not—has drawn humans toward it for millennia. It's why we find ourselves wandering out so often to look at the sky during dawn and at dusk. It's why sunset cruises are so popular at beach vacation resorts. It's why the road up to Haleakala Crater on Maui is packed at 4:00 a.m. during the high season in anticipation of the epic sunrise. It speaks to us. It's our body being drawn, unconsciously, to the energy and rhythm of the sun. When we deny it, we begin to fall out of our own rhythm. When we accept and engage it, things begin to fall into place.

To rely on the sun to live in accord with Earth's natural biorhythms, however, is virtually impossible in modern life. Everyone would have to go to bed shortly after it gets dark (for most of us equator huggers, that's around 9:00 p.m.) and wake up when it's light (around 6:00 a.m.). The real world often requires a different schedule. Maybe you're a very early riser, or you sleep during the day and work at night, or you simply decide that nocturnal pleasures outweigh the delights of dawn. (Personally, I enjoy when the house is quiet after 10:00 p.m., so I prefer a midnight–7:00 a.m. sleep schedule.) Whatever the reason, you and the sun might not be on speaking terms on occasion. This creates a twofold problem: circadian rhythm disruption and a lack of means for fixing it.

This is what Duncan Keith, assistant captain of the NHL's Chicago Blackhawks, was feeling during his 2014–15 season. His body clock was getting out of whack because he traveled a lot and worked at night in a profession where he spends most of his time during the season in darkness. A lot of hockey cities are in the frozen north, above the wall where the wildlings live, and two-thirds of the regular season schedule take place there, coinciding with the curious day-light savings custom. This meant that walking outside to get some sunlight was rarely an option for Duncan. As a result, his circadian rhythms were often out of sync with the ebbs and flows of his life. It was enough that he was noticing an effect on energy and alertness come game time.

To help solve Duncan's problem, we talked about a tweak to his routine that everyone can, and should, make to their own routine to reset their circadian rhythms. He got into the light every time he woke up—from sleep or from a nap.

The results of this blue-light tweak, with other supplement and nutrition improvements to Duncan's game-day protocol, speak for themselves: not only did the Blackhawks go on to win the Stanley Cup that year, but Duncan was named Finals MVP as the winner of the Conn Smythe Trophy. ESPN called his performance during the postseason an "indefatigable two-month surge" and "one of the most dominant . . . in NHL history." He played more than thirty minutes per game and logged more than 700 minutes of playing time over the course of the playoffs—both of which are ridiculous numbers that put him in rarefied company as a defenseman. I'm not going to take any credit for his performance—he's a fucking savage—but the adjustment to his postsleep light exposure and the rest of the tips and tactics you'll find in this book certainly didn't hurt! And it certainly won't hurt your performance either.

Movement

I haven't said anything about order for these first three essential ingredients to the perfect wake-up, but I will tell you how I start the best of my mornings: I wake up quietly. I have my morning mineral cocktail. I step outside into the rising sun. Then I sneak up on my just-waking fiancée. With ninja stealth, I make a slow and calculated attack. She protests, I laugh. I tease her in a bad Portuguese accent about her nickname "Miss2Jits" and the fact that she is a blue belt and I'm just a white belt. Eventually she's had enough of my mouthiness and we grapple to see who can gain dominant position.

To me, there is no better start to the morning than this. It's a chance to practice my "jits" and wrestle with a beautiful naked woman. While it's a disaster for keeping the fitted sheet on the mattress, it's totally worth it. If you've never tried coed naked jujitsu, you haven't really lived! (Side note: Remember how popular those Coed Naked sports shirts were? Whatever happened to those?) But this isn't just a fun little diversion to delay getting to work. There is real science behind adding a few minutes of playful activity in the morning. Even light exercise boosts circulation and improves cognitive performance. It releases endorphins and, most important of all, helps entrain that fickle bastard, our circadian rhythm. In addition to sufficient blue-light exposure, regular activity—however brief— sends strong cues to the body that it is time to wake up and get going. It helps set that internal biological clock.

Prescription

The morning prescription comes in three parts: hydrate, get lit, and move it.

Hydrate. There are no secret, scary, crazy steps to combining these ingredients into the morning mineral cocktail, but there are a couple things you want to be mindful of during preparation and consumption. First, the water should be room temperature. When you're looking to maximize mineral absorption and aid digestion, room temperature is always best for any beverage. And second, the salt needs to dissolve or stay off the bottom of the glass when you drink it. Salt is the essential component for mineralization, but since it is denser than water, it sinks to the bottom before it dissolves if you let it come to rest after mixing. Then you end up with a salty sludge at the bottom of your glass that, unless you have a tongue like beef cattle, you're gonna find hard to get out of there.

The best way to avoid that problem is to simply mix the cocktail in a shaker or a water bottle. You can make the whole thing the night before, you can make a concentrate and add the water in the morning, or you can do the whole thing from scratch every day, like a little ritual, but doing it in something with a lid allows you to drink at a pace you're comfortable with, which is important. You don't want to force the cocktail down; that only turns the whole process into something that feels more like punishment and less like nourishment. Whichever method is best for you is the method you should employ, because this is the ultimate lubricant for sliding into the day, and it would be a shame if you missed out on it.

Get lit. Upon waking, either from sleep or a nap, blast yourself with five to ten minutes of direct blue-light exposure. Ideally, you'll be able to do this by stepping outside and exposing as much of your skin as possible to that giant yellow orb in the sky, basking in its bright, warm blueness, like a cat with less body hair. When that's not possible, you'll need to adapt. Fortunately, there is a good biohack at your disposal that can do the trick.

Pro Tip—Human Charging

Light-emitting earbuds. Believe it or not, the retinas are not the only light-sensitive receptors on the human body. These receptors are also found in many locations on the brain, including the cerebrum and the hypothalamus. One of the surest ways to shine light on them is through the ears. A device called the HumanCharger25, made by a company named Valkee out of Helsinki, Finland, has pioneered this technology for consumer use. Their light-emitting device uses earbuds, like the kind you'd buy at an airport newsstand or an Apple Store, that make it feel like you're shining light straight onto your brain through your ear canals. It sounds crazy, I know, but a number of studies have shown it to be incredibly effective in reducing symptoms and increasing cognitive performance in people with seasonal affective disorder who have limited exposure to natural sunlight.

Move it. Of the three parts to this energy equation, this is by far the most difficult for people. The urge to crawl back under the blankets and slam the snooze button like a whack-a-mole is incredibly strong. The key to overcoming that resistance is understanding that what we're talking about here is not a morning workout. This is morning *movement*.

There are many ways to get this movement in. Even just light movement will increase core temperature, cortisol, circulation, and the release of endorphins that will make you more alert, and put that grogginess behind you. I want it to be fun for you, so pick what you like: light yoga, pushups, air squats, jumping jacks, a Richard Simmons clip on YouTube. Chase your dog around the house or pick your kid up and fly her around like an airplane. It doesn't really matter; it's all part of circadian entrainment. Here are some of my go-to morning movements.

▌ QUICK AND DIRTY: 1–3 MINUTES

Twenty-three burpees. Why? I like the number 23. I wore it on my back for years out on the basketball court, and to this day it makes me happy. If you are feeling frisky, add the pushup to the bottom of the burpee. If you need to break this up into several sets, go for it. Otherwise the whole thing should be over in about a minute. If twenty-three feels like a real workout to you, make up your own number. The key is simply that your heart rate gets elevated and muscles start working.

SLOW AND SEXY: 5–10 MINUTES

This is a little yoga flow I developed for the morning. I hold each position for two full intentional breaths, allowing up to one breath for the transition. Start standing with your palms open and facing outwards. Then forward fold. Walk your hands forward into down dog. Bring your left leg up parallel to your hands, into lizard lunge. Take your left hand and open it up to the sky for spinal twist. Put your hand back down. Take your leg back to high plank. Do a pushup (drop to knees if necessary). Repeat on the right side. When you complete the pushup, walk your hands back to forward fold. Roll up one vertebra at a time. Raise your arms, into a gentle backbend, then bring your hands down and your arms to center prayer pose. Repeat as many times as you like.

Pro Tip—Rebounder

Buy a dorky little mini trampoline called a rebounder to get the juices flowing. If you watched the Tony Robbins documentary *I Am Not Your Guru*, this is one of the things he uses to jump-start his biology before heading out onstage at the event venue. Proponents claim benefits to the lymph system (key to healthy immune function) due to the G-forces created from gravitational un-loading. While this has yet to be conclusively proven, regular low-leg exercise has been shown to improve lymph movement. So regardless, the rebounder qualifies. Not only that, the bouncing is going to help build coordination and balance as well, as shown in a study on fighter pilots. For me personally, I feel like it brings circulation all the way from my head to my feet. Nothing shakes off the grogginess like bouncing like the one and only Tigger. Super triple bonus points if you sing the Tigger song, "The Wonderful Thing about Tiggers", while bouncing.

The point here is not to exercise, it is to elevate your heart rate and get the lead out—all without crossing the threshold for activity that requires some form of recovery. You don't want to be sore as a result of this early-morning activity, and you don't want it to diminish your workout later, but generally speaking you want to eliminate the segregation between ordinary sedentary life and that forty-five-minute block of time where you work out at the gym. We want to add movement, activity, and play into all parts of your day, especially the beginning, to set the tone for the day to come. I think you'll find that a little play wrestling can do as much as a cup of coffee, especially if you're ticklish and the claws come out.

Now Do It

Starting and finishing are the two hardest parts of any task. Taking the first step is bringing your inertia from a dead halt into motion. Or as billionaire PayPal founder Peter Thiel would say, going from zero to one. It's like trying to push a car. The bulk of the effort is actually getting the wheels to start rolling. From there you can mostly coast and steer. Getting hydrated, getting light, and getting moving is that initial momentum. We're not asking you to wake up in the morning like a Jamaican bobsledder, jumping from the sheets into a full sprint, we're just asking you to complete three simple tasks.

Accomplish these in the first twenty minutes, and you have set the tone for the entire day. It's your on-ramp to the highway of happiness and effectiveness. It ensures you will be sufficiently warmed up and lubricated, so when we hit the gas later on in the day, you roar like the muscle car you are.

So ask yourself, are you going to hide from the day under your blankets, squander these minutes and let them pass by, lazily waking up, checking your social media, shoving another pod into the espresso machine? Are you going to succumb to comfort? Or are you gonna own it and stretch yourself a little bit? It's an exercise of will. It's an exercise of choice. It's a routine that will determine how you perform throughout the day and even how you sleep later that night.

Hydration, light, movement. That's all it takes. That's all it will ever take. With a regimen this simple, great mornings should not feel like miracles. They should not arrive like a rainbow—a beautiful surprise that is out of your control. You are the captain of your internal universe. You choose to go get the sun and the water and to move the clouds of stagnation in your body to make your own fucking rainbow.

THREE POINTERS

- Circadian rhythm influences many biological functions. To optimize circadian rhythm for performance, you need to add light and movement to the first twenty minutes upon waking up.
- Most of us are chronically dehydrated, particularly in the morning. To start your hydration off right, drink the morning mineral cocktail to ensure you are getting adequate water and electrolytes.
- We are highly sensitive to momentum. By starting your morning off with intention, you set your day off on an important positive trajectory.

2

DEEP BREATH, DEEP FREEZE

If you tiptoe into cold water, you're missing out on the rush of plunging in headfirst.

–SIMONE ELKELES

Breath and the cold are the best friends you never knew you had. In fact, you've probably been ignoring one and hiding from the other for as long as you can remember. Well, it's time to emerge from your cozy hiding spot in the hot morning shower and embrace your new allies in the fight against stress and its many cohorts. Once you're done washing and indulging, take a deep breath, then thirty more, and crank that shower knob to as cold as it can get, because each morning needs to involve the rush that comes with exposing yourself to nature's extremes for a few minutes and the willpower you cultivate in the process.

Getting Owned

Wim Hof owns two dozen extreme sports world records. He has run a marathon above the Arctic Circle with no shirt on. He has hiked past the death zone on Mount Everest, also with no shirt on . . . in a blizzard. You might think he just hates shirts, but there is a method to his madness. At age fifty-seven, Wim hasn't been sick in a decade, his joints don't ache, and he still enjoys a Heineken (or two) with dinner. His nickname is the "Iceman" but he wasn't born a super-hero, he made himself into one. He isn't a daredevil, either. He's just dared to tap the potential we all have inside, by exposing his body to the resistance of extreme natural stressors, so that it—and he—may grow stronger as a result.

Wim's uniqueness is undeniable, but there is nothing unreplicable in this man. He is not a physical anomaly, nor part penguin. He could be you or me, or anyone. Or rather, we could be him, if we made some of the same choices he has made. Instead, most of us have shied away from exposure to the acute stress of difficult con-ditions. We choose cozy over cold, automatic over intentional, and with nothing to harden us, we get soft.

Think about it. Our cars have climate control. We have jackets and scarves, and fans, and air conditioning. We can spend the whole day in our office—lunch delivered—without ever going out in the blistering Texas heat or the biting Chicago wind. If we're lucky, our homes have heated floors so when we go to the bathroom in the night our little feetsies don't get cold. Our entire culture is built on the elimination of the difficult and the pursuit of the comfortable. Everything panders to it, and we buy into it because we've got all these old scripts running through our heads from our mothers and doctors and crazy old neighbors: *If you go out in this cold without a jacket, you might catch your death. Put some shoes on, you'll catch a cold.*

Though it was always scientifically dubious, there was a time when this idea wasn't so crazy. It used to be the harshness of nature that was the greatest threat to human survival, not heart disease or driving. In that sense, one way to look at the frantic warnings of our elders is as the modern version of the prehistoric fight-or-flight stress response. For most of primate history (including our brief history as human primates) we had things trying to fight us, hunt us, and kill us—whether animal, environmental, or fellow man. Our bodily response to that stress is brilliant. We temporarily shut down all systems inessential to the necessary response. We scuttle immune response, reproduction, growth, and digestion processes in favor of musculoskeletal efficiency and cognitive performance. In other words, when threatened we push all our energetic resources to help us move well and think fast. That process—largely modulated by "stress hormones" like cortisol, adrenaline, and norepinephrine— has saved countless human asses and is probably why your grandma can't totally explain why, when you were a kid, she scrambled to wrap you in a jacket made out of a sleeping bag when it dropped below 60 degrees and then hustled you inside once you were done with whatever brought you outside in the first place.

The real problem is when the body can't distinguish between physical threats and psychosocial threats—threats to our job security, or bank account, or social status. These threats often have no concrete conclusion, and so the stress hormones that were built for brief bursts to ward off acute stress go buck wild in your brain box, and chronic stress develops. Leading neuroscientist and stress specialist Robert Sapolsky summed it up for the *Stanford News*: "If you plan to get stressed like a normal mammal, you had better turn on the stress response or else you're dead. But if you get chronically, psychosocially stressed, like a Westernized human, then you are more at risk for some of the leading causes of death in Westernized life."

That is the great irony of the modern, westernized world. Times have changed. We've advanced. Things have gotten better. So why is it that now that everything is so comfortable, we are sick all the time? America spends more on health care than any other nation, and yet we keep getting sicker. And that isn't just among the older, high-risk population. Young Americans are getting sicker too. A 2013 report by the Institute of Medicine and National Research Council found that "for many years, Americans have been dying at younger ages than people in almost all other high income countries." Survival rates of American women under fifty, for example, are plummeting in comparison to their first-world peers. How is this possible? We are the inventors of Nike, the Fitbit, and the kale smoothie, dammit! We should be terminators. We have every app and gadget in the world, all trying to make it *easy* for us. Yet everything seems so damn fraught and complicated.

And that highlights the problem, right there. You see, collectively and individually, we are in a dysfunctional relationship with stress. We have too much of the bad, chronic kind, and not enough of the good, acute kind. What makes things worse, we don't force ourselves to confront acute stress, because chronic stress has eaten away at our willpower, and as a result we don't know how to strengthen the muscles of our resolve. We become powerless to cultivate the willpower we require to make the best choices for our lives. The bad stress beats us down, exhausts our energy, and in a very real sense, starts to kill us. My friend the Olympic gold medal skier Bode Miller used to describe this state as "overwhelmed and underqualified." (He also taught me a lot about the solution—a skill I call mental override—but more on that later.) It is fertile ground for the unvirtuous cycle of stress and illness.

In fact, in a survey reported by the American Psychological Association, there was a strong correlation between high levels of stress and poor health scores. Chronic stress, which brings with it chronic inflammation, suppresses the immune system, increases occurrence of pain, and is a major correlative to depression. That's a lot. It's no wonder that upward of 75 percent of all doctor visits have a stress-related component. What *is* a wonder, however, is that less than 3 percent of doctor visits include counseling about stress. Maybe it has something to do with the 76 percent of physicians surveyed who lacked confidence in their ability to counsel patients about stress, or the 57 percent who "rarely" or "never" practice stress reduction techniques themselves. Institutionally, individually, collectively, and sometimes even me personally—we are getting owned by stress.

To fix the problems, what we need are simple strategies for reducing the bad, chronic stress and diving feetfirst into the good, acute stress. Fortunately, we can find both in a two-part regimen from that crazy Dutchman who went topless to the top of the world. Wim Hof's conscious breathing techniques and cold exposure practices are going to deliver for us the reduction in bad, chronic stress we need for greater health, and the increase in good, acute stress we need for more consistent growth in both our body and our character. The best part: we can do them at the same time, just like it happens in nature, and develop our willpower in the process.

Owning It

Wim Hof's many physical feats are astonishing even to consider, but what is truly impressive is what he has been able to teach others to do. Wim has trained groups of ordinary men and women as old as sixty-five to climb with him up Kilimanjaro. And yes, some of them went without a shirt on. He has proven in a laboratory-controlled study that he can teach people to alter the immune system's inflammatory response to pathogens—rewriting both textbooks and expectations in the process. His work on breath and cold has also turned him into a performance coach of sorts for some of the greatest athletes and performers in the world, including the biggest of all coaches (in more ways than one), Tony Robbins.

Arguably the most successful motivational speaker in history,

Tony Robbins is nothing short of a human dynamo. He's a bundle of indefatigable energy capable of nearly inhuman feats. He's six feet seven inches tall but spry and nimble. He can walk across hot coals and keep a crowd of thousands captivated during his legendary weeklong motivation marathons. All of this he embodies at virtually the same age as Wim Hof himself (they're born ten months apart), after decades of emotionally demanding work and a calendar perpetually filled with grueling international travel.

If you ask Tony, a big part of his capability springs from the fundamentals of the routine I am going to lay out for you in this chapter. As he says, "It's not exactly a gentle way to wake up, but that's beside the point." In fact, it *is* the point, because this two-part ritual—deliberate, conscious breathing exercises and cold-water exposure—goes a long way toward explaining Tony's bottomless resolve, vitality, and energy. It also explains why he's been one of the most successful people in history: he practices overcoming resistance every single day.

The Breath

There are hundreds of different breathing traditions from all over the world. Some are shrouded in arcane symbolism. Others come with complicated instructions, like the world's worst IKEA dresser: ring finger to the left nostril; spiral helix breath in lotus posture; "turn your stomach into the shape of a vase." Huh? Wim Hof cuts through that bullshit. His instructions are simple. He just wants you to get the breath in. It doesn't matter which hole it comes through, because it's what the breath does for you that matters to him. Here is his method in two steps.

▮ STEP I: THIRTY TO FIFTY POWER BREATHS
Inhale through the nose or mouth into the belly with deep, powerful breaths. Exhale without additional effort, just let the chest fall. Keep

a steady pace and make sure to focus on drawing the breath deep into your belly. Do this until you feel a slight light-headedness and a tingling sensation in your extremities. That is the sign that a shift is happening and your blood is hyperoxygenated. For most people that effect starts to kick in around thirty breaths, but it can take up to fifty, depending on certain factors.

Note: It's important not to overbreathe to the point of serious light-headedness, strong tingles, or involuntary closing of the hands. That will take you beyond the currently desired effect and into the realm of a practice called holotropic or shamanic breathing, which is a topic for a different book.

STEP 2: THE HOLD (RETENTION AFTER EXHALATION)

After the thirty to fifty breaths, or once you start to feel the tingling, draw the breath in one more time and fill the lungs to maximum capacity. Then calmly let the air out and hold for as long as you can at the bottom of the breath. You don't need to set a world record, just hold your breath until you feel that gasp reflex and you really want to breathe again.

That is one full breath cycle of what has become known as the Wim Hof method. While it is unique to Wim, it has a couple of ancient forebears from the Eastern world: specifically, Tummo breathing (sometimes called Inner Fire meditation) and the yogic tradition of pranayama, which roughly translates to "the deliberate control of breath." The part that is particularly unique to Wim is the holding of the breath with empty lungs. Temporarily depriving yourself of breath releases some of the same hormones that coffee produces, namely adrenaline and norepinephrine. This is what makes Wim's method not just relaxing, like much of the focus of conscious breathing, but *energizing*. It is why it is such a great way to start the day, and why you shouldn't melt into a puddle of terror when you realize that I'm asking you to hold off on your morning coffee for a few hours. You won't need it. This regimen is its own kind of cold brew.

The other reason that the Wim Hof method is energizing is that it reduces the chronic stress that makes you chronically tired. The benefits of pranayama on stress are fairly well documented in the literature. Most relevant for our purposes, a recent study on ninety students, randomized to three different groups—fast pranayama, slow pranayama, and control—showed that specific yogic types of fast and slow conscious breathing reduced perceived stress by an average of close to 25 percent against baseline measurements.

Think about what that means for a second: one of the major tools for coping with bad, chronic stress has literally been right under our nose this whole time. It's been a solved problem for thousands of years. And yet we breathe roughly 24,000 times a day, while almost never deliberately taking control of our breath. That sounds like hyperbole, I know, but the way we talk about our breath says otherwise. When we're angry or panicked, we're told to "stop and take a breath," as if it doesn't belong to us or we've just been giving it away. When we're exhausted or feel rushed, we need to "catch our breath," as if we don't have control of it and it has gotten away from us.

Deep Dive: Wim Hof and . . . Lamaze?

Perhaps the most compelling evidence for the power of breath to overcome massive stress load was given to us right before we were born. During delivery, mothers are asked to do two things: breathe and push. Not haphazardly or randomly, but with deliberate and conscious control. Many mothers-to-be take a class prior to delivery that teaches them how to take control of their breath. You've probably heard of it: it's a method called Lamaze breathing. In *The Official Lamaze Guide*, the tips and guidelines are simple and straightforward: "Breathing is easily subject to conscious control. Therefore, controlled breathing is easy to learn. Slow, deep breathing is particularly effective. The 'right' way to breathe is whatever feels right. There are no rules related to how many breaths per minute, whether to breathe through the mouth or nose, or whether to make sounds. The key here is that the breathing is conscious, not automatic."

Sound familiar? These are the fundamentals of the Wim Hof method. And they are the core of Lamaze breathing, because conscious breathing doesn't only reduce stress; according to multiple studies, it enhances relaxation and decreases perception of pain. If you have been through labor, you know why that's important. If you haven't, ask your mom what it was like to push a watermelon with shoulders through a hole the size of a coin purse. Then go buy her some flowers.

Breath is the rudder of our life. We have the choice to either take over conscious control or let ourselves wander aimlessly. If you are going to own the day, you must own your breath.

The Cold

The Wim Hof method of breathing—like pranayama and Lamaze—is about taking back control of your entire breathing apparatus and focusing intently on the breath. It is the simplest and most important weapon in your arsenal for reducing chronic stress and other birth-worthy stress loads. But it is not until the method is paired with cold exposure that it becomes truly life altering—a mechanism for both healing *and* growth. That is because without the cold there is no external resistance to tell you when enough is enough. There is no force outside the physical capacity of your lungs to push against to guide your sense of progress. *There is no acute stress.* This is not a revolutionary concept. We have known for millennia that resistance is the shortest path to growth. "As iron sharpens iron, so one person sharpens another," says the Old Testament (Proverbs 27:17). Put more weight on the bar, you get stronger. Run harder, you get faster. It's a form of good, acute stress known as hormesis.

At its most basic, hormesis is a biological phenomenon in which low-dose exposure to an environmental agent (called a "hormetic stressor") produces a beneficial effect, while a higher-dose exposure produces a toxic effect. The layman's explanation for this odd duality is often summarized by the famous Friedrich Nietzsche quote: "What does not kill me makes me stronger." In theory, it can apply to nearly any activity, but for our purposes we are focused on the good kind of stressors, which are natural and acute. The ones that happen quickly and then pass, which create a hormetic response that triggers the body to repair itself and adapt to handling the same or greater stress in the future—aka *grow*. Vaccination is a good example of hormesis at work. You expose the body to a weakened version of a virus, the body adapts to the stress, develops antibodies, and becomes immune to full-fledged exposure of that same virus. Mark Sisson, bestselling author and a thought leader in ancestral health, writes, "Think of hormesis as your body 'hedging its bet' and going a little above and beyond just to be safe. You don't just compensate for the stressor, you super-compensate. You get stronger/faster/healthier/more resistant to the challenge than you were before."

Cold is one of those good, acute stressors that makes us hearty and resilient, like a sherpa or a Viking. Or a Viking sherpa! Dr. Rhonda Patrick, a top investigative researcher into the benefits of various hormetic stressors like the cold, put together a brilliant 22-page document highlighting the many research-based advantages of cold exposure, including benefits for brain health, pain management, longevity, fat loss, athletic performance, immune health, and mood. People who swim in cold water during the winter, for example, had 40 percent fewer respiratory tract infections (so much for Mom's advice). Cold showers have also been suggested as a potential treatment for depression. A lot of this rests on the ability of the cold to modulate inflammation.

▨ INFLAMMATION

To give you an idea of the importance of inflammation, having a healthy inflammation response is the key predictor for making it to the age of a hundred or older. But all inflammation is not necessarily bad. In fact, we need it. At its most basic, inflammation is just the body's response to injury or threat (i.e., stressors), including tissue damage like you would get from exercise or an injury, environmental stress like heat or cold, and pathogens like bacteria or viruses. If the stressor is acute (short-lived, with ample time to recover), inflammation is a positive part of the response that makes you stronger.

Deep Dive:
Good Inflammation versus Bad Inflammation

When you work out, you break down muscle tissue and the body creates inflammation to get more cells into the area and repair the tissue, rebuilding it to be more resistant to injury. It can even happen with bone breakage; with proper time to heal, bones will become stronger at the point of fracture.

When you get sick, it is not the virus that gives you the symptoms; it is your immune system. Fatigue, mild fever, body aches, congestion—the stuff we colloquially identify as "the cold" or "the flu"—are actually manifestations of the inflammatory response. Immune cells called proinflammatory cytokines are produced and directed to the injured or threatened areas through capillaries that open to promote blood flow and help fix the problem. That increased flow, along with all the newly produced immune cells, is the actual physical inflammation. When the virus subsides, so does the inflammation. Or so you hope. When inflammation doesn't go away, it is called chronic inflammation—and that is literally like living in Dante's *Inferno*. Chronic inflammation starts to damage the body. It makes you tired and creates pain. Inflammatory cells can start attacking healthy cells, creating autoimmune diseases and overall wearing the body's energy resources thin. This leads to many disease states and is generally the root of all sorts of maladies.

What turn off the inflammation when it is no longer needed, preventing it from becoming chronic, are stress hormones like norepinephrine and adrenaline. It just so happens that the Wim Hof method is especially adept at releasing a shitload of those hormones. Cold shock has been shown to reliably release up to 300 percent more norepinephrine, and the deprivation of oxygen from breath holds reliably produces more adrenaline and norepinephrine.

But in chronic stress, with the stress hormones norepinephrine, cortisol, and adrenaline present all the time, the body becomes habituated to their presence. The tolerance that results from chronic exposure is not a phenomenon unique to stress or inflammation. As with alcohol or any drug, excessive exposure leads to increased tolerance. (In chapter 3 we will see how this happens when the constant presence of sugar in the diet makes the body resistant to the effects of insulin.) So instead of shutting down inflammation in the presence of these hormones, the body becomes less responsive. Inflammation is allowed to go relatively unchecked, which is the mechanism that turns it chronic.

With an acute stressor like the cold or a breath hold, hormones like norepinephrine and adrenaline spike enough to reduce inflammation. With inflammation low, the body can relax the chronic production of stress hormones, and you have the opportunity to break the cycle.

COLD MENTAL STEEL

While the benefits of inflammation and stress are vital, the thing that really sets cold exposure apart from other forms of hormesis is the mental edge it provides. In the smithy of life, cold exposure is the anvil against which your character is shaped and your resolve is hardened (one might say that deliberate, conscious breathing is the hammer that does the shaping), so that you might confront your chronic stress and conquer it more completely. Character and resolve are two traits that rarely get tested in modern society, and they tend to atrophy as a result. Resolve, especially, is at the heart of why we let chronic stress steal our life force and why we struggle from our first waking moments to take ownership of our days.

The Powhatan Indians—that's the tribe Pocahontas belonged to—didn't have this problem. They would bathe their babies each day in the cold waters of Chesapeake Bay to toughen them up. It was a habit they started from birth and would continue all their lives, each season, each morning. What about the winter? No worries. When the water was frozen over, they'd break through the ice and jump in. It was a daily baptism by frozen fire.

Being an American Indian was not an easy life. Not in the mid-Atlantic, not anywhere. It was a struggle, a fight to survive. So you had to practice your resolve for doing the hard things. That cold plunge bred hardiness. It created courage, defined as moving forward in the face of fear. If you can conquer freezing water, even grow to love it, you can conquer anything.

▓ MENTAL OVERRIDE

Nike's slogan "Just Do It" is genius. When you are sitting on the precipice of your cold tub, or the shower nozzle is taunting you, your mind is going to be spinning a million miles an hour, attempting to find a solution for your fear and guide you to comfort. What do you do? Just do it. The same applies for starting your workout, or talking to that pretty girl or boy in the bar, or writing your name down on the karaoke call sheet. Even though you are going to feel like a hero when you tackle any of those feats, your mind computer will still scramble to find excuses and justifications why you shouldn't. But you are not your mind computer, fueled by fear. You are the operator of your mind computer. And you always have the choice to ignore the thought output and do it. It's what Albert Einstein was getting at when he said, "You can't solve a problem on the same level it was created." You can't always outsmart the thought-machine with more thoughts. Instead, thank the machine for its efforts, take manual control of what is usually on autopilot, and fucking do it.

The more you practice this, the better you get. Bode Miller is the most decorated downhill skier in American history. He's won multiple world championships, and every color of Olympic medal. If I had to sum up the reason for Bode's success, I would call it mental override. I have seen Bode win a World Cup downhill race against the best competition in the world, on three hours of sleep and a mild hangover. How is this possible? Because he refused to indulge the thoughts that would tell the average man that it wasn't possible to win a race under those conditions. I have seen Bode turn an emotionally catastrophic event into a happy vibe in minutes. I have seen him push himself harder than any human being in training.

How was he able to do this? Just like Wim Hof: practice makes the master. As a kid he would push himself to stay longer in the sauna, when every part of him was screaming for relief from the heat. He would force himself to roll shirtless in the snow, when he wanted the cozy warmth of his cabin. When a song got stuck in his head, he would wrestle his mind until he found total, pin-drop silence. This is what made him a champion on the slopes. It is what will make you the hero of your day, and it starts first thing in the morning.

Deep Dive: Heat Is Your Friend Too

No one hates the hot and the cold equally. Those few who do move to Portland and spend their free time weaving their beards into their chest hair. For the rest of us, there is always one that produces a stronger "Aw hell no" than the other, and it is our responsibility to manage that response so we can benefit from all they have to offer us. When it comes to heat, sitting in a sauna, steam room, sauna suit, or traditional sweat lodge and sweating buckets may not seem like the greatest way to spend the morning, but it might actually save your life. In addition to reducing all-cause mortality, hyperthermic conditioning, as it is called, helps blood flow to skeletal muscle and surrounding tissue, supporting circulation and muscle growth. It can help train your cardiovascular system and lower your resting heart rate; it can even assist with detoxification, since sweat transports minerals, both good and bad, out of the body. There's a catch-22 with that, obviously. Yes, sweat can transport things like lead, cadmium, arsenic, and mercury out of your system, but it's gonna take the good stuff with them too. So when it comes to detoxification, make sure you put back all those good minerals after you're done sucking out all the bad ones. In terms of sheer effectiveness, build up to forty minutes, being mindful to stay hydrated and take as many rounds as you need to reach the forty-minute threshold. You don't need to go full Bode straight out of the gate. This is a cumulative gain, so just do your best, and make sure to listen to your body.

Prescription

Here's how:

▨ LEVEL I: THE POWER SHOWER

There are some savages in our midst who hop into the shower every morning, crank the cold knob as far open as it can go, and grit their teeth while they do their scrubbing and shampooing and teeth-brushing, until the discomfort of the cold slowly wears off and they can finally breathe normally again. I'm not asking you to do that. In fact, I don't actually think that's the most effective strategy for getting you to the place, mentally, that you should be as you prepare to start your day in earnest.

Instead, what I want you to do is to turn the shower to hot and take your normal shower. Don't dawdle, don't hide from the day under the heavy stream of hot water, but don't sprint either. Take care to wash and care for yourself in a way that leaves you satisfied. Then, once you've completed the actual hygienic part of your shower, and while the water is still hot, begin a cycle of Wim Hof breathing (thirty breaths or until you feel a tingling sensation in your extremities, whichever comes first). At that moment, turn the water as cold as it can go and let it hit every part of your body. Your reaction, likely, will be to gasp for breath. Listen to your body's reaction. Listen to the cold. It's telling you what to do: *Breathe more.* Continue with the Wim Hof breaths until your body and your breathing have calmed to their pre-cold state. When you no longer need to breathe deeply to withstand the cold, hold your breath at the end of your next exhale (this is called the "bottom" of your breath) for as long as you can, until you feel the reflex to grab more breath. If you feel too light-headed, feel free to sit down in the shower under the stream. Falling on your ass is not a hormetic stressor, it's an emergency room visit with a better than fifty-fifty shot, if the statistics hold true, of being treated by a doctor who will have no idea what you were thinking.

A typical power shower takes about ten minutes all-in, and as part of that you should aim to be in the cold water for a minimum of three minutes. If you want to go for a second or third round of breathing and cold, go for it. You can even briefly turn on the hot water to create contrast in between your breath cycles. Listen to the signals from your body, explore, and experiment. But at the bare minimum, just do your best to have three minutes of continuous cold exposure somewhere in the process.

To the uninitiated, three minutes of cold exposure probably sounds both like an impossibly short amount of time for such profound effects and an eternity to endure. But once you've done it, it'll be hard not to become a convert and three minutes will feel like a small price to pay for feeling immortal. And once you've gotten comfortable with the power shower, you can take your practice up a notch, to full cold immersion.

The Power Shower

1. Turn the shower to hot and wash.
2. Do Wim Hof breathing (thirty to fifty breaths, or until you feel tingling and/or mild light-headedness).
3. Turn the shower as cold as it can get.
4. Continue Wim Hof breaths until breathing calms.
5. Hold at the bottom of breath until the gasp reflex kicks in.

Optional: Repeat breathing cycle up to twice more, at your discretion, with cold water running continuously or with periods of warm water between cycles to create contrast.

Total cold water exposure = ~3 minutes

▪ LEVEL 2: THE POLAR PLUNGE (COLD IMMERSION WITH CONTRAST)

I would categorize the power shower as a form of cold *exposure*. Cold immersion, or "cold shock," is the next level up from that, for exactly the reason you'd expect: you are not just exposed, you are immersed, engulfed, covered virtually from head to toe, all at once. It is shocking. The best way for most people to do cold immersion is in a tub. If you have an icy river or a plunge pool, more power to you, but the rest of us have to be content being a CO_2-emitting ice-melting force of global warming in our own bathtubs. Unlike the power shower, which likely needs longer exposure to produce benefit, submersion for even twenty seconds in 40-degree water can provide the norepinephrine release we are looking for. But we're still going to shoot for two minutes, because it's the amount of time often studied for cryotherapy, and also because it is unlikely you are going to get your bath to 40 degrees.

Generally four or five bags of ice are enough to drop the water temperature in your home tub to the desired level. Hard-core enthusiasts aiming for the 40-degree mark will want more. Kyle

Kingsbury, former UFC veteran and director of human optimization for Onnit, explained that it cost him $40 in ice every time he wanted to plunge. That adds up. One solution is to freeze buckets of water in your freezer and use them to make your baths cold all the time.

A great way to enhance the process of cold shock is to include contrast. Contrast comes from heating the body once it is cold, and then cooling the body once it is hot. It sounds odd out of context, but anyone who has ever been drunk on a ski trip has done what I'm describing: it is the classic roll-in-the-snow-and-get-back-in-the-hot-tub trick.

Just like with the power shower, you can do the polar plunge every day that you feel healthy (you don't want to do cold immersion when you're sick or already under a simultaneous acute stress load). Contrast is not necessary, but for me it seems to produce the best effect. Listen to your body, not to your mind. Learn to distinguish the voices of resistance and prudence. After all, wrapped up in this concept of hormesis, of exposure to good, acute stress, is recognizing the appropriate dose. A hormetic stressor is only as good as the body's ability to fully recover from the resistance it overcomes. If the body can't, then the stressor isn't promoting growth, it's toxic and it's prompting decay. Thus, prudence dictates that you start with Level 1, and stay there for as long as you need to before moving your way up the ladder, or down into the tub, as it were. And once there, if two minutes feels too long for Level 2, set that as a goal and work toward it. Only your body will know—it's up to your brain to listen to it.

The Polar Plunge

Do the Wim Hof cycle of thirty breaths while still on dry land, or in shower after completing necessary hygiene.

1. Prepare an ice bath, or jump in water as cold as you can find. Set a timer for two minutes, or start playing a song that is two minutes long.
2. Continue Wim Hof breathing until you can breathe calmly and normally (remember, the cold will make you want to gasp for air).
3. Exhale fully, and hold your breath at the bottom.
4. If you have extensive experience (or have a buddy with you in case you pass out), submerge completely.
5. Get out of the water at the end of two minutes.

Optional: Go into a warm shower or sauna to create contrast. If you feel up to it, complete a full additional round of cold shock. Be mindful not to push too hard, as the key to hormesis is not overdoing it.

Caveat: Shallow-Water Blackout

Make no mistake, it is possible to drown in your ice bath. That's not how your hero's journey is supposed to end. The combination of full cold immersion and the breathing may induce what is called shallow-water blackout. Just as when scuba diving, the safest bet is to have a buddy or your partner with you while you plunge. If you go all the way under, put up a hand signal or raise your middle finger while you are under water. Blacking out is not a sign of weakness—it can happen to anyone—so be prudent with your cold immersion.

Pro Tip: Cryotherapy

If you want to take cold to the next level, and by next level I mean −280°F, then you can check out cryotherapy. Typically costing around $40 per session, cryotherapy works by taking one of the literally coldest substances on earth, liquid nitrogen, and using it to cool the chamber you are standing in.

You rotate around like a rotisserie Popsicle, and in three minutes your skin temperature has dropped substantially and you feel that rush of energy as the animal inside you comes alive. I've had the pleasure of introducing cryotherapy to a lot of peak performers. One of the most memorable moments was watching Bode Miller, who I've witnessed walk barefoot through the snow in New Hampshire, start to shiver. Not just a little, a lot. Like a shake weight with ears. That's when I realized that cryotherapy was a different level of cold.

Now Do It

Believe me, I am no stranger to what feels like profound amounts of stress. When I'm stressed, I tell myself I don't have the time to take an ice bath, or do the breathing. I tell myself that I just need to finish a few more things, and the stress will go away. I'm good at bullshitting myself, and you probably are too. It's good to have reference points to keep you on track. Tony Robbins has a boatload more responsibility than me, but he takes ten minutes every morning to Wim Hof–breathe and pencil-dive into a sub-50°F plunge pool in his backyard. Or crank the shower to cold if he's on the road. Or jump into a snowy river if he's at his winter home.

"If you don't have ten minutes for yourself," he has said, "you don't have a life." He's right. If I am truly owning my day, owning my life, it doesn't matter what is happening externally. To wait for the external world to change before you alleviate your stress is a fool's errand. You know what is beyond that mountain? More fucking mountains. If you're going to climb, then you better adapt. Chronic stress is less about the environment, and more about your response to it. So own it. Put yourself intentionally into the occasional fire, and take yourself intentionally out of the chronic stress oven. It's a choice, your choice. Take that power and never give it away—especially to something as capricious as fate and fortune.

I'm not saying adding the power shower or an ice bath or Wim Hof breathing to your routine will be easy. It won't be. Just like in life, you are not rewarded for the comfortable choice. You will have to mentally override the fear of the cold. Override the urges that are driving you toward cozy warmth and shallow breath. This is as essential a skill as any. Just know that as soon as the cold hits your body and your fingers tingle, what you are experiencing is the exhilaration of victory—not just over the cold itself but over resistance, over stress. What better way to start the day!

As the great swordsman Miyamoto Musashi said, "Today is victory over yourself of yesterday, tomorrow is victory over a lesser foe." If you can conquer the acute natural stress of something like freezing water, something that makes you stronger—even grow to love it—you can conquer anything.

THREE POINTERS

- ✦ Chronic stress is literally killing us, and the traditional medical model offers us very little help to deal with it. Counterintuitively, one of the best ways to deal with chronic stress is to seek certain forms of acute stress. Through a process called hormesis, acute stress will help you adapt and become stronger.
- ✦ Cold exposure is one of the best sources of acute stress, and can be accessed in showers, cold tubs, and cryotherapy. The cold also offers the opportunity to practice an essential life skill— what I call "mental override"—the ability to make yourself do something you don't want to do.
- ✦ The breath, when used in accordance with the Wim Hof method or other forms of intentional deep breathing, is an invaluable tool to modulate and adapt to acute stressors like cold shock, while also helping to melt away chronic stress on its own.

3

MORE FAT, LESS SUGAR, OR DON'T EAT

Eat to live, don't live to eat.

—BENJAMIN FRANKLIN

Breakfast isn't the most important meal of the day, but it might be your most important choice of the day. Will you continue what you have already begun well—setting the foundation for energy and health—or will you take this train straight off the rails? At breakfast, don't just think about breaking the fast. Think about breaking the habit of fast breakfast. This means fast-metabolizing foods like sugar and bread are out, fats and fiber are in. You want foods that are slow and simple for your first meal. And if you can't find them—if all you have is sugar and refined carbohydrates—then skip breakfast altogether.

Getting Owned

How many times, and from how many people, have you heard the phrase "Breakfast is the most important meal of the day"? I've heard it hundreds of times, and I'm pretty sure we have some Madison Avenue genius to thank for it. Unfortunately for Kellogg's and General Mills, it's just not true. Every meal is important. Yet as a culture we believe in breakfast at any cost, so it is the one meal where we fill ourselves with the most ridiculous shit possible. The typical American breakfast, for example, is usually some combination of refined carbohydrates and sugar made conveniently available to us, in bulk, on the run, at rock-bottom prices by the great people of the breakfast-industrial complex.

Walk down the breakfast aisle at the typical supermarket. Pop your head into the shops open for breakfast on your way to work or to school. What do you see? Nothing but cardboard and wax paper. Cardboard containers filled with "health" bars, colorful cereal niblets, sugary fruit juices, frozen waffles, toaster pastries. Wax paper filled with bagels, croissants, doughnuts (those amazing creations of human culinary ingenuity!), or, if you're lucky, some white bread or a flour tortilla wrapped around a sad excuse for protein. Those are the options made accessible to the average American: fast foods filled with sugar and refined carbohydrates.

This is not breakfast. This is bullshit. It's a blood sugar bomb. One that, when detonated, throws us entirely out of balance before we've even had a chance to set ourselves upon the day. Blood sugar is supposed to rise slowly after you eat a balanced meal full of fats, complex carbohydrates like fiber (the best kind of carbs), and protein, allowing time for the body to release just the right amount of a hormone called insulin to drop the blood sugar and help store the sugar as fuel. But when refined sugar or other simple carbohydrates push blood sugar up quickly, it is toxic to the cells and the body hurriedly floods the bloodstream with insulin, which craters our blood sugar levels, leaving us tired and irritable in the short term and at risk for a variety of health conditions in the long term.

This is not just some pesky personal problem we have to deal with on an individual basis. It can also have serious real-world ramifications. In a 2011 study of parole judges in Israel, researchers discovered that judges were significantly more likely to grant parole in the period immediately after breakfast and lunch, when blood sugar levels were rising, whereas a couple hours after a meal break, when those same levels were crashing, they almost never granted parole. It was like a real-world experiment where the hypothesis being tested was the tagline of that Snickers commercial: "You're not you when you're hungry." The irritability and discomfort of the blood sugar drop, combined of course with the mental fatigue of the work itself, led judges to be far less compassionate. For better or worse, the scales of justice were balanced only so well as the blood sugar levels of the people holding them.

But I'm the last one to blame the judges, because I've been there. Before I found my way to the Jedi side of the nutritional force, I treated my digestive system like the Death Star trash compactor. In the morning I would reach for one of my favorite "breakfast" foods: cinnamon Pop-Tarts. POP-TARTS! Sugar filling, injected between two layers of refined starch (basically another form of sugar), and coated with frosting made from whipped powdered sugar. Where did I think the nutrition was coming from—the bready part? It wasn't even bread! I would have been better off just eating the cardboard box the Pop-Tarts came in. At least that has fiber.

An hour after I popped the tart, the high from the blood sugar spike would reliably give way to the irritability, fogginess, twiredness (tired and wired), and hunger that comes with blood sugar collapse. And when that happens, what do we normally do? We step back into sugar's BDSM dungeon with a ball gag full of carbs and pay to become its bitch for yet another day.

It is this inherently imbalanced relationship that has made sugar probably the worst thing to happen to human health in the last two hundred years. As consumption of our favorite sweet thang has increased over the decades, public health has deteriorated. Obesity, diabetes, heart disease, and even cancer have been linked to sugar and the associated blood sugar swings. The numbers speak for themselves. Thirty million Americans have diabetes. Cardiovascular disease is our leading cause of death. Childhood obesity is at epidemic levels, with one out of every five children clinically obese. Only 16 percent of women and 32 percent of men don't ever worry about their weight. The great irony of all these statistics, of course, is that we have more gyms, diet coaches, juice bars, and "health food" restaurants than any place on the planet. By far. Yet despite constant worry and myriad options, we're getting owned by our diet choices.

It's hard to call it our fault, however. The fast, sugary foods making us fat and sick are perfectly engineered to trigger biological responses that are incredibly hard to resist. High-sugar foods release a massive hit of dopamine. Dopamine is a chemical reward for the brain, and as the pleasure monkeys we are, we are wired to seek it. Whether you want to call it an addiction or not, when you figure out how to release dopamine into your brain, you are going to have a hard time stopping. The same is true for sugar.

So let me stand up first. My name is Aubrey Marcus, and I'm a sugar addict. Everyone say, "Hi, Aubrey!" Even with everything I know now, living an existence dedicated to cultivating discipline and a balanced ethos, if you put a cinnamon Pop-Tart in front of me, I'd still want to eat the fuck out of it. I'd almost certainly take a few bites. The appeal is just that strong. Combine it with brands like Coca-Cola and McDonald's implanting themselves as pillars of our culture, along with really bad—I mean *really bad*—nutrition information, and it feels like we never had a chance.

Thus, the first step in your nutrition plan is simple: no sugary stuff for breakfast. Period. Instead, we need to add fats back into our diet in sugar's place. Yep, you heard me, fats. Fats fats fats fats. Get used to the word, because you are going to hear it a lot. Make this simple substitution—fat for sugar—and you will have the sustained, balanced energy to power you all the way up to lunch. And if you can't find a way to make this happen, then skip breakfast entirely. Breakfast is not mandatory, and in fact you might just be better off without it altogether.

Owning It

Diets, diets everywhere, and not a bite to eat. That's what it feels like when you look online at the landscape of diet plans and the commentary that surrounds them. Everyone, it seems, is promoting something different when it comes to nutrition: Paleo, keto, vegan, Atkins, fruitarian, Mediterranean, and countless others, each zealously claiming to be the "right diet" and the "one true way." Well, let me clue you in on the best-kept secret in the health and nutrition industry: as far as diets go, all are a little bit right, and a little bit wrong, because a good diet depends entirely on the condition and purpose of the individual. If you have familial hypercholesterolemia, for example, you are genetically predisposed to need less fat. If you need fuel to survive in a postapocalyptic vampire world and come across some Skittles, then you need to unleash your inner Buffy the Vampire Slayer and taste that rainbow! So instead of arguing about which diet is superior, what we are going to do is focus on what I call universal nutrition principles, evidence-based guidelines that most people will flourish with. These will be spread throughout the other nutrition chapters (chapters 8 and 12), and together form a definitive dietary foundation for sustained energy, weight management, enhanced performance, and sexual appetite, regardless of where you are in the goal-setting process.

The first of these principles involves shelving sugar for the foreseeable future and making friends with fat. And if you can't find the resources to get that done, then skip breakfast entirely and reap the benefits of intermittent fasting.

Universal Nutrition Principle #1: Sugar Will Fruc You Up

In 1822, according to Dr. Stephan Guyenet, people consumed on average the amount of sugar currently found in a single can of Coke or Sprite every five days. Today, we consume that amount every *seven hours*, with young males leading the way, consuming up to one hundred pounds of sugar per year! Our diabolical addiction to this sweet stuff has not only been linked to obesity, diabetes, heart disease, and cancer, as I mentioned before, but it has also been shown to degrade the skin and contribute to premature aging. There's no need to sugarcoat it anymore: extreme sugar consumption is frucking us up.

But if sugar is making us fat, wrinkly, sick, and dead, how come we can't stop eating it? One of the main problems is that often we don't realize we are eating it. Sugar hides in everything. Often it's labeled in confusing ways with innocuous names like "evaporated cane juice," "brown rice syrup," and "fruit juice concentrates." In many places, advertisers promote high-sugar foods as "healthy." I remember when I lived in Australia watching a commercial for Nestlé Milo, a cross between Yoo-hoo and Ovaltine, and seeing this sweet, chocolatey treat being sold as a type of sports drink for athletes! It's not too dissimilar from how sugar-laden beverages like Mountain Dew and Gatorade are sold in the United States, by extreme athletes crushing them in the midst of doing something totally awesome. The worst is how we market to kids. Cartoon characters and colorful boxes are like the Pied Pipers leading kids to a lifetime of sugar-induced metabolic disease. But those are the easiest sugar issues to combat, and it's already begun worldwide, with bans on television advertising of sugary junk food targeted to children in countries including the UK, Canada, Mexico, and Norway. The good ol' US of A? Not so much. We tried to self-regulate advertising to kids starting in 2006, but cartoons and Cocoa Puffs are still as friendly as green eggs and ham.

NOTHING IS SIMPLE WHEN IT COMES TO CARBS

There are two types of carbohydrates: simple and complex. What we usually call sugar is a *simple* carbohydrate. What we typically call carbohydrates, or starch, in the lexicon of diet books and nutrition programs, are *complex* carbohydrates. This isn't because starchy carbs have commitment issues; rather it refers to their chemical bonds, which take longer to break down in the body. So carbohydrates like potatoes, rice, or quinoa are just a slower form of sugar, with a few more nutrients on board, than refined carbohydrates like simple sugar (aka candy cocaine), white bread, or that stuff that holds a Pop-Tart together. And slower is always better, since it gives your body a longer and more accurate window of time to respond to the glucose, or glycogen, that all sugars eventually metabolize into for the purpose of providing fuel to every living cell, including the brain.

A lot of people use sugar's role as cellular fuel as a reason to say that sugar isn't so bad after all. But our bodies are smarter than that. If we don't have sugar in our diet, our body will get all Walter White and produce it. This is why even on an almost pure-fat diet like the ketogenic diet, the brain still has ample glucose to survive, but on a pure sugar diet, we'd turn into anxious, confused, irritable, obese, diabetic messes.

Remember, when sugar passes from the digestive tract, it enters the bloodstream, and blood sugar rises. Left alone, it becomes toxic, so as a response the body releases insulin, and the liver converts this sugar into fuel in the form of glycogen. But the liver can convert only so much before the glycogen stores become "full," much as your mobile phone battery can't store more energy than 100 percent of its capacity. So what does the liver do with the excess sugar? It converts it to fat, of course, which is the body's secondary fuel storage system.

Deep Dive—Sugar Metabolism and Insulin Resistance

When the blood contains moderate amounts of sugar, and the body has ample time between releases of insulin, things work pretty well. However, when there is a constant level of sugar in the blood, or consistent spikes of blood sugar, not only does the liver convert sugar to fat, but the body has to release a commensurate level of insulin to keep up. Naturally, if there is a fast increase in blood glucose, there will be a fast increase in insulin. Often this leads to an overcorrection, as the body is in a hurry to drop blood sugar levels. This rapid increase then causes a swift drop in blood glucose concentrations, resulting in the "crash" we dread so much and, when you have too much often enough, a tolerance to insulin called insulin resistance. When the cells become insulin-resistant, they aren't able to shuttle the sugar from the blood into the cells as efficiently, and so you aren't able to remove it from the blood. At a certain point this becomes type 2 diabetes, and the injection of additional insulin becomes necessary to reduce blood sugar.

But let's take a second to expand on that cell-phone-battery analogy, just to be crystal clear: The sugar power supply keeps flowing into your phone, representing your body, even after the glycogen battery is full. Since the battery can't charge anymore, your phone stores the extra energy as a cushiony layer of fuel supply (fat) like a phone case. The longer you keep the sugar power supply flowing without draining the battery (exercising), the larger and wider the cushion around your phone becomes. Then, before you know it, your phone is on a reality show called *My Six-Hundred-Pound Phone*, and they have to cut a giant hole in the side of your house to get it out. I don't care how much you want to be famous, that's not the way to do it.

To be fair, there is a time and place for carbohydrates, but it isn't breakfast. We'll talk more about how to intelligently work carbohydrates and even a little bit of sugar into your diet later in the book. But for now, remember the D.A.R.E. campaign and just say no to the white powder, in all its forms.

Universal Nutrition Principle #2: Fat Is Your Friend

In 1980, when saturated fat was rising through the ranks toward public enemy number one, only 15 percent of Americans were obese. Today that number is 36 percent. All across the Western world, instead of improving heart disease and obesity, we've doubled and, in some cases, as in the UK, tripled it.

How did we get here? I don't have enough fingers to point at all the people, organizations, institutions, and cultural forces responsible, but there was a pivotal moment in the latter third of the twentieth century when two influential men espoused radically different ideas about nutrition, and the wrong guy won. One man, Ancel Keys, vehemently believed that dietary fat caused heart disease, a theory that would eventually be known as the diet-heart hypothesis. The other, a scientist named John Yudkin, quietly understood that it was really sugar—pure, white, and deadly—that led to inflammation and obesity. The world chose Mr. Keys's diet-heart hypothesis, and now the bloated consequences of that decision have created a public health holocaust: when we decided that dietary fat (and its associated cholesterol) was bad for your health, we started removing fat from our foods and replacing it with sugar and vegetable oils to make up for the flavor we'd lost in the removal process. That two-pronged dietary decision began the pincer movement that landed us in the clutches of the obesity, diabetes, and cardiovascular epidemics we face today.

Placing blame is beside the point at this juncture, however; what is most important is continuing to do *good science*—work that, not surprisingly, continues to show just how wrong all those diet-heart guys really were. Work like the gigantic landmark meta-analysis in 2010 that, after a review of data from twenty-one studies that included 347,747 participants, found no evidence that saturated fat increases the risk of heart disease. In case you missed that, let me repeat—*no evidence* that saturated fat increases heart disease.

Or the research published in the *Journal of the American Medical Association* in 2006 that looked at 48,835 women who reduced their total fat intake to 20 percent of calories and increased consumption of fruits, vegetables, and grains in its place. If saturated fat was the problem, then surely replacing it with fruits, vegetables, and grains was the solution, right? Wrong. After more than eight years, the replacement of fat had not lessened the risk of coronary heart disease, stroke, or cardiovascular disease.

Or the 1998 paper before that, from the *Journal of Clinical Epidemiology*, that examined people in thirty-five countries around the world, looking for a direct link between dietary fats and cardiovascular disease. The conclusion: "The positive ecological correlations between national intakes of total fat and saturated fatty acids and cardiovascular mortality . . . were absent or negative." In other words, people in nations with higher-fat diets were not dying of heart disease.

But we shouldn't look at cardiovascular disease as the only endpoint for the science of fat. What was the quality of life of those eating more fats? William Castelli, the director of another study in Framingham, Massachusetts, that started in 1948 and is currently in its third generation of participants, has an answer: "We found that the people who ate the most cholesterol, ate the most saturated fat, ate the most calories, *weighed the least and were the most physically active*" (emphasis added). This is probably not what you grew up hearing. Nonetheless these findings have been confirmed by the recent resurgence of the ketogenic diet. A meta-analysis of over 1,200 subjects in multiple clinical trials has shown that the high-fat, very low-carb ketogenic diet helps you lose more weight than a low-fat diet.

To put it another way: if you don't eat fat, you're probably fat. This is a hard reality to accept for a lot of people. Because at a surface level it makes sense that something called fat in food would create fat in the body. Fat = fat, right? Wrong. You'll want a lot more fat in your diet than you think, despite what all those diet-heart haters have had to say about things like saturated fat and its unfairly villainized companion, cholesterol.

Deep Dive: The Truth about "Good and Bad" Cholesterol

Cholesterol is a fatlike substance your body uses in its cells and tissues for, among many other things, the production of hormones like testosterone and estrogen, which are essential to maintaining good health and protecting against certain types of cancer and depression. To do that, cholesterol needs help getting transported into the body at the cellular level. It needs a ride, basically. Think of cholesterol as cargo and the cell as the port where it needs to be delivered. The best way to deliver it is by boat, a boat made of lipoproteins, which is what most people are referring to when they measure your cholesterol. This is where the confusion and misinformation around "good" and "bad" cholesterol begins.

In reality, there is only one type of cholesterol, and it is unequivocally good for you—it is the cargo on the boat. There are, however, different types of lipoproteins—different size boats—that deliver it into the cells. There are the "bad" small boats (VLDL, or very-low-density lipoproteins) and the "good" big boats (high-density lipoproteins and large low-density lipoproteins). The big boats carry the cargo efficiently into the cell without issue, and are correlated with great heart health. The small boats don't carry as much cargo, so you need more of them, and they can get jammed up in the shipping channels (the arteries), causing all these little shipwrecks of lipoprotein and cholesterol lining your artery walls. Then, over time, pieces of the shipwrecks can get dislodged, travel to the heart, and lead to heart attacks or strokes.

What gives you more of these shipwrecking small VLDL particles? Let me tell you what doesn't, first. Motherfucking egg yolks, that's what. In a review of seventeen observational studies covering 263,938 total participants, no correlation was found between egg consumption and heart disease or stroke. Surprise, surprise, a lot of evidence points to sugar, particularly fructose and high-fructose corn syrup, as the culprit instead.

But not only was there no correlation between eggs and heart disease; eating saturated fat with associated cholesterol, like egg yolks, was actually found to increase the size of the boats, turning the dangerous small boats into larger, more benign boats and positively shifting the ratio of "good" to "bad" lipoproteins. In 1994 the official journal of the Federation of American Societies for Experimental Biology reported that subjects who consumed diets high in fat (46 percent of calories), including a high saturated fat intake, increased the percentage of the larger particles (boats) of LDL cholesterol.

And yet many of the doctors who are prescribing you medication to lower your cholesterol don't know this. A report by Credit Suisse in 2014 showed that 54 percent of doctors still believed that dietary cholesterol (like what is found in egg yolks) significantly correlated to elevated levels of bad cholesterol. It is a dangerous association that is just not true, a fact that was implicitly recognized as such less than two years later, when the newly released Dietary Guidelines for Americans did not specify an upper daily limit for dietary cholesterol, reversing a long-standing position. The body is smart; when you eat more cholesterol than your cells need, the body adjusts accordingly. What does that mean for you and me in practical dietary terms? Simple: whole-egg omelettes are back on the menu, baby!

▨ WHAT FATS (BESIDES EGGS) SHOULD I EAT, THEN?

Not all fats are created equal. There *are* bad fats. Fried oils, refined fats, and trans fats—like you find in potato chips or margarine—drive inflammation and make you feel sluggish, and should be limited or avoided. (We'll talk more about these antinutrients in chapter 8.) The good fats—saturated fats, cholesterol, triglycerides, and omegas of all sorts—are the ones found in unprocessed meats, dairy, fish, butter, egg yolks, olives, avocados, coconuts, and raw nuts, and should be sought out for breakfast. Here is a closer look at five of my all-time favorites that I regularly reach for at my first meal of the day:

WHOLE-FAT YOGURT

First of all, let's get one thing clear. Nonfat dairy of any kind is bullshit. Dairy is comprised of largely three parts: protein (where whey protein comes from), sugar (lactose), and fats. The fats and the protein are the only good parts of dairy for an adult human. The lactose is not, because lactose is just another word for milk sugar. By cutting out the fat from dairy, you are basically saying that you want to increase the percentage of sugar relative to the other macronutrients. Great plan! That's like saying you want to increase the amount of smog relative to your fresh air.

Fats make dairy taste good, and they make dairy good for us. There is a reason fat is a part of the milk that babies receive. We need it. If you look at the labels for nonfat yogurt, you will be shocked how much sugar is in there. It's not healthy, or "lean," it's slow death in a cup.

Yogurt has a variety of additional benefits beyond its macronutrient value. Yogurt is cultured, meaning it contains some of the friendly bacteria that we have in our own gut biome. Several studies show that regular consumption of yogurt enhances the function and composition of microbiota, and may even improve lactose intolerance. A healthy gut biome supports mood and immune function and can even help battle pathogenic microorganisms.

Pro Tip: Coconut Yogurt for Millionaires

My favorite place to find new foods is a grocery chain called Erewhon, in So-Cal. One day while snack-hunting I saw a yogurt with a really shoddy label that looked like it was printed on a laser-jet printer from 1992. Super Coconut Probiotic Yogurt, it was called, and it boasted "240 billion organisms." That caught my attention, but what also caught my attention was the price tag: $30 for the jar! Even for Erewhon, which regularly charges eighteen dollars for a smoothie, that was excessive. Out of sheer curiosity, I pulled the trigger anyway. Despite having extremely low sugar content, it tasted as if ice cream and coconuts had sex. After the first bite, I knew I had a dangerous new habit. And after a week of eating the stuff, I can honestly say I noticed a difference in my gut health. There are a few coconut yogurt brands, including the one from New Earth Superfoods, which I mentioned above, but the coconut cream under the Coconut Cult brand name will ship throughout the US in cold packs, so you can yogurt like a baller.

AVOCADO

Avocado may be the strongest argument against atheism I can come up with. It's creamy, fatty, delicious, and comes in the perfect to-go packaging. It is packed with saturated fats and twenty other vitamins, minerals, and micronutrients. Not only that, it has fiber too. I like to eat half an avocado with lime, sea salt, and cayenne when I want a lush, nutrient-dense snack or a quick breakfast and I don't have time to sit down to a proper meal.

BONE BROTH

Soup for breakfast? You're damn right. It's the perfect way to start your day. Bone broth may not be the miracle cure that everyone claims it to be, but it is damn good for you. When you cook it yourself, you will get a nice layer of fat that will rise to the top of the broth, full of all the vitamins and minerals from the marrow in the bones. It is an excellent carrier for a host of healthy spices, and is comprised of collagen protein, which has a unique amino acid profile, along with fats and a bunch of minerals. It contains no sugar and is one of the easiest foods to digest, making it the go-to for anyone trying to correct gut-related issues.

BACON

Bacon worship has gotten a little ridiculous. There are bacon museums, restaurants, candy bars, even bacon-themed art on Band-Aids! Part of the reason is due to the Paleo movement, which put bacon back on the plate of high-performance athletes. The other part of the reason is that fats are good for the body, including animal fats like bacon. As long as your bacon has not been pumped full of hormones or antibiotics or cured with artificial preservatives, those delicious slices of hog tummy are a fun way to get some fat and some protein on the plate. Just be sure not to burn the bacon (sorry, crispy bacon lovers), as the charring will add in some nasty antinutrients that we'll talk more about in chapter 8.

BUTTER

When I was starting my own personal health journey, I was around a lot of people who couldn't stop talking about butter. It was such an appealing concept, I decided I would try to eat butter at every single breakfast. The problem was, I wasn't sure how best to do it. I knew I didn't like how I felt when I had coffee first thing in the morning, so blending it with my coffee was out. Eating butter on its own is revolting unless you are a cute little child. So what did I do? I ordered foods that I was familiar with and I knew went well with butter. Specifically, pancakes. Lots of pancakes. Not for their own sake, of course, merely as a delivery mechanism for the butter (at least, that's what I told myself). As for the maple syrup . . . well, who can resist maple syrup when you have a buttered pancake in front of you?

What started as a well-intentioned idea blossomed into exactly the blood-sugar-spiking nightmare we've been trying to avoid. This caveat aside, butter is great to work into your diet, including breakfast. Grass-fed butter, like Kerrygold, contains CLA, a potent nutrient with its own class of benefits, along with a great serving of saturated fat to fuel you into the day. Cook your scrambled eggs in it, blend it into tea or coffee, add it to your vegetables with a little sea salt. Syrup cakes aside, think of that old-school Reese's commercial every time you look at good grass-fed butter: *There's no wrong way to eat it.*

Without good fat in your diet, you are going to be setting yourself up for some serious problems—problems made all the worse when fats have gone AWOL during breakfast roll call, and sugar and refined carbohydrates have taken their place.

Universal Nutrition Principle #3: Skipping Is Better Than Cheating

Breakfast is not the most important meal of the day. I don't care how great the tale is you're being told, or how old the wife is who is telling it to you. Most days I eat breakfast. But if I cannot gain access to good fats, and only have sugary shit and refined carbohydrates at my disposal . . . it's an easy choice. I skip it. You're going to be far better off skipping breakfast altogether and waiting until you can get a good lunch or a snack with actual nutrients involved, rather than eating a bunch of sugar.

If the body does not have adequate fuel from your food, it will pull it from *all* tissues, including lean muscle mass. This process is so efficient that morbidly obese people have been put on long, medically supervised fasts with no ill effects as far back as the 1960s. Most famously, Angus Barbieri, a twenty-seven-year-old Scot who tipped the scales at more than 450 pounds, spent 382 days on a medically supervised fast. Yes, you read that right, no food for over a year. His body just broke down all the extra fat and protein, utilizing his own nutrient stores for survival. His body metabolized not only all of his excess fat but also the protein in his excess skin to remodel the svelte young man who was emerging. The result: he lost 276 pounds.

This is not just some overly restrictive, zero-tolerance measure I'm advocating here so you avoid sugar at all costs. I'm into living optimally, I'm not a crazy, unreasonable zealot. There is a time and place for sugar—it's just never going to be at breakfast. While the classic breakfast options are perhaps the worst of any meal, the advantage is that it is probably the easiest meal to skip while complying with a principle called intermittent fasting (IF). The basic structure of intermittent fasting is that you do all your eating in an eight-hour period (for most people, noon to 8:00 p.m.) and effectively fast the other sixteen hours of the day, some of which you're sleeping through. The idea is that when the body doesn't have food, it starts to metabolize excess tissue (fat and protein) to burn as fuel, which is a good thing.

Contrary to the shitty advice that became popular over the last decade, you don't want to be eating small snacks throughout the day. That is only good for athletes training at extremely high intensity. For us mere mortals, you want turnover in your fuel supply, just like you want your body to burn off that belly fat before bikini season. Interestingly, to get this effect you don't need to fast for long periods. Even better, by simply compressing your feeding window to eight hours per day, you can get the benefits of fasting and still have lunch with your friends and dinner with your family. Every day.

> ## Caveat: IF and only if . . .
> The structure of *Own the Day* is built to accommodate intermittent fasting, and the best way to do it is to skip breakfast. But intermittent fasting isn't for everyone. If you are struggling with hormone issues, or already have trouble keeping on weight, then intermittent fasting can do more harm than good. But for a lot of us who are interested in weight management and overall health and longevity, it is worth trying for a few weeks at a time.

▓ WEIGHT LOSS

When it comes to health and fitness, the one thing people want most is to lose some fat and keep their muscle mass. Intermittent fasting is one of the few protocols that seems to do both, and it's probably the simplest. You lose fat because fasting works on both sides of the metabolic (energy burning) equation. It increases your metabolic rate, which helps you burn even more fuel. Then on the other side, by compressing the available window for eating, it typically restricts the amount of fuel you are putting in your body. Studies have seen intermittent fasting produce weight loss of 3 to 8 percent (a huge amount) and waist circumference reduction of 4 to 7 percent over periods that range from three to twenty-four weeks. That means a 200-pound man might drop to 184 pounds, just with intermittent fasting! And for those worried about losing muscle or performance, other studies have found less muscle loss from fasting than from long-term calorie restriction. And as a bonus, growth hormone levels can increase dramatically during fasting, which helps the body repair, recover, and rebuild muscle, aiding in peak performance.

▓ HEALTH AND LONGEVITY

Obviously being overweight is antithetical to a long life. But beyond just the weight loss advantage, when you aren't eating, the body takes the opportunity to jump-start cellular repair processes, such as removing waste material from cells. Just as having an oil change extends the life of your car, cleaning out your cells can help extend your own lifetime warranty. Intermittent fasting also reduces oxidative stress and inflammation, which, as we learned in chapter 2, are some of the leading causes of disease.

Prescription

The biggest mind-set shift that we need to make is away from the idea of "breakfast foods" and more toward the philosophy of breakfast as a foundation for a set of nutritional habits. Think of your breakfast choice as an act of love toward yourself for the rest of the day. It was the Buddha who said, wisely, "To keep the body in good health is a duty, otherwise we shall not be able to keep our mind strong and clear."

I'm not going to give you a set time you need to eat, or a set amount you need to eat. There is so much fuss about portion size, but if we ask ourselves honestly, we know about how much is the right amount for us, and how much is overeating. You don't want to be hungry, but you don't want to feel stuffed either. (We'll learn in chapter 8 how using calories as a measure of anything is a problem.) As far as your macronutrient balance, just focus on substituting good fats for the sugar and simple carbs. Eat whatever protein and fiber you like; as long as you add fat and cut the sugar, you are going to be in good shape. It is also generally going to be better to reserve the more complex and hard-to-digest foods for later in the day, since the morning correlates to the lowest levels of digestive enzymes and gastric acid. Eggs are easier to digest than red meat, for example. This is also why I like smoothies for breakfast, as everything is already premasticated by the teeth of the blender.

If you decide to give intermittent fasting a shot beyond those days when you simply have no quality breakfast options available to you, the easiest way is simply to skip breakfast every day and wait until lunch to have your first meal. But there are other ways. One way is to eat normally for six days and fast completely for one day. During any fast period, it is fine to drink liquids that don't have calories, and even an MCT (medium-chain triglyceride) oil or coconut oil is acceptable as a fuel source (see chapter 6 for more information on these valuable oils). Another way is to eat normally for five days, and then for two days eat a very restricted ketogenic diet. This could include bone broth, butter, MCT oil, half an avocado, some low-sugar green veggies, maybe a chia seed slurry, but not much more. Supplements are also fine to take on fast days, though some supplements can be harsh on an empty stomach. Whichever method works best for you is the one you should pursue. Just remember, it never hurts to give yourself a full break.

Below are four choices for your owned breakfast.

Classic Breakfast with Greens

SERVES 1

FOR THE EGGS
2–3 free-range eggs
1 teaspoon water
1–2 tablespoons grass-fed butter

FOR THE BACON
4 rashers of uncured bacon

FOR THE GREENS
75–150g of mixed greens
3 tablespoons Balsamic vinegar
1 tablespoon Dijon mustard
1 clove garlic, minced
120ml olive oil
Salt and pepper to taste

FOR THE EGGS

+ Crack the eggs into a bowl. Add water, and whisk until slightly frothy.

+ In a nonstick pan, melt butter over medium-low heat. Do not scorch the butter!

+ When butter is melted add the egg mixture. Cook until no liquid egg is visible.

+ Season with sea salt and pepper (black, white, or red), to taste.

FOR THE BACON

+ Place rashers in a cold pan and set over medium heat.

+ Cook until the fat in the bacon is translucent, turning once halfway through. Do not let the meat get too crispy. Keep it bendy, like Gumby, dammit. If you want to be a bacon baller, lay out the bacon on a foil-lined baking sheet. Heat the oven to 200°C/400°F/Gas Mark 6, and bake that belly for 10–12 minutes on the middle rack. Keep an eye on it since cook times will vary by oven and with bacon thickness.

FOR THE GREENS

+ Wash the greens, dry completely, and place in a large mixing bowl.

+ In a separate bowl, mix the vinegar, mustard, and garlic. Whisking constantly, add olive oil to the mixture. Pour slowly! Add salt and pepper to taste.

+ Drizzle over greens to desired coverage, and toss.

+ Save the remaining dressing in an airtight container and place in the refrigerator. This stuff will last a while.

Bone Broth and Avocado

FOR THE BONE BROTH

240–350ml bone broth   Sea salt to taste
Ginger to taste   Pepper to taste
Cayenne to taste

FOR THE AVOCADO

1 avocado   Sea salt to taste
½ lime   Chilli powder to taste

FOR THE BONE BROTH

✦ Buy this at the store, don't be a hero. Pork, chicken, turkey, buffalo, and beef are all equally great choices. Just make sure you get the best kind possible: one from pasture/naturally raised animals that has been simmered for 6–8 hours.

✦ Follow the instructions on the packaging, and season with ginger, cayenne, sea salt, and black pepper.

FOR THE AVOCADO

✦ Slice a ripe avocado in half lengthwise, being careful not to slice your hand in the process (blood is not a good garnish).

✦ Squeeze the lime over the top, season with sea salt, dust with chilli powder, and dive in.

Choco-Maca Magic Shake

Time to prep: 5 minutes

20g chocolate protein powder
(no sugar added)

180ml unsweetened organic almond
milk

180ml spring water

1 tablespoon almond butter (or your
favorite nut butter)

1 teaspoon chia seeds

75g organic blackberries

1 tablespoon MCT oil

Ice as desired

✦ In a large blender, combine the protein powder, almond milk, and spring water. Pulse quickly to incorporate—this will help reduce clumping and pasting of the protein powder up the sides of the blender.

✦ Add the almond butter, chia seeds, blackberries, and MCT oil. Top with ice to the fill line.

✦ Blend and serve.

Açaí Breakfast Blast

SERVES 1

Time to prep: 5 minutes

300ml sprouted rice milk

1 heaped tablespoon unsweetened coconut or grass-fed, full-fat dairy yogurt

20g vanilla protein powder (no sugar added)

1 packet açaí berries, frozen

1 handful spinach, frozen

1 heaped tablespoon raw peanut butter (or your favorite nut butter)

1 teaspoon flax seed

Ice as desired

Blueberries, for garnish

Psyllium husk, for garnish

✦ In a large blender, combine the rice milk, yogurt, and protein powder. Pulse quickly to incorporate—this will help reduce clumping and pasting of the protein powder up the sides of the blender.

✦ Add the açaí berry packet, spinach, peanut butter, and flax seed. Top with ice and blend until smooth and of desired consistency.

✦ Pour into a glass, then sprinkle fresh organic blueberries and psyllium husk on top for a healthy garnish and fancy flavor.

Now Do It

Ideas are like a backhoe that we drag across the brain. The longer we carry an idea, and the more times we access it, the deeper that idea becomes grooved in our psyche. When I talk to people in my father's generation, getting them to understand that dietary fat isn't going to make them fat is an incredibly challenging task. They have heard— and believed—the contrary for decades. I can show them the science, I can walk them through the metabolic mechanisms, I can pull up my shirt and pose down like a shredded manimal, but somehow, some way, they will still leave the conversation unconvinced, and they don't know why.

You may be feeling something similar right now. How could this be? How could the nutritionists have been *this* wrong about a core tenet of nutrition like this? Well, it happens all the time, because scientists are people just like you and me. Except sometimes it's worse, because when being right about something is your career, you have even more reason not to admit you might have been wrong.

Physicist Max Planck famously said, "A new scientific truth does not triumph by convincing its opponents and making them see the light, but rather because its opponents eventually die, and a new generation grows up that is familiar with it." This theory was confirmed by the National Bureau of Economic Research when they did a meta-analysis of 452 scientists who died at the peak of their prowess. When the old guard died, there was a flood of new papers from unrelated newcomers that became more referenced (a sign of successful peer review and acceptance) than the papers of their predecessors or living associates. Sometimes it takes mighty death itself to advance the field past the gatekeepers of the accepted paradigm.

I don't want to wait that long. Flexibility of thought is one of the greatest attributes any human being can have, scientist or otherwise. It's the ability to take those deeply engraved opinions, and overwrite them with new and better information. Our brains are malleable enough for that task; you just have to bring the goal into awareness.

So you may just have to rewrite everything you know about breakfast. Wheaties as the breakfast of champions? Maybe champion of falling asleep at your desk at ten thirty in the morning. No champion I know is eating Wheaties for breakfast, or anything close.

The peak performers I know eat a breakfast that aligns with the universal nutrition principles we've discussed in this chapter—more good fats, less sugar, compressed feeding windows—adapted specifically to the needs of their training or their personal goals.

Make this change in your mind first, and then your plate second. It doesn't have to feel like a sacrifice, not even for your taste buds. After all, I'm still telling you to eat butter and bacon, right?

THREE POINTERS

- ✦ The abundance of sugar in our diet is arguably the worst thing ever to happen to human health. Being aware of the many forms of sugar and minimizing sugar ingestion is key to managing the blood sugar swings that will throw off your day.
- ✦ Dietary fat and cholesterol have been unfairly villainized. To restore metabolic health and optimize weight management, adding dietary fat back into the diet, starting with breakfast, is essential.
- ✦ Breakfast is not the most important meal of the day. If you don't have good fats and protein available to you, rather than eat a bunch of sugary or starchy foods, you can skip breakfast and reap the benefits of intermittent fasting for weight loss and longevity.

4

ESSENTIAL SUPPLEMENTS

To all my little Hulkamaniacs, say your prayers, take your vitamins and you will never go wrong.

—HULK HOGAN

With the stress of modern life, even the best diet can use some help—and no, an adult gummy vitamin doesn't count. Not all supplements come as a capsule, and they are certainly not all created equal. You need to have a guide. The supplements you'll learn about here supercharge your energy and health, and come with undeniable scientific research to back them up. They represent the minimum effective dose of kicking ass. Follow these prescriptions, and you'll have greater control of your human machine.

Getting Owned

Imagine yourself living ten thousand years ago. You're sitting around a campfire with your clan. Your skin kissed from the sun. The kill from that day's hunt is roasting on a spit, above a roaring fire. You will eat the whole animal, organs and all. In the meantime you're gnawing on a collection of foraged roots, tart berries, and leafy vegetation you found, grown in pristine mineral-rich soil on which you and your clan cohabitate. Your water came from a nearby stream or from captured rain in a clay pot. You're squatting on your haunches or sitting on the ground, but so is everyone else around you. You're outside, fresh soil under your fingernails from the day's gathering. Everyone is barefoot. The day is over, and there is nothing left to do but enjoy the company, eat your food, and gaze at the stars. You will sleep with the darkness just as you woke with the dawn, in rhythm with nature.

Fast-forward ten thousand years. If you're lucky, you cut up pesticide-aided vegetables and throw them into some factory-farmed eggs that are frying in butter and cheese made from cows fed a steady diet of nutrient-stripped corn. Once the food is done, you have to eat quickly, because work beckons. You've got to dash from your climate-controlled home to your climate-controlled office, where you'll be hunched over a screen all day, or maybe standing in one place for eight hours answering inane questions. You check your phone to make sure you're not already late, and a fresh set of attention-stealing alerts greet you. You finish eating and wash your hands with antibacterial soap before heading out the door.

Whenever I bring up the topic of supplements, I ask people to imagine these two scenes—because they point to two of the biggest arguments in favor of supplementation.

First: our stresses are more in number and different in kind from what our ancestors faced. We've talked about it earlier, but it's worth repeating: we deal with more chronic stressors than our ancestors did, most of which our bodies are not designed to thwart—and it shows. Our ancestors weren't stressed about staying up all night answering emails. They didn't have cinnamon Pop-Tarts. They didn't take metal-laden pharmaceuticals or put toxic chemicals under their armpits to deflorate that pesky human smell.

Second: our environment is robbing us of a lot of the nutrients, minerals, and microbial defenses that used to come into our diets by default. Again, think about that first scene. You were eating animals that fed on wild vegetation full of nutrients. Your own plants were grown in fertile soil, packed with minerals without the need for artificial fertilizer. You ate organs and fats, and fish caught from streams. Your hands were dirty from the soil, full of probiotic bacteria and hormetic immune challenges.

And the way we live now? We're sterile. We're clean. We have fruit-washing spray. It's not bad enough that we've swapped out fats for sugar in the modern diet; a disturbing percentage of the food we're eating is so processed that even insects won't eat it. All that artificiality and hypersterility have robbed our bodies of the natural conditioning and the necessary bacteria that come from being outdoors and eating food that grew in the earth or ran, swam, or flew on it. Instead we become prey to the bacteria—ever sicker, ever more vulnerable. Add to that the problems of soil that's been overfarmed, and animals that are undernourished, and you've got a recipe for a food supply and an environment that leaves our bodies wanting more. Put simply, it leaves us at a disadvantage.

The final reason to take supplements is that even if you have a perfect diet, there are nutrients available that you can't find in the produce section of your grocery store. Herbs, exotic vegetables, vitamins and minerals from every corner of the globe, all shown to optimize performance in clinical trial research. Why not give your body the advantage?

Correcting Disadvantage

Thanks to an absence of fermented foods in our diet, germophobia, and an overreliance on antibiotics in our medicine to treat mild infection, our gut biomes are a mess. This is no small matter, because the gut is our "second brain," and it is where 80 percent of our immune system lives, controlling neurotransmitter and hormone balance and acting as the gatekeeper to inflammation response. In a way, our gut is more *us* than anything else, since the 100 trillion bacterial organisms in our guts far outweigh the amount of "human" cells we have in our body. When you think about the gut that way, a suboptimal gut biome is the essence of deficiency.

Even worse, many of us may have started at a disadvantage. Thirty-two percent of kids these days are born via cesarean section. It is now commonly held that the immune-system challenge from commingling of intestinal (fecal) bacteria in the birth canal is an important initial hormetic stressor to build a healthy gut biome and kick-start infant immunity, and we've removed that first gut gauntlet for nearly half our children, to their detriment.

Additionally, studies show that almost half the people living in the United States are magnesium-deficient. That's right, half! And what's the problem? Oh, nothing . . . except that low magnesium has been linked to diabetes, hypertension, sudden cardiac death, headaches, asthma, and a lot of other ailments. But you know what happens before any of those more serious situations? You just feel like crap. Your body slows down, and it sends up warning signs in the form of irritability, fatigue, loss of appetite, weakness, and muscle twitches. Our ancestors wouldn't have had to worry about the amount of magnesium in their blood—but we do.

What happens when an entire species that was accustomed to living outdoors and hunting and gathering suddenly decides that indoor living is the way to go? We all become deficient in vitamin D. That's right: over a billion people are deficient in vitamin D. The list of consequences for vitamin D deficiency feels like a roll call at the sick ward: depression, fibromyalgia, Alzheimer's disease. And that's just the tip of the iceberg. Vitamin D is so closely tied to immune response and hormone function that those billion people are sicker and weaker than they need to be—just because they don't get enough sunlight. It's a *free* supplement—and yet not only are we not taking it, we're actively avoiding and defending ourselves against it. Think about that the next time you go slathering on sunblock with SPF Geisha Face.

Vitamin D and magnesium are involved in hundreds of chemical processes and are thus a couple of the more standard vitamins and minerals people know to look to supplement. Does that mean that supplementing with magnesium and vitamin D will prevent you from getting every disease ever? Of course not, but your risk profile increases with deficiency.

There are other crucial supplements. Our diets are chronically deficient in fish oil and omega-3 fatty acid. We aren't getting enough B vitamins, nor are some of us able to process what we do get. And then there are all the tiny micronutrients from plants too tedious, too bitter, and too exotic to harvest for a meal.

Supplements can help you because good supplements work. But there isn't a single pill that's going to fix everything that ails you. Anytime you see someone promise you that, let them know you think they are Number 1 by raising your middle finger right in their grill. What supplements do is upgrade the places in your body that aren't easily optimized by food and exercise alone. Done right, these supplements can bring you better health, clearer thinking, and energy that your ancestors would have envied.

Owning It

We are entering the golden age of nutrition and supplementation. Yes, our stressors are many, and yes, we have traveled far from the ancestral blueprint. But we can do things that no hunter-gatherer could imagine. We can research every clinical trial ever performed, and every active form of a vitamin . . . on our phones. We can walk into Whole Foods or, even easier, shop online and get delivered to us the most exotic nutrients the world has ever produced. The hidden secrets of Amazonian plant doctors, now available on Amazon Prime. In a single formula you might have traditional herbs from Europe, India, Japan, Siberia, North America, and South America . . . conveniently blended in a plant-based capsule. All of them studied together for efficacy against placebo by accredited American research institutions. We may have dug ourselves into a hole, but we have a helicopter full of solutions to pull us out of it.

But let me be as clear as Crystal Pepsi on one important point before we go any further: to supplement, according to the dictionary and to science and to common sense, is to *add an extra element or amount* to something. What it does not mean is to replace that something completely.

A supplement is something that *enhances or completes something else*. It is anything that you do to intentionally boost your nutritional profile or increase performance. I would argue that getting twenty minutes of sun is a supplement (it increases vitamin D). That eating pumpkin seeds before you have sex is a supplement (it increases nitric oxide, which increases blood flow). That dark chocolate is a supplement when you feel the blues (it has four psychoactive mood-boosting chemicals). None of these supplements, however, are *substitutes*.

Supplements of any kind, but especially the supplements we are going to talk about in this chapter, are not a substitute for solid food and physical activity. Don't have any illusions: you can't just take a pill and own the day if you eat like a sloth and move like one too. The first move to give you every advantage should always be improvements to diet and lifestyle. (We'll cover these in great depth in chapters 8, 10, and 12 specifically.) Eating more oily fish can boost omega-3 fatty acid levels. Eating Popeye levels of spinach and taking daily magnesium sulfate (Epsom salts) baths may help improve magnesium deficiency. But sometimes those aren't options, or you're doing those things and it just isn't enough. Bridging that gap, between deficient and optimal, is a good reason to take a supplement when regular daily methods aren't enough.

Even really successful, high-performing people are often handicapping their own potential just because they aren't supplementing. Take mixed martial arts legends Donald Cerrone and Tyron Woodley. Donald has nearly set the record for the most wins in the UFC, and Tyron defended his UFC championship belt at the highly competitive welterweight division multiple times. They are at the top of their sport. They are in peak physical condition. They work with the best trainers in the world. They use the best gear. And they are people who need every edge they can get—because the guy in the cage with them is trying to take their money, their health, and their ranking, by pummeling them into submission. And even though Donald has a soft spot for Budweiser and Hot Tamales, these warriors prepare like the champions they are.

When I first started working with Donald and Tyron, they were as *anti*supplement as it gets. I wasn't surprised: both of them had supplement sponsors in the past, but what they tried didn't make them feel any better. With the combination of artificial ingredients, unhealthful binders, strange colors, and unnecessary fillers, most "sports" supplements are awful. So these two pros figured they were better off going without. And with stories all around them about companies spiking their products with illegal ingredients to boost effectiveness, they felt they were safer facing a drug test without any of those things in their system.

Those are all valid reasons not to take supplements—except that it meant they were leaving serious athletic potential on the table. When they agreed to try the protocol we designed for them, it was like a switch flipped. Donald went on a huge win streak, blazing through the 170-pound division and putting on some of the most impressive fights and finishes of his career. It included an incredible four-hit knockout combination straight out of a video game that went viral like chlamydia through a freshman dorm. Tyron started his supplementing right as he began training for a rematch with one of the most dangerous strikers ever to fight in the UFC, Stephen "Wonderboy" Thompson. He said he felt on fire, the best he'd ever felt in training camp. And it showed: his cardio was impeccable, and he defended his belt successfully. If I were a betting man, I'd say that when you're reading this, he still has that strap around his waist.

Fundamentally, whether you're an MMA fighter or an M&A attorney, supplementing is about taking control of what you need to own *your* day. And what you need—no matter your goals, your situation, or your drive—always comes down to two common threads: combating mineral and nutrient deficiencies and increasing performance.

Essential Supplements

Throughout this section we're going to talk about the major areas that everyone should focus on, and then in the prescription we'll get down to brass tacks on how to get it done.

GREENS BLEND

Everyone agrees that we need a balanced spectrum of vitamins and minerals in our diet, and the best way to do that is to eat a varied diet. Consume the bountiful diversity of earth-grown foods: shellfish like oysters, grass-fed beef, leafy greens like Swiss chard, and brassica vegetables like cauliflower, on top of a whole complement of spices and herbs.

Of course it isn't always easy to eat this way, even with the best of intentions, which is why it should be no surprise that the lion's share of our dietary deficiencies is precisely in the area of vitamins and minerals. As I see it, you have two supplement choices: you can take multivitamins, which traditionally are notoriously hard to absorb, or you can reach for a multinutrient "green food" mix, which will cover a lot of your nutrient bases.

A good greens blend is going to be nutrient-dense and should have a good mixture of freeze-dried foods containing small amounts of many vitamins and minerals, as well as enzymes, antioxidants, and other beneficial stuff you'd probably never put in a salad—herbs, fruits, grasses, leaves, and maybe even a flower or two. When at all possible, I always recommend going with a quality greens mix because you can be sure the vitamins are being delivered into your system in a way similar to how they arrive in your normal food. Which is to say, they aren't synthetic, they're natural.

I liken taking the greens blend to raiding the shelves at Home Depot when you're trying to maintain your house. When the body is looking for something to repair itself, it'll go to the shelves in search of the best tools, and if the right nutrients are available, it will make the proper repairs in the most effective manner possible. If it doesn't, it will simply pull from the discount bin by the register and use a glue gun and duct tape and hope for the best. By taking in these greens, you're giving your body the run of the store.

While every greens blend is different, and therefore not a lot of studies have been done, there is no doubt that supplementing with vitamins and minerals is beneficial. If you don't get enough of these nutrients you are more likely to be sick, violent, and all other manner of unpleasantness. As stated above, the problem with some multivitamins is that the form of the ingredient used is sometimes dissimilar to those found in food. So when it comes to a "multi," going green is usually the way to go.

MAGNESIUM

Just like calcium, magnesium supplementation has been shown in clinical research to assist with facilitating healthy bone mass, the performance of athletes, supporting men and women during exercise, even improving blood sugar regulation through diminishing insulin resistance. But what you are gonna notice is *less*. Less stress, less static, and less antsiness throughout your body. You're gonna notice everything relax, and get a little more quiet. It's probably why the most popular magnesium supplement in the world is simply called Calm. Magnesium is involved in thousands of chemical reactions. In the Home Depot of nutrient supplementation, magnesium is the hardware section. There's something there that connects to every aspect of your body temple.

KRILL OIL: SUPPLEMENT OMEGA-3

The reason some of your breakfast options today contain chia seeds, flax, and grass-fed beef or dairy is that those are some of the simplest nutritional sources of omega-3 fatty acids. The other, and probably the best, is oily fish. If we lived in Japan, that would be in your breakfast as well, but instead we'll save it for lunch.

Chia and flax are not the easiest things to find on the menu, and fresh, organic oily fish is equally difficult in many parts of the world. So in lieu of that, you can supplement your diet with fish oil or, even better, krill oil. I remember the first time I tried a higher dose of krill oil, somewhere in the 5-gram range. I took it at night, and it felt like the oil's essential omega-3 fatty acids (EPA and DHA), along with its intrinsic antioxidant astaxanthin and its brain-healthy nutrient phosphatidylcholine, were running through my bloodstream like a fire hose, just blasting out all the inflammation in my body. It works because these hard-to-find fatty acids balance out the omega-3 to omega-6 ratio, and as a result reduce normal systemic inflammation.

In chapter 2, we learned about inflammation, but here we're more concerned with how it feels. Simply put, it sucks. It feels like inner heat. It can cause your joints to ache and your brain to be a little fuzzy. Why krill oil and not fish oil? Studies show that with krill oil you get the same metabolic effects at lower doses. Translation: it's just more potent. And as a bonus, krill oil has even been shown to help the ladies out on their menstrual cycle. Since I am clearly unqualified to discuss the menstrual cycle, the abstract of the study says that krill oil is "significantly more effective for the complete management of premenstrual symptoms compared to omega-3 fish oil."

SUPPLEMENT VITAMIN D

Thanks to our friend the sun and our skin's remarkable ability to make a ton of vitamin D out of its ultraviolet B rays, vitamin D is free for all. Usually all you need is twenty to thirty minutes of direct sun exposure to your skin. Unfortunately, not all sun or all skin is created equal. Twenty minutes of sun for one person in one place can be an entirely different (and potentially worse) experience than thirty minutes of sun for another person in another place. The sun puts us in a bit of a predicament that way: too much sun is bad for the skin, but not enough sun means we don't get adequate vitamin D.

So how do we measure? How do we find the line? Typically, we don't. We can't. Even if we could, it would just confirm something we already know: more often than not we are significantly deficient in this critical vitamin that is important for over two hundred bodily processes, concerning everything from optimal mood to bone health. Vitamin D supplementation has been shown in clinical research to help reduce body fat mass, maintain muscle mass and reduce fractures, and correct mood-related issues.

Kevin Estrada, a professional hockey player, was in a devastating water plane crash that ended his career. He lives in British Columbia—where it rains all the time and there's a lot of cloud cover—and began to feel run down. His body was still broken, he had low energy, and his mood felt off. Vitamin D fit all the criteria of a supplement that could really help him. When he got his blood checked for vitamin D, of course Kevin was deficient.

He started taking vitamin D supplements, along with its ride-or-die companion vitamin K_2, at 5,000 micrograms of D a day and sometimes even higher. That's a relatively high dose, but it started to turn things around with his mood and his energy levels. It was as close to an instant fix as he'd ever thought possible, and it's the kind of supplement most of us need if we want to consistently perform our best.

SUPPLEMENT PROBIOTICS

I take a lot of different probiotics for a lot of different reasons, but the one that saved my ass—literally—is a yeast-based strain called *Saccharomyces boulardii*. When I traveled to South America and particularly Peru, I'd spend my time in the Amazon rain forest. As much as I enjoyed those trips, there was one factor that sucked some of the joy out of it—from the back. I'd return from each trip and spend the next two weeks getting reacquainted with the finer points of porcelain toilet production as traveler's diarrhea made its way through my system. As careful as I was with the water, inevitably I'd consume certain foods and vegetables, and some nasty bug would get into my GI tract.

At one point, I'd had enough. I loved, and maybe even needed, those trips to the jungle, but I didn't want to come back and have to count steps to the bathroom. I started researching probiotics to support my gut, and I came across *S. boulardii*. I brought some with me on my next trip to Peru—and it was miraculous. I had no issues while I was down there, and no issues upon return. The studies back it up: whether it's Crohn's disease, or irritable bowel, *S. boulardii* is the shit for problems with your shit.

Napoleon once said, "An army marches on its stomach." He wasn't just talking about what went into soldiers, he was just as concerned with the amount coming out. And while we are not locked in a land war with Russia (yet), and you are probably not regularly contending with Montezuma's revenge, we *are* at war against nutrient deficiency. I can assure you that you are only going to make it as far as your gut takes you. Not only is the gut largely responsible for our immune system, and perhaps even our personality, through the regulation of hormones and neurotransmitters, more simply it is responsible for digesting and disseminating our fuel source from food. A lot of weight-management issues have to do with the gut. A meta-analysis of studies showed significant improvements in obesity with probiotic supplementation. If you want to feel more like yourself again, and get that human machine humming from the inside, this supplementation regimen is essential.

There are also important impacts on regulating mood. The burgeoning field of psychobiotics, in which targeted gut treatments are being explored to assist with all sorts of medical conditions, is one of the hottest fields in medicine. It is my personal opinion, along with that of the psychiatrist Dr. Dan Engle, that the role of gut biome transplants, in which a healthy person's microbiome is transplanted and seeded into another person, is one of the frontiers of medicine.

It's why you're seeing the increasing use of probiotics, yogurts advertising the cultures they have, the trend toward fecal transplants, and the chatter about the gut . . . everywhere. Bestselling books. Blogs. News stories. The gut biome is hot—and with good reason.

ACTIVE B VITAMINS

When Kobe Bryant or LeBron James—or a young Aubrey Marcus, starting shooting guard for Westlake High School—needed to play a basketball game with the flu, there was one vitamin to reach for: B_{12}. B vitamins are involved in everything, from the conversion of nutrients into neurotransmitters like serotonin to proper mitochondrial function. You can feel it when you take a good B vitamin: there aren't any questions. You will have more energy, more resilience, more bounce in your step. Think of it like this: "I've got your back, B."

Not everyone handles the absorption of B vitamins well, however. A good portion of people, for instance, struggle to uptake the essential B vitamin folate, or folic acid, and supplementation with a methylated version, like 5-methyltetrahydrofolate, can make a huge difference. One study showed that people suffering from major psychiatric conditions like schizophrenia or depression were deficient in folate, and benefited from methylfolate supplementation. Generally speaking, the methylated form of vitamin B, methylcobalamin, is more easily absorbed by the body, so pay attention to your body and make sure you supplement with B vitamins that are packaged the best for your system.

Pro Tip: IV Vitamin Therapy

IV vitamins have been used in emergency-room care for years. Ask any medical student or young ER doctor how they deal with a bad hangover, and they will give you two words: banana bag. They are referring to a standard IV solution bag that contains many of the vitamins and minerals you need. The advantage of the IV is that it bypasses the gut, ensuring that the vitamins are delivered into the blood. A lot of places have popped up extending this service, not just to the sick but to the healthy (or the hungover). One of the best is a program developed by functional medicine wizard Dr. Craig Koniver called Fast Vitamin IV. It offers not only the usual suspects, but a whole host of amino acids to further assist with recovery.

Whether it is a dose of vitamin B_{12} to give you additional energy and pep, or glutathione to help restore your liver, or just a plain old banana bag to cover your bases, IV therapy is only going to get more popular. And as the price goes down, the only question you really need to answer for yourself is: Is the juice worth the squeeze?

The Emptor-iest of All Caveats

If you're not taking supplements, you're missing an opportunity, plain and simple. But taking the wrong supplements is just as bad, and sometimes it's worse than taking no supplements at all, because not all supplements work. We have all tried some that didn't do shit. Some are not strong enough; some have herbs that don't do what they say, or vitamins that won't absorb. You can spend hundreds of dollars on things that basically create more expensive pee, with no performance gains to show for it. The key is to find a good company that makes quality products.

I personally take products from several other places besides Onnit, including Sunwarrior, Healthforce Superfoods, NuMedica, and LivOn. Unfortunately, our industry is full of brands peddling a ton of garbage, so it is extra critical for you to choose wisely when it comes to supplements and the companies that sell them. Believe me, I understand the potential for elephantine bias in those words, as a supplement maker myself, but it doesn't make them any less true or the need for me to say them any less urgent. This isn't Supplement Supermarket Sweep, after all. We can't have you just running down the aisles of your local GNC with your arms out, scooping bottles into your basket without reading the labels and figuring out who made what's inside.

Here's what you need to know and look for when you're shopping around for each of the supplements we've just recommended:

Avoid supplements that make medical claims. Supplements are technically categorized as a food, not a drug, by the Food and Drug Administration (FDA). Foods can benefit your health, but drugs treat medical conditions. Therefore, a supplement company cannot advertise that its product is able to fix a medical condition or a disease of any sort without the bitch slap of justice eventually finding its mark upside their head. Remember that product Airborne, which was supposed to keep you from getting sick while flying or teaching elementary school? Well, those exaggerated promises cost its makers to the tune of $23 million.

If a supplement is claiming a miracle cure for a real medical condition, you know at least one of two things. The company making it is either about to get sued, or run by amateurs too small to get noticed by the FDA and too insignificant to be penalized by the Federal Trade Commission (FTC). Both of those are red flags, especially the latter. Amateurs can produce supplements and get them on the shelf without actually following the rules. It's kind of like those unlabeled cookies wrapped in cling film at the counter of the gas station. Who makes those things? While this informality occasionally results in delicious cookies, it's not what you want for supplements. Supplements must be controlled by a variety of FDA checkpoints during the development and production process.

First of all, every ingredient needs to have something called GRAS (generally recognized as safe) status. If it's not on the GRAS list, it shouldn't be in the formula. Second, there are strict laws concerning how the food/supplement is produced. This is called good manufacturing practice (GMP). Every supplement needs to be produced in a GMP-compliant facility until it is fully packaged and sealed, preventing contamination. These facilities are regularly audited by the FDA and additionally audited by the manufacturing brands. Finally, every supplement is tested for microbial and metal contamination twice before it is released to the public: each ingredient is tested individually, then the finished batch is tested. You can be fairly confident that supplements making medical claims have not cleared these rigorous regulatory hurdles on their way from some dude's basement to your kitchen counter.

Avoid companies that don't perform randomized clinical trials on their own products. If a company hasn't performed any clinical trials, it is a sign that either they are cheap or they don't believe their stuff works. As a point of reference, we spent over $400,000 to get our nootropic formula tested twice by the Boston Center for Memory against placebo. There was plenty of research on the ingredients already published, and in chapter 6 you'll read about one in particular. But we wanted to do more than just suggest that our product would work. We wanted to test it in the most rigorous method possible—randomized clinical trials, run by someone who had no stake in whether Alpha Brain worked or not. That's important: it's so easy for great marketers to convince you that a product will help your memory or help you lose weight; it's a lot harder to show—with evidence, data, and testing—that it actually does so. While it usually isn't feasible to run tests on every single product, if a company hasn't run independent clinical trials on *any* products, they are not for you.

Watch out for supplements filled with caffeine. One of the big ways those great marketers make you think that what you're swallowing is doing what they say it will is by juicing it with caffeine. The caffeine gives you an instant hit when you take it, and you end up saying to yourself, "Well, it's definitely doing something!" And it is: it's sinking its little hormonal claws into your adrenal system and memorizing your credit card number. There are plenty of good ways to take caffeine. They usually don't involve supplements. So avoid most supplements that contain heavy caffeine; it's there to cover up the weaknesses of the core product.

Prescription

Since all supplements are different, and you are different, I'm not going to give you specific amounts to take here. The first step is to supplement your lifestyle in the most natural way possible. Get more sunshine, spinach, and fish, and eat all the weird foods you can. We'll talk about more of that in chapter 8. Then when it comes to dietary supplements, the best practice is to talk to a health-care practitioner, dietitian, or functional medicine specialist.

It's also important not to expect miracles or dramatic overnight changes. Your problems weren't built in a day; the solutions may not come so quickly either. Since I am acutely aware of how my body functions and feels (hey, it's my job!), I can usually feel a difference the same day I take a supplement, but I have also learned that sometimes it takes weeks before you accrue the whole-body benefits. Track how you feel over time. Do that however you like: use an app, keep a journal, send yourself an email at the end of each day. Just make sure to get a sense of whether and how something you've taken is affecting you.

Pro Tip: Don't Make Me Think

Sourcing all these things can be intimidating, but I encourage you to see what's out there. We've done a lot of the work for you, though, with formulas that pack all the key vitamins and minerals, along with greens and krill oil, plus a host of herbal nutrients in convenient day and night packs. We also offer a complete care kit for your gut that includes probiotics you can take with any meal. All the packs are sleek, easy to travel with, and absolutely comprehensive. I could pretend that I don't think ours is the best solution, but that would be withholding information from you just to avoid seeming biased. It's what I use, and it's the starting point for our pro team and many of the customers we serve.

Now Do It

What is a supplement really going to do for me? That's the question you were probably asking as you worked your way through the material in this chapter. It's definitely the question I get most often when I meet new people and tell them what I do. If it's the right supplement, the answer is . . . something. The clinical research backs that up.

Suppose your mood is a little better from the vitamin D. When your daughter asks you "Why, Daddy?" for the tenth time, instead of getting snippy you can answer her with a tickle and a smile.

Suppose you have more mental energy from the B vitamins. Instead of surfing Facebook at work because your brain is too tired, you actually start working on the long-term project that is going to take your career to the next level.

Suppose your joints don't ache after the krill oil. Instead of sliding onto the couch when you get home, you go for a nice long run to clear your head.

Suppose you can relax better after mineral supplementation. Instead of being stressed all night, you read a book that changes the way you think about some aspect of your world.

Suppose you don't have to worry about getting diarrhea when you travel that world. Maybe you book that trip to Peru and come back a different person.

Small things have big consequences. Over time, those consequences compound. We are the accumulated momentum of all our choices. Some of those choices are binary. Go to the gym or not: that choice in that moment is going to change your day. Over time that choice will change your life. We tend to ignore the importance of fractional benefit because we lose sight of the concept of the tipping point—the little benefit that tips the cup to release a flood of benefit. It may be a 2 percent difference in force or momentum that flips the coin from heads to tails, or yes to no.

Supplements stack the odds in your favor. You will survive without them. But will you *thrive* without them? Will you be your best? Probably not. You're likely leaving some level of performance on the table. What is that costing you? That's for you to find out. Whether that means scheduling time in the sun, eating mad greens, taking Epsom salts baths, or purchasing some supplements from a reputable source, the key is to treat yourself like a pro. Because you are a pro . . . you are professional at being you. You get paid for it, right? So be the best fucking you that you can be.

THREE POINTERS

+ There are two primary reasons to supplement: to remediate potential deficiencies, and to gain access to unusual or hard-to-find nutrients. You don't need to think of supplements as something that comes in a capsule, either. Getting the right amount of sun, sleep, and food is itself a kind of supplementation, and the first line of defense.

+ The key things to consider supplementing are greens, probiotics, B vitamins, krill oil, vitamin D, and additional minerals.

+ While dietary supplements are generally safe, and more regulated than you might have heard, they are not all created equal. Look for companies that engage in clinical research on their products and use natural forms of ingredients when possible.

5

DRIVE TIME, ALIVE TIME

If time be of all things the most precious, wasting time must be the greatest prodigality.

—BENJAMIN FRANKLIN

Your commute does not need to be the most dreaded and frustrating part of your day. On the contrary, it can contain some of the most enjoyable and productive minutes of your morning and your evening. But only if you stop looking at your commute as a prison sentence—and see it instead as an opportunity. It's a choice to turn the dead time where you can't do anything to alive time where you are learning, growing, or practicing mindfulness. It's a simple distinction: alive versus dead. Choose to be alive.

Getting Owned

One of my favorite comedies of all time is *Office Space*, directed by Mike Judge, the genius behind *Beavis and Butt-Head*, *Idiocracy*, and *Silicon Valley*. It's about a software engineer named Peter Gibbons who has basically had it with his boring life, his unfulfilling relationship, and his dead-end job. Early in the movie, he goes to a hypnotherapist with his soon-to-be ex-girlfriend to get better. He tells the therapist that the reason he's there is that every day is the worst day of his life. His nemesis is a clueless middle manager who passive-aggressively hounds him about making sure he uses the proper cover sheet on his TPS reports. Later on, talking to his neighbor about what he'd do with a million dollars, he says he'd sit on his ass, relax, and do nothing. Peter's neighbor, like a redneck Confucius, reminds him that you don't need a million dollars to relax and do nothing. "Take a look at my cousin," he says. "He's broke, don't do shit."

Know where *Office Space* starts? In the car. On the way to work. In the span of ninety seconds, we see Peter go through anger, frustration, panic, desperation, exasperation, and defeat as he tries to navigate gridlocked traffic on the way to a job he hates. Mike Judge made this the very first scene in the film because he knew millions of people would immediately identify with Peter's plight and every single emotion he was experiencing. *Office Space* came out in 1999, and not a lot has changed about our daily commute since. Actually, that's not true. One thing *has* changed: our commute has gotten worse.

Since 1980, when the US Census began tracking them, commutes have gotten 20 percent longer. And it's not just one part of the country—it's all of it. The average New Yorker spends nearly 70 minutes commuting to and from work each day. In Washington, DC, the average lobbyist, cabinet secretary, and government worker spent 32.8 minutes getting to work. On the West Coast, it takes the average Oakland resident 29.9 minutes to get to her desk, and the average worker in the Inland Empire 29.8 minutes. Three percent of the US population commutes more than 90 minutes *each way*.

And that's just America: the land of long drives, suburbs, and five-lane highways. In Western Europe, where they supposedly have superior public transportation and are more "enlightened" about the environment, the average commute is actually *longer* than America's most congested cities. Better grab another éclair for the road!

You would think that in the age of the Internet, when we can work from wherever we'd like, all of this would have improved. You'd think that with Uber and ride-sharing apps, the roadways would be less congested. But you'd be wrong. We spend a lot of time in our cars.

What makes that so problematic—what sends Peter down a rabbit hole of difficult emotions at the beginning of *Office Space*—is that more often than not, our time in the car (or on public transportation) does not actually feel like our own. It feels like the Bataan death march with cars. It feels like a prison sentence. It's no coincidence that bad traffic is called grid*lock*. You're stuck, homie. With a bunch of other vehicles just like yours, with nowhere to escape, and there's nothing you can do about it.

And because this time doesn't feel like it belongs to us, we tend not to take advantage of it. We don't utilize it, we endure it. *We waste it.* Which is one of the reasons why, whether we realize it consciously or not, our commute ends up being the time when we are most angry during the day. Foaming-at-the-mouth angry. According to a study conducted by roadside assistance giant AAA in 2016 (probably trying to figure out what contributed to all the wrecked cars they were towing away!), over 8 million drivers exhibited extreme versions of road rage, while close to half of all drivers exhibited some form of rage while driving. This includes the usual program of honking aggressively, flipping people off, yelling through the window, purposely tailgating, and slowing down in front of someone who is purposely tailgating you (that's the *professional* asshole maneuver, FYI).

We're basically getting into a vehicular bar fight every day. And this is at the *start* of the day. We've already talked about how important it is to set the tone from the get-go for how the rest of the day will proceed. Imagine kicking it off with a shouting match through your car window with some numbnut who cut you off. Whether or not you find yourself on the giving or receiving side of road rage, or whether your commute is short or long, it is likely the worst part of your day.

What a waste! This is a full hour of your day we're talking about here. Sixty shiny waking minutes. The whole thing incinerated in distraction or frustration. Believe me, I know what it means to be stuck between home and work, in a kind of dreaded vehicular limbo. And I know it's even worse on the way back. That's when you know you're moments from home. That's when every moment of waiting becomes pure torture. When every accident, every stoplight, every slow merge, every brief pause, is keeping you from the rest of your life.

Nothing about this is good. But it's also something we have the ability to address. We can take back that time. We can *choose* to do something with it, to own it instead of being owned and beaten down by it. Because owning the day isn't as simple as drinking the right fluids or eating the right foods, it's about having the right mind-set. It's about coming to terms with the fact that at every moment in your life, you have a choice.

You can choose to hate your commute, to loathe your fellow drivers, and to waste that time zoning out for thirty to ninety minutes. Or you can choose something different and turn that mind-numbing, soul-sucking commute into time when you are improving and expanding.

Owning It

The author Robert Greene has a useful, simple way of thinking about *all* time: it's either alive or dead.

We've all experienced dead time. Dead time is basically everything I just got finished describing. It's every second of Peter Gibbons's life until he goes to the hypnotherapist. It's when we're stuck somewhere we don't want to be, and we give ourselves over to it. We're stuck in line, stuck in a job we don't like, stuck in jail, stuck behind someone driving too slow, and we either give up or give in to the emotions that these situations create within us. If you're like me, you can feel yourself start to burn with impatience. If you're like Peter, you twitch, you fidget, you flail. You just want it to be over! Why can't they just move faster? Gah!

Then there's the opposite: alive time. This is a feeling of purpose and progress. You're doing *exactly* what you want to do at that moment. You are firing on all possible cylinders, and you feel like any task before you could be accomplished with ease and energy left to spare. You are on fire—and you know it.

What Greene says, and what I agree with, is that any time can be made into alive time, because alive time is a choice, just as dead time is a choice. It might sound a little abstract, but think about it: you've already made a series of choices since you woke up this morning— you've gotten up, gotten moving, braced yourself, eaten right, taken supplements, and now you're on your way to work. You chose how to use those other minutes. You chose what to think about, what to put in your body, how to feel. You owned that time. Why can't we do this at *any* time? Why can't we do this with our commute, even if having to get to work or to school isn't a choice? The truth is: we can. And it's the secret to turning your commute into something you relish rather than something you dread, something to look forward to rather than check out from and waste.

Bringing this time to life is a two-step process. It requires preparing and opening your mind, then flexing and filling it. Or, as I like to call it: mindfulness and mind*fill*ness.

Mindfulness

You've almost certainly heard the words *mindfulness* or *mindfulness practice* at some point in the last year, and if I had to guess, you didn't get a clear idea of what those words meant from the person using them—usually some Silicon Valley entrepreneur on some podcast complaining about how difficult it was for him to find time to appreciate all the money he was making until he built a rock garden or bought a beach house so he could finally build his rock garden. And I bet you turned off that podcast thinking that mindfulness is some special enlightened feeling that takes place in some Edenic location for busy, hypersuccessful people (translation: not you). Either that, or you turned it off thinking that mindfulness is total bullshit.

Here's the truth: while it is the hottest word out there, referenced in every Medium post and talked about at every conference as some kind of miracle cure for all your problems—anxiety, apathy, focus, loneliness, male-pattern baldness, world hunger, you name it— mindfulness is pretty uncomplicated at its core.

Mindfulness is simply being aware and conscious in the present moment. That's it.

Mindfulness is tuning in only to the sensations of life around you. It is real and serious and sustained focus on the here and now. It's not what's going on in the world. It's not the dozens of angry, frustrated drivers boxing you in on the crowded freeway. Nor is it what you have to do in fifteen minutes when the train pulls into your station. Or the creeping stress of your job—it's *especially* not that.

In that sense, mindfulness is a type of nothingness: it's *not* your bank account, it's *not* your hopes, it's *not* your fears, it's *not* any kind of coulda, woulda, shoulda. In that same way, mindfulness is a kind of everythingness: it's you. All of you. Right now. This second, because the only thing that exists is this second.

If that sounds kind of fuzzy, here's a way to make it more concrete. The next time you're supposed to be doing something and you catch yourself focusing on something else, that is a moment when you're *not* mindful. You probably have more of those moments than you'd like to admit. But that's why mindfulness as a practice can be so powerful. It can help bring you back to the present moment, and in doing so expand and prepare your mind for what lies ahead of you for the rest of your day. This is the essence of Zen philosophy. In classic Zen training the masters proposed four very simple practices: archery, calligraphy, pouring tea, and arranging flowers. The goal was not to create an impressive result—a bull's-eye, a masterpiece, the perfect matcha latte, a good-looking vase. The goal was the process itself. Could they devote every bit of their focus to the task at hand, without letting their mind wander? Could they take the perfect shot, make the perfect stroke, the one where 100 percent of their mind, body, and spirit was unified in the task at hand?

When I was reading *Zen in the Art of Archery*, this was a concept I had a hard time understanding. To me, the perfect shot was the one that hit the bull's-eye. Bam, suck it! But for the Zen masters the result didn't matter. At least not immediately. The only thing that mattered was my total and complete mindfulness on nocking the arrow, pulling the string, aiming, breathing, and releasing. Eventually this would lead to not just one lucky bull's-eye, but a lot of purposeful ones. Yet even that wasn't the point! The point was about life. Instead of rushing from one thing to another, always focused on the past and the future, why not just be here now (nod to Ram Dass). Zen mindfulness was then, and is now, the answer to the problem of meditation.

Meditation, another buzzword with all the associated apps and gadgets, is really just a strategy for mindfulness. But meditation has an even bigger branding problem, conjuring images of monks on a mountain, and *especially* long, boring sits with our eyes closed—because most of us have tried meditation and failed to reach the promised nirvana. The problem with meditation is that it typically requires a controlled environment. You need spare time, a body that doesn't ache when you sit still, a quiet space, dim light, your favorite incense. But that's not real life. At best that's an hour out of your day where you step into an alternate universe to practice your spells, like the Marvel hero Doctor Strange. While being a wizard is undeniably dope, when you need mindfulness the most, those conditions aren't going to be there. That's what the Zen masters realized, and what Native American–trained tracker turned author Tom Brown realized. You need mindfulness you can take with you, on the road. Literally. So he developed a practice that I call the wide peripheral gaze.

THE WIDE PERIPHERAL GAZE

Open your eyes as wide as they go without engaging any muscles of the face. Keep your focus relaxed in the center of your vision. With your mind only, become aware of everything happening at the periphery of your vision. Up, down, left, right. Things might be a little fuzzy, that's fine. Then, still without focusing on anything at all, become aware of everything. Each leaf moving in the wind. People walking by. A bird in the distance. Wrinkles in fabric. See everything, focus on nothing. Every moment something will be different, always changing, just like life. It is life. Breathe with your belly. Become aware of all things happening at all times. Become the observer of every detail in the environment, ignoring nothing, yet focusing on nothing. That strange feeling you have now—of a clear mind, of freshness and lightness? That is mindfulness meditation. Nothing more and nothing less.

A lot of you might be thinking that pretty much everything I have said in this chapter sounds like I should be whispering it to you on a microphone made out of healing crystals. Fair enough. But mindfulness and meditation isn't backed by crystals, it's backed by gold-standard science. Study after study reveals that mindfulness practices have tangible real-world results. One study of over 17,000 medical records shows that those engaging in mindfulness practices are 43 percent less likely to need any form of hospital care than those who do not. Another meta-analysis of thirty-nine studies totaling 1,140 participants showed "robust" effectiveness of mindfulness-based therapy for a range of conditions, particularly those conditions related to anxiety and depression.

But here's the beauty of what I'm asking you to do: you can do it during your commute. The same time that you could be wasting, or raging, you can be practicing mindfulness. Turning dead time to alive time.

Each morning, it takes me about twenty minutes to get to the Onnit office from my home in Austin (yes, that's right, I have a commute too!). When I'm getting owned by my commute, I turn on the radio, then check my Instagram or email at every stoplight. By the time I arrive at work, I am as high-strung as a man on a wire. On the mornings I own it, I try to be present. This can take different forms, depending on a variety of circumstances, but most often it boils down to focusing on my breath, practicing a wide peripheral gaze meditation, and being hyperaware of my body and my surroundings. Sometimes I'll just look at the different shades of green in the leaves, or see all the cars, the people inside, the street art, without looking at anyone or anything in particular. I'll let my mind relax, free from all the decisions I am about to make. Call it *Zen and the Art of Getting to Work*. Best of all: it's free, it's easy, and it requires no commitment other than choice.

Mind*fill*ness

Mindfulness brings the dead time to life, but what I call mindfillness is what animates that time and makes it productive. It *fills* the mind that you've just focused and opened. This is a practical choice as much as a purposeful one, because if your commute resembles that of the average American, thirty minutes is way too long to do breath work *and* drive *and* try to stare out the sides of your head like a gecko. If you can do it, I applaud you. But most of us, myself included, don't have that kind of focus every day, so we need some other options to use this time well instead of wasting it; to go from being owned by our commute to owning it.

That's why I want you to use the rest of the time on your commute to learn something. Sure, you could just turn on the radio and drive around singing at the top of your lungs. That's definitely an option, and everyone has days when they just have to crank it up and break it down. But what if you devoted those spare minutes to studying something, to broadening not just your gaze but your horizons as well? Imagine what you could do with all those added-up minutes.

TRAVELING UNIVERSITY

The iPhone is a traveling university. It's not cheap—but it's way cheaper than an MBA. There are no tests at the end of the year, and you can pick your classes. That's why the first thing I do after my mindfulness practice is fire up my phone and put on a podcast.

There are thousands to choose from, depending on your interests. In the prescription, we'll get into the details. But for now, I'll tell you what I'm *not* listening to: the news or talk radio. I don't run a hedge fund, and I'm not in politics, so the idea that I, an average person, should be following breaking news in real time is ridiculous. While I think it's important to be an informed citizen, I'm not interested in making myself miserable by plugging into the 24/7 news cycle of endless outrage and conflict. For the same reason, I strongly suggest you resist talk radio of *all* political persuasions. The point is to learn something, not gorge on nonsense. Far too much media is designed to provoke and distract—the opposite of both mindfulness and mind*fill*ness—and so when people think they are informing themselves, they are in fact falling for a giant con. Psychologists even have a term for it: narcotizing dysfunction. In fact, the more you follow the news, in some cases, the less likely you are to be an active, involved citizen, because you've confused consuming information with acting on it.

If you can avoid the news glut and find your way to some informative podcasts, you'd be surprised how much you can learn. Every day I have someone coming up to me and telling me how a podcast changed his life. Sometimes multiple times a day. I believe it to be the single most influential force in media today. I built the entire Onnit empire on the back of podcasts, and you can use them to help you build whatever life you want too. It was Jim Rohn who said, "Formal education will make you a living; self-education will make you a fortune." In my case that has been literally true.

One of the added bonuses about podcasts is that often there are incredible interviews with authors of books. I love to read, and I love audiobooks. But I don't dare start a book until I have heard the author on a podcast. I'm not gonna give a book my time and money until I have a really good reason. If I like the interview and there is more to learn, I'm a one-click buy away from my Kindle or my Audible account (digital or audio). An average book takes about eight hours of listen time, and if your mind is sharp you can speed that up to six hours by moving to 1.5x speed. For most of us, that is going to be a new book every two weeks. Talk about leveling up! (We'll cover more of my strategies around actually reading books in chapter 14.)

Even if podcasts or audiobooks don't change your life, I can promise you this: the twenty minutes you spend listening to a high-quality podcast will feel a lot like when you find a $20 bill in a coat you haven't worn in a while. Unexpectedly you feel just a little bit wealthier, even though technically you'd had that money all along! In the same way, taking that half hour of mindless time and learning something from it will make you feel like you just got away with something—and you did. You managed to wring some value out of time that you would have wasted. It'll feel amazing, and it should.

Prescription

Some of you might work from home. You might not have a commute. Great, even better. The commute serves as a transition between your profession and the rest of your day. Go ahead and make this transition anyway. If you live and work in an apartment building, put on some headphones and go for a walk. If you're at home, head out into the yard or the porch, or walk a few streets. Practicing both mindfulness and mindfillness without actually having the distraction of driving is ideal. For the rest of us, relegated to trains, planes, and automobiles, here is the plan.

STEP 1: WOOSAH MOTHAFUCKA

As soon as you get in your car take six deep breaths. Expand your lungs as much as possible, and focus your breath into your belly— that same place where the dragon hatches and tells you to melt the traffic in front of you like you were Khaleesi on a bad moon day. A study published by the Japanese Society of Hypertension found that when you take six deep breaths over the course of thirty seconds, your blood pressure ends up lower. This will help center you, and act as a prophylactic frustration vaccine. Then, if at any other time during the drive or life you feel the dragon coming out, cool him down with six more breaths. Remember, it's not two breaths, not five breaths, it's six. SIX!

STEP 2: WIDE PERIPHERAL GAZE

The bane of driving is distraction. The opposite of mindfulness. First practice the wide peripheral gaze when you are stopped. But some of us might be inclined to explore it while driving. After all, every driver's safety class tells you to keep your eyes forward but be aware of your periphery. The goal is to notice even more of your surroundings than ever before. That little squirrel that might run out into the road, or the person not looking when they are backing out. If skillfully employed, you should be in the fucking zone! The big now. The place where martial artists fight from and surfers surf from. But if you feel that this puts you at a safety disadvantage, or you are the slightest bit uncomfortable, then only practice the wide gaze while stopped.

▧ STEP 3: LEARN SOME SHIT

Now that you've opened your mind, it's time to fill it. Open your favorite podcast app on your phone and fire up a morsel of mental magic. Since you've made it this far, I feel pretty good recommending the *Aubrey Marcus Podcast*. We explore all elements of human optimization, diving a little deeper and getting a little weirder than even this book will do. As for other inspiration and stimulating conversation, I obviously love *The Joe Rogan Experience*, Tim Ferriss is essential listening, and Lewis Howes's *School of Greatness* podcast seldom disappoints. If you need a true kick in the ass, check out Jocko Willink. If you're in the mood to think about diet and lifestyle, I listen to Ben Greenfield's and Shawn Stevenson's podcasts (and we even created one that ex-fighter and biohacker extraordinaire Kyle Kingsbury hosts). If you are looking for a great story, nothing beats the real-life tales from Daniele Bolelli's *History on Fire*, or Dan Carlin's *Hardcore History*. For love and relationships, check out Chris Ryan and Dan Savage. If laughter is your thing (it's pretty much everyone's thing) check out *The Fighter and the Kid*, hosted by Brendan Schaub and Bryan Callen, or *The Jason Ellis Show*. And finally, to dive deeper into practical spirituality, check out Duncan Trussell's *Family Hour*.

Now Do It

My mother, who was a professional tennis player, finishing as high as the semifinals of Wimbledon, always said that flying was the most relaxing thing she ever did. In the days before personal computers, phones, and Wi-Fi, there was literally nothing to do on a plane. There weren't really even consumer headphones or devices to use them with in the 1960s. This was the era of libraries, and she was often traveling around foreign countries, packing only her tennis bag, so she didn't have books either. She couldn't train, she couldn't work on anything, she was free to just . . . be . . . present. It was heaven for her. That is what your car ride can be.

Finding these pockets of peace is a critical life skill. We have to build them into the ideal day; we can't just expect to find them. Why shouldn't you be able to sit in the driver's seat of your Corolla or the orange seat of the M train and find peace and serenity? Like all things, you have to work for it. You have to make the time, you have to make the moment into the moment you want it to be.

But here's the upside: if you can do this right on your routine ride into work, this is all the meditation you will need for the day. It won't matter if you work at some fancy place like Google that offers multidenominational meditation nooks. Soon your commute will be a trigger for mindfulness instead of a trigger for road rage. It will be productive instead of destructive.

If you are going to own the day, you have to own the hour, and you have to own the minute. These minutes are precious things. They are the only currency we spend every day whose value fluctuates wildly. Spend your minutes investing in your future self, filling your emotional coffers, and building value and enjoyment, or spend minutes depleting your emotional bank account. Remember what Peter Gibbons wished for if he had a million dollars? To sit and do nothing. He had that opportunity every time he got in the car. His wealth was right there in front of him. We all have the same amount of the only currency that matters: time. To spend your minutes well—that is the only goal of a life well lived.

THREE POINTERS

+ There is a fundamental choice when it comes to your commute. You can choose alive time where you are growing, learning, and improving, or dead time where at best you are wasting your time. Those who consistently choose alive time will have a significant advantage in life.

+ To expand your mind and gain actionable information during the commute, check out podcasts or audiobooks, which offer an opportunity to learn that is as valuable as any expensive education.

+ To combat the potential negative impact of the commute, as well as to practice greater presence and peace of mind, use conscious breathing techniques along with mindfulness practices like the wide peripheral gaze.

6

THE POWER PLANTS

The problem with tobacco is inhaling it.

—DON HOWARD LAWLER

Plants are not just a vital natural source of essential nutrients and minerals. When used properly, they can also provide mental energy and clarity and unlock greater work capacity as well. Grab an optimized coffee or a nootropic whenever you need a little pick-me-up. Indulge in nicotine to take your work to the next level. Each of these plant-based substances offers something to supercharge your efforts that you can look forward to throughout the day.

Getting Owned

When you hop off the plane in Cusco, Peru, it's immediately clear why the Incas revered the sun. Over two miles closer to this celestial orb than at sea level, the sun there is intensely bright and the air is shockingly thin. The effects of altitude can be so intense that airlines place baskets of leaves for you to chew on at the counter outside the boarding door right as you enter the terminal. The leaves are from the coca plant. They have been used for millennia by the indigenous cultures and shown in clinical research to prevent altitude sickness and boost aerobic energy, which can flag if altitude sickness kicks in. When used the natural way—put in your mouth like chewing tobacco so the many alkaloids can enter your bloodstream through your gums—coca leaves have numerous health benefits and very few side effects.

This highlights one of the many beautiful things about the human experience: we have a body perfectly designed to enjoy the foods and drugs that come from the earth. We have a tongue that tastes the earthy, rich flavor of coffee, and the astringent smack of a good cup of tea, while our blood cells simultaneously deliver the complex molecules therein to our brains—stimulating production of adrenaline for energy, acetylcholine for focus, dopamine for pleasure, and serotonin for happiness.

Who among us wouldn't want a little bit more of any of those? According to the authors of *Stealing Fire*, the answer is nobody. Everyone wants a little bit more, and they always have. The authors, Jamie Wheal and Steven Kotler, make the convincing argument that harnessing these endogenous chemicals, whether from activity or ingestion, is a fundamental evolutionary drive. The problem is that these feelings can be *too good*, and the evolutionary drive for more of them can drive us right off a cliff.

You could argue that in some instances, it already has.

The feeling of hyperfocus, boundless energy, mind-bending pleasure, and euphoric happiness is so good, and people want it so bad, that we refine these plants into drugs and pharmaceuticals to make them hit harder, and hit faster. This only makes people want them more, which incentivizes us to make them stronger, and before you know it, we've become addicted. That's when the people who have had no experience with these drugs in their natural form and who are completely unaware of what plants can do become scared of their effects and try to outlaw them in *all* forms—concentrated, synthetic, natural, whatever.

This isn't the fault of the plants, obviously. The plants are not the enemy. They are allies—tools to be used for enhancing performance and the enjoyment of our lives. Nope, this is our fault. We have turned plants that can help us reach our fullest potential into toxic drugs that reduce it, and then accepted a daily existence of suboptimal functioning as a consequence.

Our altitude-fighting friend the coca leaf is a notorious example of this phenomenon, because one of the alkaloids it contains is cocaine. Cocaine comprises around half of 1 percent of the total coca. It's not a statistically insignificant amount, and it's not so much that they should change the name of the plant to the "cocaine bush," but what happens when you chemically isolate, purify, condense, and concentrate it? You get a different animal entirely. You get the powder that is highly stimulating, deleterious to health, and regularly . . . well, you watched *Narcos*, right? It is estimated that close to 900,000 people are addicted to cocaine in the United States alone. As recently as 2015, there were an estimated 1.5 million cocaine users over the age of twelve. The year before, there were more than 5,000 cocaine overdose deaths—the most since 2007.

I've watched cocaine take beautiful bodies and colorful dreams, then dry them and white them out, just like we do to the lush green coca leaf. I have friends with similar stories who can trace their origins back to the poppy. Poppy tea was a mild pain-relieving folk medicine. Then it became opium. Then it became heroin. Then it became OxyContin, Vicodin, Percocet. Over 36 million people abuse these prescription opiates. Two million of them are addicts in the United States, with more than 20,000 overdose deaths in their ranks every year. And that's just from the pharmaceutical version. The street drug, heroin, claims another 11,000.

The history of tobacco is no less tragic. It went from dried leaves that you burned or chewed, holding the plant in your mouth, to carcinogenic little tubes called cigarettes that are packed with tars and chemicals you breathe deep into your lungs. Cigarettes steal an average of thirteen years from a smoker's life, and have contributed to a kool 20 million deaths since 1964. What's worse, they also kill innocent bystanders. The CDC estimates that 41,000 people die every year from secondhand smoke.

Even caffeine has gone from something you found in tea leaves and coffee beans to a refined synthetic drug we put in cans of soda and Red Bull or, worse, Redline.

In all these cases, what began as powerful plants used in their natural form to combat everything from pain to fatigue became some of the most destructive, addictive substances in the world because we humans, in our drive for more, stronger, faster, fucked them all up. Then in many cases we banned them altogether, effectively removing them from the pantheon of performance allies.

That seems to be how it goes with consuming plants in modern society; it's a slippery slope from appreciating them to full-on getting owned by them. If you've ever met a full-blown addict, it's easy to see who is in charge there, and it's typically not the human being. Needless to say, restoring a proper relationship with plants is crucial, not only for our survival but for this single day in front of us.

Owning It

To this point in the book, many of the strategies we've covered have been designed to fill holes and get you back to even. They are the table-stakes changes that we all need to make to repair deficiencies that have accrued over time and prevented us from being our most effective self. But here's the thing about that: mastering these twenty-four hours is about more than simply being effective; it's about giving yourself the chance to be a boss.

A Peruvian-trained *vegetalista*, or plant doctor, once told me that the plants were entities so evolved and benevolent to humanity that for them to manifest in human form, with all of our capricious emotions and failings, would be a step backward. I don't expect you to take that literally, but it is a beautiful metaphor. Plants are the steady, constant ally of all animal life. Not a single animal would be alive if not for plants. Plants hold no grudge if we do them wrong. They give us the air to breathe, the food we eat, and, on occasion, much-needed medicine for mind, body, and spirit.

We have coevolved with plants, our bodies adapting to receive their benefits over time, as a tree bends toward the light. Plants can be an incredible ally in this way, and if you are going to truly own your day, truly give yourself a chance to do amazing things, then your work starts here, with the help of three powerful plants that can supercharge your efforts, take you to the next level, and help you not only achieve your full potential, but exceed it.

Note: I am replacing the "Prescription" section in this chapter with sections called "Final Thoughts" that offer some guidance and suggestions for each of the power plants we discuss. A relationship with any plant or drug is a very personal choice: the goal here is to have an honest conversation and exploration, and leave you with some actionable information should you desire to pursue it.

Caffeine—Coffee, Tea, Yerba Maté, and Guarana

All right coffee lovers, I've held you back long enough . . . now is your time! Finally, you can drink from the cup of joe, make your daily offering to the Star of Bucks, and crush some well-timed, well-fortified caffeine.

Caffeine is one of the most ubiquitous plant substances ingested in the world. There is evidence of tea drinking as far back as 2737 BC, and right now in North America 90 percent of adults will have some kind of caffeinated beverage before the day is through. There is a pretty good reason for this: as we discussed in chapter 1, caffeine releases all three stress hormones—adrenaline, cortisol, and norepinephrine—plus mood-boosting serotonin and pleasurable dopamine. No wonder a good cup of coffee feels somewhere between a warm hug and a hard drug. With caffeine's natural ability to block a compound called adenosine—one of the main factors that make the brain register fatigue—a cup of coffee is basically a piping-hot crucible of alertness that can help you forge an exceptional day.

For this reason, caffeine is the universal drug of choice for the all-nighter and the not-enough-sleep-that-day crowd. You can't go into a police station or a firehouse on an overnight shift without seeing a pot of coffee, or a Keurig ready and waiting. Not only does it keep people awake, caffeine has been shown to delay the time it takes for muscles to reach exhaustion, increasing physical performance by 12 percent, on average. For a firefighter, that could very well be the difference between Tommy the Cat making it out of that burning apartment building alive and Tommy the Cat burning through all nine of his lives at once.

While it is certainly possible to get caffeine from a variety of plant sources, including guarana berry and kola nut—the original source for "cola"—the real players in the game are tea and coffee. We're going to break down the advantages of each, so you have a better idea which ally to reach for in which situation.

Tea

Like the Michael Jackson song, most caffeinated tea comes from the same plant, it don't matter if it's black or white. Or oolong, green, matcha, sencha, pu-erh, or any of the fancy delicious teas that I love. They are all the same species, *Camellia sinensis*, just prepared different ways, with roughly the same impact on alertness and physical performance.

The only real outlier in the universe of teas is yerba maté, a mainstay in Argentina that the gauchos borrowed from the indigenous tribes who harvested the leaf from the rain-forest holly. Yerba maté has some distinct advantages; it doesn't get overly bitter as it steeps, so you can really nurse the caffeine out of it, especially if you have a gourd and a metal straw to mash it up with, as in traditional preparations. You get triple hipster points if you carry one of these in your satchel.

Maté is great, and I do have a sentimental spot for a good cuppa black or Earl Grey, probably because my mum picked up the habit of teatime at Wimbledon (pinkie in the air, don't care), but if you are looking for maximum benefits, the king of all the teas is unequivocally matcha. A tea that has an entire Zen ceremony dedicated to it in Japan. With 66 milligrams of caffeine per 8 ounces of prepared tea, matcha has more caffeine than black tea but less than a cup of coffee, making it the Mama Bear of afternoon pick-me-ups.

To make matcha, before harvest the leaves are covered in shade to prevent direct sunlight. This spikes the chlorophyll as the leaves struggle to draw energy from the sun. Along with chlorophyll, which helps matcha fight bad breath, the leaves produce more L-theanine, an amino acid that improves cognitive function on its own. L-theanine naturally balances some of the potential negative effects of caffeine like anxiety or jitters, and some studies have shown that the combination of caffeine and L-theanine has unique advantages for brain function, including heightened activity in the alpha frequency brainwaves (we'll talk more about this in chapter 9) that play a big role in things like focus and attention span. The leaves are then ground up into a luscious green powder of the gods that you can stir or whisk into hot water, or make into any variety of delicious beverages, like the MoMatchajito, which I'll share with you below. The result is a smoother ride, with greater focus, than any other natural caffeine source.

MoMatchajito

Juice of ½ lime

3 sprigs mint

1 teaspoon matcha

3 drops liquid stevia

240ml sparkling water

INSTRUCTIONS

+ In the bottom of a cocktail shaker, muddle the lime and mint.

+ Add the matcha, stevia, and 60ml of sparkling water.

+ Shake briskly and pour into a large glass.

+ Add ice, if desired, and top with the remaining sparkling water.

+ Stir and serve.

Coffee

Despite having gotten extra fancy in recent years in cities like Austin, where I live, coffee has developed much more than a cult following; it is a full-blown religion, with an army of very devout parishioners. According to the National Coffee Association, for example, Americans drank 400 million cups a day in 2016. Yes, that's more cups of coffee than there are people. When you consider that Mormons and *most* babies don't start their days with a piping-hot cup of java, that means regular coffee drinkers are typically knocking back more than one cup every day.

Grown on trees in a specific band of heat north or south of the equator called "the coffee belt," the bean is removed from the coffee "cherry," dried, then ultimately roasted and ground to varying degrees of fineness, after which nearly boiling water is poured or pressed through it until the original black gold drips through the bottom for your drinking pleasure.

While coffee shares some of the enhanced *physical* performance characteristics of all caffeinated substances, and includes a healthy amount of antioxidants and nutrients, where it really shines is its influence on mood. Specifically, drinking coffee has been correlated to a decreased risk of depression. People who drink caffeine at amounts easily found in coffee have a 13 percent lower chance of depression, and are 45 percent less likely to commit suicide. Perhaps this is due to the serotonergic qualities of coffee, or perhaps it is just that happier people drink more coffee—the jury is still out. What we do know is that coffee helps protect the liver, and in one study where participants drank three cups a day for three weeks, it was even shown to help support gut health—which could be another explanation for why coffee may assist with depression, since so much of our immune system and neurotransmitter growth occurs in the gut.

Whether we're talking about tea for increased focus or coffee for elevated mood, to do caffeine the right way, you have to manage your timing and your tolerance—that's why you're drinking it now instead of first thing in the morning—and you have to slow down its absorption into your bloodstream so it doesn't spike you into the ceiling and then drop you through the floor like you're glued to a giant Super Ball. To do that, you gotta mix it with fat (just like we did with breakfast) into something I call optimized caffeine.

Deep Dive: How Fat Slows Caffeine

Why fat with caffeine? Fat is one of the slowest foods to digest (metabolize) in the human system. When you mix caffeine with fat, the body can only effectively metabolize the caffeine as fast as it can metabolize fat. To break down fats, the stomach has to wait for a secretion of bile from the gallbladder. There is a natural rate-limiting factor on this mechanism of action, which forces a slower drip of caffeine into the system. As the caffeine-spurred hormone levels rise slowly, they fall slowly, spreading out the arc and diminishing the spiking and crashing sensation that can come from naked caffeine.

LET'S GET FAT

Adding good fat to caffeine is not a new concept. In Tibet, where the conditions are cold and harsh, the work is long, and people need fuel throughout the day, they have been putting yak butter in their tea for ages. We used to do it too, back in the day when we put cream in our coffee and tea. But then it became half and half. And after that it became skim milk and a bunch of sugar, or worse, two pumps of artificially flavored high-fructose corn syrup. Unfortunately, this progression, which we thought was doing our body a favor, was actually doing the opposite; substituting a harmful anti-nutrient combination of lactose and sugar for an important macronutrient in the fat-rich cream.

In recent years, we've begun to smarten up, thanks to guys like nutrition expert Robb Wolf. When the world was busy squirting cow sugar (aka skim milk) into their coffee, Robb went the other direction and started recommending adding fats like butter, cacao butter, or MCT as supplements to your morning coffee. Not only does that taste delicious but the feeling of time-released caffeine through fat's slower absorption rate has fueled the butter coffee craze. Still, there are far too many of us trying to get by with low-fat almond milk, soy milk, or rice milk in our coffee and tea, none of which are going to do shit but sweeten our drinks, because none of those "milks" possess the slow-digesting fats necessary to slow down the metabolizing of caffeine.

In a pinch, full-fat dairy like whole cream will do, but better than that is to whip out a blender and add a serving of grass-fed butter, coconut oil, or cacao butter to make a frothy fatty latte, and get those fat macronutrients into your life! Perhaps the best fat source for your caffeine, though, is MCT oil.

Pro Tip: Emulsified MCT Oil

MCT stands for medium-chain triglyceride, a form of saturated fatty acid. These triglycerides are found naturally in coconut and palm oil, but coconut oil provides the best source, free of the environmental cost of destroying palm forests. MCTs serve multiple health benefits, including evidence for improved cognitive function, weight management, and up to 5 percent more energy. Boom! For high-intensity athletes and those following a higher-fat, lower-carbohydrate diet, MCTs can serve as a vital source of energy due to the liver's ability to easily metabolize MCT into fuel.

One of the problems with regular MCT oil, as with any of the other fats mentioned, is that typically fat doesn't mix into water. Only fats that are emulsified, like cream, will mix with a simple stir. Otherwise you have to blend them in, and I know at my house a clean blender is as exciting as finding your favorite pair of underwear folded neatly at the top of the drawer. MCT oil is arguably the best fat in the world, and using it as an emulsified creamer that can be stirred into any drink, hot or cold, is a game changer. There are some good brands starting to offer it now, so, wherever you can get it, emulsified MCT is hands down the best, simplest way to mix fat with caffeine.

Final Word

I've got ninety-nine problems, and caffeine might be one of them. Like most good drugs, caffeine has its issues: tolerance and addiction, to name two. Dehydration and sleep disturbances, to name two more.

We probably all know people with a really high caffeine tolerance. I remember watching billionaire hedge fund trader Paul Tudor Jones drink a glass bottle of Coca-Cola prior to bed, when I was lucky enough to visit him at his Maryland hunting lodge as a child. I know my good friend, former fighter, host, comedian, and podcaster Brendan Schaub can drink coffee pretty much all day and hardly feel a buzz. If either of those hard-charging, successful gentlemen stopped drinking caffeine, they might have a problem. That's what the research shows, at least. After reviewing 170 years of data, a Johns Hopkins study in 2004 recognized caffeine withdrawal and the associated headaches, fatigue, and nervous system dysregulation as a full-fledged medical disorder. Dehydration, which comes from the body trying to pass the caffeine quickly through the system, and sleep disturbances, which result from caffeine's six-hour half-life (half of it is still in your system six hours past ingestion), certainly contribute to those symptoms and the overall disorder diagnosis, but the fundamental fact of the matter is that caffeine is a drug. It's one of the funnest, friendliest, most social drugs we know of, but it is still a drug that can do real damage. Four cups of coffee or 400 milligrams of caffeine spread through the day is generally considered safe, but as little as 500 to 1,000 milligrams of caffeine at one time can be a fatal overdose, especially if you have a preexisting condition that makes you more susceptible to caffeine's effects.

As with any drug, the point is to not overdo it. Don't drink too much, so you don't build up an unmanageable tolerance. Don't drink too much *too often*, so you don't get addicted. If you want to reset your tolerance, research indicates that if you take a week off, you'll be back to normal. And don't drink too late, so you don't hamper your ability to enter deeper sleep states. Avoid those pitfalls, while adding good fats to your caffeine to flatten and extend its effects, and you are set up to enjoy one of our favorite pastimes and take advantage of all the mental and physical benefits it has to offer.

Tobacco

If you're anything like my editors, you probably saw the word *tobacco* in bold print and figured this section would be one word long: DON'T. As you can see from the ocean of ink below this sentence, that is not the case. How could it be, when you consider that as of 2012, an estimated billion people smoke tobacco, and countless others consume it in alternative ways, including traditional ceremonial use? We have to talk about it, and get to the bottom of the mysteries of tobacco, because the problems we have with it as a society have little to do with the plant itself, and more to do with how you get it inside you.

All tobacco consumption carries the stigma of the misuse of cigarettes—aka Death Sticks—and the companies who manufacture and peddle them. It's understandable when you consider that cigarettes are the most ubiquitous tobacco product, and the evidence is pretty clear that smoking cigarettes is dumb if you like life. The tricky part for us, as we talk about owning this day and taking our work to the next level, is that nicotine—the active component of tobacco—while carrying its own risks, has a ton of performance benefits.

For one, nicotine puts you in the fucking zone, also called "flow." In mechanistic terms, nicotine fits into the same receptors in our brain as acetylcholine—the powerhouse neurotransmitter responsible for attention and memory—and is correlated with the alpha frequency brainwave state, similar to that produced by matcha tea, characterized by effortlessness, alertness, and creativity. An analysis of forty-one studies on nicotine and cognitive performance concluded that nicotine safely improved fine motor skills, attention, accuracy, response time, short-term memory, and working memory. That's some Neo in the matrix shit, right there. It might also be why you see baseball players and elite military units lean on chewing tobacco as part of their routines. Hitting a ninety-miles-per-hour fastball from sixty feet away or pinging a moving target with 5.56mm ammo from sixty yards away both take an incredible amount of focus, dexterity, accuracy, and muscle memory.

So the game, then, with tobacco isn't about determining whether or not it's useful, it's figuring out how to get the nicotine safely into your system while doing the least amount of damage. As Aldous Huxley famously said, "You don't want to burn the house down to bake a loaf of bread." So before we burn the house down, or burn anything at all for that matter, let's take a look at the options for getting that delicious dope into your brain.

Caveat: Nicotine Advisory

Let's get one thing clear: nicotine isn't for everyone. It is definitely not good for developing brains, as some data suggests that anyone under twenty-five who uses nicotine may experience some cognitive impairment later in life. But even if you are over twenty-five, you should proceed with caution. Even responsible nicotine use may cause seizures and involuntary muscle twitching, as well as abnormal heart rhythms, a slow heart rate, and fluctuating blood pressure.

Vomiting is the most common symptom of nicotine poisoning, however, and it can begin as quickly as fifteen minutes after ingestion. Beyond just poisoning, a full overdose of nicotine can be fatal. If you are going to dance with a plant as powerful as tobacco, it's good to have some respect and know the boundaries—yours and the plant's.

CIGARETTES: AKA DEATH STICKS

The nicotine in cigarette smoke increases levels of three of the most pleasurable chemicals the brain can produce—dopamine, norepinephrine, and serotonin. These are chemicals the body is capable of releasing on its own, but since smoking a cigarette is such a novel activity, some researchers suggest that the act of smoking might itself trigger the release of these chemicals based on a conditioned response, much like Pavlov's dogs that drooled at the sound of a dinner bell even when food wasn't present. This is likely why alternative nicotine delivery systems have such a poor success rate—they just don't trigger the same response—and why you should please, for the love of shiny disco Jesus, stay the fuck away from cigarettes.

You know the statistics already. You read some of them earlier. Cigarettes kill. In large part because you aren't simply taking tobacco smoke into your lungs, you are bringing with it significant amounts of toxic, carcinogenic smoke as well, thanks to all that fun stuff the unscrupulous profitmongers at cigarette manufacturers have added to their product over the years to preserve the tobacco, accelerate the burning, and increase the addictiveness. There is the bleached white paper you are inhaling, for instance, and oh, just under 600 other chemical additives, 100 of which are psychoactive. I wonder, do you think any of those 100 are addictive? I'd ask the 35 million people who try to quit smoking every year and fail within a week, but they're all out taking a smoke break. Again.

Independent of the specific health risks, cigarette smokers are also less attractive to potential partners, have a tougher time finding a job, and even when they do, end up earning less money. I could go on, but I'm gonna assume we trust each other at this point. I'm not going to give a lot of hard noes in this book, but this is one of them. Don't smoke cigarettes. There are better ways to get nicotine, and you're about to learn them.

SMOKELESS

In a groundbreaking report, London's Royal College of Physicians determined that "as a way of using nicotine, the consumption of non-combustible [smokeless] tobacco is on the order of 10–1,000 times less hazardous than smoking, depending on the product." They went on to suggest that smokeless tobacco manufacturers might market their products "as a 'harm reduction' option for nicotine users, and they may find support for that in the public health community." This evidence-based opinion has been highly contested here in the United States, primarily by Big Tobacco with their $117 billion in annual revenue to protect, so I'd go ahead and trust the good doctors across the pond on this one.

Swedish snus, a moist tobacco powder you tuck under your upper lip, appears to be one of the healthiest forms of smokeless tobacco. One study showed little difference in overall health and life expectancy between smokers who quit entirely and smokers who switched to snus. With no sweeteners and fewer additives—if any—snus is a cleaner option than many of the American snuff or chew products.

That said, the amount of nicotine you receive into your blood from smokeless tobacco can be equal to about four cigarettes, so for those of you thinking about making the switch, be mindful of the dose. For first-timers, this can really sneak up on you too, so tread lightly and make sure you have something to throw up into nearby if you aren't good at knowing your limits. We're not saying that smokeless tobacco, even snus, carries no risk at all, but there are elephantine advantages to choosing smokeless over cigarettes.

VAPING

While some research on cells in a petri dish indicates that vapor may impair cellular function, particularly around wound healing, a lot more research needs to be done to determine the actual harm of inhaled vapor. For now the best analysis comes from the same highly respected London Royal College of Physicians paper, which suggests that the hazard to health arising from long-term vapor inhalation from the e-cigarettes available today is unlikely to exceed 5 percent of the harm from smoking tobacco. That is to say, it might be twenty times safer. And while they acknowledge that there are no medical standards for the production of vapor, largely made of glycerin (though many have begun to move away from that), they strongly encourage all cigarette smokers to make the switch.

CIGARS AND PIPES

The big advantage of cigars and pipes is that you aren't meant to inhale the smoke into your lungs. To be sure, there is still *some* smoke being inhaled, and of course a lot of the same chemicals from the smoke still get into your blood through your gums, but the absence of significant smoke inhalation drops your risk for a lot of the cancers associated with cigarette smoking to virtually nil, especially, in the case of cigars, if you are only smoking one or two per day.

Pipe tobacco in a ceremonial context probably originated with our own Native American predecessors, who would smoke tobacco as a bonding ritual and to commemorate peace. In a Western context, we are most familiar with pipe tobacco in the mouths of ship captains (thank you, *The Simpsons*), European grandfathers, and old college professors. For pipes, tobacco is often steamed for hours to darken the color, then flavored and fortified with quite a few chemical additives that contribute to its mild, sweet smell and flavor. Pipe tobacco is smoked like a cigar, Bill Clinton–style (don't inhale), so despite the additives it's still a far better option for the positive mental performance attributes of nicotine than cigarettes.

NICOTINE GUM OR PATCH
This is the cleanest way to get nicotine into your system, period. With the clinical efficiency, however, the ritual and a lot of the fun is lost, which is why these alternatives don't work so well in helping people quit. But for the biohacker on a mission to optimize mental performance for short stretches, this is the cleanest way to do it.

Final Word
The bottom line is this: if you are smoking cigarettes, you need to switch to some other nicotine-delivery method like vaping, cigar or pipe smoking, gum, or the patch. And if you are interested in trying tobacco for the first time, it's extra important that you do it the right way. Even better, rotate the delivery so you are spreading potential stress to multiple different systems. Nicotine has tremendous advantages for mental sharpness and clarity when used appropriately, but when used sloppily and without clear intent, it is very easy to find yourself on a slippery slope to Addictionville.

Plant Nootropics and a Peculiar Little Moss
Nootropic is a word that has some heat behind it right now. It's hard to pronounce and harder to define, but consensus is that a nootropic is any supplement, food, or drug that improves some aspect of mental performance. For me, the key definitional aspect of a nootropic is its intention to boost mental performance, as opposed to treating some mental disease state, or deriving some ancillary benefit. Most don't consider caffeine and tobacco to be nootropics, for example. The studies show that they benefit cognitive performance, however,

so if you are intending to use them for that function, they would fit squarely in the nootropic category. One of the most popular pharmaceuticals of our generation, Adderall, is prescribed to treat ADHD, but ends up getting crushed up and snorted like a street drug to fight off fatigue and increase alertness. While that certainly can improve mental performance, the mechanism of action and intention of use is more as a stimulant, being only one single molecule away from the street drug methamphetamine. So is it a nootropic? If you are using it so that you can drink more Fireball whiskey shots without falling down on your face, then no, it is a stimulant. If you are using it to compose a symphony (do people still do that?), then yes, it is.

HUPERZIA SERRATA, ACETYLCHOLINE, AND OTHER SAT WORDS

The main plant nootropic we are going to focus on is something called *Huperzia serrata*, or club moss. *H. serrata* grows wild in Asia and has likely been used in local medicine for thousands of years. It has a very specific and well-defined mechanism of action, has an excellent safety profile, is not a classic stimulant, and targets one neurotransmitter in particular: acetylcholine.

We have talked a bit about serotonin and dopamine, but we haven't talked much about acetylcholine. Acetylcholine helps neurons (brain cells) communicate better with each other. *H. serrata* contains a compound called huperzine A, which acts as a . . . drumroll for a big word, please . . . acetylcholinesterase inhibitor. What that basically means is that it delays the breakdown of acetylcholine in the brain, providing a temporary surplus of the neurotransmitter and extending the duration of its action. A meta-analysis of the use of huperzine A for the treatment of Alzheimer's and related symptoms has shown marginal benefit. And as would make sense, studies done on this compound show benefits similar to what you would find for any natural or synthetic substance designed to increase available acetylcholine: namely memory and learning performance.

I first learned about *H. serrata* after a visit to New York at the demand of my parents in my late twenties. They were worried that I was partying too hard, and about to destroy my brain. One glance at my social media, and I realized that argument was futile. They may have a point. So I agreed. What I didn't realize was that by agreeing, I was submitting myself to four days of testing, often hooked up to pointy hairnets with wires coming out. When all was said and done, the doctor told me that my mental hardware was okay, but the operating system was in serious need of support. He said the levels of all four of my major neurotransmitters were depressed—a sign of sleep deprivation, stress, and too much alcohol. Way too much. So he gave me a combination of some things to try: some 5-HTP for serotonin, some *Mucuna pruriens* for dopamine (did I really need more dopamine?), some L-theanine for gamma-aminobutyric acid (GABA) modulation, and then this stuff that sounded like the name of an Argentinian soccer player, called *Huperzia serrata*, targeted toward acetylcholine.

As much as I wanted to convince myself that my brain didn't need any help, the supplements worked. I was sharper, happier, and simultaneously more relaxed. But it was the *Huperzia serrata* that really changed the game. The feeling was foreign at first . . . and then it was like the gears in my brain caught, and suddenly I was operating on a higher level than I usually did. I was hyperfocused and aware, but still calm. My heart wasn't racing, but I was awake—more awake than usual. I felt elevated in my thinking, able to form fluid, lyrical sentences whose internal logic held together no matter how far my thinking took me. I wasn't just able to articulate complicated ideas, I was able to focus on complicated tasks as well. Even my mind-body coordination seemed improved, as if I was reacting faster to external stimulus.

It was this experience with the plant that eventually led me to place *Huperzia serrata* at the heart of supplementing high brain function. This little power plant you've probably never heard of, when combined with the right nutrients, can help with word recall and solving complicated tasks, and even assist with the speed at which you register external stimulus, which is one of the reasons why it has become a staple performance enhancer for our athletes, from Super Bowl champions to Sunday tennis club soldiers.

Final Word

We live in a get-shit-done world, and our brain is our biggest ally. Supporting the brain with nutrients not only will help you perform better but can keep your brain healthier over the long term. *Huperzia serrata* is a tool in your arsenal, a screwdriver in your set, and while you don't need to take it every day, on the days you need to be at your best, *on days you want to own,* you should have it available. Whether you wild-harvest and brew them into a tea or buy them in bulk online, nootropics like this humble little fern-looking moss have contributed to a lot of beautiful things being made, not the least of which can be your perfect day.

Now Do It

It was Saturday, late morning. I had gotten some good sleep the night before; my wearable sleep tracker, the Oura ring, showed an 84 percent sleep efficiency out of 100. I'll take that any day. I woke up and put in my HumanCharger earbuds. I did twenty-three burpees. Power shower. I had a great breakfast. I took my supplements. I sat here trying to write some of the pages of this book, and I couldn't get going. I had literally done everything to perfection, but I still needed help. I knew it was time for the caffeine. I decided on mixing up some coconut-almond-flavored black tea with some heavy cacao-infused coconut cream. I brewed up the tea, put in a huge dollop of cream. Steeped and stirred. As I started to sip, I noticed a familiar feeling in my bowels. It was a trained response, triggered as much from the taste as the effects. Yep, I needed to take a shit.

If you're a caffeine person, you don't need me to link to a study here. The adrenaline triggers the desired bowel response, and the healthy fats ensure that everything is going to move along its merry way. And this is good. Because when you take a big bowel-emptying dump, you are literally a different person. The balance of cells, bacteria, and microorganisms that reside in your body shifts by billions. No wonder good authors like James Altucher recommend taking a dump if you are stuck with your writing. A lot of times it feels like writer's block is literally sitting in your large intestine. Remove that obstacle, and the words start to flow. Everyone reading this book is benefiting from my postpoop clarity, brought about by three plants—tea, cacao, and coconut. This is the power of plants, in real time.

The love affair between writers, caffeine, and nicotine is both universal and eternal. Why? Writing is a beast. It is the birth of pure ideas into the messy symbolism of words. Your creation may get rejected, debunked, ignored. So when confronted by a beast like the pearly white snarl of the empty page, you need to call on your allies. If I'm writing, working late, podcasting, or playing chess in the boardroom, it is caffeine, nicotine, and Alpha Brain that I bring to the front lines.

But of course these plants aren't just for the hard tasks, they are also allies for the love of life. At sunset, I will smoke a good cigar and look out on the playground of my yard, with the foxes, the rabbits, the lizards, the snakes, the falcons, and all the plants in my garden that feed and nourish me—sending out gratitude in the form of smoke rings for the gift of being alive. I'll have a cup of coffee Thanksgiving morning with my mother as she bastes the turkey and we chat about her latest spiritual adventures. I'll take some Alpha Brain before a round of golf in a desperate attempt to shoot under 100, until I finally surrender with a laugh at my 107.

It doesn't really matter what you use the plants for, as long as your relationship with them is healthy. Your goal is to be better—at your work, at your relationship, at being alive. It's the same with anything. These plants are miraculous, powerful allies that can help you achieve amazing shit (sometimes literally), but they can also have power over you if you allow them to. If they are controlling your life, consider the well-established practice of harm reduction, and find ways to transition to a less harmful method or frequency to limit your downside exposure. To check myself, I'll pause with them for a week or sometimes even a month. Just to make sure I'm not convincing myself of anything that isn't true. Know the plants, know yourself, be honest, and decide the terms of your relationship with them. If it can be healthy, it will enhance more than just your performance, and you'll have an advantage in everything you do for as long as you live.

THREE POINTERS

+ Caffeine is ideal to alleviate sleepiness and improve your mood. To do it the right way, look for natural plant sources, make sure you don't interrupt your sleep, and blend with fats to help slow down the release into your body.
+ Nicotine on its own can be beneficial to focus, attention, and the enjoyment of your day. The problems come with the delivery. Never inhale smoke! Instead, look for other means like vaping and absorption through the gums or the skin to get you in the zone.
+ Nootropics have been proven to assist with memory and cognitive performance. *Huperzia serrata* is a great place to start and is a part of one of the most rigorously tested formulas on the market. If you don't know about nootropics, now's the time to find out.

DOIN' WORK

Whatever is worth doing at all is worth doing well.

—PHILIP STANHOPE,
4TH EARL OF CHESTERFIELD

We are built for work. It is never going to go away, nor would most of us ever want it to. It is part of the balance of life, and however you define it, you will always have work to do. To derive as much meaning, pleasure, and value out of this inescapable part of life as possible, you need to know your mission—whether it's related to the work itself or not. Then you need to own your workspace, and work as effectively as possible. Because what makes work feel less like labor is when you know why you are doing it, and how to do it well.

Getting Owned

I once had a boss who decided that his employees were cheating him on the amount of time they worked in the office. He complained about the few extra minutes at lunch, in the morning, grabbing coffee, going to the bathroom. Because he was paying for that time, any bit of it not used for work was therefore theft in his mind. Every day we were actively *stealing* from him.

Trying to clamp down on wanton thievery, like a Chinese buffet clamping down on wonton thievery, our boss instituted a time-measurement policy where all salaried workers, including executives like myself, had to fingerprint in and out of the office. The policy worked, kind of. Nobody took those extra minutes for themselves anymore, just like our boss wanted. Instead, we all stayed at our desks, just like he hoped, and fucked off five times as much on the Internet. Whoops. When I walked around the office and looked at employee computer screens, I was more likely to see Facebook or YouTube open than Photoshop or an Excel sheet. This loss of productivity wasn't something unique to our unhappy workplace. Companies have lost billions in revenue and workers $3 trillion in labor thanks to hours lost to Facebook alone since the site crossed the 100-million-user mark in 2008.

But even that, I think, misses the point. Time is the wrong metric to use when we evaluate work. Because it's not just about how much *time* you work, it's about how *effectively* you use that time. Before the fingerprint scanners, we were pretty effective, because we were reasonably content. What my boss didn't understand was that any productivity issues we had weren't time-related, they were process- and passion-related. So when he made it about time, not only did it feel like a punishment, it made all of us miserable, which resulted in a massive decrease in effectiveness—much of it purely out of spite!

That's the thing about work: it is simultaneously our greatest inner virtue and our biggest pain in the ass. When the balance gets upset, we get unhappy and it tips us into a negative space: workaholism on one end, Facebookaholism on the other. In my mind neither of those things should happen, because work—by which I mean the act of completing tasks for some purpose other than pure pleasure—is not the be-all and end-all. Work is just what we do. We are cut out for it.

Just look at the human body: the proportions of our upper and lower torso; the length of our arms; opposable thumbs; prehensile digits; the musculature in the abdomen and the lower back. Then look at our brains, solving puzzles for the future with the tenacity of a caffeinated child prodigy palming a stack of Rubik's Cubes. You know how I know that humans built the great wall of China? Because our bodies basically make us walking construction cranes, and our minds love nothing more than to play Legos with real life.

Unfortunately, over the centuries, we've allowed our unique capacity for work to define us as living beings. And somewhere along the way, we got so far out of balance that now 80 percent of people are dissatisfied with their jobs. The average person works 90,000 hours in his life. That's a long time to be miserable. Especially because if you hate your work, you are going to spend even more hours being miserable just thinking about how much you hate it. For the 40 percent who say their job is "very or extremely stressful," quickly those 90,000 lifetime hours of suck become 150,000. And before they know it, they are truly slaves to the hamster wheel of work.

How did we get here? Is it because people have gotten lazier and more entitled? I don't think so. Is it because they are blowing their work/life balance? Probably in part. In the United States, workers only take an average of 57 percent of their paid vacation days. That's crazy. You've got 90,000 hours to knock out, take the chance to chill on the beach when someone gives it to you. Or just stay at home and tell everyone you are in Bali. You know how nice it is to be home with no obligations? It's like heaven. But at least it's better in the West than in Japan, where 10,000 workers per year drop dead at their desks as a result of sixty-to-seventy-hour workweeks. The phenomenon is so prevalent that it even has a name—*karoshi*—proving once again that when it comes to forms of honorable suicide, no one fucks with the Japanese.

I think the biggest problem with all the dissatisfaction is that in most cases people are bringing the wrong mentality and the wrong expectations into their workplace. They think if they work long enough, and make enough money, eventually whatever happiness they are postponing will just sort of arrive. If that were true, then why do studies show that the peak income correlated to happiness is $83,000—surely not enough money to solve what most of us would consider to be typical problems? It's because there is no amount of work you will do that will finally make the work go away, and definitely no amount of money you can make that will solve all your problems. And the sooner you realize that, the sooner you can look for happiness in places where it might actually be found.

Many of you have already far surpassed that magic salary number. For you it may not be mo' money, mo' problems, like Diddy said (it's still Diddy, right?), but it's definitely mo' money, *different* problems. Those of you who are still working your way up to $83,000 are probably saying *Give me those rich-person problems any day, homie.* And I hear ya. That's why I had no intention of stopping at $83,000 a year either, and why guys like Gary Vaynerchuk admit that they were willing to "eat shit" for twenty years to be where they are today.

What sets guys like Gary Vee apart from the rest of us, though, is that he enjoys his work. He doesn't just embrace the grind, he relishes it. He's working toward something, and that something matters to him. That is why he is such a colossal force. That's also how I've been able to grow Onnit at an average of 40 percent a year since 2012. When people come visit the office, you know what they say?

It's not "Man, Aubrey, your employees are working so hard." It's "Man, your employees are so happy." And happiness is a magnet for success. Happy people do better work and draw other happy people to them. I never have to beg people to stay late to finish a project, or volunteer to work a trade show. Because I am constantly supporting their personal journeys of self-optimization, financially, physically, and emotionally. And it's not just my company; these principles are being adopted by many of the best and biggest companies in every industry.

The worst thing in the world is to feel like you are getting owned by your job or your employer. So what is the formula for owning your profession and being happy at work? Sure, working at a company you love helps. But it isn't essential, because you are the master of your internal environment. The formula has three parts: you need a mission you believe in, you have to own your space, and you have to work effectively.

Owning It

The unhappiest time of my life was right after college. I started a marketing company, and my only client at the time requested that I work full-time in-house. Desperate to prove something, not just to him but to myself, I poured my heart and soul into my client's company. And even though I wasn't very good at marketing yet, we started to see some serious progress. Through a few good ideas and relentless effort, online revenue went up 800 percent over the course of three years. What was my reward? A demotion. For reasons completely unrelated to me or my performance, I was being punished for my success. Despondent and demoralized, I quit.

For the next year or so I cobbled together enough work with other clients to work my way out of the darkness. That was the nature of the marketing hustle. In a single day you could go from comfortable to desperate. There were very few easy days. Eventually, comfort came calling again. My first client wanted me back and offered me a gigantic monthly paycheck to come back in-house. I weighed my options carefully. The last year I worked there had been the most emotionally challenging time of my life. I knew that if I went back, the same thing would happen again, and any shot at being happy in my work would go down the drain.

Mission: Implacable

I needed a strategy. I needed a *mission*. A very clear "Why?" that was just my own, that would function as a lodestar to help me chart a course through the treacherous, volatile waters of this particular workplace as I made my way toward the overarching objective of my life.

Everyone needs a mission. Imagine the totality of your being, your work product, your energy, your will, expressed as a force. You could say that every force has a fundamental desire, which is to be applied to maximum effect. A bowling ball's "desire" is to knock down all of the pins. The sun "desires" to burn bright and hot, radiating energy to distant planets where it draws seeds from the soil and puts warmth on skin. As humans we desire to apply our force—*our work*—to the maximum effect possible. Our mission is what we want that force to accomplish. While the meaning of life might be complicated, your mission in life should not be complicated. What are you, in this lifetime, on this planet, in this body, here to do? What do you want more than anything else?

My mission was to start a movement to help as many people as possible reach their potential. I didn't know what the brand looked like yet, nor how I was going to do it, but that didn't matter. What mattered was articulating and believing in the mission; finding that bright star in the vast darkness of the night sky and then following it day in and day out.

Once you have your mission, your next step is to sort out how your work can serve the mission. I'm a firm believer that there are two kinds of people in this world: those who need to find purpose and meaning in what they do for a living, and those who find purpose and meaning elsewhere and use work as a means to those ends. You can find yourself in either group by happenstance at any moment, which is why it's so important never to lose sight of your mission. If you need to have meaning in what you do, your profession should directly help your mission. If you want to save the oceans, become an oceanographer or marine biologist or a plastics chemist who changes the game. If your mission lies outside your work, you should look at your profession as the minimum effective way to gain the resources necessary to work toward your mission. Neither path is better or more valid than the other. I know numerous people from both sides who are equally happy or equally miserable, depending on whether they've found their mission and know which camp they're in.

I'm fortunate that I have created a situation where I have purpose in what I do for a living—but that wasn't the case when my old employer came calling the second time. Except I had a plan. I just needed to buy enough time and gather enough resources to start Onnit. I didn't care if I was appreciated at my new-old job, I didn't need a pat on the back. I just needed to do good work and get paid. In service of my mission, I was able to smile through the suck, and learn from the dysfunctional management so I didn't make the same mistakes once I got my own thing off the ground. In short, I intentionally went into a toxic work environment day after day in order to emerge with the resources necessary to build my dream. The plan succeeded.

YOUR MISSION IS YOUR PURPOSE

Ralph Waldo Emerson once said, "The purpose of life is not to be happy. It is to be useful, to be honorable, to be compassionate, to have it make some difference that you have lived and lived well." Emerson is right, though I think the piece of that equation he failed to mention is that if you do all those things—be useful, honorable, compassionate—happiness tends to be the result. In his book *Tribe*, war reporter Sebastian Junger talks about how Londoners would reminisce about how they felt when the bombs were dropping. They had a purpose, they had a mission: survive and win the war. This, then, is your job. To figure out your mission so you can own not just this day, but every day after it.

Humans are happiest when they are working toward something. When they have a sense of purpose. Knowing your mission will help to turn your work from drudgery to a victory. Without a mission, it will take superhuman effort just to keep up the inspiration and motivation to make all the right choices necessary to own the day.

So what do you want to do? What does your best self want more than anything else, want so bad that your inability to stop thinking about it will make it impossible for anyone to stop you from achieving it? Think about it, because in a few chapters we're going to ask you to write it down.

Own Your Space

My office is my sanctuary. I have a Zen fountain. I have my favorite candle burning. I have a mini trampoline, a foot massager, a fridge full of endless kombucha, and a couple different places I can sit or stand. I'm fortunate to have my own office, in that I can curate the space exactly how I want. It is perfect. Not everyone is as lucky as I am. But owning your space is not just about the things in your office, it's also about how you engage with your space, and how people interact with you while you're there. Any one of those three things can make a huge difference, positively or negatively, not just on your mission but on your productivity and your overall happiness, so they should be given equal consideration as you rethink how you work.

CAN YOU SMELL WHAT'S COOKIN'?

Everything in the entire building may belong to the company that signs your checks, but ultimately you own your space. Sure, you may not be able to have a mini trampoline, or a Zen fountain, but there is one thing you can do with any space, however large or small, and that is control the smell. Ooooh, that smell. Let me smell that smell!

What your workplace smells like makes a difference. If you ask employees at Onnit HQ, the scourge of the office is the microwaved tilapia phenomenon. Putting two-day-old meal-prepped fish into the microwave offends every culinary sensibility a reasonable human being should have, and it creates a stink bomb that lasts for hours and sticks to every conceivable surface like napalm. It's virtually inescapable, so when it happens, our usually Zen and cheerful employees erupt into finger-pointing and complaints, myself occasionally leading the charge. The result is a cascading loss of effectiveness and overall happiness. Studies shows that bad odor is not only distracting but in some cases can elicit emotions like anger and disgust.

Interestingly enough, if the smell of fish is the biggest disruptor of workplace productivity, research indicates that it is lemon (the same thing you use to disguise fishy taste) that might increase productivity the most. In Japan, according to the author of a book titled *The Healthy Workplace,* a large fragrance and flavor company investigated how smells affect the accuracy of typists. Their research found that "54% made fewer errors when they could smell lemon, 33% fewer with jasmine and 20% fewer with lavender." Lemon-jasmine-lavender tea for the win!

This is not news to anyone who has a little bit of experience smelling the roses—or all the other extracts from various plant roots, leaves, seeds, stems, and blossoms, otherwise known as *essential oils.* Essential oils have been used therapeutically for more than six thousand years. What we now call aromatherapy has officially been around for a century. The exact mechanism of action is still a mystery to researchers, but what they do know is that certain oils, when inhaled or massaged into the skin, have been shown to reduce anxiety and stress, blood pressure, nausea, even depression. We've all had jobs that induced those symptoms—sometimes all at once—and it's a relief to know there is something natural out there that can help us combat them.

You don't *have* to use just essential oils to get the desired effect, however. Depending on your situation, you could use a lemon-scented candle or an oil diffuser. You can rub lemongrass on your palms and smell, or simply put a fresh-cut lemon at your desk (that you squeeze into your water!). If you want to get fancy with the essential oils, try blending lemongrass and basil oil, or lemon and peppermint. Kick it up a notch, because the real power of smell and essential oils isn't in their acute ability to relieve negative sensations, it's in their ability to create positive ones. I call them "trigger scents." And they work by reverse-engineering the process by which, according to scientists at the University of Maryland Medical Center, "the 'smell' receptors in our noses communicate with parts of our brain that serve as storehouses for emotions and memories." Ever smell something that brings back a memory? Maybe it's a perfume or cologne that reminds you of your ex. Or maybe it's the smell of a food that brings back memories of a happy childhood. For a lot of us, "Grandma's house" had a certain smell that could trigger a nostalgic state of wistfulness. That is one of the powerful characteristics of scent, one you can use to your advantage at work by either piggy-backing on positive memories you've already made or making new ones and deliberately associating a scent with them.

For years, when I was meditating I would burn North American white sage or the South American wood palo santo. After ten-plus years of steady meditation practice, smelling either of those scents, even just for a few seconds, will help put me into a meditative state. So when I know that I have a crazy week at the office ahead of me, filled with thousands of little decisions and dozens of fires to put out,

I spark one of those scents, knowing that it will trigger the mind-set I need for greater balance, contemplation, and contentment.

You can do the same for all kinds of states. Suppose that every time you know you are going to (try to) enter a flow state, you have a certain essential oil that you smell. After a while your brain will link that flow state to the scent. Eventually, you will be able to use that scent in reverse, helping you to invoke that desired flow state, just like I use sage and palo santo to elicit a meditative state.

How do you want to feel about your workspace? Do you want to imbue it with energy? Do you want it to be warm and cozy and safe? Experiment with the oils that make the most sense to you for your environmental goals at work and create a trigger scent. Have fun with it. Make it your own. And if you're one of those people whose spirit animal is a junkyard tomcat who doesn't want to be bothered, just keep a microwave at your desk and zap a tilapia fillet every hour or so. No one will bother you ever again!

PUNCTUATE YOUR DAY WITH PROPER POSTURE

One of my worst habits is poor posture. I'm a slumper. I'm a slouch. And I pay the price. My head pushes too far forward, putting strain on my neck and the supporting muscles. My traps are always too tight because my hands are elevated too high. My joints are less and less flexible the harder I work. If I'm writing, I can sit for upward of twelve hours a day. My spine ends up bent like a question mark (?) when I should be sitting like an exclamation point (!).

All of this is not good. Sitting for more than three hours a day can cut two years off your life expectancy, even if you exercise regularly. I'm way beyond three hours. So I work on it. I stand up more. I fix my posture. I know how important this is, so at my company we made Varidesk and all forms of ergonomic chairs, including stability balls, free upon request. I see more and more utilization every day, which is good for my employees as human beings and good for me as their boss.

The Washington State Department of Labor and Industries re-viewed 250 workplace ergonomics case studies, and they found not only regular increases in productivity where meaningful ergonomic intervention occurred but also a dramatic reduction in strain-related injuries and absenteeism. It makes sense. For many people, work is already stressful enough—who wants to spend eight hours in what amounts to a stress position? If you work at a company, send them this research and see if they will get you what you are looking for. If you own the company, what you invest in your employees will always yield a great return, so take a good hard look at your ergo-nomic options. In the meantime, take matters into your own hands today and start straightening out that question mark of a body into an exclamation point of pride.

Sitting, Standing, and Movement

The key to good ergonomics is to vary your position regularly from sitting to standing, and to move your body in between to make sure that your muscles don't cramp or tighten.

When you are sitting, even if you like to slouch, spend some time with classic good posture. Engage your core to straighten your back, rotate your pelvis forward (like you were trying to move your taint to the front of the seat) and push your chin back to straighten your neck. This may be uncomfortable at first, so treat it like resistance training. Just do a little bit every day, until it becomes easier and easier. If you have the flexibility, bring your feet up to a squat in the chair, or cross your legs, eventually advancing from "Indian style" to what the yogis call "full lotus," where the outsides of your ankles rest on the inside of the opposing thigh.

A bosu ball, if you have one at your disposal, forces much of this better posture by virtue of its shape and elasticity. You have to sit up straight with your small balance muscles engaged, or the ball will roll out from under you. Try slouching into it while you work, and it will only be a matter of seconds before you land flat on your back. This is advanced ergonomics, though, so it's best to work up to that.

When standing, once again rotate your pelvis forward, pull the chin back, and ideally take off your shoes and spread your toes so all of those little piggies make contact with the ground. A lot of foot problems come from shoes forcing your feet far narrower than we were biomechanically engineered. And once foot problems settle in, they start to travel up the posterior chain as you try to compensate for the discomfort.

Pro Tip: Better Shoes and Toe Spreaders

There is nothing dorkier than wearing your five-finger Vibram shoes to the office, or out to dinner. I love my Vibrams. Each toe can move independently, my foot can spread out, and I get to build strength from the ground up. I work out in them 90 percent of the time, and feel like Arnold training barefoot at Muscle Beach. But I still can't bring myself to wear them outside the gym, where I spend the other fifteen of my waking hours. So the answer is to purchase some wide-toe-box shoes. Companies like Altra and Kuru have sprung up who make some great training, casual, and running shoes with a wide toe box so you can move your feet a little more like nature intended.

To help correct years of unintentional foot binding, you can also check out toe spreaders like those made by Yoga Toes or Correct Toes. They feel a bit like getting braces on your toes, but after a while you'll start to reap the benefits.

Movement, usually in the form of some light, resisted stretching, is something you should do both seated and standing. When you get up from your desk, do a few squats, some light spinal twists, or some calf raises. Open up your ribcage with one of those big "good morning world!"–type yawn stretches. In yoga, this looks like the first part of the sun salutation.

While you're seated, there are a number of movements you can do:

Chin retractions. The goal of the chin push is to push your chin down and back, elongating the neck and setting a better alignment for your head on your shoulders. Do three sets of ten reps, holding a duration of two seconds each time.

Draw the shoulders down. Holding your chin in the position you just patterned, reaching your hands toward the floor, draw your shoulders down to your sides, stretching and lengthening the traps, which are one of the main places many of us hold our stress, especially if we are holding our hands too high when we type. The shoulders tense up, and then they get tight, which leads to tightness in the neck and the traps (and eventually headaches). Gently push your ear down toward your shoulder, increasing the stretch on the opposite trap. Hold for 10 seconds at a time. Do ten sets for a total of 100 seconds.

PEOPLE ARE STRANGE, WHEN YOU ARE STRANGER

We are each part of an energetic bioorganism in both our home and work environments. We may have our own bedrooms or our own office, but we do not exist in isolation. We are social creatures and emotional beings who are incredibly adept at detecting others' emotions. If you are having a bad day, if you are stressed, if you are *elated*, people will pick up on what you are going through. The recent discovery of mirror neurons in the brain, which reflect the emotional state of the person with whom we are interacting at any given moment, has uncovered how this process works neurochemically. It's basically a hardwired version of empathy.

Any of us who have been around someone who is frantic can recognize this phenomenon in action; if we're not careful, that chaos rubs off on us. Same goes for when someone angrily honks their car horn at us, and it makes us angry as well. I remember I shared my office for a few months with a coworker. He was prone to bouts of stress and anxiety, and I would hear him letting out deep sighs. This was good for him, but it was bad for me. Every time I heard him purge the energy, it would make me aware of his emotional state, and before I knew it, I was mirroring his emotional energy with my own behavior. Initially, it was really frustrating because it felt like the emotional version of a sick person coming into the office and coughing on everything. He was sighing his negative energy all over my desk.

Eventually we chatted about what I call "energetic hygiene" and determined that the best thing for him to do was head outside and blow off a little steam on his own when he needed to, then reenter the office. In reality, I'd already determined for myself the actual best thing, and that was for him to get the hell out and give me my office back! But I didn't propose that right away, because just as important as being cautious about our energetic hygiene is being a good teammate.

▨ THERE IS NO "I" IN TEAM, BUT THERE IS A "ME"

We talk a lot about teamwork in our society. *Teamwork makes the dream work!* But we don't talk nearly enough about how to be a good teammate, or how to judge whether you are working well with your team, or how to know who is actually on your team. Even if you work on your own, at some point or another you are going to be interacting with someone who supports what you do. If it's not a coworker, maybe it's your spouse, or even your dog. If you don't walk your dog, then he's gonna shit in your house, and so you traded a nice sunny walk in support of your teammate for angrily cleaning up the pile of shit he made, left to his own devices. It's the same when we don't communicate with people at work and support them in the ways that are most useful to them as opposed to most obvious or convenient to us.

I learned that lesson the first time I was invited back to the UFC locker room before a fight to hang with a fighter that we were working with. I thought we needed to keep things intense. It seemed obvious to me. What I didn't appreciate was that the fight was already intense enough, and getting intense is easy for a fighter. Staying loose enough to have snap in your punches, and keep your adrenaline from dumping too early, *that* is the challenge. So the best thing the people in a fighter's corner can do, leading up to the walkout where shit gets real, is crack jokes.

Laughter is the diffuser of intensity. One of the greatest Buddhist teachers of our time is the Jamaican-born Mooji, the "laughing buddha." He got his name because people will travel from all over the world to see him with their problems, and by the time they are ready to tell him what's wrong, they start laughing. He has an incredible gift of pointing out the silliness and futility of many of our emotional challenges, which diffuses them immediately. In fact, evolutionary biologists credit laughter with exactly that purpose: diffusing what would ordinarily be tense situations. The moment you can laugh about something, the threat is over. If anyone is in an energetically challenging place, instead of indulging it, or telling them to fix it, be a good teammate and shoot for laughter. Farts count, but only if they are loud. A good teammate announces his farts proudly.

Work Effectively

I know that I am a streak worker. I can accomplish a normal week of work in a day. But I can only do one of those days twice a week. My goal is to learn to operate at that high capacity without the burnout that forces me to need so many recovery days. I want to be able to turn on that skill at will, rather than waiting around for inspiration like I'm holding a bingo card, hoping the letters FLOW line up. The best way for me to make that happen is to get into a rhythm with some easy housekeeping tasks, then go in hard on the most important thing on my to-do list, by saying no to things of lesser priority and blocking out distractions that could get in the way.

ABOUT THOSE EMAILS . . .

The first thing I do when I start the workday is check my texts and my emails. While it is true that email has been shown to be a hindrance to workplace productivity—70 percent of people react to new emails within six seconds of notification, and it takes about sixty-four seconds to return to the original task after every email—any book that tells you to do something else besides look at your emails when you get to work is bullshit. Because you won't actually follow it. In your email you might discover something that you need to devote all your time to that day. I've had that scenario develop dozens of times. A website outage. A supply problem. A human resources situation. Something that, if I don't give it immediate attention, will do exponential damage. I have to check my emails, or I am going to be stressed about it. For the most part, it's annoying housekeeping work, but it's also a chance for some easy productivity wins that help reduce some of the noise that so often drowns out the all-important signal.

This doesn't mean that I *answer* any of my emails, however. This is one case where technology is really helpful. In Gmail, which is industry standard if you want anyone to take you seriously, there is a star system. They have yellow stars, blue stars, and a whole progression of simple, clickable icons by which you can sort your emails. I use three of them: blue stars, yellow stars, and green check marks. If an email needs a reply, it gets a yellow star. If it's time-sensitive, personal, or just more important, it gets a blue star. A blue-starred email takes priority above all yellow stars. And then, if it's something I want to keep handy because it contains useful information but doesn't need a response, it gets a green check. This process takes about five minutes. If it doesn't get a star, it isn't going to get answered. Then, assuming there is nothing urgent, which usually there isn't, I get on with the most important stuff.

GO IN FOR THE KILL

The writer Nicolas Chamfort once jokingly advised that if you swallow a live toad first thing in the morning, nothing else will seem too challenging for the rest of the day. I'm not sure that's true, but he's definitely right about one thing: if you start the day off with the hardest thing you need to accomplish, you are going to enjoy the whole day a hell of a lot more. How are you going to really relax when the thing that you are dreading the most is still to come? How often do you not get to it when you put it off until later? How well do you usually sleep that night? The answers to those questions are, in order: *You're not*; *A lot*; and *Like shit*.

Still, the human tendency is to put off the hardest thing to the last minute. Procrastination may create urgency, but at what cost? The stress of the large task will occupy valuable brain capacity as it builds momentum until finally you can't take it anymore. It will force you to overlook and ignore and lose on the little things that could have been small victories. It will turn your task from art to math, as you count the minutes remaining and divide by the amount of work you have left. So why do we always procrastinate, then? We're missing the skill you learned in the shower thanks to Bode Miller: mental override. The ability to make yourself do the thing you know you should, even when you don't want to.

It is what Steven Pressfield talks about when he says that he doesn't wait for the muse to show up, he sits his ass in the chair every morning at 9:00 a.m. and starts writing, so if the muse decides to come, she knows where to find him. In the words of General George Patton: "Accept the challenges so that you can feel the exhilaration of victory."

LEARN TO SAY NO

The sports psychologist Dr. Jonathan Fader, who advises the New York Mets along with many other high performers, is fond of sending out a framed picture of Dr. Oliver Sacks speaking on the phone. Behind Sacks on a large piece of yellow paper is the word "NO!" written in block letters. Dr. Fader wants clients to hang this picture up in a prominent space near their computer, to remind them that they must say "No!" a lot.

I want you to do something similar in your own office. Put it up next to the piece of paper with your mission written on it, so in the morning and after lunch, when you are reviewing your emails, you feel empowered to ignore most of them, answer only those that are most important or urgent to you, and to respond with a (more polite) no to those making demands on your time and energy that do not service your mission. No, I'm not interested. No, I can't attend. No, I'm not available. No, I won't do that. The more you say no via email, the more effective you will be. I want you to have that sign so you're able to say no to other things too: no to self-doubt, no to fear, no to procrastination. . . . but most of all, say no to distraction.

BLOCK OUT DISTRACTIONS

The key to blocking out distractions is . . . *Oh, hey girl, what up?* If you are a pro, you can't afford those kinds of distractions. That's why when LeBron James or Kevin Durant gets off the team bus before a game, he has his headphones on and eyes fixed forward as he walks straight to the locker room. They do this not just because it's part of their daily routine, but also because they can't afford to get distracted—by people they recognize, by fans wanting to take pictures. That stuff is for after the game. Now? They have *work* to do.

By leaning on routine and blocking out all distractions, athletes like LeBron and KD are fighting off momentum killers so they can focus on the most important task at hand: getting to work and getting the job done. *Being effective.*

So when it comes to productivity at work, first things first: invest in an expensive pair of noise-canceling headphones or a white noise machine. You want to drown out what's going on out there, so you can focus on what's going on in front of you.

Second, turn off every kind of notification you can. Notifications are the sticker burr in the sock of effectiveness. They are the pebble in the shoe. Except worse, because they come with interesting sounds and customizable buzzes and bouncing icons, all sorts of habituating dopamine triggers designed to grab your attention . . . and keep it. But your attention is precious, because attention is time, and that is the only resource you cannot renew. So guard it well.

There are a lot of fancy software apps that can block things from your computer, but I just go old-school. I figure if I don't have the willpower to block out my own distractions, I won't have the willpower to write. Similarly, I want to train my will to be stronger than the opportunity. So I minimize all the tabs on my browser other than what I'm working on, and make sure that no notifications are going to pop up. For my phone, I turn on airplane mode, put on some trance-inducing tunes, and off we go to the happy, purposeful, productive land of effectiveness.

Prescription

There are three things to focus on when it comes to owning your workday:

1.   **Know your mission.** When I get in to work, I know my mission because I have it on a journal I keep in my man purse with me at all times. (We'll talk about journaling in chapter 14.) I used to call it a satchel, but one day a flight attendant called it a purse, and I realized that instead of defending my manliness and calling it a satchel, I would just go with purse. Man purse. Anyway, my mission and my objectives for the day are right there with me. Once you figure out your mission, write it down and put it somewhere you'll see it.

2.   **Own your space.** The first thing I do is turn on my Zen fountain and my oil diffuser. I create a variety of different scents using seven or eight different essential oils. Sometimes I mix cedar oil with a drop of rose, for that masculine vibe. Sometimes I mix peppermint and bergamot. I'm like a chef coming up with the daily special. Do the same for yourself,

whether it's re-creating a trigger scent you already have positive associations with or experimenting with new scents that might become tomorrow's trigger scent for owning the day today.

As the day goes along, I get up regularly to go for a walk or bounce on the rebounder. Make sure you practice good posture, get up from your desk on a regular basis, move around and support your teammates, whoever and whatever they may be. Don't let a question-mark-shaped spine turn your productivity or your effectiveness or your professional integrity into a question mark as well.

3.   **Work effectively.** When it is time to grind . . . I power through my morning email review, tell everyone I'm unavailable, turn off my cell phone and go to my supersecret bat phone, and then I leave the office. I have too many people coming in and out and too many distractions to really be efficient on larger tasks while I'm there. I'll go to a coffee shop, or café, or somewhere I can focus without distractions. Preferably some place without highly attentive servers who will feel like they aren't doing their job if they leave you alone too long. Once there, do whatever you have to do to minimize distractions and get down to whatever is the most important objective of the day.

Now Do It

You ever hear the cliché, "If you do what you love you'll never work a day in your life"? It's bullshit. I love what I do. And I generally feel good after a full day of work. But it's fucking *work*. Sometimes it's brutal. It's demanding, it's exhausting, the pressure can seem insurmountable. And that's all to be expected. Anytime you are pushing the boundaries of what you are capable of, it will be work— *hard work*—because you are coming up against the internal points of resistance within your mind and your soul. If it wasn't work, it would be a problem, and I'd be worried.

Daniel Cormier, a dominant light heavyweight UFC champion, has a saying: "Embrace the grind." Training for a UFC fight sucks. It sucks so much worse than your job. You have a whole group of people trying to kill you every day, trainers sucking the last bit of energy out of you, media up your ass; a lot of times you are away from your family, and the grand finale is a weight cut where you starve yourself of all food and water and then stand on a stage in your underwear in front of dozens of cameras and sometimes thousands of people, like a show pony. Then, after all that, you may still get your ass kicked and spend the night in a hospital. If that is the life you chose for yourself, if that is part of your mission, you better embrace it.

What you will find, once you embrace the grind, whatever your grind may be, is that all of a sudden it isn't so bad. It is never pain that is the problem; it is the suffering caused by the resistance to that pain. Eckhart Tolle describes this in his world-shaking book *A New Earth*, when he talks about the only three states of mind anyone should tolerate: acceptance, enjoyment, and enthusiasm. To accept is to embrace, to meet without resistance or judgment or preference. To enjoy is to move past acceptance and actually have fun while you are doing it. And enthusiasm sits beyond enjoyment, where you are bringing your intent, and your passion, into what you are doing.

So when you approach the workday today, you can power through just like you always have—slouching through distractions, procrastination, and then ultimately panic—or you can do it better. You have a choice. You have questions to ask yourself that only you can answer. Can you support your body while getting shit done? Can you optimize your workflow to accomplish even more? Can you embrace the grind? Can you make it better for your team? That is owning it. It's not how many hours you log or how many words you churn. The question is, can you do it well? If you follow the steps in this chapter, you can and you will. You're not at work to fuck around. You're at work to do work. Go, hero, go.

THREE POINTERS

- More important than enjoying every minute of the work you do is knowing why you are doing it. This is your mission, and being certain of that mission will allow you to flourish even in challenging situations.
- To own your work, you have to own your space. This means cultivating optimal conditions for yourself within your environment by paying attention to your posture and movement, as well as the energetic and olfactory conditions of your workspace.
- Working effectively means accomplishing your best work with the minimum amount of resistance. To do this, you need to minimize distraction, learn to say no, and develop a process of prioritizing what you need to tackle first.

8

EAT A WEIRD LUNCH

Tell me what you eat, and I will tell you what you are.

—G. K. CHESTERTON

It's called a lunch break, so let's break with the ordinary. It's become a cliché for important people to have the same lunch every day, a way to reduce their decision load. Ugh, boring. What kind of awesome day rings in the halfway point without the spice of variety? No more. Lunch is an opportunity to reframe and restart your day. It's not an obligation to cross off the list. It's also an opportunity to get your body the micronutrients it needs to keep you feeling great. The way to do that isn't with something ordered off a cart. It's by experimenting and exploring. It's by taking my hometown's motto to heart, and *keeping* it weird.

Getting Owned

My favorite lunch as a young man was the Carl's Jr. Double Western Bacon Cheeseburger. I would order it two, sometimes three times a week, and with that first hot, steaming bite, every time I'd think to myself: *What is this creation of the fast food gods? This Zeus Burger that has me slobbering like a pit bull in a butcher shop?* Back then I thought the sandwich was a savory flavor explosion designed by supergeniuses, proof of man's inherent dominion over nature. I would gleefully crush it with reckless abandon, then bask in the postcoital euphoria of a multiple flavorgasm . . . for all of about a minute and a half.

Then I would literally feel sick to my stomach and drag ass the rest of the afternoon. Why? Well, let me tell you what that sandwich *really* was. It was meat and bacon that had been shot full of hormones and antibiotics and raised on Monsanto corn. It was yellow "cheese" that was somewhere in between milk and Nickelodeon "gak," engineered not for flavor but for its ability to "melt" over the "all-beef" patty like a coat of high-gloss latex paint. It was sugary BBQ sauce for tang, and breaded onion fried in canola oil for crunch, all of it sandwiched between two fluffy slices of refined blood-sugar-spiking carbohydrates.

How many of you fall prey to similar guilty lunch pleasures or worry that you have poor lunch habits? Not sure? Then answer me this: How many of the following things do you do, or have you done, on a regular basis at lunchtime?

1. Decided what to eat based on how many/few calories it has.
2. Bought a sandwich from Subway because it's "fresh."

3. Eaten some form of fried starch like chips or fries as your "side."
4. Eaten a meal whose only colors are different shades of white and brown (yellow cheese doesn't count).

If you are anything like I was, you've done all those things. Many times. You found yourself owned by cravings and convenience, only to be left battling inflammation, brain fog, low energy, and mood dysregulation, all of which prevent you from crushing it during your afternoon work session.

There are a number of reasons for this. With an estimated 75 percent of the world's food produced from only twelve plant and five animal species, the lack of biodiversity in our diet is failing to support our "second brain." Additionally, our culture's maniacal focus on calories instead of nutrients has left our bodies unbalanced and undernourished. Last, and I think most important, when it comes to the midday meal, the typical lunch is often packed with what I call antinutrients, and far too few of the essential micronutrients you get when you eat weird foods in all colors of the rainbow from fertile, mineral-rich soil.

Eventually I got to a point where I was sick and tired—literally and figuratively—of only being productive for the first half of my day and missing the giant opportunities I had to fulfill my mission and achieve the things I dreamed about when I closed my eyes at night. So I changed my lunch. And that's what you're going to do too.

In this chapter, we're going to walk you through the right kind of lunch. You're gonna spice it up. You're gonna make it interesting, exciting . . . even weird. It's not gonna be the same every damn time. It's gonna take a little effort to prepare before you dive right in and devour it, but it's gonna be worth it. And you're gonna be doing your body a solid.

As Orson Welles once said, "Ask not what you can do for your country. Ask what's for lunch."

Owning It

Take a deep breath. Lunch is about to get weird. But before we have some fun with it, we have to get fundamental. We have to address the nutrient profile of your overall diet and how that connects to your lunch. We need a solid foundation of macronutrients that provide the fuel for your body and the building blocks for your growth—all those proteins, fats, fiber, and carbohydrates that come from air, land, and sea. Once we have a handle on those, then we can dive into the weird foods that provide the key *micro*nutrients that take you from functional to optimal. And finally we can go to war against the antinutrients that are regularly undercutting the benefits of both your macro- and micronutrient consumption.

Universal Nutrition Principle #4: Calories Are Bullshit, Macronutrients Matter

Nutrition coach Mike Dolce has captained thousands of dramatic weight-loss and body transformations in his career, helping people from all across the spectrum: tall, short, white, black, male, female, Team Edward, Team Jacob. If there is one message that Mike has preached most consistently over all those years, it's that if you are counting calories, you are setting yourself up for failure, because calories aren't real, and humans don't actually "burn" them.

The calorie, as a unit of measurement, is based on the amount of heat produced when food is burned in a metal oven called a calorimeter. Last time I checked, our bodies are not metal ovens. They can become *Dutch* ovens, with the appropriate amount of chipotle and chill, but even then we need a fully made bed to get there. What the body actually does is break down food in complex metabolic pathways, utilizing amino acids for muscles, shuttling nutrients into cells, and storing energy. When we work out, we don't "burn the calories" from the last meal we ate, like a coal-powered engine. Energy in the body comes from a chemical called adenosine triphosphate (ATP) that the body generates from a variety of sources, including glycogen, ketones, protein, and fat that our body had previously stored.

That's a very science-y way of saying that calories are bullshit. Still, this is how most people think about calories: Food has them. If you eat more than you burn when you work out, you get fat. Full stop. If it were only that simple! Does that mean you can eat any amount of food you want? Of course not. But it probably does mean that you can and should eat more of the right macronutrients than you currently consume.

The biggest surprise to many of Mike Dolce's clients, in fact, is just how much food he tells them to eat. Convinced by years of diet fad brainwashing of the calorie-in, calorie-out hypothesis, his overweight clients are shocked that when they eat more food than they ever have, they start losing weight. These anecdotes are plausible because when it comes to food and owning your health, it ain't about the calories, it's about the nutrients.

The body needs good macronutrients to trigger the hormonal signals that help you start losing weight. A 100-calorie pack of crackers is not going to be as good as a small handful of almonds, or a couple pieces of grass-fed jerky, or any of the weird foods we're going to talk about in this chapter. That is a nutritional truism that holds for more than just weight loss, as well. Solid macronutrient intake is essential for optimal organ function, musculoskeletal function, and general bodily effectiveness.

PROTEIN: BUILD YOUR HOUSE

Protein is a key building block within our bodies. Technically, proteins are chains of different amino acids that break down and rebuild to help us form our muscles, skin, joints, even our eyeballs. If the body were a house, it would be in a constant state of renovation, and protein would be the building materials. When the body starts to run out of those materials, it starts to age and degrade until it breaks down rather than building up. Eating enough protein (especially complete amino acid protein) as a regular part of your diet ensures that you supply your body with the building materials it needs to keep those internal load-bearing walls strong and, thanks to its role in promoting stable blood sugar levels, keep those lights on and burning brightly.

That said, the big question with protein as a macronutrient isn't whether it's important; it's what constitutes enough and whether there is such a thing as too much. In a study including both young and elderly subjects, a meal consisting of beef that yielded 30 grams of protein elicited significant increases in muscle protein synthesis after an overnight fasting period. Interestingly, a meal yielding 90 grams of protein did not elicit any greater responses in muscle protein synthesis. What makes those numbers so significant is when you put them in the context of a Western diet and standard American portions. Thirty grams of protein is only 4–5 ounces of beef, or about the size of the palm of your hand. An 8-ounce steak is 50 grams of protein by itself, and that's usually the smallest option on most restaurant menus. So if you are totally looking for gains, bro, try hitting that 30-gram mark, because more is likely just going to be unnecessary extra work for your organs, and your wallet.

> **IDEAL SOURCES:** Grass-fed beef, wild-caught salmon, free-range eggs, sprouted pumpkin seeds, hemp seeds

■ FIBER: SLOW AND STEADY

If I were Dietary Fat, I would fire my PR agent and hire the one they have working for my friend Dietary Fiber. While fiber is technically a carbohydrate, everyone and their mother—especially their mother—has heard of the importance of fiber. But not many people know exactly why. To understand fiber, you have to understand the different types, and how each can be beneficial to your body. We are going to focus on three main types: soluble, insoluble, and fermentable (prebiotic) fiber.

Soluble fibers mix with water and form a gel-like substance. If you've ever had chia seed pudding, or a chia slurry, you have a good sense of what this looks like. It almost has the consistency of Jell-O. Soluble fiber, like its unjustly maligned friend Dietary Fat, offers a variety of metabolic benefits when this process happens in the body, including slowing down the uptake of nutrients just long enough to help level out blood sugar spikes. You'll learn more about how to use soluble fiber to hack your cheat meal in chapter 12.

IDEAL SOURCES: Chia, flax, asparagus, guar gum

Insoluble fiber plays an important role in making sure your digestive tract has enough substance to push through the system efficiently and completely. Some of the most common sources of insoluble fiber are plants without much nutrient density but whose cell walls are made of cellulose. Like our friend psyllium, they act as a bulking agent, which helps speed the complete passage of food and waste through your gut. Basically, they become the plunger at the bottom of the push-pop that makes it easy to shove all the shit out. *All right, who's hungry?*

IDEAL SOURCES: Avocado, sprouted barley, mixed greens, popcorn, psyllium

Fermentable fiber/resistant starch is often called a "prebiotic" because your friendly neighborhood gut bacteria are able to digest (ferment) it to use as food. Whereas *probiotics* actually contain more friendly bacteria to help populate your gut colony, prebiotics provide the food they need to thrive. The most common fermentable fibers include beans, the "magical fruit," and as with all forms of fermentation, produce everyone's favorite bodily byproduct: gas. Not all fermentable fibers are created equal, of course. Some will be more efficient and tolerable for your body than others, and you'll just have to experiment to find out. Though I suspect you, or whoever you might share a bed with, already know. Personally, my favorite prebiotic fermentable fiber is dandelion greens. My body tolerates them very well. My least favorite are Brussels sprouts, which turn my digestive tract into a fart factory.

> **IDEAL SOURCES:** Chickpeas (hummus), dandelion greens, chicory root, onions

A lunch with these fibers well represented will promote gut health and aid digestion. A healthy, well-firing digestive tract is key to preventing the kind of heavy bloat and discomfort that can derail what would otherwise have been a smooth, productive afternoon.

CARBOHYDRATE: SPEED KILLS

With the exception of fiber, carbohydrates are basically sugar. But it is not their sugary nature that makes them dangerous, it is the speed at which they are delivered into your system. We talked about this in chapter 3, so I won't belabor it; just remember that your goal when it comes to carb consumption is to slow them down as much as possible.

The speed at which you digest caffeine depends on what else you've consumed with it. Chewed-up food—or chyme—will digest at the rate of the slowest-absorbing nutrients within it. Fat and fiber take longer for the body to process than sugar or starch, and are therefore two of the best nutrients for slowing down digestion. The best way to eat carbs, then, is to eat things that already have the fiber in them—things like yams, sweet potatoes, quinoa, sprouted or fermented grains, and some fruits.

A lot of people who are sensitive to their carb intake look at the composition of fruit, being largely sugar, and they come to the conclusion that fruit is bad. What they fail to realize, though, is that fruit is full of fiber. The fiber is a big part of what gives fruit its solid-state structure. Without it, most fruits would just be juice balloons ready to spill out all over the place. That relationship between the fiber and the sugar in fruit plays out in the body as well. Fruits don't just flood your bloodstream with sugar; the fiber in them slows down the absorption of the sugar in the gut, which basically spreads out the glycogen battery charge over a longer period, giving you longer to burn down your battery power. Remember, anything over 100 percent charge of your glycogen stores converts to fat, so if you can charge your body at a pace similar to the one you drain it at, you'll be fine on the fruit front.

So if fiber and fat slow down the absorption of sugar, what do you suppose produces the fastest absorption? Well, something that has neither fiber nor fat. The liquid greased lightning of sugar: soda. If you just do one thing for your nutrition, for your workday, and for your world, stop drinking conventional soda and stop giving soda to your kids. Sugar-sweetened beverages contributed to a staggering 60 percent increase in childhood obesity. Sugar-sweetened beverages that use fructose, like fruit juice concentrates and high-fructose corn syrup, are the worst of the worst. Fructose cannot be used in any other immediate functions of the body, so it immediately converts to glycogen or fat. When it comes to sugar, and especially fructose, you need to get them out of your diet so you can get their effects out of your day.

> **IDEAL SOURCES:** Yams, sweet potatoes, sprouted or fermented grains, certain fruits

FAT: FUEL THE BURN

We've briefly discussed how high-fat diets like the ketogenic diet can help you lose weight. One way they do this is by curbing hunger through increasing the signal for satiety, the feeling of being full. This diminishes the desire to overeat, sometimes starting as early as the first bite of hunger-satiating fat. Your liver can convert saturated fat in your diet to cholesterol, but contrary to what you might have been told, cholesterol is not going to kill you. There are studies showing that even in the elderly, high cholesterol can be protective. In these older populations, the higher the cholesterol, the lower your risk of heart disease. Not to mention that cholesterol levels that are *too low* are actually associated with increased risk of death . . . from other causes, like cancer and suicide. This likely has to do with the fact that saturated fat and cholesterol are the starting point for the production of many important hormones, including testosterone and estrogen. Whether you're male or female, having robust hormone levels has been linked to most aspects of healthy living: mood, body composition, libido, and energy level. Without good fat in your diet, without enough cholesterol, you will be setting yourself up for some serious problems.

> **IDEAL SOURCES:** Coconut oil, animal fats, avocado, grass-fed butter, egg yolk, olive oil, MCT oil, cacao butter

YOU ARE WHAT YOU EAT ATE

As critically important as macronutrients are to your overall health, it's equally important that they come from as many high-quality sources as possible. We've all heard the expression "You are what you eat." Well, that's literally true. You didn't grow from magic, or because that's just what babies do. You grew because you ate stuff. But that's only half the story, because the stuff you ate grew because *it* ate (and metabolized) stuff too. You aren't just what you eat, you're also what what you eat *ate*.

Double Western bacon cheeseburgers, technically speaking, have a macronutrient profile you could get away with, especially if you threw one bun off and made it a convertible. But if that is all you ever ate (like I wanted to when I was young), you would literally be made up of reconstituted and metabolized double Western bacon cheese-burgers. You would be a cheeseburger human. Carl's Jr. *Junior.* Which might be all right, depending on what what you eat ate. Did the cow who so kindly donated the patty and the cheese eat grass and weeds full of nutrients and conjugated linoleic acid (CLA)? Or did it eat genetically modified corn, packed with fructose? Did the onion come from nutrient-rich soil, or was it commercially farmed on refertilized ground that was regularly doused in Roundup? Was the bread refined wheat—basically cotton candy in the shape of a bun—or was it a sprouted grain, watered from mineral-rich springs or rainwater?

Multinational food manufacturers have tried to convince us that stuff like this doesn't matter that much, but a cursory glance at the difference between natural foods and those that have endured even a modest amount of processing is all you need to know that this matters a lot if you want to own your day and own your life. Look at the higher concentrations of healthy fats like CLA in grass-fed beef versus conventional beef. Or just look at the food, period. Often you can actually see the difference in nutritional quality. Wild-caught salmon, with higher natural levels of the colorful antioxidant as-taxanthin, have a much deeper pink flesh compared to farm-raised salmon, which would be unrecognizable without the red dye added for coloring. Free-range chickens produce eggs with rich orange yolks, whereas factory-farmed chickens lay eggs with almost sickly yellow yolks. Even corn and berries, when grown organically, can have up to 50 percent more antioxidants. And veggies, well, they are only as good as the soil and water that made them grow. Anyone who has sampled the merchandise at a good farmer's market can tell you that it is not to-*may*-to versus to-*mah*-to. It's tomato versus *what the hell is that?*

All of which is to say, whether it's macro- or micronutrients you're after, going conventional with your food isn't going to get you very far. You've gotta get weird.

Universal Nutrition Principle #5: Eat Weird Foods

Jonathan Swift said, "He was a bold man that first ate an oyster." Damn right. I wonder if ol' Curious Jorge was actually hungry or just feeling destructive when he came across his first oyster? I can imagine him finding this sea rock that seemed to have something alive inside it, smashing it open, and giving it a good sniff. It smelled like the ocean, so he poked it with his tongue. It was slimy . . . yet familiar. Then, fuck it, he eventually slurped the whole thing down for desperately needed sustenance. What is certain is that he had no idea how just a few oysters could supply 1,000 percent of his daily vitamin B_{12} needs, along with hefty supplies of vitamins A and E, copper, selenium, zinc, and essential fatty acids. Add in a bottle of sauv blanc, and he would also have the world's first afternoon patio brunch, but that's a whole different discussion.

This is the essence of weird foods. And the more diverse they are, the more diverse the micronutrients you consume, the closer you'll be to optimized performance, and the farther away you'll be from the deleterious internal conditions that always seem to throw the brakes on the rest of our day.

MICROBIOME-ASSISTIVE FOODS

Besides taking a supplement to fix our screwed-up guts, the next best thing we can do is dramatically increase the type and variety of foods we eat, because with that diversity comes a more robust and more diverse group of microbiota. The more diverse and plentiful your microbiota, the more potential health benefits they can contribute to the body. To get there, you need to hunt down prebiotic foods that feed the good bacteria that already exist, encouraging them to flourish, and probiotic foods that increase the ranks of those friendly bacteria.

Prebiotic foods are those that feed the bacteria already present in the gut. Fueling those little dudes, which outnumber the rest of the body's cells ten to one, is pretty important and why foods rich in fermentable fiber and resistant starch are so key. They survive the digestive enzymes in the stomach and small intestine and deliver their payload—principally inulin, among others—to the large intestine, where they can feed critical strains of probiotic bacteria like bifidobacteria, which keep things efficient in the bowel system by helping reduce constipation and boosting the immune system.

While lunch is not usually the time for a bunch of starchy carbohydrates like french fries, surprisingly there may be a way to keep potatoes on the lunch menu in a useful, prebiotic fashion: potato salad! When you heat and cool potatoes (or rice), you turn some of the digestible starches into resistant starch via a process called retrogradation. In addition to feeding your friendlies, the retrograded starch will have a diminished effect on elevating blood sugar levels, which will help you ward off the afternoon drowsies.

The key with any prebiotic food is to start small and build up. If you eat too much right off the bat, you are going to have serious gas.

IDEAL SOURCES: Jerusalem artichokes, blueberries, almonds and pistachios, and especially high quantities in chicory root, dandelion greens, and onions

Probiotic foods add more friendly bacteria into your system, the ones that not only break down food in the stomach but also start breaking down food outside the stomach as well. Their helpful bacteria and yeasts feed on the sugars and resistant starches in the food, converting some of the sugar to organic acids and making the food easier to digest. Eating a probiotic food is kind of like hiring new intestinal factory workers who start working before they even reach the factory floor. They work a lifetime, multiply, have children during the fermentation process, and then when you finally consume the food, you add some of their numbers to your own intestinal factory. It's a win/win.

The best place to find these probiotics is in cultured or fermented foods. Fermentation not only introduces a bunch of healthy probiotics, it also increases nutrient bioavailability and digestibility, making tolerable many foods like dairy, soy, or plants like cabbage that would normally be irritating to the digestive tract. Fermentation is a traditional practice around the world, and commonplace in many of the world's blue zones. If you haven't heard that term, blue zones are areas of the globe whose populations enjoy the highest levels of health, and studying those populations can give great insight into some best practices we can all apply.

> IDEAL SOURCES: Miso, kimchi, sauerkraut, kefir, kombucha, dark chocolate, Greek yogurt

PROTECTIVE FOODS
There are a lot of different protective foods, to the extent that any nutrient-dense food you eat is probably doing something to benefit or bolster one of the systems in your body, but two classes of food stand above the others for their essential protective nature: omega-3 fatty acids and antioxidants.

Omega-3 fatty acids are called essential fatty acids because the body can't produce them and needs to source them from food. As we learned in chapter 4, these aren't normal fats; these compounds play key roles in regulating inflammation and other processes like blood clotting. While both omega-3 and omega-6 fatty acids are important, the problem develops when the ratio gets out of line. Research by Dr. Stephan Guyenet suggests that the ratio in healthy nonindustrial populations is somewhere from 1:1 to 1:4 omega-3 to omega-6, respectively. Unfortunately, in our typical diet the ratio is more like 1:16, and we need to correct that, not just with supplements but with diet.

> IDEAL SOURCES: Chia, flax, and sacha inchi seeds; wild-caught fish like sockeye salmon, sardines, and mackerel; grass-fed beef (as long as it isn't grain-finished)

Antioxidants have been touted, at one time or another, as a cure for everything from cancer to the common cold. While the hype for antoxidants as a panacea was definitely overblown, what is absolutely true is that they reduce oxidative stress in the body by eliminating free radicals, hungry molecules on the hunt for electrons to quench their unending molecular thirst. When free radicals pull electrons from normal cells, those cells die, as part of the inflammation process. Cell death is a healthy function that keeps deranged and damaged cells from wandering around aimlessly, but when there is too much oxidative stress, and there are too many free radicals roaming around like Pac-Man ghosts, you start to get more inflammation than you need or want. That is when it is time to reach for the antioxidants. With electrons to spare, there are several powerful classes of antioxidants that can blast thirsty radicals like a fire hose at a skinhead rally:

Polyphenols help reduce something called C-reactive protein, which is a marker of inflammation. The best sources for polyphenols are chocolate, red wine, and green tea.

Anthocyanins are immune boosters present in dark fruits like blackberries, blueberries, açaí, black currant, and cherries, as well as black rice and aubergines. Like Tupac and Kendrick always say, the blacker the berry, the stronger the anthocyanins.

Curcuminoids have earned a lot of buzz for their ability to reduce inflammation. Found primarily in turmeric—whose yellow root gives curry powder its color—not only do they reduce oxidative stress, they are specifically valuable for the brain and may help reduce the burden of age-related brain conditions. Unfortunately, on their own, curcuminoids are hard for the body to absorb, but when you combine the turmeric with black pepper or the extract BioPerine, the absorption can skyrocket up to 2,000 percent.

Garlic is one of these mysterious foods that has been used therapeutically for millennia. It contains multiple antioxidant compounds that, among other things, subdue the common cold like a Brazilian jujitsu black belt. A large twelve-week study found that garlic supplementation reduced the number of colds by 63 percent versus placebo. That is awesome by itself, but even better when you consider the average length of cold symptoms for those who were sick was also reduced, from 5 days to just 1.5 days in the group taking garlic. Another study backed up those results and found that a high dose of garlic extract can reduce the number of days someone feels sick with cold or flu by 61 percent. To get the maximum benefit, load up on garlic in the winter or if anyone in your house is getting the sniffles.

Sulforaphane is an antioxidant compound produced when raw cruciferous vegetables like broccoli, Brussels sprouts, and cabbage are chopped or chewed. Evidence suggests that sulforaphane may help inactivate and eliminate carcinogens as well as help decrease DNA damage by reducing inflammation, the underlying cause of many diseases. The highest concentration of sulforaphane is actually in broccoli *sprouts* rather than broccoli itself. As it turns out, it's not uncommon for sprouts to be more nutritious than their more mature form.

> **IDEAL SOURCES:** Dark chocolate, red wine, green tea, berries, black rice, turmeric and black pepper, garlic, broccoli sprouts

▓ VITAMIN- AND MINERAL (MICRONUTRIENT)–RICH FOODS

Here's the deal: pretty much every vegetable or well-sourced protein contains good vitamins and minerals. But if you're going to get all the trace micronutrients you need to really get your body and your brain humming on a regular basis, you need to vary your dietary intake and pull from the WTF-is-that? part of the salad bar. Here are a couple of winners:

Cauliflower is so hot right now. Go to any modern food joint and you'll likely see some kind of unique preparation: cauliflower rice, cauliflower flan, cauliflower pizza crust, General Tso's cauliflower. It's become the grain of vegetables, with the added benefit of 900 percent fewer carbs than rice, and contains all the usual vitamin and mineral suspects, along with brain-healthy nutrients like choline.

Seaweed/sea veggies contain high levels of ocean minerals, including iodine, magnesium, manganese, iron, and other trace minerals. One great way to add in seaweed besides eating sushi or miso soup at your favorite Japanese restaurant is to purchase kelp or dulse flakes. I have a great seasoning that includes sesame seeds and seaweed flakes that I sprinkle on all my stir-fry meals and even put in my bone broth. The seaweed snack game has really found its groove with sea crackers and dried nori, as well.

Organ meat (liver, heart, kidneys) sourced from free-range animals is one of the world's most nutrient-dense superfoods. While the taste and texture can be a challenge to overcome, the benefits make it worthwhile; it's packed with the most bioavailable forms of both vitamins and minerals. Don't be shy about doing your best Hannibal impression and eating some liver with fava beans and a nice Chianti.

Universal Nutrition Principle #6: Go to War with Antinutrients

You know that old saying, "Two steps forward, one step back." When it comes to diet and health, antinutrients are the one step back, and they are just as important to avoid as the two steps forward we need to make with macro- and micronutrients. These toxic compounds generally lead to oxidative stress and inflammation, which, as we've discussed at length already, is one of the most harmful conditions our bodies deal with on the regular. And since most of us are too chronically stressed out to be able to count on simply shutting off inflammation, limiting the inputs that trigger inflammation is the next best thing.

Sugar, of course, is the biggest antinutrient of them all. If you'd like to revisit how excessive sugar horsefucks your health, head back to chapter 3, but here we are going to cover the other dietary super-villains so that you might avoid limiting or reversing your progress.

▨ TRANS FATS AND VEGETABLE OILS

Artificial trans fats (vegetable oils bonded with hydrogen) were created by food manufacturers to extend the shelf life of packaged and processed foods so they could sell more food, more cheaply, and farther away. The strategy worked, ballooning their bottom lines. Unfortunately it also started killing us in the process, causing massive systemic inflammation that was the precursor to all sorts of chronic health conditions. In 2015, in recognition of this fact, the FDA took the remarkable step of removing trans fats from GRAS status (generally regarded as safe) despite the explicit trans fat labeling requirements already in place.

The biggest problem with most vegetable oils like canola and safflower is that they are so high in omega-6 fatty acids, skewing the omega-6 to omega-3 ratio so disproportionately that the only way your body doesn't slip into a pro-inflammatory state when you consume them regularly is if you start every morning with a salmon-sized suppository full of fish oil. These oils are in all kinds of foods, including baked goods, fried goods, spreads, and sauces. The most offensive, though, are the fake butters and margarines; these are so packed with pro-inflammatory, cardiovascular-disease-inducing vegetable oils that people who replace their butter with margarine are more likely to die from heart disease, according to the Framingham heart study we first discussed over breakfast in chapter 3.

So here's the move: anytime you can't believe it's not butter, or you see something with trans fats, throw that shit in the trash. Even if it says "0 g trans fats" on the packaging, double-check that the ingredients don't include anything listed as "partially hydrogenated ____ oil," because that shit is trans fat. Companies get to claim zero, because the FDA allows them to round down for anything that contains less than 0.5 grams per serving. Spare yourself the fraction math and just throw it all out. Simple, done. No further discussion necessary. And as for canola and safflower oil, just do your best to limit your intake and vote with your dollars for products that don't contain them.

▇ FRIED OR BURNED FOODS

When you're cooking for your health, even if you're indulging in some delicious pan-fried foods, you want to make sure you don't heat your fats—olive oil, butter, coconut oil—to what is called their "smoke point." This is where healthy fats start to turn unhealthy, because once they burn, they start to produce toxic compounds called aldehydes, which, interestingly, are also in the class of compounds that accumulate when we drink too much alcohol, making us feel hungover.

This chemical conversion process is why I told you to keep your bacon bendy. When you burn it or fry it on high heat, the sodium nitrite that naturally occurs in bacon, as well as the nitrates that are often added for preservation, can turn into a nasty carcinogen called nitrosamines. Not only is this bad for your system, but it also ruins one of nature's tastiest, porkiest gifts.

To this point, asking you to hold off on your coffee until after breakfast has probably been the biggest bummer for most people, but I suspect asking many of you to eliminate the crisp bacon isn't much better. Well, guess what, it's about to get worse, because part and parcel with not burning your bacon is not charring your meats. I know that dark crust on burned ends and bone-in ribeye steaks is mouth-watering good, but for the sake of optimizing your lunch and reducing the carcinogenic effects on your body over the long term, let's go ahead and dial all that back for a little while.

Pro Tip: Fry with Avocado Oil

Avocado oil has the highest smoke point of all cooking oils. With a nice mild flavor, it's great for any kind of sauté or stir-fry. And with a smoke point upward of 500°F, you'll be hard-pressed to scorch it unless you crank the burner to 11 and then forget about it.

▊ PESTICIDES

While major players in the agricultural-industrial complex will defend their use of pesticides on crops, you would do well to proceed with caution when you consider that numerous studies over the years have demonstrated disturbing links between pesticides and a host of gnarly shit.

One study found pesticide residues were four times more likely on nonorganic crops, while organic produce saw a 48 percent lower presence of cadmium, a toxic metal, than their nonorganic counterparts. In a study of 1,139 children, researchers found a 50–90 percent increased risk of ADHD in children with the highest levels of pesticides in their urine, compared to those with the lowest levels. Another study noted a correlation between those gardening with the pesticide rotenone and the development of Parkinson's later in life.

Does all this mean you need to go run screaming from the conventional produce section at your local supermarket? No, just understand that pesticides are not good for you and that eating organic as much as possible will be the surest way to avoid the antinutrients conventional produce contains.

▊ CHEMICALS

There are all kinds of chemicals found in food, but perhaps the most ubiquitous are the food dyes. An analysis of over fifteen clinical trials, compiled well over a decade ago, showed that artificial food dyes increased hyperactivity in children. And yet they still remain in food.

Tartrazine, also known as FD&C Yellow #5, found in many of those tasty mac-and-cheese boxes and cheese singles marketed to kids, is particularly ugly, having been correlated with behavioral changes including irritability, restlessness, depression, and difficulty sleeping.

It's not just food dyes, though. A huge study looking at 1,873 children showed that food dye in conjunction with sodium benzoate, a common preservative, also increased hyperactivity. Is it any wonder we are handing out ADD medication to our kids like candy? Blame it on culture all you want, but it might just be what's in your pantry that's the problem.

Reversal: Eat Real Food

If anyone is trying to trick you into eating something by making it a different color, you probably don't need to eat it. Real food is delicious. Any of your favorite processed foods could be replaced with a healthier real version, for just a little bit of time.

▨ HEAVY METALS

We're not talking about Metallica. We're talking about death metal. Namely, your own death from metal. Remember our indefatigable old friend Tony Robbins from chapter 2? Well, his favorite thing to eat was tuna and swordfish steaks, and it almost killed him. The reason? Mercury poisoning. Like most larger and longer-living predatory fish, tuna and swordfish are extremely high in mercury, and over time those metals can build up in the tissue and wreak havoc. In a study of 129 Brazilians, for example, higher levels of mercury were associated with a decrease in fine motor skills, dexterity, memory, and attention. Further evidence suggests that low levels of mercury toxicity are linked to diseases like depression, anxiety, and even

Alzheimer's and Parkinson's. Interestingly, canned tuna has a much more reasonable level of mercury than a bigeye tuna steak, so if the preservatives and additives are not off the charts, and you need your chicken of the sea, snagging some cans off the grocery store shelf may be your best option.

If you are concerned about heavy metals, whether because you live in a polluted environment, you had a bunch of dental work thirty years ago, or you are a sushi addict who is 25 percent spicy tuna roll by weight, definitely get your blood levels tested. In addition, consider adding a daily dose (about 15g) of cilantro to your diet. Packed with vitamins and minerals, cilantro (or coriander leaves, if you're not from North America) in moderation has been shown in several studies to have the unique ability to help the body chelate (a fancy word for "eliminate") heavy metal accumulation. In the animal model it has even been shown to prevent the accumulation of metals. Either way, it is important not to overdo it with cilantro chelation because the metals can become mobilized during the elimination process and enter even more sensitive tissues. To prevent that from happening, you want to open up all the channels of detoxification. In other words, make sure you are drinking plenty of water to flush urine, having regular bowel movements, and sweating to release the toxins. Sauna and hot yoga are great ways to ensure you are moving enough sweat.

PHYTIC ACID AND OXALATE

Phytic acid and oxalate (or oxalic acid) are natural chemicals found exclusively in plant species that protect and assist the plants in which they're found but inhibit mineral absorption when consumed by humans.

Phytic acid, found in all edible seeds, grains, and legumes, helps protect the seed and stores phosphorus that young plants use to grow. When ingested by a human, it prevents full absorption of key minerals like iron, zinc, and calcium.

Oxalate is found in particularly high concentration in leafy greens like kale. It is part of the plants' natural antipest defense mechanisms, but binds with minerals, particularly calcium, when consumed and makes them less available for use in key cellular processes.

Fortunately there are strategies for mitigating the antinutrient properties of both these sneaky little devils. Sprouting or fermentation disable and degrade phytic acid in plant seeds so that the grain can burst through, increasing vitamins like folate, vitamin C, and vitamin E, and nutrients like lysine, a crucial amino acid for immune health, in the process. The tastiest version of this process is probably sourdough bread. The fermentation of the dough promotes phytate breakdown to a much greater degree than typical yeast fermentation in normal bread, resulting in a delicious delivery mechanism for a slab of REAL butter and mineral-rich sea salt.

The best way to handle the oxalate in your leafy greens is simply to boil or cook them, which significantly reduces the amount of oxalate, in some cases by up to 90 percent. Adding calcium to your dietary regimen can compensate for the calcium lost to the oxalates, as well.

Caveat: Fuck Your Gluten Sensitivity!

If there is one thing I have learned in my personal and professional journey, it's that the mind is a powerful thing. Nowhere on the nutritional landscape is that more true than with gluten. Poor, poor gluten. What did gluten ever do to you to earn such disdain? I don't know about you specifically, but I can tell you what it did to six out of the seven friends of yours who claim to be gluten-intolerant: it didn't do anything, besides deliver years of bready deliciousness.

Let's go inside the numbers. Up to 1 percent of people have legitimate celiac disease, which is a full-on gluten intolerance marked by nasty symptoms like digestive discomfort, bloating, diarrhea, constipation, headache, tiredness, skin rashes, depression, and smelly, smelly shit. Beyond celiac

OWN THE DAY, OWN YOUR LIFE

cases, the percentage of the population that registers as gluten-"sensitive" sits somewhere in the 0.5–13 percent range. That's a huge variance. One that's virtually impossible to pin down because it's hard to track these self-reported conditions and separate them from the nocebo effect (the negative placebo effect that happens after you hear about how bad gluten is for you). A 2015 study by gastroenterology researchers in Italy took nearly 400 people with self-diagnosed gluten intolerance, put them on a gluten-free diet, and tracked their progress to see how their symptoms improved. This is what they found: 26 people had celiac disease; 2 had a wheat allergy; and only 27 of the remaining 364 people were diagnosed as gluten-sensitive. That's 55 people out of nearly 400, or less than 15 percent, who actually had gluten issues.

So why do so many people report feeling better when they cut out gluten from their diet? Well, it's not because of the gluten. Sometimes it's some other stuff in the grain, like fermentable oligosaccharides, disaccharides, monosaccharides, and polyols (FODMAPs), or herbicides and pesticides such as glyphosate. But usually it's simply that they've stopped eating a lot of the junky, refined carbohydrate-rich foods that spike their blood sugar and produce fatigue on the way down. I'm not saying that you, personally, aren't gluten-sensitive or gluten-intolerant. I'm not calling you a liar. But if you haven't thoroughly tested it, well then, ain't nobody got time for your "sensitivity."

Prescription

I dare you. I double dare you to go buy an old-school, retro lunchbox—one of the metal ones with the thermos that can keep soup hot for a week and a half—and bring that clanker to work or to school with you, filled with the best lunch you've ever made in your life. In an ideal world you have prepped your food earlier in the week, so packing that Incredible Hulk lunchbox full of all your weird foods will be a snap. Then, if the sun is shining, you're gonna take yourself out somewhere you can relax, and you are gonna open it up and feast. You're gonna eat for twenty minutes, maybe put on some headphones and nap for thirty minutes (we'll get to that next), and you're gonna love life.

PLAN A

Here are some dishes you can mix and match for Plan A:

Chipotle Beef Bowl

SERVES 1

Time to prep: 5 minutes
Time to cook: 15 minutes

1 tablespoon avocado oil

120g seasonal organic peppers (bell, Hatch, and hotter ones if you can take it—remove the stems and ribs if you can't), sliced

1 small organic brown onion, sliced

1 teaspoon chipotle seasoning blend

175g grass-fed ground beef

Sea salt

Black pepper

30g organic broccoli sprouts

15g fresh organic coriander, chopped

2 tablespoons full-fat Greek yogurt

30g pico de gallo

✦ Heat the avocado oil in a medium frying pan over medium-high heat. Add the peppers and onion, and sauté for about 5 minutes, stirring occasionally, until they start to get soft.

✦ Add the chipotle seasoning blend and beef. Lower the heat to medium and cook, stirring often, until the beef is no longer pink (7–10 minutes).

✦ Season to taste with salt and pepper.

✦ Serve over the broccoli sprouts, and top with the coriander, yogurt, and pico.

Probiotic Ceviche

SERVES 2

Time to prep: 15 minutes
Time to marinate: 2+ hours

225g boiled prawns, deveined, peeled,
   and tails removed

½ organic avocado, diced

40g kimchi

1 small organic red onion, diced

30g organic pomegranate seeds

Juice of 1 lime

Chilli sauce

¼ teaspoon sea salt

1 tablespoon seaweed flakes (see note)

✦ Chop the prawns.

✦ Combine the prawns, avocado, kimchi, red onion, and pomegranate seeds in a large bowl.

✦ Add the lime juice, chilli sauce (to preferred heat level), and sea salt, and stir to combine.

✦ Refrigerate for a minimum of 2 hours to let the ceviche marinate.

✦ Before serving, sprinkle on the seaweed flakes.

NOTE: You can find dulse or nori flakes in most supermarkets, or use the Japanese seaweed seasoning blend furikake.

Bacony Asparagus with Sauerkraut

SERVES 2

Time to prep: 3 minutes
Time to cook: 10 minutes

2 tablespoons leftover bacon grease

450g organic asparagus, trimmed and chopped (see tip)

75g sauerkraut

+ Melt the bacon grease in a large frying pan over medium heat.

+ Add the asparagus, and sauté until tender (about 10 minutes).

+ Serve on a bed of sauerkraut.

TIP: To avoid eating the woody ends of asparagus, grab a spear at either end, then snap. The asparagus will break at the top of the woody section, leaving you with only the good stuff.

Garlic Green Beans with Cashews

SERVES 2

Time to prep: 5 minutes
Time to cook: 10 minutes

2 tablespoons avocado oil

450g organic green beans, ends trimmed

1 tablespoon chopped organic garlic

1 teaspoon garlic powder

40g raw organic cashews

Bragg Liquid Aminos (see note)

✦ Heat the avocado oil in a medium frying pan over medium-high heat.

✦ Add the green beans, garlic, garlic powder, and cashews. Cook, stirring often, until the beans are tender.

✦ Season to taste in the pan with the liquid aminos.

NOTE: Bragg Liquid Aminos is a protein concentrate made from non-GMO soy. You can find it with the soy sauce, or you can swap in organic tamari or coconut aminos.

Turmeric No-Tato Salad

SERVES 2

Time to prep: 5 minutes
Time to cook: 20 minutes

1 head cauliflower

2 tablespoons avocado oil

Sea salt

4 tablespoons Primal Kitchen Mayo

2 tablespoons Indian curry powder or
ground turmeric (or more, to taste)

+ Preheat the oven to 190°C/375°F/Gas Mark 5.

+ Break the cauliflower into florets.

+ On a baking sheet, toss the cauliflower with the avocado oil, and sprinkle with sea salt.

+ Roast for 20 minutes or until the cauliflower starts to turn soft and golden brown.

+ In a medium bowl, mix together the mayo and the curry powder or turmeric.

+ Add the roasted cauliflower to the bowl, and stir to combine.

Sautéed Garlic-Mustard Dandelion Greens

SERVES 2

Time to prep: 2 minutes
Time to cook: 5 minutes

2 tablespoons avocado oil

1 bunch organic dandelion greens, ends trimmed and chopped into bite-size pieces

½ teaspoon garlic powder

½ teaspoon mustard powder (or more, to taste)

Sea salt

✦ Heat the avocado oil in a medium frying pan over medium-high heat.

✦ Add the dandelion greens along with the garlic and mustard powders.

✦ Sauté, stirring often, until the greens are wilted (4–5 minutes).

✦ Season to taste with salt.

Chia Pudding

SERVES 1

Time to prep: 1 hour

3 tablespoons chia seeds
250ml unsweetened organic almond
  milk

1 tablespoon cashew butter

✦ In a bowl or mason jar, stir together the chia seeds and almond milk.

✦ Refrigerate, but keep stirring every 15 minutes or so until the seeds begin to absorb the almond milk and form a pudding. (This will take about an hour.)

✦ Before serving, swirl in warmed or room-temperature cashew butter.

PLAN B

But what if you can't meal-prep today and make something deli-cious? Even the best days don't run like clockwork the whole way through. In that case, you need to know what restaurants in your area serve properly sourced and sufficiently weird food. In Austin we have a restaurant called Thai Fresh, which serves all grass-fed, free-range meat with seasonal veggies from local farms. You get all those weird and awesome Asian spices and fatty coconut milk and fish broth, combined with great nutrients. I eat there for lunch twice a week. What's your Thai Fresh? Find it, make friends with it, and feast.

PLAN C

The platinum baller-on-the-go alternative to making your lunch or ordering out is to subscribe to a meal delivery service. Nearly every city of reasonable size has one or more meal deliv-ery services these days. Some are built around a specific dietary philosophy—low-carb, Paleo, even full keto—and many offer cus-tomizable options for you to choose from.

Now Do It

Humans are funny creatures. Having lost our instinctual guidance, we have to make choices with our minds constantly. Some of these choices require willpower, and when life gets rocky, that's when our willpower turns to Rocky Road. The decision to delay or restrict immediate pleasure for future gain or the greater good is controlled by a part of the brain called the frontal cortex. This part of the brain continues to develop even through our twenties, reaching maturity well beyond the time we have a car and a credit card.

With an immature frontal cortex, and the means to acquire a dou-ble Western bacon cheeseburger on the regular, even if we know it isn't good for us, we still might do it. But it's not just those wild teens and troubled twentysomethings who may not have a powerful frontal cortex; like any part of the brain (or entire body for that matter), it gets stronger largely through exercise. Every time we make a choice for our future good, our frontal cortex is strengthened. Every time we fail, the groove that slides us into post-food-orgy shame is also deepened.

This is why lunch is important not only for the body but also for the mind. But it doesn't have to be a wrestling match with yourself. Make eating weird foods a game, take some of the pressure off. The world is full of awesome food, so stop thinking about what you can't have and get excited about what you can. Expand that list by seeking out restaurants and foods you've never tried and giving them a go. I'm not talking about a new toaster strudel flavor or a new gastropub either (it'll have the same crudo and Brussels sprouts appetizers as all the other pubs), I'm talking about a new concept or a new type of nut, or fruit, or vegetable. Something like rutabaga, or macambo, or pili nuts.

Tag me in your weird foods that you love and we'll share the journey together. If you can build upon the momentum of these positive choices, the payoff will extend far beyond the implications of this single meal.

THREE POINTERS

- ✦ Rather than counting your calories, focus on the nutrients you are putting into your body. You want to ingest plenty of macronutrients like proteins, fats, and fiber. Remember, you are what you eat ate, so source your macros well.
- ✦ Micronutrients are abundant in a diverse diet. Seek out these "weird" foods and benefit from a host of protective and performance-enhancing nutrients.

✦ Equally important as what you put into your body is what you keep out of it. Avoid antinutrients that come from highly processed, refined, burned, fried, or artificial foods and colorings. These are the succubi of the food world and are to be resisted.

9

THE BINAURAL POWER NAP

Let's begin by taking a smallish nap or two . . .

—WINNIE-THE-POOH

Doing the most is not always doing your best. When the natural post-lunch lull comes rolling in, the best thing you can do is listen to your body. Instead of fighting it, go with it. Recharge the battery with a thirty-minute power nap, aided by brain-wave entrainment, and return to owning your day with a clear sense of purpose and mental clarity.

Getting Owned

The passengers riding the Metro-North in New York in late November 2013 figured it was just another normal train ride, the same holiday trek many of them had been doing for decades.

Then the people at the back of the train felt the crash, and the lights went out. Bodies and limbs flew. Windows shattered. Everyone could hear the sound of wrenching metal and screaming and feel gravel and dust in their faces. The governor of New York would tell CNN that the whole thing "looked like a toy train set that was mangled by some super-powerful force."

After the cleanup crews completed their work, they'd found four dead bodies. Sixty-three other people were injured. It was the worst disaster in the history of the Metro-North.

The cause? The conductor fell asleep at the wheel.

I know, I know . . . that's dark as fuck. Especially after starting the chapter with a quote by Winnie-the-Pooh. But I tell this story because the reality of the modern world is that after lunch far too many of us are that conductor, and our workday is the train—derailed, out of control, and ground to a screeching halt. If we're going to change that, we need to accept that we're a nation of tired people.

There's countless reasons for it—food, phones, work, stress, light, the quality and length of sleep, and much more—but the end result, regardless of the cause, is the same: too many of us walk around in a kind of permanent fog, from the moment we wake up until the moment we go to sleep. One of the main goals of this book, one of the only ways to reliably own this day and own our lives, is to get rid of that damn feeling. But before you can fix a problem, you have to admit you have one.

In a selection from a *Guardian* article titled "The Exhaustion Epidemic," the author retells the story of a conversation she had with a friend. They were talking about the old and simple ritual of hosting dinner for friends, and how deeply it's been affected by how tired we all are:

> [My] friend . . . a consummate hostess and an excellent social barometer, [said]: "Ten years ago I would have been horrified if a guest fell asleep at dinner. Now it happens all the time. And you just think to yourself, 'I understand, everybody is so tired, working late, travelling, more pressures, worrying about things.' Now when I ask people to supper, I'm never offended when they tell me they have a hell of a week coming up and could they please wait to see how they feel. Nor do I mind when one half of a couple comes on their own."

That's how bad it's gotten! We're falling asleep at our friends' dinners and skipping time with the people we most want to be with because we don't have the energy anymore. Our relationships, our vitality, our productivity, are all being captured in the gaping maw of exhaustion. Obviously, I'm not the first person to draw attention to this problem. It's become fashionable to talk about sleep these days (we'll talk about it more in chapter 15). But too often that's all we do: talk about this quiet crisis. We lament its costs but almost never actually *do* anything about it.

We read story after story about the need for a good solid amount of sack time, but how many of us end up staying up late staring into a screen, watching the hours tick by and compressing the amount of shut-eye we can get? We know the slide toward sleepy time begins with how we wake up and fuel ourselves. We feel it pick up speed during the middle of the day, and through our yawns we feign superiority over the "lazy" cultures that still have a siesta in the afternoon. But secretly we're envious, because that is exactly what our body is telling us to do. But do we listen? No, we stick to the script and fight through the exhaustion. We mainline coffee and energy drinks, we throw water on our faces, some of us pop some pills, and still we end up looking like one of those puppies in your Facebook feed whose owners record them fighting to stay awake, only to fall over into their food dish.

This is the postlunch drag. That strange period where the beginning of the end of the workday has yet to begin, but you're too far past the end of the beginning to think you can start fresh. You've seen the commercials about it. *Do you know what 2:30 feels like?* Yeah, you do. Everyone, including yours truly, has felt that post-lunch energy dip. It feels terrible. Like walking and thinking through sand. Like anywhere in the world is a better choice than being in the office right now. You come back to work from lunch, often grudgingly, every cell in your body telling you to turn out the lights in your office and pull a George Costanza—napping under your desk, hoping you don't get caught.

Sometimes I suspect that if most people snuck out after lunch and stopped working, it would have no visible impact on national productivity, because for so many people nothing gets done after lunch anyway. They limp toward the end of the day feeling overly warm, generally uncomfortable, and interminably slow. This is a phenomenon I'm not just curious about from a science and health perspective. I have a lot of people who work for me—so when the afternoon doldrums take hold of people in my office, it has a literal cost. As an employer, as well as a person motivated by total human optimization, I'd prefer for a full third of the workday not to be a complete waste of time for everyone involved. More specifically, I want to find a way for people to be doing their *best* work in the afternoons.

The good news is that this is very possible, which is why we're going to focus our efforts here, where the right actions (especially when preceded by the right meal) can combine to have an immediate effect on your day and yield a productive, restorative period right after you've finished lunch. This period can make or break the rest of the time you have at work and your time afterward at home. If you're deliberate about how you spend this time, if you resist the inertia of the day and listen to your body's signals, then just as you do in the mornings, you can take what is for everyone else a rough patch and turn it into a period of smooth sailing.

Owning It

When you feel yourself slowing down after lunch, your body is sending you a signal loud and clear that it needs a rest. As my man Kris Kristofferson once said, "You don't paddle against the current, you paddle with it. And if you get good at it, you throw away the oars." I take that to mean there is no shame in going with the flow and taking a nap. But don't take my word for it. Look at history. It's filled with famous nappers who were also famously productive. Winston Churchill, John F. Kennedy, Ronald Reagan, Napoleon, Albert Einstein, Thomas Edison—all regular nappers. For some of them, their schedules actually had the nap time built in! In other words, people in their lives knew that they were going to take a break in the mid-afternoon, because they knew what the afternoon lull did to them, and not a soul faulted them for it.

Or if history isn't your thing, look at science. Naps have been shown to consistently outperform high doses of caffeine for cognitive tasks and even motor performance. They've been shown to improve logical reasoning, reaction time, and immune function. Basically, if you take a nap instead of a coffee break, you'll be better at seeing the signs that it would make sense right now to take a nap instead of a coffee break. It's a virtuous cycle, recommended to both military pilots and astronauts based on a study that showed napping doubled levels of alertness. My favorite study, though, is a 2008 British experiment in which they compared a nap, a cup of coffee, and more nighttime sleep, to see what would happen to people's afternoon energy levels and concentration. The nap—yes, the nap!—won.

Naps have even been indicated to decrease levels of frustration and impulsiveness. Imagine how much more compassion we might have seen out of those Israeli parole judges from chapter 3 if they'd only taken a nap after lunch before returning to the bench. Is it any wonder that some of the biggest companies in the world—household names like Uber and Google—extol the virtues of napping? They know what it can do for their employees, and they know that letting their workers catch a few extra Zs during the day could mean more $$$s for them after it's all said and done.

READY, SET, NAP!

Much of this book might seem like it's about rewiring or overhauling your day, but a lot of what we're doing is just tuning ourselves in to the messages our bodies and brains send us—that we've stopped listening to. That overwhelming exhaustion you feel suffocating your brain in the afternoon is no different. It's not an accident; it's a signal for your body, telling you to stop and recharge. While a lot of times the dip in energy is exacerbated by poor lunch choices, it is actually a part of the same circadian cycle that governs our waking and sleeping hours. You are supposed to get sleepy in the afternoon. The last thing you want to do is run away from this, or any other of your body's signals. Naps are a powerful way to get back into the groove after lunch and prepare you for a fulfilling evening at home. There's no shame in that game.

So what is the perfect length of nap? That depends. A full sleep cycle is usually around ninety minutes, and is ideal on a day that you have really lost out on a lot of sleep. But thirty minutes is generally the upper limit of what most people have available, and so it is exactly the length of time that sleep expert Nick Littlehales recommends for a controlled recovery period (CRP). You won't typically enter deep sleep in that time, but your body will prioritize REM sleep and leave you feeling mentally refreshed. This length is almost universally what I target during my day, and recommend to all the pros we work with. Any longer than thirty minutes, and I risk getting pulled from the middle of a deep sleep cycle—which can be very disruptive if not allowed to run its course all the way to the end. Not to mention that a ninety-minute nap every day might get you fired for sleeping on the job. If you don't have thirty minutes, feel free to take what you can get: a little rest is better than none at all.

▨ MY FAVORITE BIOHACK

How many of us have struggled to relax or fall asleep after a stressful day? How many times have you lain awake, waiting for your brain to slow down and turn off? The same problem applies to naps during the middle of the day, to a greater degree in many cases, because our brain waves are not in the ideal place for restfulness.

Brain waves are a physiological reaction to our environments. They can help us optimize mental functioning for our current situations. There are five common brain-wave states—gamma, beta, alpha, theta, and delta—and each one is put to its highest and best use in different situations. If you are navigating daily decisions, slipping into beta frequency is the most useful. If you need to surf a big wave or write your novel, alpha frequency is helpful. And if you are trying to rest, theta frequency is most powerful. Unfortunately, it can be a slow and frustrating process trying to rely on our environment alone to get us naturally into any one of these brain-wave states, so sometimes we have to be more purposeful about it. We have to target a specific brain-wave frequency.

That's where brain-wave entrainment comes in. Entrainment can help round the corners so you can reach your intent faster and more effectively. In plain English, targeting theta and delta waves can help you take your naps to the next level. (It will also score you a point on the 30–35 sleep cycles you are trying to accomplish per week; more on that in chapter 15.) One of my favorite ways to do this is with binaural beat technology. Binaural beats are an auditory biohack designed to facilitate brain-wave entrainment. While the effect of any form of music on a human individual is highly personal and therefore resistant to generalization, a variety of research shows potential improvements for everything from cognitive performance to enhanced relaxation. Data aside, of all the biohacks in the world, if I had to personally choose to keep only one, it would be my binaural beats.

Wearing headphones, you listen to an audio track that pumps one frequency or tone in one ear and a different frequency or tone in the other ear. The difference in the frequency between the left and right ear determines which of the five brain-wave states you entrain. You can find binaural beats tracks for sale online or on YouTube, but to get you started I have hosted two of mine for free at aubreymarcus .com/beats.

These days, I know that in thirty minutes' time, I can dip my brain state and body back into the restorative parasympathetic and slow-wave waters, and then emerge refreshed. As a naturally shitty sleeper, I regularly knock out a thirty-minute CRP on days when I don't reach my sleep goals during the night shift. It's gotten so automatic for me, in fact, that I do it a minimum of five times a week. It's starting to be an everyday thing. On nights where my sleep is really screwed and I sleep less than five hours, I might do two 30-minute CRPs with my binaural beats (one at 2:00 or 3:00 p.m., one at 6:00 or 7:00 p.m.). I do them in the sun, on the grass, on my couch, in a chair, it doesn't matter. Often I receive reports that I was snoring, but I am not asleep. A shred of consciousness remains, and if anyone was to ask me a math problem in the headphones, I could solve it. I may not desire to speak it, but when we finished the experience, I could give them the answer. I'm somewhere between waking and sleeping—and I'm restoring my body all the while.

The more we learn about brain waves, the more we understand how important they are in generating desired states of consciousness. Binaural beats are a very basic technology, not too dissimilar from a rhythmic beat of a drum, but the tech is sure to improve. With the increasingly chaotic environment in which we live, assistive technology like these beats can be a game changer for a lot of people. By its very nature—with headphones and a twenty- to thirty-minute session—brain-wave entrainment is perfect for a post-lunch nap. Give it a shot and use it to slingshot you through the rest of your day.

Prescription

If you read chapter 8 and did what we told you to do, you rocked a sick-ass lunchbox to work or to school with a fantastically weird lunch full of micronutrients inside, and now it's working its way through your system. Besides being extra nutritious and minimizing the blood sugar swings that follow a traditional lunch, the other benefit of that lunch is that you don't need an entire lunch hour to track it down, buy it, eat it, and get back to the office. You can consciously crush it in fifteen minutes, and the rest of that time is now yours. I want you to use that time to take a nap if you're feeling a little sluggish.

1. Pick a time in the early afternoon.
2. Lock and load your theta waves binaural beats track.
3. Find a cool, quiet place—under a tree outside, Isaac Newton–style, under your office desk, Costanza-style, in your car with the A/C on, cabbie-style, it doesn't matter too much.
4. Set your alarm for thirty minutes.
5. Hit play on the binaural beats track and close your eyes.

I don't know what's crazier: that something so simple can have such a profound effect on the rest of your day or that something so simple can have been so easily discarded by our culture. Regardless, we're bringing nap time back so we can attack our remaining waking hours with a purposeful, productive vengeance.

Now Do It

At some point in your life someone called you lazy for sleeping. Maybe you were napping in the middle of the day. Maybe you were waking up late because you were up late. Maybe you just liked to sleep, dammit! Whoever that was, even though you love 'em, you gotta shake that off like a dog you just squeezed too hard.

Sleeping is not for lazy people, it is for productive people. The discipline comes not in what time you wake up, it's what time you go to bed. You should sleep in if you can. You should nap if you can. In fact you should plan for both of those things!

Shrug off what American culture tells you about napping, and look at the actual science. It is also important to note that sleep is not a binary thing, awake and asleep. There are all different shades of parasympathetic activation that help the recovery process for mind and body.

When the Navy SEALs are going through BUD/S training, which is designed to select only the strongest among them, they are given very short recovery periods, not long enough to properly sleep. This is not dissimilar to what they might find in the battlefield. Maybe you can't fully go to sleep when you are in a dangerous position. But you can recover your mind, so that you can be sharp. Being able to modulate and control your brainwave patterns is crucial to a high-functioning, ass-kicking life. Life is push, pull. Gather, go. Exert, recover. So rest, Padawan, the Force needs you at 100 percent.

THREE POINTERS:

✦ Ditch whatever you have been told about naps being for lazy people. Naps have been scientifically proven to be one of the most effective ways to stay alert and perform at a high level.

✦ Binaural beats are a great way to get the benefits of napping without having to fully fall asleep. By entraining your brain waves to more restorative patterns, you activate that restorative parasympathetic response you are looking for.

✦ Don't think of sleep as just what happens at night. Admit when you are tired and get comfortable with napping during the day to supplement your daily intake of sleep.

10

TRAINING

Your body is your slave; it works for you.

—JACK LALANNE

Healthy is sexy, and there is no single better thing you can do for your health than exercise. In trying to make us sexy without the methods that make us healthy, conventional training, with all its conveniences, has failed us on all accounts. So it's time to take an unconventional approach to physical conditioning, using unconventional tools in search of unconventional results. Instead of beach muscles and machine weights, we're going to climb a training pyramid together that builds durability, cardio, endurance, strength, and power in service of long life, well lived and totally owned.

Getting Owned

What if I told you there was an actual miracle drug? It could make you skinny. It could make you sexier. It could build your muscles. It could relieve stress. It helps you live longer. It helps you sleep. It relieves depression. It alleviates pain. It can even help you remember things better. And the kicker? While you can pay for it if you want, you don't have to. It's totally free.

It's called exercise. And it's a goddamn miracle. Yet 80 percent of Americans fail to take the recommended dose, because it's hard. Even for those of us who have embraced physical training, it can be hard to get out of bed for that run or make the left turn toward the gym instead of the right turn toward home after a long day at work. The mighty Joe Rogan, slayer of elk, slinger of jokes, and swinger of kettlebells, still has trouble motivating himself to exercise. He calls the voice inside him that tells him to skip the workout his "inner bitch." As an insanely busy man with demands on his time pulling in every direction on a constant basis, he has to set out to conquer that inner voice *every single time*.

I feel what he's saying. As soon as that first drop of sweat hits my brow, I'm good, but getting to that point has gotten the best of me hundreds of times. And if this is what we experience on a regular basis as lifelong athletes, I can only imagine what it's like for those who aren't just overstressed, undernourished, and overweight but also tired, sad, and in pain. And believe me, there are *millions* of those people. As much as 10 percent of the American population is depressed. The CDC estimates that a million Americans suffer from chronic fatigue. Over 100 million suffer from chronic pain, 20,000 of whom die every year from an overdose of the pain pills used to mask it.

Exercise can change a lot of that, as long as two things happen: (1) you actually do it, and (2) you actually do it *right*.

Getting in there and doing it is as much about motivation and inertia as it is about understanding why you should do it. We all know that training can help you lose weight and look all jacked like a Spartan from *300*, but the true gains from physical conditioning come from the insanely broad hormetic response our bodies' systems produce when put under the good kind of stress.

+ If you're tired all the time or suffering from chronic fatigue, exercise can help you restore good energy levels.
+ If you're down in the dumps, or downright depressed, it can improve your mood.
+ If you're not sleeping well, it can dramatically improve your sleep quality, by as much as 65 percent!
+ If you're in pain, and that is impacting the quality of your life, training is the drug for you.
+ If you're a healthy guy, training will help you perform better in bed.

Welcome to exercise, the miracle drug. For the miracle to happen, though, you need to know how to take your medicine, and unfortunately a lot of people overdose right out of the box, because the dragon they are chasing is not the one who is the vision of health, but rather the one with rock-hard abs, massive traps, and spindly legs, who has done more "curls for the girls" than there are girls on this earth.

The problems typically start when people who don't work out hit a point where they say, "Enough is enough, I'm getting in shape!" Usually it's because they spent New Year's Eve alone again, or they went to a party in clothes that they'd nearly eaten their way out of fitting into. Then comes the annual spike in gym memberships around the world in January, when that New Year's resolution still carries the hope of personal renewal. With all kinds of energy and motivation to get super shredded so they can get super laid, the well-meaning yet out-of-shape jump in a group class with a workout above their fitness level, or they go see an overzealous trainer, and they overdo it. What happens? The same thing that happens when someone who hasn't seen any sun for four months lies on the beach in Mexico for ten hours in a day. They get burned. After struggling through the session, they are so sore they can't work out for another week. That doesn't bother some of them initially, because they think that soreness means their training worked. They're one step closer to their goal. But even if that were true—which it isn't—what good is soreness if it keeps you out of the gym? Then February arrives. Any momentum they may have built with those first sessions has completely dissipated, and their hopes for personal renewal start heading in the same direction as their gym membership renewal.

This is the conventional trajectory for most people in modern society when it comes to training. It is a trajectory that has been shaped and defined by conventional wisdom and conventional methods, seeking conventional results. And all of them have let us down. If we want to own our physical health, and own the day as a result, we have to abandon our conventional approach to exercise and think and act unconventionally. In fact, fuck exercise. Let's start there. Exercise is for puppies and babies. We need to *train*. Train for a healthy body, because healthy is what matters. And training is what adults do who have goals and a mission to own the rest of their lives. Training *unconventionally* is how you do it with a smile on your face.

A note on timing. We have placed training in the afternoon, which is usually the best time to lift heavy and push a hard workout. But for those of you who prefer morning workouts, especially the more anaerobic or high-intensity, you may want to modify the breakfast recommendations to make sure you eat a full breakfast like the meals we recommend. Other than that, morning training and afternoon training remain very much the same.

Owning It

All right, let's be honest. Most of us aren't professional athletes. We don't work out because our paychecks depend on how long we can run, how much we can lift, how hard we can hit, or how fast we can move. Some of us work out simply because we enjoy it, some of us work out for health, but all of us work out because we want to look good naked. The problem is that when we focus on this goal, rather than on actually training the body to function properly, we build imbalances. I see it every day with new members who sign up to train at our academy. Men like good pecs, so they overdevelop their chest in comparison to their back. Then those big strong pecs start pulling their shoulders forward, straining their rotator cuffs and front deltoids until their shoulders blow out. Then by the time they are forty years old, they can't even do a pushup anymore, and instead of the chest filling out their shirts, it's their gut. Women don't usually have that issue. Theirs is different. They often look at an area of their body they don't like and immediately start trying to reduce the fat or cellulite there, to the exclusion of most of their body-moving muscles. Unfortunately, fat loss doesn't work that way, so they get frustrated with the results, and working out begins to feel like a waste.

The truth is that we are all attracted to healthy bodies. After all, what else would our ancestors be looking for in a mating partner? Of course, a healthy body can come in all shapes and sizes, but it does have a certain set of characteristics: the joints are mobile and fluid; the muscles are strong and flexible enough to perform a variety of tasks; the frame is capable of carrying weight, a little more, or a little less, without unnecessary strain; the tissue is healthy and supple. If you meet all or most of those criteria, you are what is called, in evolutionary terms, "fit," and in Aubrey Marcus terms, "sexy AF." I don't care about your body mass index or whether you look like an Instagram model. Healthy is sexy.

So we're gonna make sure you look sexy, by focusing on building a healthy body that is going to enable you to be the hero in any story you want to write. The foundation for this is going to be unconventional training.

Train Unconventional

If you want conventional nutrition, conventional sex, or conventional anything . . . this is the wrong book for you. Because conventional is boring at best, and ineffective or harmful at worst. The same goes for training. Capitalizing on the desire to make working out "easy," "simple," "fast"—like a fucking breakfast burrito—a whole host of fancy equipment sprang up in the latter third of the twentieth century promising to turn librarians into barbarians. You see the momentum of that movement in all the big-box globo gyms like 24 Hour Fitness, Equinox, Gold's, Planet Fitness, and all their other regional spawn. A bunch of expensive machines with levers and stacks of weight that isolate movements and muscles so that we can flex our way into narcissistic ecstasy.

But quietly, among the top athletes, a torch stayed lit. With a fundamental understanding of human movement, and a sentimental nod to the ancient traditions of the past, unconventional training was kept alive, waiting for its return to its proper place in the pantheon of physical conditioning. I became friends with one of the keepers of that flame when, in 2008, I met Roger Huerta, a rising mixed martial arts star and UFC title contender. We started working out together, and I noticed something different about his training. He didn't do what everyone else did. He used kettlebells, bands, ropes, bags, anything he could get his hands on. Sure, sometimes he hit the barbell, or tossed up some dumbbells or did sprints on the treadmill, but mixed in with his training was something else that people at Gold's Gym weren't doing. And just as his training was unconventional, his results were unconventional. He was fighting more frequently, and beating fighters of arguably higher skill, by having better conditioning, and more heart. The heart he was born with, the conditioning he built.

Unconventional training covers the use of the kettlebell, steel mace, sandbag, battle ropes, steel club, barbell (you can breathe a sigh of relief now, my meathead friends), and the most old-school of them all: body weight. But it was really Roger's use of kettlebells that first caught my eye and allowed unconventional training to capture my imagination. If you're an athlete of any kind, kettlebell training better simulates the constantly shifting center of gravity you encounter on the field, mat, or court than most conventional lifting does. Other objects, whether a ball, obstacle, or opposing player, rarely stand still during competition. Using kettlebells teaches your body to stabilize itself and produce force despite the chaos of movement. It works the back side of your body you don't see in the mirror and the deep inner core where the courage lives along your spine.

Exercise scientists were equally intrigued by what kettlebells could do. In 2013, researchers at the University of Wisconsin–La Crosse examined the effects of kettlebell training on healthy male and female volunteers—ages nineteen to twenty-five—all of whom were experienced in strength training. The subjects had their strength, aerobic capacity, and balance tested with conventional exercises first and then spent eight weeks training with kettlebells, performing lifts that included swings, snatches, cleans, and presses. Afterward, the same battery of conventional lifts were used to measure progress. After eight weeks, the subjects' strength improved, but core strength in particular jumped 70 percent. Aerobic capacity increased 13.8 percent. The participants' ability to balance also improved significantly, which the researchers cited as being especially valuable to grown adults who take up strength training.

The breadth of gains that kettlebells produce is stunning, but each of the unconventional tools and methods we will cover in this chapter offers its own unique benefits. Each has its own strengths. Together all of them have a few things in common. They focus on movement patterns that mimic and support movements that help us in everyday life. They allow you to move into positions that—if you're used to doing machine circuits or barbell training at your globo gym—you're probably not very familiar with. Training in this way corrects muscle imbalances and weaknesses, improves mobility, and allows you to perform any task you undertake better. Put more simply, they make you better at life.

Caveat: The CrossFit Phenomenon (Competing versus Training)

With more than 13,000 boxes—the term that CrossFit uses to describe its stripped-down gyms worldwide—you cannot ignore the CrossFit movement. It's a polarizing force that undoubtedly has produced some of the fittest humans in the world. It's also turned the activity of working out into a source of social and even tribal identity. While CrossFit has a lot of strengths, and in many ways has embraced the philosophy of the unconventional training movement, due to a stubborn inclusion of highly technical Olympic-style barbell lifts, a one-size-fits-all workout plan, and social pressure to perform in training as if it were a competition, it has produced a rash of injuries. And while injuries are part of life for a mixed martial arts fighter or an extreme athlete, they don't need to be part of life for you or me.

The bottom line is that CrossFit can be a fun, crazy workout that will get you in shape and introduce you to a community. But be careful. Use your own discretion about what you should and shouldn't do. If it doesn't feel right, don't do it. Remember, it's training, and as good as it feels to put your name on the board, it feels worse to put your name on the sign-in sheet at the ER and not be able to train for a while. If you are going to do CrossFit, own the workout yourself. Listen to your body, do what you feel like you should do, and don't get caught up and in over your head.

The Tools of the Trade

▓ BODY WEIGHT

HISTORY

Body-weight exercises have gone by another name for millennia: *cal-isthenics*, an ancient Greek word that translates roughly to "move your ass already" and describes the discipline of using your body's weight as a way to develop strength, stamina, and your overall physique. Calisthenics used to be a huge part of physical fitness, especially for women, in the nineteenth and early twentieth centuries, and remains a key part of physical training in the military.

ADVANTAGES

Body-weight exercises are inherently joint friendly and safe because the loads you lift (your body parts) are never more than you can normally stabilize. They are also crazy convenient and practical, since you need very little space to do them in and you don't need a gym to scale them up or down in difficulty. Whereas with weight training, you need to add weight to progress, body-weight movements can be progressed and regressed as necessary by simply changing the angle of your body. Pushups can be done with hands on an incline to make them easier or with feet on an incline to make them harder. Leg exercises can be done with both or one limb at a time. Tools like the suspension trainer make this easier, but all the basic exercises can be done and modified with body weight alone.

SIGNATURE MOVE

Sit Through

KETTLEBELL

HISTORY

Kettlebells debuted in eighteenth-century Russia, where they were used as counterweights to measure grain and other dry goods. It wasn't long before workers started challenging each other to lift the heaviest ones, and kettlebells eventually found their way into the hands of circus strong-men. After World War II, the Soviet Red Army adopted kettlebells as a means of training its soldiers, and by the 1970s kettlebell lifting had grown in popularity to such a degree that it became an official sport of the Soviet Union. Now you'll find at least a kettlebell or two in almost every major gym that includes free weights.

ADVANTAGES

A kettlebell's center of gravity lies six to eight inches away from your grip, making it harder to control. As a result, practically any exercise you do with it—from conventional strength movements like presses and squats to more unique kettlebell exercises like swings and snatches—is going to require stricter form and more muscle activation than you could get away with using a dumbbell. Kettlebell lends itself to flowing motions, like the long cycle from kettlebell sport, which allows for the maximum amount of weight to be lifted overhead in ten minutes of any exercise in the world. Kettlebells are incredibly versatile and are also great for building strength and power with heavier bells.

Kettlebell Swing

▨ STEEL MACE

HISTORY

Developed by Hindu warriors over two thousand years ago, the mace, or *gada*, was used as a weapon of war. To condition the muscles of the shoulders and back, and thus become more effective in battle, warriors practiced swinging heavy maces as a part of their daily morning regimen. The tradition  was picked up by the Pehlwani wrestlers, until it became adopted by the strongman community in the twentieth century.

ADVANTAGES

The steel mace is the most unbalanced of all tools, with a heavy head and a very light handle. This forces maximum correction and adaptation of the body to maintain balance. In motion, the specialty of the mace is rotation, which forces stabilization and counterrotation, all in the same movement. Excellent for conditioning the shoulder girdle and connecting muscle groups in compound movements for maximum power, the mace is a favorite among the MMA athletes who come through our gym.

SIGNATURE MOVE

Mace 360

CLUB

HISTORY

The club dates back to the Hindu warriors, who used it similarly to the steel mace. It was also a part of strongman contests in Persia, and wrestlers and other martial artists throughout the Middle East and Asia adopted it for strength training. Club swinging grew in popularity until it became part of Olympic  gymnastics in 1904, where it endured until 1932. Clubs have seen a resurgence since the beginning of the twenty-first century, and are recognized for their ability to develop strength and mobility simultaneously.

ADVANTAGES

A club's handle is an extension of the club itself; it's not set off from the load as it is on a sandbag, kettlebell, mace, and other implements. That makes the club act as more of an extension of your arm, which allows for a very natural motion and the opportunity to countertrain unilateral movements such as golf swings, to restore balance to the body. Clubs aren't really "lifted," they're swung, so generating and resisting that momentum is great for developing endurance as well as mobility. Swinging a club can gently pull your joints into greater ranges of motion while forcing your body to stabilize it at the same time—the optimal way to improve flexibility that you can access during activity (or, simply, in life).

SIGNATURE MOVE

Club Pullover

■ SANDBAG

HISTORY

Sandbags have been used by wrestlers and military personnel for ages. They're a classic example of old-school farm-boy strength—the idea that simple manual

labor done out of necessity can have an ancillary, even unintended, boon to strength and conditioning.

ADVANTAGES

The sandbag offers the perfect introduction to strength training with an external load. Whereas kettlebells and clubs could cause discomfort or injury if you lose control of them and allow them to smack into your shoulder or knee, the sandbag is soft, and any contact it makes with you will be light. Unlike the other unconventional tools, the load in a sandbag is nearly alive—it's always shifting, challenging your stability no matter what movement you perform. It's hard to grip because of its shape, and works your core and balance hard.

SIGNATURE MOVE

Clean and Press

ROPE

HISTORY

Battle ropes were pioneered by a trainer named John Brookfield. Thick ropes akin to the kind used to lower an anchor on a large ship, battle ropes are highly versatile  and one of the newest and most unique pieces of equipment to enter the fitness industry.

ADVANTAGES

With a rope, it is not only how heavy the rope is, but how much effort you put into it that creates the work rate. This makes it one of the safest implements to train full-power movements at maximum capacity. You can dial it back for longer aerobic cardio sets, or dial it up for sheer anaerobic explosiveness. Ropes are extremely low-impact on the joints, and allow for a wide range of movement to be applied. You can shuffle side to side, do squats or lunges, jump, do a burpee, all while maintaining an alternating wave. Ropes are about the closest thing you can get to sprinting for your upper body.

SIGNATURE MOVE

Lateral Wave

▓ BARBELL

HISTORY

The barbell has a multifaceted origin story. One of the earliest examples was a globe-ended barbell used by Austrian strongman Karl Rappo in the early 1800s. Gym owners in France and Germany began experi-  menting with barbell training until ultimately Kasper Berg developed the seven-foot barbell, still the standard today, and this device was entered into the 1928 Olympic Games. Once it had a foothold in the

Olympics, it spread quickly across the world, becoming the standard for weightlifting competitions worldwide.

ADVANTAGES

The advantage of a barbell is the ability to load up weight. A lot of weight. What you do with that weight determines whether the tool is helpful or not. Conventional barbell training includes the bench press, squat, deadlift, and some of the more complicated Olympic movements like the clean and jerk or the snatch. For a lot of these movements, it takes years to master and condition your joints to bear the load correctly. However, everyone can benefit from barbell training, particularly if they broaden their perspective on how the barbell can be used. It doesn't always need to be loaded heavy, or evenly, nor does it have to be held horizontally.

SIGNATURE MOVE

Suitcase Deadlift

The Training Pyramid—Your Ideal Fifty-Minute Workout

While it is possible to divide up a workout in myriad different ways over the course of a week, month, or twelve-week fight camp, for the purpose of this book, we want to create an ideal, option-filled, unconventional fifty-minute workout that trains multiple kinetic systems, targeting a series of functional health priorities, that you can repeat with slight variations three or four times every week. You can think of the kinetic systems and their associated health priorities as the strata of a pyramid, like the old debunked food pyramid that taught you to build your diet around pasta and bread . . . except this one won't try to kill you.

▓ DURABILITY (MOBILITY + FLEXIBILITY)—15 MINUTES

At the base of the pyramid, where you will naturally consume most of your training, is mobility and flexibility, which, combined, we call durability. There are a lot of ways to build durability that don't require setting foot in a gym. You can work on your mobility and flexibility pretty much anywhere. A big part of the corrections in posture we talked about in chapter 7 related to the effects of sitting too long at work, for instance, are aimed at supporting mobility and flexibility in your joints and your spine, which is the center of your nervous system.

Flexibility allows you to bend, not break, under the pressures of life and the stressors of a workout. Mobility allows you to complete wider ranges of motion without unnecessary compensation or additional pain. When you start training your muscles, mobility and flexibility become of even greater importance, since the constant contraction of muscles can create additional tightness and inflexibility. To combat that, you always need to bring your muscles through a full range of motion, and in some cases, apply pressure to the muscles with a foam roller or a lacrosse ball for a kind of self-massage called self myofascial release.

Deep Dive: What Is the Fascia, and Why Do You Release It?

Think of your fascia as the cling film that surrounds the meat of your muscles. Except it isn't like dumb old plastic, it is a network of nerves responsible for instructing the muscles exactly how they should contract. These nerves in the fascia can sometimes get stuck in the on or off position, causing undesired tension and body position. A muscle in constant "on" will pull your bones and joints to unfavorable spots, creating stiffness and limited range of motion. Self myofascial release loosens up that dense tissue and helps get you right.

The goal of mobility and flexibility practices is to live pain-free, and continue functioning for a long time to come. If you do nothing else, just getting up, moving around, putting your joints through a full range of motion, and massaging out your muscles will increase your durability and lead to a longer, vibrant life.

CARDIO—10 MINUTES

The second tier of the pyramid is the cardio system. Have you ever seen someone get winded and have to take a break climbing up a few flights of stairs? Or stop, hunched over, sucking wind, after chasing their kids for a few moments? That's because their cardio is weak. Cardio is short for cardiovascular fitness, which describes how effectively you can deliver and utilize oxygen to produce energy in your muscles. To move a greater capacity of oxygen-rich blood from your lungs throughout your body, your heart rate and breath rate go up. And as long as your lungs and heart can pump enough oxygen into your muscles, you can keep moving—at least until other mechanical forces, like muscle breakdown, and chemical forces, like lactate, cause you to stop. This is what is called your aerobic capacity. It's also called VO2 max, but that sounds like the name of a really fancy shampoo brand, so let's just stick with cardio for now.

You may have heard of high-intensity interval training. That term is as hot right now as Hansel from *Zoolander*. Basically, it amounts to repetitive, high-intensity bursts of effort that typically entrain multiple power systems, including cardio. So while high-intensity interval training (HIIT) is an effective way to build your cardio base, and has been shown to improve VO2 max and peak anaerobic power output, there is still a strong argument for including traditional steady-state cardio like running, swimming, biking, rowing, and the elliptical machine into your workout. It's good for variety, for laying the foundation for greater endurance, and for those beginning training or coming back after a long layoff. Many of the burnout stories you hear from people jumping into the gym right after the New Year happen because they passed up cardio and went straight to a HIIT full-body workout or circuit that wiped them out. Our focus with ten minutes of steady-state cardio in your workout is to get the heart rate up, so when you begin to tax your muscles in the rest of the workout, you are putting enough hormetic stress on them to produce greater endurance, without increasing the risk that you will never come back to the gym again.

▨ MUSCULAR ENDURANCE—8 MINUTES

The third tier is muscular endurance. The difference between cardio and muscular endurance for practical purposes is whether it is your aerobic capacity (your lungs) or muscle fatigue that is limiting your workload. Often they coincide, but sometimes one is more significantly strained then the other. When you say you are "winded," it's usually your cardio. When it's your quads burning during cycling or your biceps fried from rowing that cause you to stop, that's muscular endurance. This is when any muscle group gets fatigued from repetitive use.

Muscular endurance serves both absolute strength development and long-distance/time endurance, helping us to repeat a sustained muscular effort, over and over, for a moderate time with moderate power output. What does that look like? Middle-distance running (soccer), swimming, hiking up a mountain, mixed martial arts, power yoga.

To train muscular endurance, unconventional tools work great. Their impact on controlled range of motion, rotation (which we do in all movement), and multidirectional/multiangular movement is immense, while also offering a generally lighter resistance load, rather than a maximum heavy lift, for higher repetitions in a more sustained period of work. This helps create a solid foundation for strength gains while also minimizing potential risk of injury.

▨ STRENGTH—5 MINUTES

Strength is the body's ability to move a maximal load through muscular recruitment and contraction. How many bags of groceries can you carry from the car to the house? How many 737 jets can you tow if someone put you in a harness? Strength is not truly defined by those absolute numbers, however. Rather, it is measured holistically in relation to your body's frame and natural capacity. My strong is different from your strong, because we are different humans.

Strength training is not often thought of for its benefits beyond getting strong and building muscle. It does those things, but strength work also contributes to weight loss, a stronger heart, and increased bone density, as well as providing a good space to develop better body mechanics. Strong is also super sexy. All of which support performance in both life and sport, while ensuring the ability to do so at a higher level over the long haul.

▓ POWER—3 MINUTES

Power is the final tier, the tippy top of the pyramid. If strength is when force acts against resistance to create movement, then power is the rate (or speed) at which that force is enacted to create the movement. This is perhaps the most important system for athletes, so many athletic training regimens highly prioritize power development. It is how hard you can throw a punch, how explosively you can jump, how far you can throw a ball. It is generating the maximum amount of force possible.

The power system is important—it wouldn't be included in the training pyramid if it weren't—but it is by far the most taxing on the body, so for noncompetitive athletes, you don't need to spend a lot of time training it to own the day and be effective in life. You simply need to develop enough power to draw on when you need to sprint to the bus, jump out of the way of a bicycle, or defend yourself if necessary. Sprinting, plyometrics, and unconventional tools like battle ropes are all great easy, low-skill ways to train full-body power development.

Prescription

I don't know you. I don't know how you slept last night, how your body feels, whether you have any injuries, or what your fitness level is or isn't. But by committing to own the day, you are going to do something to move your body. We broke down what that might look like into three levels.

Level I: Have Fun and Just Get Moving

If you are just getting started with training, or if you feel like you have a long, intimidating road ahead, start out by slowly working your way into the shallow end of the training pool (sometimes literally) with elemental work that is fundamental to human movement. For me, there are a few things that are fun, including playing a game of any sort. Followed perhaps by doing some animal crawls across the turf, or dropping in for a little vulgar vinyasa at Black Swan Yoga. Here are three different ways you can get started:

TIME TO PLAY

Remember playing tag, or tug of war, when you were a kid, and only stopping when you were panting for air? This was the inspiration for Primal Play, a method developed by movement coach Darryl Edwards. The beauty of playing a game is that when you are engaged in something fun, you forget that you are working out. Here are a few of my favorite games that create bonds and break a sweat:

SHOULDER TAG

The goal of the game is to tag the other players anywhere in the shoulder. It's kind of like fencing and tag had a love child, with cardio, mobility, endurance, and hand-eye coordination each playing an important role. Boxing trainer and Olympic bronze medalist for Great Britain Tony Jeffries played this game every session with his mates leading up to the games. He credits it with his speed and movement, plus they always had a laugh. Play to ten clean touches, or go for three minutes, then tell me how you feel . . . once you catch your breath.

CROSS-HOP

Clasp right arms with someone of similar size, by doing what amounts to a forearm handshake, where your palms should be on the inside of each other's arm. Then lift your right foot off the ground behind you by bending your knee. The goal is to tug or push your opponent using your clasped arm until they are forced to drop their foot to the ground or release their grip on your arm. A lot of hilarious hopping ensues, making this game as much about strength and cardio as it is about plyometric power. Make sure to switch arms too, so you don't create imbalances.

PALM PUSH

In this game you line up facing your opponent. Palm to palm, you push or withdraw your hand until the other person is off balance. The goal is to get the other person to take a step, or to touch any other part of your body besides the flat part of your hand. This isn't as intense a workout as the other forms of play, but definitely one of the most fun.

ANIMAL MOVEMENTS

Undoubtedly the most well-paid, the most followed, and perhaps the most well-known mixed martial arts fighter of our epoch is Conor McGregor. The Notorious, as he is called, has won title belts in two weight classes in dramatic knockout fashion, and more than held his own in one of the highest-money boxing matches of all time, against perhaps the greatest pound-for-pound boxer of all time, Floyd Mayweather. His secret? According to him, it's hard work. And part of that hard work is doing ground-based, or animal flow, training with legendary movement specialist Ido Portal. This type of movement often has you moving on all fours across space, a practice Conor often takes when entering the octagon itself. It improves flexibility, balance, and spatial body awareness, as well as perhaps a little bit of something else special. I incorporate animal movements, specifically the bear crawl and the ape walk, into almost every one of my workouts.

BEAR CRAWL

I prefer the straight-leg version of this movement, with your feet and hands flat on the ground, and arms and legs extended. Starting from this position, you move your right foot up close to your right hand, but slightly behind and to the outside. Then your right hand moves up, then your left foot, then left hand. It's great for strengthening hips, hamstrings, and butt, as well as upper arms.

APE WALK

This movement is a lateral movement with bent knees, flat back, in which you push your weight onto your hands, and shuffle both feet to the right. Then release your hands and come to a straight-backed squat with legs still bent. Put your hands down again and repeat. Make sure to go in both directions for this. It's a great warmup and hip opener that will work the quads as well.

■ YOGA—THE ALL-IN-ONE

Yoga is everywhere. And for good reason! It's one of the best ways to connect mind and body, and access levels of higher consciousness. A lot of people view yoga as stretching, like it's some kind of ancient Indian calisthenics. While stretching is part of the practice, the magic of yoga is the utilization of breath to push through self-imposed limitations. As you practice, you start to hear your mind squealing, *That's far enough. I can't do that. What are we doing later?* Anything to take you out of the intensity of the present moment. But you stay steady with your intent. You focus on your breath. You release stray thoughts with each exhale. You bring in life force with each inhale. You drown the fire of the mind with a generous ocean of respiration and perspiration.

You can go all the way into the spiritual side of yoga, you can wear all white, you can take it really seriously. Or you can just breathe, stretch, sweat, and connect to the best version of yourself. If you're just starting out, that's where you should aim with your yoga practice. That was the idea behind Black Swan Yoga when we acquired it in 2014. You're as likely to hear Drake as you are wind chimes, because you're as likely to be seated next to a next-level practitioner as you are a retiree looking to stay mobile. And you can be sure, with the inclusion of an infrared heating system, that the sweat flows freely, puddling up with the remnants of the parts of yourself you are leaving behind as you end your session in shavasana, with the mind a quiet and humble servant, and your body at rest with the full force of mindfulness.

Pro Tip: Yoga Anywhere

When my fiancée travels abroad for work, she does yoga almost every day. In Amsterdam, in Prague, in China, and all other sorts of places that aren't known for their yoga. Yoga doesn't need a fancy studio, it doesn't even need a mat. They didn't have mats in India. But you should have some instruction to get the most out of it.

Level 2: The Own-the-Day Workout

We have created two workouts specifically for this book, derived directly from the philosophy built into this chapter generally and the training pyramid specifically. The first is perfect for beginners and people at an intermediate fitness level, and relies solely on body-weight movement, making it easy to do at home, in a dorm, or in an airport hotel room. The second is designed for those between the intermediate and advanced fitness levels and uses a single kettlebell (find the right weight for your ability) to make the workout similarly easy to knock out.

■ BODY WEIGHT—BASIC TO INTERMEDIATE

CARDIO—STEADY STATE (10 MINUTES)

Run, bike, dance, row, swim, jump rope, shadow box—pick any one or any combination and go with it.

MOBILITY (10 MINUTES)

The following drills should be performed in a circuit fashion for as many rounds as possible in the allotted time.

Egyptian, 5 reps each side

Lunge Twist, 5 reps each side

Standing Leg Circle, 5 reps each side

POWER (3 MINUTES)

Alternating Split Jump for max height, 10 seconds, followed by 20 seconds rest; 6 sets

STRENGTH (5 MINUTES)

Frog Pushups, 5 seconds down and 5 seconds up, 5 sets of 3

MUSCULAR ENDURANCE (8 MINUTES)

Alternate between the following two exercises, 4 sets

Plank, 40 seconds, then 20 seconds rest

Sit-Through, 40 seconds, then 20 seconds rest

STRETCHING, RELEASE (5 MINUTES)

Kneeling Hip Flexor Stretch

Kneeling Hamstring Stretch

Shoulder Bridge

▨ KETTLEBELL—INTERMEDIATE TO ADVANCED

CARDIO—STEADY STATE (10 MINUTES)

Run, bike, dance, row, swim, jump rope, shadow box—pick any one or any combination and go with it.

MOBILITY (10 MINUTES)

The following drills should be performed in a circuit fashion for as many rounds as possible in the allotted time.

Windmill, 5 reps each side

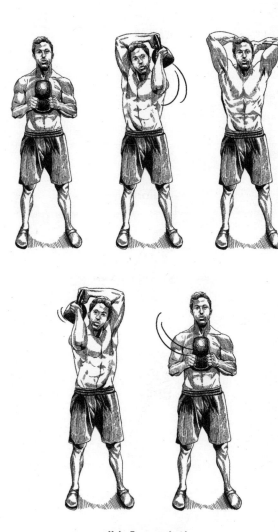

Halo, 5 reps each side

Bootstrapper, 5 reps each side

POWER (3 MINUTES)

Sumo Squat Jumps, 10 seconds, then 20 seconds rest, 6 sets

STRENGTH (5 MINUTES)

Super Slow Presses, 5 seconds up, 5 seconds down, 5 sets of 3 reps

MUSCULAR ENDURANCE (8 MINUTES)

Perform the following drills for as many rounds as possible in 8 minutes:

Kettlebell Swings, 15 reps

Single Arm Thruster, 5 reps each side

STRETCHING, RELEASE (5 MINUTES)

Couch Stretch

Pigeon Pose

Standing Forward Fold

Level 3: Work with a Pro

To really take your training to the next level, you'll need additional resources beyond this book. Check out www.OnnitAcademy.com for some ideas on where to get started.

Now Do It

Your body is the only car you are ever going to drive. It is up to you whether you want to supercharge that bitch and make it purr like a kitten and roar like a hemi for the next 200,000 miles, or whether you're going to let it rust out into a junker at a metal scrapyard. I assume, if you're reading this book, that you want the former. You want to be behind the wheel of a healthy, fine-tuned sex machine.

I won't lie to you—getting there won't happen quickly. But don't get frustrated. You just have to start. You just have to do a little bit of work. Make the commitment to put one foot in front of the other and get to the gym. Find ways to hold yourself accountable, either with a workout buddy, a trainer, or just social media. Trust me, the moment that first drop of sweat hits your brow, you are going to start getting help from your body. The animal inside you wants to move. It wants to work. It wants to thrive. It's all a game of momentum. One well-executed workout will leave you feeling more capable for the next, and so on, and so on, until you are ripping through workouts in fifth gear with the top down and the music blasting.

I don't care how you motivate yourself to get your workout in, as long as you don't use shame and self-judgment. I don't want to hear about you berating yourself into the gym by telling yourself how ugly or lazy or stupid you are. Not only is that not true, it's not going to work, and it's going to alter the effects of your workout, in the opposite direction that positive motivation produces. Don't believe me? Cue the science!

In 2007, a couple of researchers in the psychology department at

Harvard, Alia Crum and Ellen Langer, decided to test the effect of mind-set on exercise and health. They chose as their subjects eighty-four hotel maids across more than half a dozen hotels who did more or less the same amount of work each day and little or no exercise. They split the group in two, telling one half that the work they did cleaning rooms was good exercise and, in fact, satisfied the surgeon general's "recommendations for an active lifestyle." The other half of the group was told nothing related to their work. They were the control group.

Four weeks later Crum and Langer checked back with the maids and discovered that the women who'd received the positive messages about their work actually perceived that they were getting more exercise than before, even though their behavior hadn't really changed at all. Not only that, but they also displayed significant physical changes, including decrease in "weight, blood pressure, body fat, waist-to-hip ratio, and body mass index."

What might be even more astounding was a controlled experiment in which researchers asked ten volunteers to simply *imagine* flexing their biceps as hard as they could five times a week. To prevent unintentional tensing of the muscles, they placed sensors on the biceps. What happened? The test group increased actual bicep strength by 13.5 percent in just a few weeks, whereas the control group, who didn't perform the mental gymnastics, gained nothing. The gains persisted over three months even after the mental training stopped.

That is the power of positive intention on your health and fitness. You can be sure negative motivation can have an equally deleterious effect. So if you are having trouble using your mind-set to get you into the gym, at least start by using your mind to imagine you are there. And when you do, think about your physical conditioning, and go big! Squat boxcars full of imaginary children and pull 737s with your teeth like your name was Magnus and it was 1984, when steroids were "good for you." Your mind is the ultimate unconventional tool in pursuit of unconventional results. Listen to it, harness it, and go own your workout. Remember, healthy is sexy, and it's about time to get frisky.

THREE POINTERS

- ✦ Exercise is a miracle drug—you just need to take it. If you haven't been training regularly, the key is to start slow and simply get moving. Even if you are a seasoned vet, mixing in some play can keep the enthusiasm for training high.
- ✦ Conventional means of exercise are going to create conventional results. And if you go to your local shopping centre and look around, that isn't going to cut it. Try out unconventional equipment like kettlebells, clubs, maces, and ropes.
- ✦ An ideal workout trains multiple power systems, including mobility, flexibility, endurance, cardio, power, and strength. Use the training pyramid as a model to ensure you are training in a well-rounded and sustainable manner.

RESET AND RECONNECT

We do not stop playing because we grow old; we grow old because we stop playing.

—GEORGE BERNARD SHAW

You've been gone all day—but now you're home. It's time to really be home. That means work has to be put fully aside. Put your phone on the charger, leave your computer in the bag, and connect with your life. You're gonna quiet down the mind, and raise up your spirits. You're gonna kiss your lover, wrestle your dogs, or push a few notes through a musical instrument. Most important, you're gonna enjoy yourself. If you spend a day without laughter and a smile, you haven't owned the day. Because there is no destination in a well-lived life, there is only the journey.

Getting Owned

Our bodies and our genes were formed in tribes. Thousands of years ago, we ate and played as a group, slept shoulder to shoulder, and secured food as a clan. The idea of going off on your own to "find yourself" wouldn't have just seemed crazy—it would have seemed downright dangerous. The tribe was how you survived.

For our bodies, then, being around other people is as much a part of our nature as air or water. Which might explain why so many of us today feel so starved, not of those essential life-giving elements but of the life-sustaining bonds that we used to have with other people in our tribe.

Being in close-knit groups is what being a human is about. We're social creatures—and even though many of us have hyperactive digital social lives and flesh-and-blood social connections, the fact is that at no time in human history have so many people felt so alone. Our bodies can feel and sense this loneliness, and they are responding the only way bodies know how: by making us sick more often; by sinking us into deep depression; by throwing off our hormonal balance; and by making us find chemical substitutes for the human contact that we so crave.

This isn't anecdotal—it's data. Middle-aged *and* older adults have up to a 30 percent greater risk of dying from all causes when lonely and living alone. Not so long ago on the scale of human history, we used to work together, communicating and striving for a common goal. Now we can work from home on our computer, get our food delivered by a stranger, and peer through the peephole of our own experience at the kaleidoscope of social media and all its pretty images of people seeming to have way more fun than us. Is it any wonder that loneliness is rapidly becoming a public health crisis on the scale of obesity and substance abuse?

But if loneliness kills, the opposite is also true: being together heals. Research shows that there is a 50 percent higher likelihood of survival in people with strong social relationships. In fact, I think of togetherness as some of the best medicine we can give ourselves, the kind that releases life-enhancing chemicals in our brains and leads to life-affirming stories for our spirits. You know what is just a straight-up good time? Connecting with people you love. Playing and learning with your chosen family, your tribe. Cooking them food, having them bring you wine. Doing something fun together. Taking the opportunity to reset from your workday and enjoying yourself.

Here's the mistaken assumption of a lot of hard chargers: that wanting to come home and be with your family and friends and loved ones is just a sign you aren't badass enough to crush it. If you can't work from 6:00 p.m. to midnight, you have no chance against the wolves of Wall Street or the scions of Silicon Valley. I've known wolves and scions . . . most of them are miserable. They are getting owned by their own ambition and expectations.

So don't confuse owning the day with figuring out ways to squeeze out more and more productivity in less and less time. Owning is not about working more. It's about living a full and fulfilled life— one that speaks to what our bodies need most, which, yes, includes meaningful bursts of productivity, but also includes the rich and joyful connection that other people give us. If you don't connect with others, then you can't own the day. Plain and simple.

Owning It

You are a human being, not a human *doing*. This time after work is a time of transition—from the thing that you do to the person that you are. In that way, you need to think about this initial period when you come home as a way of disconnecting both from work and from the stuff in your day that you've *been working for*—your dream home, your kids' college fund, that promotion, that boat.

There is always more to do in service of your goals, and if you don't know what to do with them when you're off the clock (I'll show you in chapter 14), it's very easy to let yourself slip into another round of work. Instead, you have to give yourself permission to enjoy this break you've earned. It doesn't take much to blow past these moments and turn family time into work time by another name: jumping straight into dinner or scolding your kids about homework or doing chores or turning on the television. All of it misses the point. This is a time to be with the people you love.

There was a time in America when we wouldn't have had to be as emphatic about this point. In an earlier era, we used to do things socially—people were in bowling leagues, played music with each other, sat on their porches and talked. Ironically, in a world of social media, we've gotten considerably less social. The result has been an epidemic of existential angst and loneliness. The easiest way to solve that in your life is to actively seek out in-person connection and community after work. Go to the dog park. Play in a sports league. Create true family time.

It actually matters a lot less *what* you do and much more that you simply *do something* social. Whatever it is, be around people and be present while doing so. We are social creatures, and we thrive on community. Especially after a hard day's work, this is your reward: don't just let the drudgery of daily existence wash over you when you walk through the front door. You should be excited about this time. It's time you've been given to reconnect with yourself and with your tribe.

Connect with Yourself

You've spent much of the day working hard and training hard. If you're like most of us, your mind is still humming. Perhaps it's the inner critic judging you on today's performance, or the premeditator planning tomorrow's attack. Maybe it's the worrier, doing what he or she does best. Maybe it's the ego, ranting "How dare you?" to everyone who didn't bow to its grandeur. When we say connect to "yourself," it is a tricky thing. Because you are many different selves. But there is one self that remains when the multiplicity dissolves into the singular: let's call that the true self. Presence, embodied. To connect to that self, to be that self, you need to find a way to harmonize everything else, to take all the discordant tones from all of the different voices in your mind and turn their hum into one beautiful note that is exactly you. It is the essence of the waking flow state, mindfulness in motion. And with any harmony, sometimes the best way to get it is to add an instrument.

PLAY AN INSTRUMENT

I thought I was a musical disaster. Like a Chernobyl-level nuclear disaster—bad enough that if I picked up an instrument and put myself to it, the ears who heard me play would grow three lobes in radioactive protest. I believed that until I was thirty-one years old. Then I picked up a Native American flute. Anyone who heard me play that first week would have probably agreed: it sounded like the outtakes from a greased pig–catching contest. I'm surprised my backyard wasn't full of neighborhood dogs some of those nights. But slowly I started to get the hang of it. One by one, notes started to connect, and music started to form. The more I got out of my own head, the more harmony I created.

All music starts from nothing. Paradoxically, as I become more still in my mind, the music becomes more alive. But sometimes the hum of my other selves wins the fight for oneness, and I have trouble giving myself permission to get comfy and lift the flute to my lips. In those moments, I need a little help quieting down their perpetual angst, and so I will reach for a chemical state shift to make it happen. A little glass of wine or a few puffs of my favorite flower almost always do the trick.

◼ IF YOU WANT TO GET HIGH, NOW'S THE TIME

This is a health book that green-lights drinking a glass of wine or lighting up a bowl of sticky marijuana flower. Most health books don't do that, and guess what, you do it anyway. Half of Americans drink alcohol, and half of a quarter of Americans smoke weed. I'll let you guess which side of the survey I'm on for both of those statistics. Because intrinsically you and I see the value proposition as positive—unless you are addicted, of course, in which case the addiction is dragging you by the nipple rings through what you pretend are your own choices. So if you are into alcohol and marijuana, you aren't breaking the law, and you still want to own your day, after your workout is the perfect time to have a drink or smoke a little of the sticky icky.

The key is: a little. There are both emotional and physical reasons for this. On the emotional level, you've just completed the "hard work" part of your day. It's nice to save a mini-celebration to reward yourself for the discipline. It's something to look forward to, a way to connect and harmonize with yourself. But you don't want it to get sloppy and get away from you. Having too much has a way of taking that internal discord you've been trying to harmonize and setting the voices against each other like a cockfight where your mind is the ring.

Choosing to intoxicate after training is potentiated by the fact that you're likely going to be mildly dehydrated, meaning that you are going to have less blood volume. This means that the same amount of active ingredient in your blood will have a proportionally higher concentration. With alcohol, you are going to have nothing in your stomach to slow down the absorption rate, so you won't need as much to drink to get the buzz you want. And with liver glycogen levels so much lower after a workout, the sugars in the alcohol will metabolize easier, which means that a glass of wine is not that bad for you at all—maximum bang, minimum bucks—but two or three can send you down a less-than-conscious path. The general rule with any intoxicating substance, particularly alcohol, is to use the least amount necessary to achieve the desired effect. This has a couple advantages: (1) it's cost-effective, and (2) it limits any negative side effects like toxicity to the liver or lungs. In short, you want to be your own cheap date, and the best time for that is postworkout.

Same goes with weed. When inhaled, the active ingredients of marijuana, THC and CBD, don't pass through the stomach, but smoking with lower blood volume and an empty stomach still exacerbates their effects. (This is likely why platinum rapper Master P, in his weed anthem "Pass Me Da Green," proclaimed that "Real smokers don't blow no green on empty stomachs.") A lot of people treat how much they consume as a badge of honor. I get it, I've been there too, I was a frat dog—KAPPA SIG! But I've also grown up and learned the hard way that it's a dumb metric.

Deep Dive: On Cannabis and Pain

Many of us are uncomfortable in the skin we are in. The source of that discomfort is pain—physical pain, emotional pain, spiritual and psychic pain, just fucking pain. When the pain gets bad, we'll reach for anything to alleviate it. A recent study by Alan Krueger at Princeton University revealed that nearly half of unemployed working-age men in America are addicted to opiate painkillers. The problem with these painkillers is that they are highly addictive, and push you toward dissociation from your body rather than a heightened connection to it. Cannabis is different. A 2015 *Journal of American Medical Association* meta-analysis of nearly eighty cannabinoid trials across more than 6,400 participants found a 64 percent reduction in chronic pain. Other analyses of multiple double-blind clinical trials confirm the value of marijuana for chronic pain reduction and pain scale assessment. But it's not just the aches and pains of a hard day's labor that cannabis can alleviate; it has benefits for a banged-up brain as well, particularly the high-CBD strains. Dr. Dan Engle, author of *The Concussion Repair Manual*, says of CBD, "In my practice treating concussions and post-concussion syndrome no supplement has been as effective as CBD." "Bazooka" Joe Valtellini, a former world champion kickboxer turned commentator, was forced into retirement after repeated concussions. CBD has been the only thing that keeps his headaches away. With opioid use spiraling out of control, the state-by-state wave of legalization of medical marijuana and CBD might have come just in time, because nothing is a bigger buzzkill for productivity and personal connection than headaches and chronic pain.

Here's how the pros use it: in the modern world, the pros use it because cannabis is renowned for its ability to connect us with our creative inner self. One analysis of over thirty surveys found that more than 50 percent of users report enhanced creativity when using cannabis. That's definitely a big part of why I experiment with cannabis. When it comes to owning my day, I want that marked benefit to performance *and* the increase in overall enjoyment of life that comes with being creative. And it's not just me. Steve Jobs used marijuana and hashish to make him "relaxed and creative." World-class athlete and nutrition coach Ben Greenfield gets down with a vape full of that Washington State high-CBD good-good and a glass of elderberry wine sourced from an elderberry tree literally in his own backyard. Even when he's training to run an Ironman or the next Spartan Race, this is his jam. By dinner, the effects of the vape and the wine have worn off or settled into harmony, and he can finish out the night strong, playing his ukulele, teaching his kids, and connecting with his wife.

What is important to always remember is that we have a healthy relationship with all powerful plants. That is not always the case. One of the most vocal and eloquent advocates for the legalization of cannabis, Graham Hancock, talks openly about how he fell into a poor relationship with it, something more like a dependency than a decision. You will have to judge for yourself, based on how your mind and your body respond to it, whether cannabis is right for you—whether it stimulates connection and creativity, or demotivates you and incentivizes Doritos. Just take it slow and see how it goes. Especially when you eat it. Because I will 100 percent laugh at your 911 call when you think that you are going to die from eating that second cookie. Remember, people have been using ganja for 8,000 years—you don't need to eat all the weed tonight.

Connect with Your Tribe

With all the noise in our own heads, it's no wonder that we sometimes choose to be alone rather than to connect with people. But a funny thing happens when we connect with others; we start to realize that we are all pretty much the same. We all have fears and thoughts that we can't shake out of our head, beliefs that we stubbornly hold on to, and things that keep us awake at night. When we start to open ourselves up to people, we transcend that crushing loneliness. Connection cures us. And those with whom we connect most tightly and most regularly become our tribe.

One of the great blessings in my life is my ability to connect with so many different people. It makes me a better leader in my company, it makes me a better friend. Honestly, I've become so attached to these feelings of connectedness that I look for company no matter where I am. Yet deep down, I'm an introvert who requires bouts of solitude to recharge. But, man, do I love people! People are awesome—even though, just like trees stretching hard to find light, they can get a little bent in the trunk and twisted as they take on trauma and search for love.

Still, it's easy to let connections dissolve and friendships atrophy. The dopamine hits from social media and our email in-box make living your whole damn life online or at work seem almost . . . worth it. But it's not, and you can't, and you shouldn't try. You'll get so much more out of a meal with a small group of friends than with a big group of clients who are footing the bill. You will be filled with more light and love hearing about your family's day than you ever will by adding another thousand Twitter or Instagram followers.

Just trust me on this: unplug and reconnect. These connections will help you own your day and love your life. I know they have for me. I know that it's a love of people that's helped me thrive as a person, succeed in business, and achieve the balance I have in my life. My friends have helped me when things have gotten difficult, and I've paid it forward for them too. Sure, those probably seem like the most practical elements of friendship, but you would be shocked at how many people I meet who would agree with this idea and have no idea what to do with it. No idea how to connect or where to find common experience that produces uncommon bonds. Fortunately, I have a few ideas.

LISTEN TO MUSIC

Ladies and gentlemen, it's time to rock out with your cock out and jam out with your clam out (or not, if there are kids around). Music isn't just fun—it's *scientifically proven* fun. The research shows that when music is playing at home, people become physically closer. People are literally 12 percent closer when music is playing than when it's not. They actually measured this! When the music's going, people are a third more likely to cook together and almost 90 percent more likely to invite people over. They are more likely to laugh together, and here's the kicker: they are more likely to say the words "I love you."

Oh, and then there's the most important connection of all: in a study conducted by the speaker company Sonos, in conjunction with Apple Music and the neuroscientist Daniel Levitin, couples reported a stunning increase in intimacy when listening to music, and a nearly 40 percent increase in what they hilariously called "awake time" in bed. I'm guessing that doesn't mean reading *Harry Potter*. So go ahead, and pump . . . up the volume.

GET SILLY!

When did we stop playing? At some point, the backpack of responsibility weighed down our shoulders and made us get serious. "Grow up," says the world. How about fuck you! Take that backpack off and play! Join a Skee-Ball league. Raid a bouncy castle. Buy a pinball machine. I have two pinball machines (my favorite is Avatar).

My whole backyard, in fact, is built like an adult playground, with a slackline, a trampoline, knife targets, volleyball, Frisbee golf. I have a dartboard, a pool table, foosball. The gym at Onnit HQ is a playground too. We have a loop in our jujitsu room designed to allow adults to play the hot lava game, where you pretend the ground is lava and you have to travel a lap without touching it.

If you've forgotten how to play, that's one of the great things kids are for. They can remind us what we've forgotten about the heart. Get on the level with someone younger than you and let loose. It's not only going to be fun. Research shows that if you act younger, your biological markers actually start to reverse.

Harvard psychologist Ellen Langer writes in her book *Counterclockwise* about an experiment where she took eight men in their seventies and put them in an environment where everything around them—from the music to the television, the car in the driveway, the newspapers and magazines in the house—mimicked what life was like two decades earlier. A week later the men, who'd arrived frail and on walkers and canes, were playing an impromptu game of touch football on the lawn. It wasn't just their bodies that felt younger— the men in the test group scored 63 percent higher on an intelligence test. It was a powerful testament to the power of the mind and the placebo effect. Youth might really be a state of mind after all.

So play. If you believe you are too old to play, you will *become* too old to play. If you stay young in heart, spirit, and belief, you will stay young in body and mind as well.

PLAY WITH PETS

People are not the only living creatures who are members of your tribe. And games are not the only things you can play with. In America, especially, pets are truly man's (and woman's) best friend. I have a pet dog. She's an Alaskan Klee Kai, and her name is Lobita,

Spanish for Little Wolf. She's my best furry friend and I love her because in the daytime, she's more like a cat, content to do her own thing, but first thing in the morning, she is a little kiss bomb ready to explode. Who doesn't want to have a shower of love and licks first thing in the morning?

There are selfish reasons we love our pets, of course—they're a ready-made solution to loneliness—but the positive research on pet ownership is truly compelling. Dr. Robert Sapolsky, for example, has shared findings that dogs and humans have coevolved to mutually produce the connection hormone oxytocin. Pet ownership has also been shown to reduce blood pressure and resting heart rate, and pets have helped kids with no brothers or sisters develop greater empathy, higher self-esteem, and increased participation in social and physical activities. Pets are the exercise of the animal kingdom—a miracle drug with ears.

That said, pets are a responsibility. But with services like Rover available for immediate on-demand dog watching in real homes, the downside of owning a dog or a cat has been greatly diminished. I used to tease my friends who would pass on an epic vacation because they couldn't find a babysitter for their dog. But now, as long as you are willing to pay a few extra bucks, you can have it all. A happy pet, and your freedom!

Let's keep it simple: get a dog and get ready for cuddles. You won't regret it.

Prescription: Connect with Yourself

The first thing you do when you come home from work, or emerge from the "productive" part of the day, is reset. While the mindfulness on the ride home should have started the state shift, the last thing you want to do when you get to your house is jump back on the computer and keep the stress train rolling. You need a proper reset. For me it's the flute, or another instrument you'll learn about in chapter 15, the didgeridoo. And when I play, after a few moments I am no longer Aubrey Marcus, I am just wind and energy that is transforming into sound. It is the easiest and fastest way for me to get out of my head, and connect to my unified voice.

Since it's the perfect time to enjoy a glass of wine or take a few puffs of cannabis, occasionally I'll go there too. Or drink a cup of kava, the relaxing herb they drink in Fiji, or even light up a cigar. This is a signal that for right now, I'm clocked out and off duty. If you don't like any form of intoxicant, then maybe grab a stevia soda (Zevia cream soda is the best) and just enjoy the moment.

The key is to create the conduit to connection. Find yours, and not only will you tune your body to the key of yourself, but you will open up in ways that make reconnecting with your tribe feel like second nature, and make loneliness feel light-years away.

Connect with Your Tribe

Jesus, the great Christian mystic, said, "Do unto others as you would have them do unto you." This is the golden rule. Let's take it one step further, to the deeper meaning: Do unto others because they *are* you. You, just living a different life. From that perspective, no one is too distant or too strange to connect with, but what still keeps us apart is that we judge people as harshly as we judge ourselves. We find people lacking like we find ourselves lacking. However, if we can learn to truly see others, we can also learn to truly see ourselves.

I want you to imagine someone who has annoyed you, and to see that person as yourself living a different life. Jump inside his body, not as a resident, but as a visitor. Use that power of imagination to visualize all the forces that shaped him into who he is. His family, his environments, the food he ate, the pets he loved and lost. Just like a tree that stretches roots to the water for nourishment and extends its leaves to the sun, what has he been stretching toward? Where is his nourishment? Maybe he hasn't been getting enough. Maybe it's too far out of reach. Maybe he is curled and withered as a result. Where are you curled and withered? See this person as a little boy or a little girl, just like you. What was she like on the playground at recess? Did the kids play with her or shun her? Did she deserve to be shunned? See the world through her eyes, as if they were your eyes. And maybe you'll find that those eyes aren't so different from your eyes after all.

Now Do It

Bronnie Ware, a palliative care nurse, wrote a book about the top five deathbed regrets. These are people who lived an entire life, accumulated all that wisdom and experience, and had a chance to look back and say what they would have done differently. That is something worth paying attention to. There are three that really stand out:

1.   **I wish I hadn't worked so hard.** This sentiment came from every single male patient she cared for. Every single one.

2.   **I wish I had stayed in touch with my friends.** Our connections bring the dance to our life, and yet we find ourselves with too little time to enjoy these moments. But I think another problem is that at a certain point we stop making really great new friends. In the absence of rituals like school and sports, we don't take the time to forge deeper connections with people. Whether it is having an all-night bender in Vegas, or a ten-day journey in Peru, extreme experiences have the potential to form the deepest bonds. Go for it; leave your important adult self behind and have an adventure with people you might very well love.

3.   **I wish that I had let myself be happier.** This one breaks my heart. Not just because it came from the mouths of human souls who were out of chances to do something about it, but

because they knew—or at least they finally realized—that they had a choice in the matter. They did not say "I wish I was happier," leaving happiness as a capricious blessing from Fortune herself. Wisdom in old age led them to say "I wish I had *let* myself be happier." I wish I had made a better choice.

Sometimes that choice is a hard one to make. We can become addicted to accumulating things, chasing goals, and "being productive." Killing it. Crushing it. But you know what feels better? Owning it. Owning the joy, love, and laughter that true connection can bring to our lives. We have to choose to play. Choose to connect. Choose to be happy. Sometimes it comes wafting through the air like a unicorn's fart. And sometimes you gotta go where the unicorns are eating their magical beans, and start sniffing. That's what this pot-flavored pep talk has been all about!

THREE POINTERS

+ Loneliness kills. But combating loneliness doesn't mean having just anyone around you. It's about forging deeper connections, with yourself first, and with your tribe.
+ To connect with yourself, don't be shy about creating a little state shift. A puff of cannabis or a glass of wine after your workout and before dinner can be beneficial to the mind, while minimizing challenges to the body. Then, to really deepen the connection, pick up a musical instrument and learn to play.
+ To connect with others, collapse the judgments that separate you by seeing them as you living a different life. Then play some music, have a laugh, but most important, make the effort to cultivate the sense of community around you.

12

EAT DINNER LIKE A KING

When walking, walk. When eating, eat.

—ZEN PROVERB

After any good battle, the warrior looks forward to a feast. And that feast is dinner. Go ahead, champ, eat up and enjoy. The day is not won quite yet, but you deserve this meal. Break bread, grab some popcorn, eat some chocolate and enjoy. You deserve it not just because you worked for it—but because food is a great part of life. If you go a little too far, don't worry, we've got your back. Eat it consciously, digest it well, and prime yourself for the best kind of dessert: sex.

Getting Owned

I think a little part of humanity died circa 2013—because that was the year Soylent was born.

For the uninitiated, Soylent is a food replacement sludge created by three guys from Silicon Valley (shock of all shocks) who hate joy. Their concoction—named after *Soylent Green*, a dystopian 1973 science-fiction movie in which food wafers are made out of human flesh—is a liquid that alleges to give you all of your nutritional needs while removing the necessity for food. That, apparently, is its selling point. You drink three shakes a day, and voilà, no more food in your life! In fact, when the founders of this stuff were interviewed by the *New Yorker*, they were quoted as saying, "Food is such a large burden," and their website leads with the tagline: "Taking eating off your plate." Food is the enemy in their flavorless world, and Soylent is the cold liquid assassin that's come to kill it off.

If you are one of those people for whom food has gone from joy to chore, I think you need a hug. Food is a biological necessity, yes. But it is also a pleasure. A luxury for the masses. When did we all become that busy? When did we pack so much into our schedules that we can't even take a moment to put some food in our mouths and appreciate it? If a poet from antiquity walked through a grocery store like Erewhon or Whole Foods today, he would cease writing about anything else, and send word to the four corners of the empire that the Garden of Eden had been found here on earth. He would relish the sensory experience and revel in the bounty.

And yet we open our refrigerators and have the audacity to complain, "Ugh, there's nothing to eat!" It reminds me of the Chinese emperors that Matt Ridley talks about in *The Red Queen*, who had harems of up to 50,000 virgin women but complained ceaselessly about the burden of having sex with them all. Man, I wish there was Facebook back then. Can you imagine a Friday late-night post from Emperor Ming? "Concubine #38,877 wants to go again. FML." ☺ Talk about a whole new level of #firstworldproblems.

But we are those emperors! In Austin, we have these expansive food truck parks that are like visiting a brothel for your taste buds. You can get a Korean BBQ cheesesteak, a boudin ball with fried alligator, and a lobster corn dog in the space of five minutes. And we want to give this up? In favor of Silicon Valley's version of Slim-Fast? Of preprepared and prepackaged microwave meals, instant noodles, fast casual, drive-thru, and all the rest? None of which pay any mind to our digestion, which is really where our heads need to be, heading into the end of our day. Family time, sexy time, wind-down time, sleepy time—none of them are going to be great if your body spends the next six hours fighting what you just put in it.

Needless to say, this has all got to change.

We all need to become foodies. Not the snobby kind that will only eat endive if it's grown with compost made of koala turds and watered by the tears of butterflies. We need to be the grateful kind. The kind who enjoy ourselves, who smile when we hit the produce section and all the fruits and veggies of the world are presented with dewdrops of mist on their leaves, and keep a positive mind-set around food. After all, food isn't what makes you fat, or makes you feel bad, or holds you back at work. Food is what keeps you alive. It's what brings friends together. Breaking bread breaks down walls and builds up connections. What can be better than that?

Owning It

Okay, dinnertime. You've got two objectives: (1) enjoy yourself, and (2) get ready to have sex. And I don't mean going down on a big plate of ribs. I mean fucking, and preparing food that's going to support your sex machine.

This is the meal where you really get to have some fun. If you let yourself. See, the thing about enjoying your food is that if you are worried all the time about what you are eating, eating is gonna suck. And ironically, the more you worry about it, the worse the food will actually be for you. We're going to get rid of this anxiety and make food fun again.

The rule is moderation in all things, including moderation. We're going to teach you how to eat a full dinner that supports your digestion, supports sex, supports sleep, and sets you up for a great night. We're also going to show you ways to cheat the right way, and mitigate any damage done by too much sugar, booze, or just too much of everything. Dinner should be a celebration of a day fully owned, so let's make it that way. The work starts by believing that's okay, and that the food you're about to consume is going to nourish your body and mind. But first some good news about your "bad" habits.

▨ THE NOT-SO-SECRET MENU OF INDULGENCES

My friend Rich Roll, podcaster, author, and triathlete, is right—people love nothing more than good news about their bad habits. Well, you're welcome. Because I'm about to give you some good news about cheese, chocolate, bread, and popcorn.

Cheese has been in the doghouse of just about every nutrition movement since the turn of the century. The main knocks are that cheese is bad for your heart, and bad for digestion. We've already illuminated the bullshit around the fat-is-bad-for-your-heart hypothesis. So is cheese bad for your digestion? That depends on what cheese you are cutting! After all, in the cheese-crazed mania of the modern era, where cheese comes in cans, pastes, and little plastic pouches, we have done worse things to cheese than bulldogs have done to stuffed animals. But plastic-wrapped cheese slices are not exactly the same thing as my favorite grass-fed raw goat cheese . . . which is the G.O.A.T. of all cheese, digestively speaking.

Raw milk cheese, like raw juice, has not been pasteurized, so any of the more delicate nutrients, probiotics, and enzymes that aid with digestion stay intact. This is likely why a survey done of 2,503 raw milk drinkers in Michigan revealed that 81 percent of those diagnosed with lactose intolerance reported reduced symptoms of indigestion after having switched from store-bought (pasteurized and homogenized) milk. In addition, three studies totaling 20,000 subjects showed that the consumption of raw milk has a significant benefit in the reduction of allergies and asthma.

So why did we start pasteurizing in the first place? It's the most conservative play for mass production. Just in case there are harmful bacteria along for the ride, the pasteurization will take care of them. But most places, including Whole Foods and Erewhon, offer all types of raw cheese, and in the case of the latter grocery heaven, even raw milk.

Goat milk exhibits similar if not even greater benefits than raw milk. The reason for this is that goat milk is a lot more like the milk that came out of our own momma's mammaries. The biological resemblance to human breast milk goes all the way down to the DNA structure itself. These similarities apply to protein structure (beta casein versus alpha casein), prebiotic content (oligosaccharides), and fat structure (small/medium-chain fatty acids versus long-chain fatty acids). So what does all this mean?

A study in France demonstrated that 93 percent of infants showed less allergic reaction to goat milk than cow milk. It's delicious, it's nutritious, it's even ambitious. It's for dinner, dammit!

Sprouted or sourdough bread is the yeasty nectar of the gods. We have known this intuitively since ancient times. The Romans knew that there were two things they needed to provide to keep the populace happy: bread and circus. While I might caution against chariot races with no helmets or seat belts, I'm not about to tell you in this book that you shouldn't eat bread. I love bread. There is nothing better than a good lump of sourdough or some sprouted bread slathered with butter. Many of the best athletes and performers feel the same way. And like me, they know that all bread is not created equal, which we learned in chapter 8 when we discussed how sprouting and fermenting alleviates some of the common antinutrients found in bread. But not all times during the day are right for bread. The best timing for bread is dinner, after your glycogen stores have been depleted by exercise, and you're about to head into the winter of your day . . . sleep. So if bread and butter is your thing, do it the right way, with grass-fed butter on sprouted or sourdough. Go for it!

Chocolate is a perfect example of a really good thing that we found a way to fuck up. Cocoa is a true superfood, packed with antioxidants shown to be more effective than blueberries or açaí, along with a few really cool psychoactive compounds like caffeine and theobromine that boost mood and cognition.

Cocoa even has protein and fiber, and its byproduct—cacao butter—is one of the best natural fats in the world. It is packed with minerals, and even boosts nitric oxide production, giving chocolate its legendary aphrodisiac status. If you're talking about gifts from the gods, you have to include chocolate in that conversation. The Aztecs and Mayans did. Chocolate was sacred to them. You also have to recognize that modern food manufacturing has turned chocolate from a superfood into just another Trojan horse for pasteurized milk and sugar. Which means you have to know what you're buying when you're on the hunt for a chocolate treat.

Fortunately, the world is waking up to this problem and acquiring a taste for chocolate as it was meant to be. Using natural sweeteners like stevia or monk fruit, brands like Lily's and Lakanto are offering dark chocolate without any added sugar and minimal dairy. Chocolate is a heart-healthy food, and we should treat it as such.

Popcorn is one of those foods that, if you're like me, you had no idea how the hell it even works. Popcorn is a type of corn kernel with a small amount of water in the center. When heated, the water expands into gas and the kernel explodes. Yay! Even though it's fluffy and white, there are actually quite a few important minerals in popcorn, including much-needed magnesium along with iron and zinc.

To do it right, pop it yourself and add your own grass-fed butter and sea salt. Most store-bought popcorn contains the high omega-6 vegetable oils we warned about in chapter 8. But the big reason to eat popcorn and dispense with the fiction that it's a secret indulgence to be enjoyed in the dark of a movie theater is the whopping 15 grams of insoluble fiber that come with it, which is extremely high. It's why my fiancée dubbed popcorn "PooCorn." Insoluble fiber like that found in popcorn is great for those legendary belly-flattening poops that provide a unique window into the importance of digestion, not just for health but to start the morrow off right. With a big ol' deuce.

Universal Nutrition Principle #7: What You Think About Food Matters

I once had a very well-meaning and zealous employee who took it upon herself to advise all of our team members to do skin allergy tests. The push started innocently enough, but pretty soon everyone in the company was allergic to common, everyday healthy food. At our weekly birthday lunches, people who would normally be first in line to house some celebratory tacos or Texas BBQ would sit there staring longingly at food they had not thought twice about eating their entire lives but now had determined they couldn't even touch. All because of a skin test!

And this is true for everything. I can't tell you how many people in the wellness industry become wildly intolerant of wheat after reading a book like *Wheat Belly*. Some of these people are Italian and grew up on bread and pasta without a care in the world! But after that book, one ziti will send them running to the toilet. Their bodies didn't change at all when they received the information that ninjas were lurking in the wheat germ, ready to slit their throat. Their minds changed. And when their minds changed, their bodies changed. This is not woo-woo, this is science: the famous nocebo effect, the evil twin of the placebo effect. Like when people were told that taking a pill with nothing in it would make them run slower, and it did. And it's the most overlooked aspect of nutrition—one that to own the day, you have to master.

There's a great study where a researcher had two groups drink the same 300-calorie French vanilla shake (*Mmmm, ice cream . . .*). She made one group think they were drinking an "indulgence" shake—with higher calories and more sugar, like one you would drink from an old-timey diner. She led the other group to believe that they were drinking something more sensible with fewer calories, like something you would drink at a bourgie health spa. Lo and behold, just telling these two groups that they were drinking different kinds of shakes changed their bodies' responses to it. The spa group demonstrated a stable hormone response, whereas the "diner" group had wild hormone swings, almost three times as high as the other group. Their bodies had been tricked by their own minds.

Not unlike with training results, this is the power of our own thoughts when it comes to food we put in our systems. And yet food allergy testing has never been more popular. It has become a cottage industry—a cottage full of problems! The biggest one is that everyone who gets one of these tests done ends up seeming allergic to pretty much everything. Here's the issue with that: they are testing your skin, not your gut. Your skin cannot mimic the probiotic environment of your actual gut, so it results in a lot of false positives. Plus, they aren't always testing the difference between raw foods, cooked foods, and fermented types of the same food—which can be vast. But most important, they aren't taking the mind into consideration.

Take Timmy. He is one of a dozen personalities in a man with multiple personality disorder. Timmy loves orange juice and drinks it frequently. However, if any one of his other personalities drinks that orange juice, he becomes wildly allergic. Like hospital allergic. By simply changing the personality in control of his body, he changes whether or not OJ sends him to the hospital. Timmy's story was profiled in the *New York Times* all the way back in 1998 and sheds some light on just how far the mind can go when it comes to controlling the body.

If we tell our body something is poison, it becomes more poisonous. If we convince ourselves that it is healthy, it becomes more healthy. This is not to say that the reality of a food or situation doesn't matter. Molecular biology still exists—it's a real thing—but the mind isn't a passive bystander. It matters, too. It can be part of the celebration that dinner is about to become, or it can become the ultimate party pooper that makes dinner a shitshow.

Universal Nutrition Principle #8: Nutrition Is Only as Good as Digestion

It is as true for any meal as it is for dinner that the nutritional value of your food is only as good as your body's ability to digest it. We are talking about it here, though, because our goal by the end of the chapter is to set you up with the ultimate pro-sex meal, and the only way that pays off is if you've primed your system to digest the foods of which that meal is comprised and you aren't a bloated, tired, farting mess as a result. In addition, at the end of this section we're going to talk about how to give you the right kind of gas—nitric oxide, which will help fuel you in any kind of performance, sexual, physical, or if you're doing it right, both.

EAT SLOW, CHEW HARD

There is an old saying, attributed, somewhat curiously, to Mahatma Gandhi, that to be healthy you must "Chew your drink, and drink your food." While the Soylent guys may have taken that mantra a little too literally, what Gandhi is alluding to is the same reprimand we've all received from at least one of our parents or relatives at some point in our childhoods: "Slow down and chew your food!"

Most of the time they're chiding us because it looks sloppy or the sound of piglets at the dinner trough gets to them or they're just worried that we're going to choke. At least that's why we think they do it; they never really explain themselves.

It turns out, though, that there is a very good reason to slow down and chew your food, even if our relatives didn't know it. Chewing is the process that first starts the breakdown of big pieces of food into little pieces. The mastication of the teeth (aka chewing) offers support in physically grinding the food, breaking it down. Saliva then picks up where chewing leaves off and makes food even smaller. Remember, all food eventually has to break down into super-small particles if it's to be absorbed through the walls of your intestines and nourish your body. If you don't start in your mouth, your stomach and guts are going to have to work overtime, costing you vital energy and efficiency and wasting some perfectly good food in the process.

Have you ever gotten up from the toilet after a bowel movement and inspected your work? Of course you have. Every guy has, and I'm betting some of you ladies get in on the action too. Have you ever been able to tell, by its contents, exactly what you ate a few hours earlier? Maybe some corn kernels. Some threads of spinach. Some almond slivers or carrot chunks. If you can see it, it means you didn't digest it, which usually means you ate too fast.

But what if you're like me, and you suck at chewing? When I am stressed, I eat really fast, like a wolf devouring a freshly killed meal, which prevents me from chewing properly. I had a friend who prided himself, stress or no stress, on eating his meals as fast as his three dogs. Breaking news: he also consistently complained about intestinal pains. The other problem with eating fast is that your body doesn't have time to send up the signal that you are full as the food rockets down your throat like kids on a waterslide.

No surprise then that overeating is a big problem with fast eaters. Study after study shows that nonchewers and fast eaters are in a constant struggle with weight. One found that fast eaters are up to

115 percent more likely to be obese. Another survey of 4,000 people showed that those who ate "very fast" tended to be heavier and had gained the most body weight since age twenty. Put simply, overweight people chew less than normal-weight people, because when you chew more, you tend to eat less—15 percent less, in one study that used delicious pizza for its experiment.

One of the ways to give you more time to chew your food—and therefore eat slower and eat less—is to take smaller bites, using less efficient tools. Have you ever seen an eating competition that used chopsticks or cocktail forks? Of course not. That would only slow these animals down. That's why I force myself to eat with the most inefficient tools possible, to let my mouth start the process of making my digestion as efficient as possible. So buy yourself some extra chopsticks, and then try to eat your damn Cheerios.

▓ STOMACH ACID—KEEP THE FIRE HOT!

If you've ever watched a movie about Mexican drug cartels, you've probably seen how effective acid can be in disintegrating organic matter. Well, what works with bodies in fifty-five-gallon drums works just as well for food in the human stomach. Once you've swallowed your well-chewed food, it is principally hydrochloric acid (HCL) in your stomach that takes the food from small to microscopic. To make sure that process works as effectively as possible, you need to keep up your HCL levels.

One of the most common digestive mistakes people make is consuming cold beverages while they eat. Any beverage dilutes the HCL in your stomach, making the overall acid concentration acting on your food weaker, while the cold slows down your digestion like a snake in a snowstorm. Leave the cold drinks for well before and well after your meals.

This has the added benefit of reducing a potential reliance on antacids. People think when they have heartburn that it is caused by too much stomach acid. In actuality, it is often the opposite: there is not enough acid in their system to effectively break down the food, so it stays around longer, burning the inner lining. Taking an antacid may temporarily solve the problem, but it will adversely affect digestion, and the problem will continue into the future.

If you can eliminate your mealtime cold beverage consumption, along with eliminating antacids, you should see a meaningful benefit to your digestion from a more optimal level of HCL in your stomach. Then, if that doesn't work, look into HCL supplements to get your gut firing on all cylinders.

DIGESTIVE ENZYMES

Along with the HCL that breaks down food generally, specific enzymes in the stomach help with specific types of foods. There are enzymes for fats, dairy, carbs, protein, even the cell walls of vegetables. Having strong digestive enzyme activity that covers these bases is one of the best ways not just to hit a home run with your digestion but to ensure a longer life as well. "A person's life span is directly related to the exhaustion of their enzyme potential," says digestive enzyme specialist Jon Barron. "And the use of food enzymes decreases that rate of exhaustion, and thus results in a longer, healthier, and more vital life."

The best way to ensure good digestive enzyme activity is by adding digestive enzymes, or adding foods that contain natural enzymes like papaya or pineapple. Think of adding enzymes as like swallowing a set of keys (and sometimes a crowbar) to unlock and release the energy from the chains of complex food particles, including protein, fats, cellulose, carbohydrates, dairy, fiber, and anything else you might have ingested. Whereas the HCL melts through everything, specific enzymes will work specifically on these molecules, so good digestion depends on both.

LET'S SPEED THIS UP

Good digestion is essential for proper nutrition, but for proper post-dinner sexual activity, sometimes good digestion isn't good enough. Sometimes, whether because of limited time or limited patience, you need to speed things along down the digestive tract. In that situation, ginger is an excellent resource.

Ginger has the ability to speed up the time it takes your stomach to pass food to your digestive tract by up to 50 percent. Add ginger to your meal, and you can say so long to that full feeling in your gut and hello to that full feeling in your pants sooner. Ginger tea works, pickled ginger is great, or just a half thumb of peeled ginger boiled into a tea, or even raw, will do the trick.

GOOD GAS, BAD GAS

Eating a nutritious, delicious, digestible meal that is also good for sex is all about regulating your gas. You don't want any of the fart kind, and you want as much of the nitric oxide kind as you can.

There is truly nothing worse than preparing to have sex when you have a bowel full of gas. It's displeasing to each of the sensory organs that are part of what makes sex so pleasurable. When it's really bad, you can even taste it, which is the death knell of intimacy, and each of us, man and woman alike, has a food that produces farts that can peel paint off a wall. The key to eliminating this kind of gas is simple: limit fermentable fibers like those found in legumes, Brussels sprouts, and asparagus. Focus on insoluble fiber instead, the kind found in salads and grains like popcorn. If you can do that, you will increase the likelihood that all the explosions during sex come from the right place.

On the flip side, nitric oxide is like a natural, gaseous Viagra. Like a good therapist, nitric oxide tells the tiny muscle cells around the arteries to "relax and open up a little bit." When they open up, our blood vessels dilate, and we experience more blood flow and circulation. This is coveted by bodybuilders and porn stars alike because it gives you that extra "pump," moving the blood fast and furiously to where you direct it. In the bodybuilding classic *Pumping Iron*, Arnold Schwarzenegger famously commented that when he gets his pump on in the gym, it "feels like he's cumming all day." I don't know how I feel about that analogy, but I do know that when you get that nitric oxide flowing and combine it with the anticipation and foreplay prior to sex, all that extra blood has to go *somewhere* . . . Excited yet?

Here are some foods with high dietary nitrate levels that are easily converted into the biological signal of nitric oxide: beetroots, pumpkin seeds, Swiss chard, rocket, watermelon, red wine, dark chocolate. Eat as many of those as possible with dinner. Don't worry, we've got some recipes coming up.

Universal Nutrition Principle #9: Cheat Like a Pro

I never liked the dentists who made you feel guilty for not flossing. As if I didn't already know that the fact I was never going to floss after every meal was less than optimal! I actually feel the same way about sugar. We've spent the better part of this book talking massive shit about sugar. Well, guess what: you're still going to eat sugar, whether you know it or not. The responsible thing to do isn't to shame you about it, it's to show you how to do sugar right. Because sometimes you gotta dunk the doughnut, lick the ice cream, and monster the cookie.

This doesn't change the earlier plan, of course. You still want to steer clear of the white stuff whenever possible, but sometimes you just gotta indulge. That's the philosophy at the heart of ancient Roman Epicureanism. As a contrast to their Stoic friends, Epicureans set out to create a philosophy surrounding how to maximize their pleasure, rather than their effectiveness or accomplishment. What they realized was that constant bingeing (think hedonism) was detrimental to overall sustained pleasure levels. The pain of the hangover counteracted the pleasure of the bender. So most of the time they would sip small amounts of diluted wine, spend time with their friends, and eat simple foods. But every once in a while they would go HAM and get drunk and feast.

HOW TO THINK ABOUT SUGAR

That's a useful way to think about sugar. In general, keep the sugar to less than 5 grams' indulgence, but every once in a while give yourself permission to have a bowl of ice cream, or eat the carrot cake, or get dirty with a good chai, and not regret a moment of it. Here are the rules for eating sugar right.

1.   **Slow it down.** As we have discussed ad nauseam to this point, the speed at which sugar is delivered into the body is the crucial factor when it comes to regulating blood sugar and fighting downstream effects like obesity, diabetes, and cardiovascular disease. For overall health and optimal mood and physical performance, you need to pair any sugar you consume with something that slows its absorption into the body—and the two things that do that are fat and fiber. That's why having sugar after a high-fat, high-fiber meal is great.

2.   **Don't add gas to the fire.** There is a restaurant on Kaanapali Beach in Hawaii called Leilani's. For dessert they have this hula pie, a coconut, whipped cream, and fudge-covered frozen ice cream cake that reminds me of some of the best family vacations of my life. When I go to Leilani's, I'm going to get the hula pie—there's simply no question about that. So I make sure that I cut the carbs entirely from my dinner. No bread, no rice, no sweet potato, nothing. Just protein, fats, and fibers. Because when you add sugar to an already high-carbohydrate meal, you are adding fuel to the fire. Which of course is exactly what your brain tells you to do *after* a meal full of carbs, to stave off that dreaded blood sugar crash. Get the dessert! It's like prolonging a hangover by continuing to drink. That's how you become a drunk, and getting the dessert after a high-carb meal is how you get fat.

3.   **Know your timing.** I used to take my road bike and ride from somewhere just south of Malibu, all the way to the

Manhattan Beach pier. When I got to the pier, after a good two-hour ride, I could eat whatever I wanted. That is the beauty of a celebratory dinner after a day fully owned. If you have followed the nutritional guidelines thus far, and kept sugar and carbs to a minimum, then crushed a good workout, your liver likely has dipped into its glycogen reserve to keep you fueled, just as mine did after my ride down to the pier, and you're free to eat sugar and carbs, pretty much of any type. While a glass of wine after work might have dripped a little back into the tank, topping off your glycogen with some good ol' starch will help keep your energy tank full with diminished impact on blood sugar levels.

4.   **Quantity.** This should be fairly obvious. You don't need to eat the whole dessert. You don't need to drink the whole bottle of wine. If you have a lot of sugar, your body is going to have no choice but to overcharge your glycogen battery and store fat.

5.   **Learn your healthy sweeteners.** The artificial sweeteners on the market are horrible, often carcinogenic. But the good news is that there are natural alternatives that not only taste better but have virtually no negative impact on the body. Stevia and monk fruit are foremost among them. Stevia comes from the leaf of a South American plant. It is impossibly sweet, but can carry a bit of a bitter aftertaste if not alchemized with the food or beverage properly. Monk fruit is a great option for confections like chocolate because it can be crystallized, like sugar. Native to Southeast Asia, it won't spike your blood sugar, and can be used as a substitute for almost all sweeteners. Instead of the slightly bitter stevia finish, it contains a mild menthol finish, so I choose between the two depending on the flavor profile I'm aiming for.

6.   **Take counteractive measures.** You have earned the right to indulge in some delicious carbs with your dinner. You should embrace that and feel zero guilt about it. That does not mean

you should not also bring some friends to the sugar party that chill it the fuck out when things start to get a little crazy.

If you like ice cream, for example, adding some unusual toppings is a good way to further slow down the absorption process and sometimes even add good nutrients. Everyone screams for ice cream. The first time is when you get it, the second time is after you go hypoglycemic from the insulin dump. That is, if you even have the energy to scream. The good thing about ice cream, though, is that it already has fat, which slows down the process. But if you are clever, you can slow that down even further.

For instance, instead of sprinkling more sugar on your ice cream, try sprinkling on some psyllium, or chia seeds. One study showed that adding soluble fiber, like what is found in chia and psyllium, dramatically reduced the impact on blood glucose of high-carbohydrate foods. Psyllium has been shown to have a host of benefits on its own, including increased satiety (feeling full). Increased satiety when it comes to ice cream might be the difference between having a scoop and eating the whole pint. With mind-blowing sex on the immediate horizon, the controlled portions are important if you have lactose issues. But if you're into using all the pleasure channels, have psyllium early in the day because it is perhaps best known for epic bowel-clearing poops.

Psyllium isn't the only magic powder out there when it comes to digestion at dinner. A couple of other things can lower blood sugar after a meal, as well, through sheer witchcraft and sorcery.

Those things are Ceylon cinnamon and apple cider vinegar. Apple cider vinegar is no one's choice for the next Skittles flavor, but it has a number of great health benefits and no sugar. As little as one ounce after a meal has shown benefits in blood sugar management, likely contributing to further studies showing mild weight loss. I use Bragg apple cider vinegar, which comes in convenient bulk bottles, but you can use whatever brand you like. Ideally, it will be organic ACV "with the mother"—a cute way of saying that it contains part of the probiotic culture that produced it—adding additional support for a healthy gut biome. Add cinnamon, another blood sugar reducer, and you have a great way to combat blood sugar spikes as well. I call that concoction my "Cheater Shooter." To make it, just mix 30ml of ACV and half a teaspoon of Ceylon cinnamon into 90ml of room-temperature water and send it down the hatch.

The final measure is something a lot of us do instinctively. Go for a walk. A recent study found that people who got up and went for a walk had lower blood sugar levels and less of a peak in blood sugar than people who didn't get up after eating. One study shows that 15 minutes of low-intensity walking is enough to significantly drop blood sugar levels.

HOW TO DEAL WITH ALCOHOL

No celebratory dinner is complete without a high-quality cocktail to get you to the table, or a glass of great wine to accompany the meal itself. But just like we talked about in the previous chapter, the key to alcohol is only having a little. Not necessarily because I'm worried that you will become an alcoholic; it's more because the last thing you want to do is feel like you're owning this day at the expense of the next one. Then you're not really owning the day at all, you're overspending and borrowing from tomorrow. That said, we all make mistakes, so if you find yourself looking at the bottom of a liquor bottle and staring at the prospect of a really tough tomorrow, don't beat yourself up, just work to beat down the hangover and prepare yourself for some good sleep and a better morning.

THE ULTIMATE HANGOVER CURE
Step 1: Rehydrate, Duh
Alcohol is dehydrating. Along with the loss of water is a loss of minerals. You need both. Drink a liter of natural spring water with the addition of a total of 5 grams of Himalayan salt within the first two

hours of waking up. Keep drinking water heavily until you pee at least twice. Additional magnesium is also a really good idea before bed, as it further assists with step 2, the reduction of acetaldehyde.

Step 2: Reduce the Toxic Burden of Acetaldehyde

Excessive alcohol puts a strain on the body, requiring the utilization of vitamins and minerals to assist with recovery. One of those crucial minerals is molybdenum. Never in the history of TV medical dramas has the mystery ailment been severe molybdenum deficiency, but molybdenum is essential for the body's production of chemicals that neutralize acetaldehyde. What the hell is acetaldehyde? It's one of the main toxins that the body produces as a result of alcohol ingestion. If we have been drinking, we are likely depleting our stores of molybdenum rapidly, increasing our acetaldehyde sensitivity. It's one of the reasons we feel hungover in the morning, and why our bodies then begin to crave molybdenum-rich foods like legumes. In Texas, at least, classic hangover food is tacos, nachos, and burritos—all of them chock full of beans. In the Mediterranean? Hummus, made from chickpeas. Even after a night of crushing Jack Daniel's or ouzo, our instincts can be incredibly accurate, cutting across cultures and cuisines. But rather than gorge on nachos, the best idea would be to supplement with some molybdenum (300 mcg) prior to bed, and again in the morning. Studies have shown it to reduce regular aches and pains, which if nothing else will make tomorrow's walk of shame a little easier to endure!

Step 3: Balance Your Neurotransmitters

Alcohol is a gamma-aminobutyric acid (GABA) agonist, meaning that it produces more GABA in the brain. This is what results in the good, loopy feelings from drinking. Another neurotransmitter, glutamate, has the exact opposite effect on GABA. When you drink alcohol, after you are done with the flood of GABA, you experience a glutamate rebound where the body overcorrects for the problem with the release of excess glutamate. This is why you wake up so quickly and sleep so poorly, and it's what leads to the anxious, light-headed, cracked-out feeling you can get from a hangover. To combat this, you should take things that support the GABA system. This is precisely why the "hair of the dog" seems to work. At least on a neurotransmitter level, you are getting more GABA in your system to balance out the glutamate.

L-theanine, which occurs naturally in green tea, is great at mimicking the effects of GABA. Matcha, as we described in chapter 6, is the best source.

Pro Tip: Glutathione Push

Come Monday morning, a line down the hall at the office leads into a pop-up clinic in our gym that offers glutathione straight into the veins. Glutathione is known as the master antioxidant in the body, and it dismantles all forms of toxicity, including our nemesis acetaldehyde. Glutathione is not only the preferred defense against acetaldehyde but, as an added benefit, will support the rest of your body in dealing with oxidative stress. The problem is that the stomach neuters glutathione like a brothelkeeper from antiquity, so the only way to get it into your body effectively is to absorb a liposomal form through the tissue, or inject it into the veins. The latter is undoubtedly the most effective. IV vitamin therapy clinics are gaining in popularity all over the United States. A Google search of your local area with those terms should find you some results.

Prescription: Make Your New Favorite (Pro-Sex) Dinner

There are two important tasks that lie ahead of you: sex, and sleep. These meals are designed to help you with both. It's also finally time for a few carbs. Praise Ceres, goddess of the grain! Research shows that adding in some carbohydrates after training is good for testosterone. If you are like most of us, it is also good for your sanity, and helps you sleep. It's the adult version of cookies and milk.

As for sex, these nutrient-dense, digestion-friendly meals are packed with foods that help with the production of nitric oxide. So let's get cookin'!

Sensual Steak Salad

SERVES 2

Time to prep: 15 minutes
Time to cook: 25 minutes

FOR THE DRESSING

60ml balsamic vinegar
60ml avocado oil

Dash of mustard powder

FOR THE STEAK

1 teaspoon fennel seeds
2 teaspoons garlic powder
1 teaspoon black pepper
1 teaspoon salt

225g grass-fed steak
  (ribeye, New York strip, or fillet)
225g Brie

FOR THE SALAD

140g rocket
140g Swiss chard, chopped
140g spinach

2 medium beetroots, steamed, peeled,
  and sliced
30g raw or roasted pumpkin seeds

✦ Make the dressing: Shake, blend, or whisk together all the ingredients until thoroughly combined.

✦ Make the steak: Combine the fennel seeds, garlic powder, black pepper, and salt in a small bowl. Rub evenly onto both sides of the steak.

✦ Grill or cook in a hot cast-iron frying pan until the steak reaches your desired level of doneness. If you are a real foodie, that's medium-rare. (For an inch-thick steak, that's 5 minutes on the first side, then another 4 minutes on the second.)

✦ Let the steak rest for 10 minutes so it doesn't dry out when you slice it. Slice the steak and Brie to the same thickness.

✦ Make the salad: Toss the greens and beetroots with the dressing, then sprinkle the pumpkin seeds on top.

✦ To serve, divide the salad onto two plates. Alternating slices of each, stack the steak and Brie sideways on top of the salads.

TIP: This blend of garlic, fennel seeds, black pepper, and sea salt is also sold premixed as Canadian or chophouse seasoning.

Sourdough Garlic Bread

SERVES 2

Time to prep: 5 minutes
Time to cook: 10 minutes

1 loaf sourdough bread
1 stick grass-fed butter
    (you won't need it all)

1 tablespoon garlic powder
    (or more if desired)

+ Preheat the oven to 180°C/350°F/Gas Mark 4.

+ Slice the loaf of sourdough down the center.

+ Spread the bread liberally with the butter, and sprinkle on the garlic powder.

+ Place in the oven and bake until the bread is golden brown, about 10 minutes.

Love Pasta

SERVES 2

Time to prep: 10 minutes
Time to cook: 20 minutes

2 servings quinoa pasta

2 tablespoons extra-virgin olive oil

1 teaspoon minced garlic

1 medium onion, diced

2 free-range chicken breasts, diced

2 small courgettes, diced

1 tablespoon dried Italian herbs

½ teaspoon chilli flakes, or more to taste

30g raw pumpkin seeds

400g tin organic stewed tomatoes

70g rocket

70g Swiss chard, chopped

Sea salt

Freshly grated Parmesan, for garnish

✦ Make the pasta according to package directions. Drain and set aside.

✦ Make the sauce: Heat the oil in a large frying pan over medium heat. Add the garlic and onion and sauté for 5 minutes, stirring often.

✦ Add the chicken, courgettes, Italian herbs, and chilli flakes. Cook, stirring occasionally, until the chicken is browned on all sides (about 5 minutes).

✦ Add the pumpkin seeds and tomatoes, cover, and simmer for 10 minutes, until the chicken is cooked through. Remove from heat and stir in the greens.

✦ Cover and let sit until the greens wilt (about 3 minutes). Season to taste with salt.

✦ Toss the sauce with the pasta, then divide the pasta into two bowls.

✦ Top with the Parmesan as desired.

Game-On Stew

―――――――

SERVES 4

Time to prep: 20 minutes
Time to cook: 8 hours

1.8kg buffalo or grass-fed beef bones,
    with the marrow, cut

2.27l filtered water

1 bottle organic dry red wine

6 garlic cloves, peeled and chopped

450g game meat, cubed

450g small purple potatoes

2 medium carrots, peeled and chopped

1 medium yellow onion, sliced

1 tablespoon sea salt

1 teaspoon black pepper

3 bay leaves

+ Make the bone broth: Simmer the bones in 2.27l of filtered water for 3 hours.

+ Add the red wine, garlic, and meat. Simmer for 3 hours.

+ Add the remaining ingredients, and simmer for 2 hours.

+ Before serving, remove the bones and bay leaves.

Jammin' Tandoori Salmon with Tzatziki

SERVES 2

Time to prep: 5 minutes
Time to cook: 10 minutes

FOR THE TZATZIKI

125g full-fat Greek yogurt

¼ teaspoon dried dill

2 garlic cloves, peeled

¼ medium cucumber, chopped

Sea salt

FOR THE SALMON

350g sockeye salmon
  (or another wild-caught salmon)

1 tablespoon avocado oil

1 lemon, sliced in half

1 tablespoon tandoori seasoning
  (or more to coat liberally)

½ teaspoon coarse sea salt

✦ Preheat the oven to 190°C/375°F/Gas Mark 5.

✦ Make the tzatziki: Blend all the ingredients together in a blender or food processor until mostly smooth. Season to taste with salt.

✦ Make the salmon: Coat both sides of the salmon in avocado oil, then place it skin side down on a baking sheet or in a roasting pan. Squeeze on the lemon juice, then coat with the tandoori seasoning. Sprinkle sea salt on top, and bake in the preheated oven until the salmon is cooked to medium. (That's 10 minutes per inch of thickness.)

✦ Divide onto two plates and serve immediately.

Spicy Creamy Greens

SERVES 2

Time to prep: 5 minutes
Time to cook: 5 minutes

1 tablespoon avocado oil

1 teaspoon berbere seasoning (see note)

30g raw pumpkin seeds

140g rocket

140g Swiss chard, chopped

140g spinach

Primal Kitchen Ranch dressing

✦ Heat the avocado oil in a large frying pan over medium-high heat. Add the berbere seasoning, pumpkin seeds, and greens. Sauté, tossing often, until the greens are cooked as you like them.

✦ Douse in Primal Kitchen Ranch dressing, divide onto two plates, and serve immediately.

NOTE: Berbere seasoning is an Ethiopian spice blend that contains paprika, cayenne, fenugreek, coriander, cumin, black pepper, cardamom, cinnamon, organic clove, ginger, and turmeric. You can buy it premixed.

Mashed Potatoes

SERVES 2

Time to prep: 5 minutes
Time to cook: 20 minutes

4 medium potatoes, peeled and chopped
3 tablespoons grass-fed butter

50g grated mature cheddar
Sea salt

+ Boil the potatoes until fork-tender, then drain. This should take about 15 minutes.

+ Return them to the pot, add the butter and cheddar, and mash.

+ Season to taste with salt.

Popcorn with Grass-Fed Butter and Chocolate

SERVES 2

Time to prep: 5 minutes
Time to cook: 5 minutes

50g organic popcorn kernels
2 tablespoons grass-fed butter
Sea salt

Lily's stevia-sweetened chocolate
(choose your favorite flavor)

✦ Pop the corn in an air popper while you melt the butter.

✦ Drizzle the melted butter over the popcorn, add sea salt to taste, and toss in chunks of the chocolate. Eat immediately. Wash your hands before making love to your partner. Or not.

Say Grace Like a Scientist!

In *Island*, Aldous Huxley's last novel, about a utopian island called Pala, Huxley talks about saying grace as an act of gratitude to be done not with words but with your senses. It's a concept I regularly borrow in my own life, and one that I want you to apply, since it encompasses the principles of modern nutrition science.

Before you eat, prepare the very best bite on your fork. Take a moment to look deeply at all the food on your plate. Think about where it came from (a reinforcement to eat food sourced in a healthy manner). Think about the energy required to grow that food—the nutrients, the sunlight, the other plants and animals ingested by your food. Take time to bring yourself to a state of mindfulness and reduced stress. Think about how that energy will translate to energy in your own body and what you are going to need that energy for (a reminder about portion control . . . and that you're about to bone down!).

As you put the bite in your mouth, if the food is lacking in any of these categories, forgive it. You never want to think that what you're about to eat is poison, or bad for you, or will ruin your diet. Instead, tell your body that what it is about to eat is nourishment. Then look at the food, smell the food, and savor it. When you taste it, chew it until there is nothing left, and your tastebuds have flirted with every ingredient in this orgy of flavor.

That should be your first bite, and how you say grace: it's a piece of mindfulness, a nutrition reinforcer, and a way through the placebo to ensure that your food will be digested and absorbed optimally.

Now Do It

When any relationship breaks down, it's usually due to lack of communication. This is especially true with our bodies. It sometimes feels like we are speaking two different languages. Our body produces gas, or sends a signal that we are hungover. What does that mean? What does our body want? Then, conversely, we demand that our body perform the tasks we want. But simultaneously we might be telling our body that something we ate is poisonous. How does our body respond? If there is one relationship that we all need to repair, it's the one with our body. Here's the way I like to look at it. If we broke our bodies down into the trillions of cells that they are, and imagined those cells as our loyal subjects, and our conscious mind as their ruler, what kind of ruler would we be? Most of us would be sadistic tyrants. We feed our cells things that aren't helpful, we chastise them for the appearance they create, we force them into unnatural positions for long periods of time, and then we take all manner of drugs to shut out what they are trying to communicate with us.

We talk to psychiatrists and read books about restoring healthy relationships with our parents, with our friends, with our lovers, but perhaps the most dysfunctional relationship we have is with our bodies. We've gotta change that. Our body has our back. Yeah, sometimes it fails. Sometimes it disappoints us. But it tries its hardest always, whether we believe it or not.

The key to restoring our relationship with our bodies is the way you maintain any good relationship: you learn and you listen. A lot of this book has been spent explaining what causes some of the signals your body has been sending. So now when you listen, hopefully you are better at translating that into corrective action. When anything isn't happening the way you want, first ask, "What is my body telling me?" Pain, inflammation, gas, fatigue, those are all modes of communication. Listen to these messages from the deep. Remember, it's not your body's fault; it always speaks the truth.

In the same light, we need to start sending the right messages back to our body. If we want it to act like everything is going to be okay, we have to communicate that everything is going to be okay. Not verbally, but emotionally. Emotions are the way we translate our thoughts to our body. It is the Rosetta Stone. So when we have the cake and we smile and we laugh, and we celebrate, our body is going to respond better than if we have the cake and tell ourselves what a weak-willed piece of shit we are.

If you're going to own your life, you have to take responsibility for all the relationships in it. And there is perhaps none more important than the one with your body.

THREE POINTERS

+ Don't believe everything you have heard about food. First, it was probably wrong. Second, if you believe the bad advice, you will make it feel correct. The mind communicates through the body via your emotions surrounding your choices. Learn to harness the power of belief to your benefit rather than your detriment.
+ Digestion is the foundation of nutrition. It is what delivers the food you eat from your stomach into your cells. To optimize digestion, eat slow, chew hard, and increase levels of HCL and digestive enzymes. For peak sexual prowess with minimal gaseous distraction, eat pro-sex foods that contain nitric oxide.
+ If you are going to cheat, do it well. Learn to minimize the cost of an indulgent dessert or a high-carbohydrate meal by timing it after a workout and taking steps to mitigate the ensuing blood sugar spikes, like by taking a walk. If you want to indulge in a few extra adult beverages, add molybdenum-rich foods, hydrate, and boost levels of glutathione.

MORE, BETTER SEX

"Sex" is as important as eating or drinking and we ought to allow the one appetite to be satisfied with as little restraint or false modesty as the other.

—MARQUIS DE SADE

You're done with the daily grind—except for a little bump n' grind. What day isn't made better by some action with someone you care about? Even if that someone is you. People don't have nearly enough sex—no wonder as a society we are so frustrated. But we not only need to have more sex, we need to have better sex. As you'll learn, you may not be able to have one without the other.

Getting Owned

Look around you: sex is everywhere. Always has been, always will be. It sells movies, magazines, cars, boats, vacations, beer. Today it even sells cleaning products. In 2017, Mr. Clean ran a Super Bowl ad that showed their iconic bald guy sweeping not just the floors but the proverbial panties off unsuspecting housewives. There's a reason sex is always everywhere. We're never having enough of it. So we crave it, and we jump at every tantalizing suggestion of it—a fact that advertisers and media conglomerates are fully aware of, and use to their advantage.

Wanting more sex than we normally have is part of the natural order. It's when we start having less sex than we normally should, which we're seeing now, that things really start to go sideways. Statistics show that even millennials, who should be in the prime of their biological sex drive, are having less sex than ever before. That is despite the fact that, at least in theory, sex is just a right swipe away. Those in committed relationships aren't doing any better. The average couple has sex only once or twice per week. *A week!* The average couple is also a couple of fucking liars—those self-reported statistics are about as reliable as the number of people who say they love to read and to hike on their dating profiles. Sorry, sport, but the aisles of my local Barnes & Noble are about as empty as the trails at your nearest national park.

So how do we explain this paradox? On the one hand, we're a species designed to be obsessed with sex. And it's seemingly more available than ever before. And yet, even with ample demand and accessible supply, we aren't doing enough of it. What gives?

As with anything, it's a choice. Sex isn't happening because we are not making it a priority, and there are a lot of reasons why. For one, it might be because the sex we're having is just not that good. In American culture at least, guys talk about "scoring" or "getting lucky," even with their wives! If men are using this adversarial, zero-sum language to describe sex, it's no wonder women want to have it only when men choose to do something incredibly romantic. You know what all this tells me? The sex isn't very good. Regardless of whose "fault" it is, it's clear that the sexual expectations of the average woman—who holds the power of sexual choice in the standard relationship—are so low that you gotta play all the games and win both Showcase Showdowns to make her feel like the price of putting up with suboptimal sex is right. If the sex was usually good, language and behavior like that wouldn't occur as often, because *everyone* would be getting lucky. Both people would win.

So why aren't we better at sex? The answer is actually shockingly simple: we've never been taught. As a culture we are absolutely devoid of any kind of practical sexual education, both for teens and adults. What do we have instead? Well, we usually start with lectures on how dangerous and bad and frightening sex is. Sex Ed should be called Sex Dead, since really it's just a mechanism for adults to convince children that if they have sex outside of marriage or love, there is a 100 percent chance either they or their dreams will die.

> *Jimmy had unprotected sex after prom with a girl he liked, but didn't like it, and the next morning he woke up dead of AIDS.*
> *Sally wanted to be an astronaut, but she had sex once in high school, and now she's got three kids and gives handjobs for crack.*

Once we navigate the gauntlet of Sex Dead, most of us have parents who are so uncomfortable with the subject of sex that you can literally hear their testicles and ovaries drying up and shrinking back into their stomachs when you ask them about it. At that point, the only options left are cool uncles and porn (they usually come as a set), which is probably how most men learn how to have sex. Learning how to have mutually fulfilling sex by watching porn is like learning how to be a great boxer by watching *Rocky* films—it might be good for motivation, but the technique is wildly exaggerated, and the expectations are completely unrealistic. Whatever you're into, it's not gonna look like it does in the movies.

All of this leads to an unsurprising and troubling problem: all of us are insecure about sex. Is it any wonder why? If we've been told sex is dangerous, and all the sex we have ever seen is porn, and every pop song talks about filling Magnum XL condoms and a "juice box that is always wet," how are we supposed to feel about ourselves (and sex) after the first several times we do it and perform like an amateur at an open-mic night? If we even manage to find the break in the curtains through all those folds in the fabric, the bright lights might trigger a massive case of stage fright and flop sweat, at which point we're lucky to get one good line out before they're laughing at us instead of with us. Just the thought of it is enough to give you a condition.

As a mentor to a lot of young men, I hear from a shocking number of twentysomethings with sexual dysfunction. They are putting so much pressure on themselves to perform that they psych themselves out. Many of them end up just avoiding sex, making excuses to themselves and their lovers. Or they do it in dangerous ways, like by ingesting copious amounts of mysterious gas-station boner pills. Just ask former UFC light heavyweight champion Jon Jones about that.

My fiancée, host of the sex and relationship docu-series *Love Undressed*, tells me she too hears frequent reports from the ladies of otherwise healthy males failing to achieve and maintain an erection. Stuff like this doesn't happen to any other animal species but humans, because so much of our sexual behavior is about what's going on in the head on top of our shoulders instead of the one inside our pants. I know, because that used to be me. (Told you this book would be honest, didn't I?)

I have always been hard on myself. In sports, I would replay every missed shot, every mistake, a hundred times, chastising myself end-lessly. But the good thing about sports is that if you make a mis-take, you can go practice and fix the problem. With sex, there are no scrimmages, no preseason training, no two-a-days. Every day is game day. So in my early twenties, after a few bad episodes with a girlfriend who made me feel unworthy if I failed to perform to her standards, I was sexually incapacitated. I remember turning down countless sexual advances from women I was interested in, simply because the potential pain of failing to perform outweighed the pos-sible pleasure of the sex. It was a truly awful period of my life.

But insecurities aren't just for the boys. Women have become insecure about their smell, the shape of their vagina, their vaginal wetness, and even the color of their asshole! (A small but important aside: If there is one procedure that is completely absurd, it is getting your asshole bleached. I don't care if it is so dark that it blocks out the sun like the undereye warpaint of an NFL middle linebacker, you don't need to bleach your asshole. This is a prime opportunity to love the skin you're in.)

Finally, there are the physical things that prevent us from both wanting the sex we need and having the sex we want. On a physical level, our hormones are way out of whack. Everyone has read those now-famous studies about how testosterone has dipped in the USA and worldwide. That's just one part of the problem. It's a *symptom*, not the ultimate cause, of our stilted sex lives. Just as our neuro-chemistry has been thrown out of whack for sleep and food, we also aren't optimized for sex. We aren't, for example, priming our pumps the way we should for the chemical foundation for arousal, nitric oxide. The result: our insecurities and insufficiencies continue to get the best of us.

We need more sex, and we need better sex. The better the sex we have, the more we'll make it a priority. And that's important. Men who have sex less than once a week have been found to be twice as likely to experience erectile dysfunction. So while this won't be a guide to optimizing your Bumble profile, for anyone who has a partner available now or in the future, this chapter will explain the keys to having more sex and better sex. And in the process hopefully you'll also rediscover something that is one of the great joys of the human experience—a chance for pleasure, fun, connection, and chemistry that has never been equaled by a drug or a pill or a potion.

Owning It

If you have any doubts about what you'll have to do to "own it" during sex—or if you've reached peak frustration and are ready to just embrace your self-imposed celibacy—think again. Aside from all the self-evident benefits (uh, orgasm feels awesome!), sex is also important for our well-being. It relieves stress, stimulates endorphins and hormones, and is crucial for sexual health. Correlations also exist between improved aspects of mental health and immune function, and according to a recent report, frequent sex may help with depression, wound healing, aging, prostate health, and pain tolerance. It's the next best miracle drug after exercise.

The reality is, sex and reproduction are at the core of what it means to be human. To incentivize it, to make sure we do it and propagate the species, is it any wonder that we've evolved so that sex makes our bodies and our minds feel so great? We're designed to do the deed, to *like* the deed; now we just need to rediscover the desire to do more of it and do it better.

More Sex

More sex is something that everyone can get behind (or on top of, or underneath) regardless of age, gender, or sexual orientation. When couples are asked why they don't have more sex, often you'll hear them say they don't have the time. I call bullshit! If you want to have sex, you will find the time. And as for the right time, there is no shortage of books with tips and strategies for the best time to have sex, yet all of them boil down to one essential reality: it depends on who you are. For most of us, though, the best time to have sex is going to be the most convenient time, which is usually after dinner (and why this chapter sits where it does in the book). The kids will be off to bed, your guests will have gone home, and you'll have the benefits of a postdinner testosterone spike courtesy of the pro-sex meal you prepared. Then, once you do whatever self-care you need to feel clean and confident and sexy (we'll talk more about self-care in the next chapter), you'll be ready to get after it. The real way to ensure regular visits to Pound Town is to optimize your physical and mental states of readiness. That means managing both your hormones and a phenomenon known as hedonic tolerance.

HORMONES DRIVE THE SEX MACHINE

The drive to have sex is largely regulated by our hormones, particularly testosterone and estrogen. While a bit of an oversimplification, think of testosterone like the gas, and estrogen like the brakes. Too much gas, you might drive right off a cliff. Too much brakes, you won't get anywhere. Interestingly, this applies both to men and women, regardless of the fact that we each have an abundance of one hormone over the other. And it is finding the right balance that becomes the essential thing for getting where you want to go, as fast and as often as you want to go there.

Caveat: About the Pill . . .

Because testosterone is so often in the headlines, we tend to think men have an easier time controlling these hormones than women do. But actually, it's the reverse: for women, there is a more direct and ubiquitous form of hormone manipulation. It's called the birth control pill.

According to the CDC, 28 percent of all women using contraception are using "the pill." That's well over 10 million women in the United States alone. The pill works by creating a hormonal environment that mimics pregnancy, thus preventing ovulation or the release of the egg. When taken correctly, it is over 99 percent effective in preventing pregnancy and 100 percent effective in convincing guys that they can finally throw away their condoms and bareback it.

Needless to say, when the hormone-based birth control pill was invented, men and women rejoiced. As they should have, when you consider its many benefits. There is just this one thing: changing the hormone balance in the female body mimics what happens with low testosterone in men. Adding estrogen and progestin to the body in pill form often leads to reduced sex drive and, according to a recently published study tracking a million Danish women, even depression.

And to make matters worse, another study showed that women who were on the pill were attracted to partners with similar immune traits, and repelled by those who were different, which is the exact opposite of what should happen with a hormonally balanced, normally functioning attraction system. So Jane meets Tommy while she is on the pill, and she is passionately attracted to him. Jane and Tommy get married, and Jane gets off the pill. All of a sudden her body is screaming "No!" because she is less sexually attracted to him on multiple levels. The pill not only scrambled her hormones but tricked her into choosing a biological mismatch as well.

While I'm not saying that the pill should be taken off the table as a birth control option, every woman should go into it knowing the potential hormonal downside and pay attention to how her body responds. Especially if sex is important to her.

Like so many of the tweaks we need to make to optimize our functioning and own our days, finding hormone balance is easier said than done at first, because it is a moving target. Testosterone, for example, decreases naturally with age, and estrogen levels can easily spike due to diet choices, exposure to pollutants like BPA found in plastic water bottles, too much stress, and even carrying excess body weight. The combination can leave even the sturdiest and most robust of people sexually inert.

Fortunately, there are numerous ways to naturally boost testosterone and hit the gas so your sex machine gets going again. Here are three:

Eat fat. To synthesize hormones like testosterone, the body requires adequate production of saturated fat and cholesterol. The connection between the two is so strong that one study showed that you can get testosterone levels to drop with a low-fat diet and bounce back on a high-fat diet. We should have hammered this point home by now, but just in case you need to hear it a different way, here you go: eating healthy fats won't make you chubby, but it will definitely help you get one.

Get sleep. Sleep is the time when the testosterone factory is open for business. The restorative sleep cycles are when the body can prioritize things like necessary hormone production. Research even shows that every additional hour of sleep you get bumps up testosterone levels 15 percent or more, while those who experience sleep disturbances tend to have curbed testosterone production.

Lift heavy. When training under anaerobic conditions such as lifting heavy weights or sprinting, you are signaling to the body that you are the type of animal that needs to produce testosterone to flourish. Even in experienced lifters, whose bodies are used to the stress loads they endure, their testosterone increases with heavy lifting. So don't skip out on leg day if you want to boost T production, because larger muscles contribute to higher testosterone.

▦ HEDONIC TOLERANCE AND THE SPANKING MONKEY

The sex experts agree: masturbation is healthy (and we all do it). It provides a lot of the same benefits as sex, and it's available on demand. Like Netflix. And like anything (including Netflix), it is possible to take something healthy and go overboard, to go from hormetic to toxic in the blink of an eye, or the push of a button.

Scientist-turned-consciousness-explorer John Lilly discovered this for himself when he gave a rhesus monkey access to an orgasm button. He inserted wired catheters into the orgasm center of the monkey's brain, rigged a button that would neurologically trigger an orgasm, and handed him the controls. What he soon found was that over the course of a typical day, Sexually Curious George would spend sixteen hours straight pressing the orgasm button and eight hours sleeping. The monkey took breaks to eat too, but only briefly, and only enough to sustain himself. Lilly had basically discovered how to turn a rhesus monkey into a fourteen-year-old human boy.

While orgasm is definitely a signature of a life well lived, if we spend all of our time spanking the monkey like . . . well . . . monkeys, we will miss out on the diverse human connections that lead to the sex we really want, and we will find ourselves fallen victim to the principle of hedonic tolerance, whereby the more of something pleasurable you experience, the less pleasure you will take from it with each successive experience.

Hedonic tolerance happens with everything—sex, drugs, food, extreme sports. The first year you started drinking alcohol, it made you feel better than it does now. Eating ice cream for the first time in a while is better than finding yourself at the bottom of a Ben & Jerry's pint for the eleventh day in a row. If you are masturbating constantly, not only will you diminish the amount of enjoyment you experience from the act itself, but you'll diminish the joy of sex too. A tour of online support-group message boards for sex addicts and their horrifying stories of endless pornography consumption and marathon masturbation sessions is all you need to know that the key is all things in moderation, including moderation . . . and masturbation.

Better Sex

The key to better sex is not in the *Kama Sutra* (though it's a pretty good read). It's not some proprietary sexual position you can only learn by attending a love doctor's seminar at an airport hotel. In fact, it's only partially related to the act itself. The majority of the pathway to better sex lies in the quality of your interactions with a potential partner all the way up to the point that sex occurs.

▚ BETTER ATTRACTION

When you break it down, physical attraction is really nothing more than a genetic and immune system assessment. Our bodies instinctively scan the bodies of those around us and produce an instant Maury Povich response—*You can(NOT) be the father!*—based typically on the presence of healthy genetics and differing acquired immune characteristics. And while this process might start with the eyes, using symmetry and bodily health as the big visual cues, it ends with the nose, thanks to the power of pheromones.

Pheromones are a chemo-signal that translates your immune system profile into a scent, designed to attract mates with different coverage than your own, and repel those with similar characteristics. In a study conducted on 100 college students, women were asked to smell the T-shirts worn by a variety of men. The women were demonstrably more attracted to men who had a different acquired immune system than them, while those with similar traits were described more like a "brother" or "father." The evolutionary advantage of this mechanism is fairly obvious: not only does this help prevent incest, it increases the survival rate of the child by breeding more robust immune coverage.

We have a problem, though. We modern humans mask our scents with perfectly engineered deodorants, antiperspirants, perfumes, lotions, and body sprays. This confuses our natural attraction system and sets us up for a random chance at attraction when we get down to places where you can't hide the smell anymore. If you're one of those unfortunate souls whose milkshake keeps bringing all the wrong boys (or girls) to the yard, you might want to consider going easy on the colognes and perfumes and scented lotions.

BETTER COMMUNICATION

Let me tell you the most important, game-changing, life-altering way you can use your tongue to improve your sex life. To make words. And use them to talk with your partner about sex.

Why is it so hard to talk about sex? To talk, as Salt-n-Pepa said, about you and (s)he, about all the good things and the bad things that may be? Well, for one, all those bad things are a minefield of insecurities. She says, "I like it when you touch me this way," and he thinks, *Oh, so you haven't liked how I touched you all those other times?* So let's just set things straight.

Everyone is different. Everyone likes different things. No matter how skilled you are (or think you are) as a lover, you will never truly know your partner unless you communicate. What are their desires, fantasies, boundaries, insecurities? What are yours? We all just need to relax a little bit and lay it all out there on the table. Maybe you aren't into the same things, maybe you are. But if you shame your partner into lying to you about what gets them off, they are way more likely to do it behind your back.

Creating an honest discourse is absolutely vital, but it's not just communicating with our partner that matters, we have to be willing to communicate in general. You gotta take sex out of the closet for it to bloom into its full potential. Open up about it, talk to your friends, and if your friends are uptight, listen to podcasts. Dr. Chris Ryan and Dan Savage both produce great sex podcasts. Make it as regular a discussion as your conversations about food, sports, politics, the weather. You might learn a thing or two . . . or twelve.

Like Larry Flynt famously said, "Relax, it's just sex!"

▓ BETTER POLARITY

Despite panning from all the critics for its shallow, predictable storyline and flat characters, the erotic power-exchange novel *Fifty Shades of Grey* sold more books than all the Harry Potter series combined. The popularity of what was once thought of as "fringe" sexuality went full mainstream. Why? Because it was about polarity, and polarity is sexy.

The metaphor comes from the idea of a magnet, in which there are two sides. Both sides are equally powerful, but the magnet will only be attracted to its opposite polarity, and repelled by the same. One of the reasons that power exchange is so exciting is that it exaggerates polarity. Take Mr. Grey, the young, physically perfect, controlling billionaire in the novel. He represents a very dominant polarity. Take Ana, the shy, demure, almost virginal college grad. She represents a very submissive polarity. There is already plenty of room for sexual attraction there. But then when Mr. Grey turns on his role of master in the power exchange, his dominant energy is heightened. When Ana submits to his will, her submissive polarity is exacerbated, and they both fall madly in lust, while the whole world squirms in their seats reading about it. If *Fifty Shades* were the business book of sex, it would be *Good to Great*.

As with the story, the basic premise of polarity or power exchange is that one partner takes the dominant role, and the other takes the submissive role. This is not gender-specific, but generally in a single session the roles don't switch. There are a lot of toys and props associated with power exchange, but they are just different ways to create the underlying conditions. One doesn't need to get lost in the props. The masterpiece is in the power dynamic itself.

In a relationship that struggles with polarity—let's say a couple that has two dominant personalities, both with strong careers, and similar characteristics in bed—adding power exchange can be the air that allows the flame of passion to ignite. There are many methods and means by which you can play the game, but these are the basic strategies:

1. **Delayed gratification:** The submissive delays gratification at the request of the dominant.
2. **Restraint:** The submissive is physically restrained, or encouraged not to move certain body parts (hands, feet, etc.).
3. **Pain:** The submissive endures trials of light to moderate pain at the request of the dominant.
4. **Observation:** The dominant can observe the submissive for longer and more explicitly than the submissive.

Not only might power exchange ignite additional passion, it might just be one of the keys to mental health. In a survey of sixty-six dominant females, they described the services they provided for their partners as "therapeutic." In a fascinating 2006 study, researcher Pamela Connolly compared power-exchange practitioners to the normal population and found that practitioners had *lower levels* of many negative characteristics, including depression, anxiety, post-traumatic stress disorder (PTSD), and paranoia. Basically, they were chill AF. A study seven years later, by Andreas Wismeijer and Marcel van Assen, found something similar, this time about traits that, frankly, all of us would like to have more of in our lives: practitioners were more extroverted, more open to new experiences, more conscientious than their nonpracticing counterparts. Practitioners were also found to be less neurotic and rejection sensitive.

Now, you don't need to go turning your bedroom into a BDSM dungeon overnight. Nor should you do anything that your partner isn't open to. But you should experiment. You should release some of those inhibitions. Build on some of those communication skills we just talked about and tell your partner what does and doesn't turn you on. One of the more striking things from research about sex and power-exchange communities is how easily and often they are able to get into the flow state—a state of mental transcendence. In the words of Ron Burgundy, it's science.

So if you've toyed with the idea of trying any of this, but found it too taboo because of cultural stigmas or your own hang-ups, let that stuff go and give yourself a shot at better sex. You might find you have the perfect capstone to your day.

BETTER SKILL

I have very little interest in being a sexual golf pro and coaching you on your strokes, so I am not going to waste your time running down a bunch of "techniques" that you can find in other books and *Cosmopolitan* magazine articles about driving that special someone crazy for days. Instead, what I want to offer you is a single skill that both women and men can employ, and that can bring a disproportionate amount of pleasure compared to the effort it requires.

It is all about mastering the squeeze.

For a man, purely physical sexual pleasure comes down to friction. Controlling the rhythm and pressure of the friction during intercourse is a skill that women, especially, are able to practice by squeezing the muscles of the pelvic floor. First discussed in the published research of an American gynecologist named Arnold Kegel in 1948, these exercises eventually took his name. A Kegel, as it is called, is a contraction of the pubococcygeal (PC) muscles, which is pretty much what you do to stop yourself from peeing midstream. If a woman can master the contractions of the PC muscles during intercourse, she can vary the friction to speed or slow the climax, taking the vagina from purely passive participant to pulsating pleasure pocket.

For men, the goal of the squeeze is something different. Training the PC muscles has been shown to increase the hardness of erections. The control of contractions works as a kind of pump to increase blood flow through the shaft. But the real magic happens when a man is able to use this skill to indefinitely delay ejaculation.

The problem with the male orgasm is that it usually only happens once, and if it happens too soon, it can leave a partner unsatisfied. Mainstream advice for men is pretty simple: "Think about baseball," the idea goes. Yeah, right. If you can think about baseball while a sexy woman is moaning and writhing underneath you, using her own PC muscles to play with the friction, you are either a sociopath or a salary cap data geek like the guys from *Moneyball*.

Better methods for orgasm control are required. The way I see it, you have three choices. The first choice is simply, when you are getting close, to slow down or stop, shift your focus to oral or manual stimulation for your partner, and then restart when the engine isn't quite so hot. This is basic brinksmanship, as the terminology goes. Or you can take manual control of the PC muscles that actually control the ejaculation, and keep them contracted so that they are unable to activate the launch sequence to release the ejaculate. It will take some time to build up the strength to execute, but the payoff is worth it. It carries very much the same pleasure of the orgasm, but without the release, and there is still the same biological urge to continue having sex.

For those looking for a Kegel training regimen, check out the app Kegel Camp; otherwise practice three-second contractions in sets of ten, as often as you think about it. As you advance, practice holding the contractions longer than three seconds. In the meantime, while you build up your Kegel strength, there is a third method that can accomplish something similar.

THE MILLION-DOLLAR SPOT

The legend goes that a man who struggled with premature ejaculation paid a million dollars to a Taoist sex master to learn of a spot he could press on his body to manually prevent ejaculation. This probably never happened, but the spot is not a myth. It's your perineum, located between testicles and anus, and its contractions are what propel the ejaculate forward. By applying manual pressure with two fingers to this spot, you can delay or prevent the ejaculation.

When you do Kegel exercises, this is the spot you're strengthening. Sure, it feels weird; but remember, no one can see you practicing. After a few years of practicing your Kegel contractions in the car, you may be able to delay ejaculation the way you take a phone call in that same car: hands free.

BETTER PHYSICAL PERFORMANCE

Sexual performance is both a physical and a mental game. We've already talked about some of the psychological factors that can interfere with sexual performance, but when it comes to the physical aspect, it's all about making sure that the blood is gonna flow where you want the blood to flow. And as we discussed in the last chapter, the chemical that controls that is a molecule called nitric oxide.

Nitric oxide affects blood flow to your whole body, including your genitals, by regulating the restriction or dilation of capillaries. More nitric oxide equals more dilation, equals more blood flow. For dinner we talked about eating pro-sex foods that contained nitric-oxide-boosting qualities, and this is why. It's basically natural, full-body Viagra (which itself actually works by capitalizing on the local release of nitric oxide during sexual pleasure and enhancing the effects).

Based on the research, one could argue that nitric oxide is *the key component* to your sexual stamina, sexual pleasure, and health. More blood flow to the erectile tissue (penis, clitoris) equals more surface area available for pleasure. It's a pretty straightforward equation. The key is to find and take advantage of ways to increase your nitric oxide intake. Besides eating enriched foods, fresh air and sunlight have been shown to increase nitric oxide. Even laughing or watching funny movies can increase it. Interestingly, watching stressful or scary movies caused a restriction in blood flow, proving that if you're in it for the sex, *The Conjuring* is not the way to conjure a massive boner. A comedy will always be the best option when you're ready to Netflix & Chill.

BETTER MENTAL PERFORMANCE

The brain is the most important sex organ we have. Period. If your head isn't in the game, your body is not going to be in the game either. Trust me, I've been there. So how did I get out of my funk? Compassion, both from myself and from my lover. If you see some-one you love being really hard on themselves for making a mistake, like missing a shot in a basketball game, forgetting a line in a play, or playing a note off-key, what is your response? To make them feel worse about themselves, tell them how bad they suck? Or is it to have compassion, and shrug it off? I can tell you which one yields a better result! Sex is no different than any other performance.

If you have an unsatisfactory sexual performance, then treat yourself or your lover the same way you would treat someone in a sport. Have a laugh about it, smile, and don't make it a big deal. If you remove the punishment for failure, you will remove the fear of failure. If you remove the fear of failure, you remove the activation of the parts of the brain you don't want to be activated.

The other way to take the pressure off is to expand the definition of what constitutes successful sex. Starting sex with satisfying oral sex, or even a sensual massage, ensures that the experience will be pleasurable beyond the simple act of intercourse. In short, it takes the pressure off the things that are hardest to control—namely erec-tions and vaginal wetness.

Last, just as with any sport, the key is to be in the moment. When I coach a fighter, like the great Cody Garbrandt, on the mental as-pects of a great performance, I tell him to be in the moment. Feel the canvas beneath his feet, the energy of the crowd, and don't think about anything in the past or future. Just be there in the big now. It's the same with a lover. Focus on the smells, the sounds, the feel-ing of it all. Don't think about what is going to happen in five min-utes or what happened five minutes ago. Just be there. That's all you gotta do.

Prescription

More sex, better sex. That is both the prescription and the goal. Simple enough, right? Hopefully what we've just spent the last few pages talking about will help you own the bedroom on your journey to own the day. To help get you over the hump, here are a few other things you can do.

OPEN UP AND TRY ONE NEW THING

If you have a regular sexual partner, the first intercourse you need to focus on is with your mouth. You gotta talk. Create a space where you can discuss openly anything that is on your mind. Your fantasies, your boundaries, your motivation, everything. Then mutually make a decision to help each other get better.

Experiment, push the boundaries, gently—or not. Get out of your comfort zone, but always be ready for feedback. Great lovers aren't born; they are made out of good listeners. Besides, there is nothing you can implement from this chapter without the consent of your partner, so talk about it. Talk about what you read, talk about the studies; maybe they can read the chapter themselves. Then every time you talk, make a plan to try something new. Could be something little, could be something big. When it's done, communicate how it went, how it felt. This can become a really exciting part of your sex life and certainly lead to more, better sex.

TAKE PORNOGRAPHY FASTS

The first time I took an intentional pornography fast was at age thirty-four. That meant I'd had pretty much twenty straight years of occasional porn, with a few weeks here or there when I accidentally lost access. Not any different from most guys I know. The reason I took the fast was unrelated to anything having to do with sexual optimization, however; it was part of a spiritual practice.

The task was to go twenty-one days without thinking a sexual thought. No fantasies, no masturbation, no sexual contact, nothing.

I wasn't even supposed to dream about sex, but on the eighteenth day, my unconscious mind disagreed with me. I had a wet dream. A grown man, having a wet dream—I just started laughing at myself in the morning. In any case, on day twenty-two, when Whitney picked me up from the airport, I was enraptured. Our connection crackled with electricity. Every piece of her skin was tantalizing, every smell intoxicating, and the touch? Forget about it. When we made it to the hotel room (barely), it was one of the best sexual experiences of either of our lives. We still think about that day now, *years* later.

So based on that experience, I'll regularly fast from all sexual images and thoughts. Sometimes just for a few days, sometimes a week. Just as fasting from sugary foods helps bring out the sweetness of all food, fasting from overly indulgent sexual imagery helps bring the excitement back to all sexuality. It is the ultimate weapon against hedonic tolerance, and I highly recommend it. My only advice is to make sure that you set a goal that you can keep. Be realistic and stick to it. Start with one day if you have to. Start with six hours if twenty-four feels like an eternity. Build upon your successes rather than complain about your failures. And remember, the fast is going to just make the feast all that much better.

■ EVERY DAY FOR A WEEK CHALLENGE

Here is something simple that puts it all together: have sex every day for a week, each day trying something new. You are going to fast from all other forms of pornography, and just focus on your partner. If you run out of ideas, read a good book on sex, or listen to a sex podcast. See what happens, and tell your friends. We aren't gonna make this world a sexier place all by ourselves. If we want more, better sex, we need to include *more* people and help them be better too.

Now Do It

When I was thinking about what holds people back from having better sex more often, one word kept rising to the surface: ego.

The biggest obstacle to improving your sex life is the ego. Think about it. When we're single, the reason we don't talk to more potential mates is that we are afraid of rejection. Or sometimes we choose the wrong mate because of our ego. We choose people we are not compatible with because their status or attractiveness will make us feel better about who we are, and maybe make others think better of us too.

In relationships, we don't ask our partners what they like, because even the idea that we aren't already exactly what they want is too much for our fragile ego to handle. The ego leads us to believe, sometimes consciously and sometimes not, that we were born as the kings and queens of all sexual performance. Of course, this only leads to all of us walking around terrified of *not* performing. We are afraid of how we look, or smell, or taste because the ego has wild expectations. We might not even admit to ourselves that we are not having as much sex as we should because the ego doesn't want to admit our sex life needs some help. We might lie to ourselves about our addiction to pornography; we might be seeking high-risk, low-yield sex to unhealthily fulfill an emotional need. All things the ego will brush over, bury, or rationalize away.

The truth is this: the ego likes to hold us to an unrealistic standard of perfection. It is always thinking about what happened in the past, or will happen in the future. Well, guess what? Sex isn't perfect! Not our genitals, not our partners, not us, and not the act. Sex is sweaty, messy, constantly changing, and happens only in the now. It's different every time, and that very uniqueness is the beauty of the act itself.

Tell your ego to back off. Tell it that sex is not who you are, it's just what you do. So relax, take the pressure off, and get back to having fun. Open up all your sensations and perceptions. Don't rush anything. Communicate, broaden your scope of sexuality, and make a promise to yourself that no matter what happens, you won't think less of yourself, or your partner. It might be a hard promise to keep, but if you do, I promise it will keep you hard. It just takes practice. The kind of practice that even Allen Iverson wouldn't complain about.

THREE POINTERS

+ The tongue is the most important sex organ on the body. Not because you lick with it, but because you communicate with it. Let down your ego. Talk to your partner about your likes, dislikes, and fantasies. Laugh if something you didn't expect happens. Don't take it too seriously. Your sex does not define you.
+ If you enjoy your sex, you are going to have more of it. The more sex you have, the healthier you will be. Limit your indulgence in pornography, explore power exchange, be adventurous, and level up your sex game by mastering the squeeze.
+ Ensure you are creating favorable sex conditions by supporting hormone balance, and managing nitric oxide. Remember that sex begins with attraction, and attraction begins with the nose, so be careful with masking your natural smells and pheromones.

14

TURN OFF, TUNE IN

The cell phone has become the adult's transitional object, replacing the toddler's teddy bear for comfort and a sense of belonging.

—MARGARET HEFFERNAN

You have to unplug to recharge. This is going to sound easy—but it might be harder than you think. Your phone has become an extension of you, so for some of you, doing this is going to feel like cutting off your own hand. I don't care. It has to be done. Then you can download your thoughts onto the pages of a journal, and really unwind before heading to sleep. This is the opportunity to give a gift to your mind, body, and spirit—the chance to take a deep breath and . . . relax.

Getting Owned

What's the longest stretch you can remember going without your phone? And I don't mean without phone *service*, I mean without the physical object. Without that little glowing rectangular box of magic and infinite wisdom. I'll bet the answer isn't something you're proud of.

Don't worry: you're not alone. Everywhere I go, I see people superglued to their devices. I see moms on their phones while their kids are screaming at each other. I see people on phones at concerts, the theater, even the movies (FYI, there's a MASSIVE screen right in front of you, put down the tiny one). I see people on dates who are more interested in the screen than in the human sitting across from them. In the bathroom at the airport or the bar, I see guys with a tighter grip and a deeper focus on their phone than on their shaft, unaware of the piss splashing off the urinal and onto their shoes. I am a very busy person, but I have neither sent nor received an email in my life that couldn't wait for thirty seconds and a hearty shake.

When these devices went from something that makes life more convenient to something we need to use even while relieving ourselves, I don't know. But whenever the shift happened, it happened completely. We are now a different species because of our devices. We are slaves to them. They own more of our attention than nearly everything else in our lives. Studies show that most of us check out phones between fifty and seventy-five times a day. Other than breathe and blink, I don't do anything that many times in one day.

Our phones have invaded our psyches. Watching the power display on our screen drop into the red produces something called "low battery anxiety." People who are afraid—literally *afraid*—to be without their phones have been diagnosed with "nomophobia." A recent study showed a correlation between self-described addictive phone and internet use and anxiety + depression scores. These are real things. Joe Rogan calls it "the spell of the glass." We've become enchanted, bewitched, seduced by the pull of the screen.

Even if it all seems somewhat shocking, in one way, it makes complete sense. We are walking around with the most advanced, most sophisticated, best-designed Pez dispensers in human history. That's right: you have in your pocket a device designed to release your brain's favorite chemical candy—dopamine. Your brain can't get enough of this stuff, and your phone is right there to give it to you. Dopamine, or the "reward chemical," is released not only when we receive communication from a friend or social validation, but also simply from the act of self-disclosure. A recent study showed that self-disclosure—talking about yourself or posting about yourself on social media—releases dopamine powerful enough to override even financial incentives. In other words, there are actually people out there who, given a choice between banking a stack of cold, hard cash and posting a selfie of cold blue steel, would really have to think about it first.

It would be all well and good if the phone was just pumping you full of dopamine all day, but as all of us know, the phone has its own cost, ranging from the real to the metaphysical. Phones are stopping us from feeling that full range of emotions that makes us human and helps us to know ourselves, because they take us out of those moments and thrust us into the whirl of information.

And if that weren't enough, they're also giving us heaping helpings of dopamine's evil twin: cortisol, the stress hormone. Check your email right now, and you'll feel it. That knot in your stomach? The twitch in your back? The sudden hit of anxiety about that deadline that's around the corner? You know how it feels. Your face scrunches up, your breath shortens, and before you know it, you are pulled into the thick of work—even if you're thousands of miles from your office. The data on this is, at this point, irrefutable: the longer one spends on email in an hour, the higher stress levels are. To be fair, stress *has* a purpose. Along with its cousins adrenaline and norepinephrine, cortisol makes you more equipped to handle a temporary challenging situation. But should we really let ourselves count email on that side of the ledger? Even if there isn't a stressful email waiting, the act of checking can increase stress. And that's what you have instant access to when you have your phone nearby. You have a ticking stress bomb in your pocket that is quite literally designed to create the opposite conditions for sleep, which is where we are headed ultimately in our day.

I've started to think about phones the way that bad guys in far-away places must think of drones: they are always lurking there, the dull background hum of our lives, hovering everywhere we go, ready to strike. We can't ever escape them; they have eyes on us wherever we go. We pay a huge cost in never turning the phone off—and the cost is that we never turn our brains off, at least not fully, in the way they were designed to be. A lot of us start the day and end the day with a screen in our face—blasting us with information, entertainment, people, problems, and all of life's complexities.

As hard as it is to imagine, it wasn't always this way. I remember when the phone was used for a simple purpose: to connect two people so they could hear the sound of each other's voices. I didn't have a damn library in my pocket, so the actual library was interesting. I wasn't able to read the news constantly, so I enjoyed talking to people who read the paper. I remember having to actually fill those moments of boredom or aloneness with my own creativity. But yeah, I had to print out maps to go places. You could try and meet up with a friend somewhere and never find her. You could actually get lost. The phone, and the connectivity it enables, is both a luxurious and futuristic convenience as well as an annoying and addictive leash. It's not just phones either. It's televisions, laptops, wearable devices, iPads. In the war for our time and attention, these devices have all established their beachheads and created so much static in our lives that many of us find it impossible to separate the signal from the noise.

So what do we do? I know it's much easier to say "Go ahead and turn off those devices, killer" than it is to actually do that. But we have to try, which is why we're going to start small, with the evenings. We're going to treat these times, and the people with whom you share them, as a special kingdom, and the devices to which you have been tethered until now will be the barbarians at the gates.

It will seem deceptively simple at first—"Yeah, Aubrey, I get it. Off switch. Awesome. Roger that"—but I would bet some decent money that when you start this process, you'll go through stages of withdrawal. I'm not saying you'll get the shakes and tremors, but I think you'll be surprised with how intense the pull of these devices is. Regardless, I know you can defeat them, if you want to. We're here to show you that it's worth it.

Owning It

I am a realist: asking too much is akin to asking nothing at all. So go for it. Revel in that last spell of the glass. Soak in that last hit of dopamine as you refresh your Facebook feed, post your last Insta story, and soak in the last drip of cortisol as you check your email—because you are now about to unplug. The drawbridge is going up!

It's nighttime, and it's time to turn it all off. Power down the laptop. Go ahead, put your phone on airplane mode, DND, or simply shut it off. If you want to keep your phone on, but minimize the chance of getting distracted, look into apps like Inbox Pause from Boomerang. This will ensure you don't have any late-night stress wormholes to get dragged into. However you do it, this is important. We need to clear the static from your mental channels and reduce your anxiety load. You have a big day tomorrow. You have to own it. You can do it. It's a phone; your life doesn't depend on your next email, and if you think it does, then I'd recommend you put this book down and tend to whatever that email says. If that email didn't help (spoiler alert: it won't) then use your mental override practice, or just think how exciting it will be to check in with all your social friends and work puzzles in the morning. Either way, it's gotta be done. Then you can move on to the stuff you should be doing to wind down before sleep.

But I get it: you're saying to yourself, "But, Aubrey, I've turned it off. And all I can do now is think. Sit here and think about this and that. And I want to write stuff down, do stuff. Because I want to be a baller, like Gary Vee!" I hear you. But part of making sure you own each day is giving your brain time to recharge its batteries. We extend the same courtesy to our devices, don't we? We plug them in so they can get full again. Your brain needs the same thing.

I know that the first few evenings you do this will feel funny. It will feel so automatic to reach for your phone and cycle through news or Facebook or Instagram. It'll feel unfamiliar to just . . . sit. So let me offer some suggestions for what you can do to fill that time and charge your batteries.

Journaling

I try to journal every night. My process has two parts, both of which should fit on a single page. I start by writing down my mission and three main objectives for the following day, before then carrying on to more cathartic or freestyle journaling. Your mission could be as simple as "Own the Day" or "Make everyone around me happier." Whatever it is, writing it down gets it out of the hamster wheel of your mind and makes it real. It is a reinforcement of the overarching objective of your life. Writing things down also reduces the instinct to go over that thought again and again in your head, making it easier for you to relax. Knowing that you won't forget anything, because it's written down right there for you, also smoothes your transition into sleepy time and makes waking up to own the day a pleasure instead of a panic.

THE OBJECTIVE LAW OF THREE

Like a lot of young, ambitious, entrepreneurially minded founders and CEOs, I can very easily find myself with a Google calendar that has no white space in it for days at a time. My instinct with each success is to seek out another one; with each failure, to try again twice as hard. If I'm not careful, I can end up with more balls in the air than a troupe of all-male acrobats. The problem with that isn't the stress of it all—though stress is definitely an issue—it's that I can only ever do three things well at a time. This fundamentally violates one of my core principles: do it well, or not at all.

Yet here we are. To help myself stay truer to that principle, I started a practice of limiting myself to listing three objectives for the following day, laid out right below my mission at the top of the journal page. Ideally, these objectives are mission related, but even if they're not, even if they include minor tasks like "Finish errands for the party," thinking of them as sub-missions or mini-missions will help imbue them with the significance they need for you to get your hustle on and get them done.

Why three? I detest all forms of numerology, but three really is the magic number when it comes to our ability to focus, whether we're operating at a micro level or a macro level. Research on working memory, for example, pegs the sweet spot for the number of things we can hold at once in our conscious at three or four. And since we're not trying to stretch the elastic limits of your brain as you wind down toward bed, three is square in the center of the bull's-eye. It's why at the end of each chapter we have limited our pointers to three, and why fellow health and fitness CEO Josh Bezoni abides by the law of three in his own life, only allowing himself to focus on three things at the same time. Maybe that's why he grew his company to twice the gross sales of Onnit in half the time! He was doing less, not more. The question isn't whether he could handle four or five objectives. Of course he could. The question is, at what point do you start sacrificing your greatness for goodness?

▩ CATHARTIC WRITING

If you looked back at my journals, you would think that I was a very troubled individual. The reason is a normal one, though: I journal the most when I'm going through something difficult. I think that would be true for most people who journal regularly. The first instinct of most people who are surfing through life on a rainbow of unwavering love is to share their joy with the world, not the blank pages of their journal.

The beauty of writing, especially in a place meant only to be read and reviewed by you, is that it allows you to organize your thoughts and make sense out of the nonsensical. In this sense, journaling has allowed for pure, unfettered catharsis that has also allowed me to indulge myself in the creation of a lasting monument to my emotional pain. Not only does this give me a running tally of all the things—both external and internal—that I have overcome on my path toward success, but just as writing down my mission gets it out of my head and makes it real, writing down my pain gets it out of my head and confines it to the page, which makes it much more manageable. It's like a Ghostbuster trapping a ghost in that little box and storing it in the warehouse. Research backs up this sentiment: people who engage in expressive writing report feeling happier and less negative than they felt before writing. Other depressive symptoms like rumination and anxiety tend to drop after writing about emotional upheavals, as well.

Channel your inner poet, and let your emotions fly. They've used up enough of your mental batteries already as it is!

Caveat: Sacred Ground

In ancient times, trespassing on sacred ground was punishable by death. I think that's a little harsh for putting your boots on a piece of dirt, but when it comes to journals, I kinda like the old rules. Reading someone else's journal is a violation of the deepest intimacy. It is a psychological rape. It is not only a betrayal of the past but also a betrayal of the future; the moment you are journaling with the worry that someone else might read it, your journal is worthless. It has fallen victim to the Heisenberg Uncertainty Principle: it's just not the same anymore. If regular invasion of privacy is a possibility in your relationship or household, I recommend using a secure password-protected file system on your computer. The best way to do this is to create a separate email address on Gmail, and use the Google Drive feature for your journaling. Your email will not be in use, and so the likelihood of it being hacked is almost zero; plus even if someone did, they wouldn't know whose journal it was.

Enjoy "Cuddle Time"

Cuddle is the time before bed that should be the most stress-free of your entire day, where you spend time with people you care about most, even if that's just yourself. You've owned the day, you've set out your mission and objectives for the following day, and now let's let that stress and cortisol hit the floor. You're off duty. Act like it. If you have a special someone in your life, now is the time to get close to them and to do stuff together—*sans phones*. If you don't, it's time to get to know and to treat yourself better. The Golden Rule isn't just for other people—after all, you count too!

▓ (NONVIDEO) GAMING

Let's say you have a competitive nature and need a little more stimulation. Go old-school and pull the board games and card games out of the closet. They turn your brain to something challenging, but in the context of social interaction with real human beings instead of stressful digital combat that defines the blue-light-dominated phone and computer screens we cling to. I love chess and Monopoly when I want to ignite my strategic fire. When I just want to laugh, I whip out Cards Against Humanity. And when I want to let my nerd flag fly with my nerd brethren from the multiverse, it's Magic: The Gathering all the way. Planeswalkers for life, dawg!

▓ THE TUBE

A study by Australian researchers showed that every hour of watching television after age twenty-five was associated with a twenty-two-minute reduction in life expectancy. When it comes to shows like *Westworld*, or *Girls*, or *Billions*, or *Game of Thrones*, I'll take that trade. Plus it's off the end of my life . . . and that's like really far away. Some television is too good to ignore or to pretend it's not culture. Like everything, it's all about balance. So when it comes to your favorite show, cuddle up with your own Mother of Dragons or King in the North, and enjoy the fuck out of it. Just don't try to manage your anxiety or mitigate your guilt by having your laptop open, pretending to stay "productive." That defeats the whole purpose.

As for video or computer gaming, games are designed to be highly stimulating—engaging all your attention, through heightened stress and focus. Not really ideal before bed. Find another time to pwn your friends. Headshot, bitch!

▓ READING

This one isn't too complicated: reading books is one of the fastest ways to give yourself over to another world, another time, and level up your mind. It literally allows you to stand on the shoulders of the giants who came before you. We live in a world where there are near infinite books, and less and less time, so it is important to choose the right books for your mood and your mind-set.

Personally, I don't read a lot of business books because they tend to take an idea that you could cover in 5 pages and expand it into 200, with anecdotes and platitudes and truisms that I've already read a hundred times. Instead, I prefer books built on philosophical or spiritual topics, because that is the headspace I deliberately put myself in as I wind down my day. I would never abandon fiction, of course, and when I do dip my toe in the pool of history's greatest imaginations, I almost always get the most out of the classics, with one exception: the American writer Cormac McCarthy. He's probably the best writer I've ever read, including all the greats. I remember immersing myself in *The Road* and realizing, as I closed the back cover, that the entire story was a setup for one perfect paragraph on the last page. And, damn, was it was worth it.

But that's me. You might be different. Just know that there are no wrong books if you like them. The only rule you should follow is that if you start a book, and you don't like it, *do not* continue to read it just because you bought it. Life isn't the summer reading program at your local library. You don't get free passes to the water park just for finishing books, even if you hate them. The surest way to avoid having your reading time wasted is to lean on the recommendations from smart podcast guests and your own bookworm friends and mentors. Most of the best books I have read came to me through those channels; books I didn't just read cover to cover but inhaled and then sifted like I was searching for gold on the Bering Sea.

Reading's been so important to my personal growth that I take the responsibility of recommending books to people very seriously. I keep five copies of my ten to twelve favorite books in my office cabinets at all times to give to just the right person at just the right time. Giving a book that doesn't get read is a waste. Giving a book that gets read but doesn't help is even worse.

OPTIMIZE YOUR PERSONAL CARE

Brushing your teeth. Flossing. Washing your face. Stretching and rolling out your muscles. Taking a bath. Historically, for many of us, these actions have always felt like obligations, duties forced upon us by parents and doctors back when we were kids and we had no choice. And now that we're adults, *if* we do them, we do them begrudgingly and hurriedly.

What a colossal mistake. These things are not nagging chores. They are opportunities to clear out the junk, make yourself feel better, arm yourself for tomorrow, and reward yourself. Sure, there's nothing sexy about floss, but there's also nothing better than the feeling of breaking up the tight muscle fascia in your back and your legs, then giving yourself time to take that long soak in a magnesium-rich Epsom salts bath that you've been dreaming about all week. Even better, none of these things involve screens, but they can involve a partner, making them even more enjoyable.

Take my word for it: there is no better time than the period between dinner and bed for some honest-to-goodness restorative "me" time . . . or "we" time.

Caveat: What Goes on Your Body, Gets in Your Body

The skin is not made of aluminum. It is porous and designed to conduct molecules both into and out of the body. One recent study determined that laboratory skin absorption rates are generally underestimated, and that the skin contributes a good portion of contaminants that enter our body. And different parts of the skin have different absorption rates. Some of the most absorbent areas are the gums, genitals, and armpits, with rates as high as 99 percent.

So take precautions with your personal care regimen. Your teeth whitener doesn't just whiten your teeth and then you spit it out; it enters the bloodstream and tries to "whiten" your liver. The metals in your deodorant don't just change the smell of your skin; they try to "deodorize" your whole body. That petroleum-based lubricant isn't just helping your good parts slide, it's putting dead dinosaurs into your joints. The bottom line is this: if you wouldn't eat it, you shouldn't put it on or in your body.

This is especially true for the penis and vagina, which have a layer of micro-organisms that are the first line of defense, protecting your special man and lady parts. You want to do as little as possible to disrupt that balance. For women, remember that your vagina is a self-cleaning oven. Do not use anti-biotic or perfumed soaps and douches. Some studies have shown that these types of products increase your chances of infection. Instead, use all-natural products like unscented Castile soap and aloe vera–based lubricants to keep the machinery moving. And as for tampons and pads, they aren't just cotton, they also emit chemicals, like styrene, chloroethane, and chloroform. That's an average of 11,400 times that a woman who uses tampons might expose herself to toxic chemicals. Styrene, a neurotoxin, is listed by the World Health Organization as a carcinogen, and while chloroform isn't like what we see in the movies, where one sniff of a soaked rag knocks someone unconscious, it isn't exactly good for us either. What's worse, because they are listed as medical devices by the FDA, they don't have to list their ingredients. Without testing, there is no way to know what is in your tampon or pad. Bringing the natural tampon game to the next level with Apple-quality packaging is a company called Cora, and many other great natural brands like Lola can be found online.

Prescription

There are four essential steps to the restorative, wind-down period prior to sleep:

1. You gotta check out and turn off your phone and email so you can check in with yourself and the ones you love.

2. You gotta open up your journal and get your mind off the hamster wheel that creates the mental static and anxiety that prevent so many of us from owning our days.
3. You gotta enjoy the cuddle huddle: playing, watching, reading.
4. You gotta brush your damn teeth and soak your damn bones.

Here is how that looks for me:

• I'll check my social platforms to make sure all is in order, and people aren't reaching out telling me the website is broken or an unusually high percentage of people aren't telling me that I suck for some reason. All right, and also because my social media usually is really positive and it feels good.

• Then I'll check my emails, not to respond, but to star the ones I need to get to in the morning.

• Then I'll check my texts, and see who I ignored through the day, and decide if I really need to answer them. Texts are like the new email—the more you respond, the more you get back—so don't feel compelled to respond to everyone. We all need to just get over it; sometimes you aren't gonna hear back from someone, and it's not because they don't love you.

• Then I'll bust out the journal, rewrite my mission, and figure out what my three objectives are for the following day. If there is anything else on my mind, I'll write about it then and there too.

- I'll brew up a tea (Ron Teeguarden Longevity Tea, Tulsi Sweet Rose Tea, or Republic of Tea Milk Thistle). Sometimes it's a reishi mushroom latte with Four Sigmatic reishi and Onnit vanilla emulsified MCT oil (or another emulsified MCT oil).

- Then generally I'll jump into something I enjoy: a TV show, a game, or something else fun that is not also too high-energy.

- After that I'll handle my personal care, shower, and as I wait for the sleepies to come I'll start reading in orange light, controlled by color bulbs, Philips Hue, or in a pinch the nerdiest biohack of all, blue-light-blocking glasses. When the sleepies hit, out go the lights.

Now Do It

I've suffered off and on from anxiety most of my life. It feels like there is one of those Tesla electricity balls in my chest, and I can't relax. I don't do my best work under these conditions. And not surprisingly, this happens the most when I fail to turn off the day. Or when I lose sight of my objectives. Or if I haven't purged all the emotional static on the pages of my journal.

But when I do all those things and still struggle, generally it just comes down to having a little more faith. In my life, I have always overcome the challenges that were presented to me. If you're still here reading this, that means you have too. In hindsight, I can honestly say that I am grateful for every one of my failures and mishaps. I learned something valuable from all of them. I became stronger, wiser, better, because of them in some way.

With hindsight, I am batting 100 percent. But sometimes I lack the foresight to see what hindsight was going to tell me. If everything that happens to me is something I am grateful for, why am I so anxious about the future? I've always dealt with the problems that I've needed to deal with, I've always come out better, yet I lack the foresight to have the same perspective as my hindsight. It's just not having faith. It's thinking that this next disaster will be different. Guess what, it's probably not going to be different. Whatever comes, you can deal with it. You *will* deal with it. Fight that battle if it comes.

Until then, do not play war games in your mind and in your heart every night. Find a strategy that works for you and put your stress away, at least for a few hours. This might sound like a very first-world problem I'm harping on, if you're one of those people who easily gets tired of successful people talking about their struggles and failures, but the reality is that many cultures have strategies for this very problem. In Guatemala, children are given "worry dolls" that they tell all their concerns to before bed. As keepers of their worries, the dolls act as the stress release, and the child can drift into a peaceful sleep. Native American culture uses the dreamcatcher to catch any negative energy or spirits, so that the sleeper can rest easy.

But most important, be grateful that life is the kind of chef that doesn't pander to our sweet tooth. It serves up bitter and salty meals that keep us hale and hearty, and every once in a while it gives us the chocolate cake. You aren't ever going to be able to fully control what's on tomorrow's menu, but everything life has served you so far has made you the person you are today. Own that thought, and tell your stress that it can go fuck itself.

THREE POINTERS

- ✦ If you don't turn off, you won't ever properly turn on. The stress of carrying the weight of the day into the night will compound over time and slow you down. Let your phone go. It will be there waiting for you in the morning, I promise.
- ✦ One of the most effective ways to deal with stress is to pick up a pen or open a Google doc and start journaling. First you want to make sure you set your mission and objective for the following day. Then you want to purge anything you no longer want to carry, and memorialize those things you don't want to forget but also don't want to burden your psyche with.
- ✦ The last hour before bed is time to really wind down and cuddle with yourself or someone you love. It's the time for reading, a relaxing game, or maybe even your favorite show. Give your body some love with the personal care it needs, and get ready to sleep your face off.

15

SLEEP

Sleep turns the dreams about your health into a reality.

—AUBREY MARCUS

We have arrived at the bridge that takes us from today to tomorrow. How we cross it determines whether one good day will lead to another, and another. Finish your day strong, my friend. Finish it right. And go the fuck to sleep. Of course, it's not so simple. Sleeping well and sleeping right take work, too—it's not just lying down and letting it happen. But you need to do it. You own your sleep, and you own your day.

Getting Owned

She was one of the most powerful women in the world. She graced the covers of magazines and had powerful people on her speed dial. She had a Brentwood mansion and was building a media empire— and that was on top of a successful life she'd already built involved in politics and writing bestselling books. She worked so hard, she had a team of assistants on both coasts who could barely keep up with her. She was a mover and shaker, a rock star whose every decision was studied and written about. Successful by every metric we use to measure success.

But there came a moment when none of it mattered. Collapsed on the floor, her cheek cracked open, lying in a pool of her own blood, Arianna Huffington had fallen from exhaustion, hitting her face on her desk on the way down. She had pushed herself beyond what was reasonable; pulled one too many late nights; become addicted to her phone, her website, her lifestyle, and the pull and thrill of success. She had become consumed by it all—and it had all come crashing down, literally. It was this moment that Arianna Huffington points to as the one where it all became clear for her.

Huffington's doctors told her she was exhausted. Depleted to the marrow of her bones. The famous nineteenth-century German philosopher Arthur Schopenhauer once said, "Sleep is the interest we have to pay on the capital which is called in at death. The higher the interest rate and the more regularly it is paid, the further the date of redemption is postponed." Arianna Huffington was months behind on her payments, and she was looking at a fatal foreclosure if she didn't get caught up.

She isn't the only one. We are sleeping less than we ever have.

Over 60 percent of people in the United States report sleep difficulties, more than ever before. It is an epidemic, one that is largely self-inflicted. After all, how many of us just assume, when faced with a choice in our schedule, that sleep's got to be the first thing to go? "I'm just too busy," we say. Or "I'll sleep when I'm dead." Or "But Bill Clinton never slept." Some people actually feel real *guilt* for sleeping. As much of a champion as I am of personal accountability, I can't put the blame for how perversely we've been guilted into a sleepless schedule squarely at our own feet.

"The Man" shares a good deal of the blame. With the advent of the industrial revolution it became advantageous to get people to work early, and keep them there as long as possible. We still do this today: Why do you think Google has gyms and cafeterias and foosball tables all over their campus? To keep Googlers at the office! Since Western industrialized society adopted this approach to work, we have increasingly seen a good night's sleep or sleeping late in the morning as a sign of laziness or sloth (one of the cutest deadly sins) or, worse, a lack of ambition. If we get tired during the day, instead of showing our soft underbelly and sleeping, we drink more coffee or, worse, we take an Adderall (that is, the wrong kind of supplement).

The other party that shares some blame here is the media—especially the media who cover the science of this stuff. How many times have you heard that you need to get eight hours of uninterrupted sleep? It's repeated so often it has become a platitude, even though it's essentially dangerous advice—because for most of us eight hours of uninterrupted sleep is a fantasy, like reverse orgy porn (Google it). After the media starts listing all the bad things that happen if you don't get that eight hours of unbroken bliss, when you have to wake up in five or six hours, sheer panic sets in. Panic and fear are not conducive to sleep of any variety. This chapter is designed to be the antidote to that panic and fear, providing a different perspective from which to view sleep.

That said, if you're one of those slumbering unicorns who can get that eight hours, halle-fuckin-lujah to you. The strategies we're about to cover are going to give you the best chance to sleep like a stone at night. If you already are a champion sleeper, then the only other thing I want you to take away from this chapter is this: do not feel an ounce of guilt for getting some shut-eye. You need your rest. Quality sleep is a key ingredient to your health. It helps combat obesity; it improves the immune system; it's vital for optimal mental function and improves all markers of physical performance. Don't let anyone—not your boss, not your spouse, not your inner critic— make you feel bad for getting sleep. Because try as you might—and oh, you might—you can't outsmart sleep. You have flirted with the idea that you'll sleep when you are dead, but if you truly believe that, then don't be surprised when death swipes right, puts on roller skates, and cruises on over to your crib, because death is DTF.

Owning It

Thankfully, more and more prominent and successful people are talking about the importance of sleep. Matthew McConaughey has publicly talked about needing 8.5 hours per day. Heidi Klum gets *ten hours* every night. And that's with two kids. That is some serious beauty sleep. LeBron James and Roger Federer both have said they sleep twelve hours per night—half the day. Bill Gates has talked about his need for a solid seven hours of sack time per night. He's jealous, he says, of short sleepers, people who can do with less. But for him, it is crucial to get his sleep. Jeff Bezos, the founder of a multi-multibillion-dollar online empire, is right there with him: "I just feel so much better all day long if I've had eight hours."

Here's the deal I can make with you: if you take your sleep seriously, you will get more done with less stress. For some, it sounds too good to be true—like golden eggs from a goose—but the productivity and lifestyle benefits of sleep have all been very well researched and well documented. It's a "life hack" that's not a hack, just a rule of the operating system. Outside nutrition, it's the single most important ingredient to owning the day—and you need to pay attention to how to do it well.

Don't Be a Hero, Cycle Your Sleep

The topic of sleep is very personal to me. I'm a poor natural sleeper, and the busier I got as the CEO of Onnit, the more sleep became a stressor in my life. Why couldn't I just sleep like everybody else? It felt like something was wrong with me. I could not afford to have humanity's primary natural stress reliever become an additional source of stress in my life. It took some time, but finally the literature and the counsel of my peers made me realize that we're all very different when it comes to sleep. Some of us are light sleepers; some heavy. Some can take a long time to get into sleep; some can sleep at the drop of a hat.

My fiancée, Whitney Miller, was Miss United States and a sponsored surfer. She is currently a blue belt in jujitsu and the host of Glory Kickboxing. But her biggest talent has nothing to do with any of that: it's sleep. The time between when she hits the pillow and when she enters sleep is nothing short of a superpower. I remember one time I told her I was going to count how long it took her to go to sleep. I said "Ready . . . *Go!*" and she giggled and then closed her eyes. At 11 seconds in my silent count she cracked up and started laughing out loud. "It's too much pressure!" she said. I just smiled and kept counting. She closed her eyes again, and at 27 seconds, 16 seconds after she burst out laughing, I felt her body start twitching—the telltale sign of the nervous system entering shutdown. When I told her in the morning, even she was surprised. I've never been more jealous of anyone's abilities in my life!

We're not all Whitneys. But we don't have to be. The important thing is to learn what you are. Study your body. Track your timing. Take notes. "Sleep homework" might be the most important work you ever do. And if you do it right, one of the first lessons you will learn is that to do sleep well does not mean to do it all at once.

Somewhere along the line, despite anthropological research to the contrary, we got this idea in our heads that proper sleep is a monolith that you do straight through, uninterrupted. And then, because it feels so impossible to so many of us, it immediately becomes yet another thing to put on the daily checklist, to feel guilty about not doing right. Well, fuck that! Sleep should be relaxing. The last thing any of us need is the exact kind of pressure that creates unrealistic expectations and keeps us up at night stressing about why we're still awake.

The reality is, there are four phases to sleep: awake and resting; light sleep; deep sleep; and REM sleep. And while each of these phases is helpful, the two most important are deep sleep and REM sleep. In deep sleep, you release all the hormones to repair and rebuild your body. In REM sleep, you are basically rebooting the mental hard drive. A typical sleep cycle lasts ninety minutes and transitions from awake and resting, to light sleep, to deep sleep, finally ending in REM. After REM, it is common to wake up, though you may not remember it before you enter your next cycle. They key is, if you *do* wake up, not to stress. Instead, take a page from the books of other cultures, both historically and currently, who have no problem sleeping multiple times a day (something called polyphasic sleep).

Currently, in cultures like Spain and Egypt, the *siesta* or *ta'assila* is an example of a type of polyphasic sleep in which people sleep about five or six hours per night, and up to ninety minutes (one sleep cycle) in the afternoon. The !Kung of Botswana and the Efe of Zaire have a more fluid sleep pattern, basically sleeping any damn time they feel like it. In other tribal communities, our ancestors would sleep after dusk for three hours, wake for a few hours, perhaps smoke some tobacco or drink some tea, maybe have sex, and sleep again for a few hours before dawn.

This was due, in no small part, to the fact that our ancestors never conceived of trying to outsmart the phases of sleep; instead they rolled with them as a natural part of being human. Expecting eight hours of uninterrupted sleep out of themselves every night would have been borderline ridiculous, just as it is to expect it out of ourselves. Nick Littlehales and his aptly named book *Sleep* have been a major part of coming to that realization and expanding my views on sleep cycles and polyphasic sleep.

You shouldn't, for example, count how many hours of sleep you get in a night, but rather how many ninety-minute sleep cycles you get in a week (thirty-five cycles should be your target). It is a strategy Littlehales has used for some of Great Britain's best and busiest athletes and performers, including the legendary football club Manchester United and the UK cycling team.

If thirty-five sleep cycles per week is the goal, that means the typical day should theoretically include four or five sleep cycles. Fortunately, they don't all have to come at night. In the siesta model, our Spanish and Egyptian friends sleep three or four cycles at night, and one cycle in the afternoon. In Littlehales's model, sleep is even more fluid. A thirty-minute nap like the one we talked about in chapter 9, which is only one-third of a full cycle, still counts as one point toward your sleep-cycle goal. It's not extra or a bonus, it's part of your sleep regimen. So if you sleep six hours at night, you get four points. If you take a thirty-minute power nap that day, you get an additional point, bringing you to five. Do that every day of the week and you have met your thirty-five-point goal. If you get 7.5 hours of sleep one night, that's five points right there. You can put one in the bank for later with another nap, or just power through the day. Make sense?

For many of you, a schedule with sleep spread evenly and regularly across the day might not be possible. And that's okay. The point is to recognize that cycles—and not total hours—might be the way to get your body the rest you need. Even if you have to work a full day, you can find creative ways to squeeze in the sleep. If you have a night when you don't sleep much, just do the math and adjust the points. It's something we intrinsically understand when we say "catch up on sleep." Catching up is a real thing. The point of the cycles model is to take the pressure off a single day and spread it over something much more manageable—a week.

Pro Tip—Track Your Sleep

There are a lot of sleep trackers through your smartphone that track your movement during the night. But honestly, they aren't all that accurate. If you are sleeping with a partner or a dog, the movement trackers have no way of distinguishing you from the other mammals in the room. They also have limited ability to track the difference between the cycles.

So I stepped up my game and purchased the sleekest tracker on the market, the Oura ring. It slips over your finger and processes all the biometrics needed to truly give you an accurate snapshot of your sleep. It will show you how much time you were awake, in light sleep, in deep sleep, and in REM. From there you can really understand your sleep quality. What were the conditions that led to good sleep or what Littlehales would call junk sleep? Junk sleep is like junk food—it will do the trick when you're hungry, but it isn't as healthy for you as real sleep. I started noticing correlations between sleep and caffeine, room temperature, even time of last meal. It gave me the data that allowed me to really understand what I needed to do to improve my sleep, and when I needed to grab an extra nap or two.

The problem with the Oura is that some nights, you might think you got a pretty decent sleep, but the readings give you a poor score. Instead of feeling good, you mindfuck yourself into thinking that you are tired or exhausted. So it is key to remember that how you feel matters just as much as what the reading says. Master the data, don't let the data master you.

Get Your Shit Together

This is where the personal accountability part of my personality kicks back in. I cannot tell you the number of times I have worked with someone on their sleep—it didn't matter if they were an elite athlete or a regular Joe—and asked them what their sleeping environment looked like, only to find out it resembled a Tokyo robot disco more than an actual bedroom. Phones were on the nightstand within arm's reach, buzzers and dings and push notifications all turned on. Bright red and blue lights from cable boxes and electronics chargers illuminated the floor. Streetlights and sunlight poured through flimsy curtains. There were cars and noise and dogs barking. The heat was cranked to infinity . . . and beyond! And they wondered why they hadn't had a decent night's sleep in god knows how long.

Fortunately, getting your shit together in the bedroom for proper sleep is not rocket science. It's a simple matter of adding a few key elements and removing others. All of them, entirely within your control. No excuses.

▦ WIND DOWN THE TEMPERATURE

When you don't have central heat in your home, it gets cold at night. Most of our evolution was spent without central heat. So we got used to sleeping when it was cold. Still to this day, we sleep best when it is a bit colder than usual at night. Having a programmable thermostat like Nest is perfect to replicate that natural progression from warm to cool and back again. I tend to sleep from about 12:30 to 8:00 a.m., and my temperature schedule goes like this:

7:30 am

9:00 pm

Figure out whatever works for you, but go ahead and drop the temperature around the time you're going to sleep. Your body will thank you.

■ ELIMINATE BLUE LIGHTS

In chapter 1 we talked about using blue light to help you wake up and recalibrate your circadian rhythms. If blue-spectrum light exposure is good for waking, it only makes sense that you should limit and then eliminate it when you're getting ready for bed. By 10 p.m., all blue light should be out. Blue light counteracts the natural release of melatonin, the darkness signal in the brain that makes us sleepy, which is why exposure to screens is critical to regulating sleeping and waking.

The brilliant stand-up comic and filmmaker Mike Birbiglia has a great way of thinking about it. His first film, *Sleepwalk with Me*, is all about his REM-sleep disorder and how he had nearly died from his horrible sleepwalking habits. He says, "Think of sleep not as something that you crash into, but that you ease into. If your body is like a car, you want to park it, not crash it."

Everything you did in the wind-down phase, and every choice you make here, is about throttling down your engines so you can coast smoothly into the garage of your sleep.

Remember: sleep isn't binary. It's not an off switch. It's a dimmer.

POWER DOWN THE GRID

We are energetic beings. This isn't woo-woo hippie-dippie nonsense; this is science. We project an electromagnetic field, just like our electronics. Studies have indicated a correlation between sleep disturbances and exposure to EMF frequencies, so do your best to keep any high-powered devices away from your sleeping area. This includes, most important, your smartphone.

This has a couple other advantages for your sleep. First, you won't be thinking about the email you might miss or the text message you've been waiting for if the phone isn't in the room. Out of sight, out of mind. Second, you won't be tempted to blast yourself with blue light if you can't sleep. Trust me on that one, I've been there. Tossing and turning, I've counted every last goddamned sheep in Scotland and then fired up my phone to browse all the sheep on Instagram too. Inevitably, I kept going and going down the internet blue-light rabbit hole. Hours would pass, then I'd be stressed about what time it was, and instead of counting sheep I'd start counting the minutes until I had to be up.

It wasn't until I banished electronics from the bedroom that this impulse died down, and I stopped screwing with my melatonin production.

ADD GREEN PLANTS

Air quality matters! You can add high-tech filters to your HVAC system, you can bring in a humidifier or dehumidifier (provided it doesn't make too much noise and you tape over the power light), but nothing is quite like the fresh, oxygenating power of plants. They're a simple, cheap, effective way to get better sleep.

The sleep messiah himself, Shawn Stevenson, likes English ivy, NASA's top recommended air-filtering plant, and the perennial snake plant, which is nocturnal and releases oxygen during the night rather than the day. Don't worry, you don't have to turn your bedroom into the Little Shop of Horrors, where the plants are dominating your space, to get the benefits. Just a few good plants will do.

NO-FRIEND ZONE

This is probably the hardest one for most households, including in Casa Aubrey, where I have failed to heed my own advice, but I'm gonna move forward with unabashed hypocrisy, thanks to our little Alaskan Klee Kai. The rule is that the bedroom is for sleeping and for sex only. Anyone with whom you wouldn't want to do both should be strictly *verboten* from the bedroom. If you are serious about sleep quality, this includes your best canine or feline buddy. I'm sorry, but there is only one kind of doggy style you should allow in the bedroom, and it doesn't come with whiskers. Hope you have better luck with this rule than me!

Get Yourself Together

It's not just your environment that you need to get squared away to get good sleep. You need to get yourself straight as well. We've already spent time and energy regulating your nutrition and caffeine. We've been physical. You've (hopefully) had sex. So you're nearly there. All we need now is to add in the specific, sleep-related tweaks that will bring the sandman calling.

GET SECURE

Sleep is an inherently vulnerable act. You are in the worst position to defend yourself from any potential threat. Whether it is a mosquito, a scorpion, a bear, or a deranged human being, sleep is an ambush waiting to happen. Plus, it is fairly normal for people to be a little wary of the things that go bump in the night. Even in a protected house, some instincts are just hardwired. Make a ritual out of locking your doors and setting your alarm if you have one.

If you still want to err on the side of an abundance of caution, when you actually go to bed, the most secure sleeping position is going to be lying on your side, with your dominant hand on top. In the unlikely event that you have to fend off an attack, this will give you the chance to do your best Liam Neeson impression and showcase your very particular set of skills.

SLEEP POSTURE

Not only is sleeping on your side the most secure position, it is also generally the best position for breathing. Sleeping on your back is more likely to lead to snoring and sleep apnea, and sleeping on your stomach is going to cause shallower breathing, not to mention a lot of low back issues. There are exceptions, of course, particularly for those who have structural alignment issues. Regardless of which positions you end up rotating through during the night, you'll always want something that encourages a neutral neck position, which is generally a lot less pillow than you think it is, despite what the world's finer hotels would have you believe.

As with everything else, test, try, take notes, and repeat what works.

NOSE BREATHING

Sleep apnea affects an estimated 22 million people in the United States. It's a condition in which the airway gets partially obstructed, mildly suffocating the sleeper, forcing her to wake up and readjust. It is massively disruptive to sleep cycles as well as any unlucky partner in the bed with normal hearing who has *selfishly* not grown accustomed to sleeping next to what you could easily confuse for a chain saw with a sputtering motor, about to run out of gas.

Nose breathing isn't just good for cardiovascular training, it's also your first line of defense against apnea's assault on fluid sleep. There are a couple options to assist you on the nose-breathing front: you can pursue medical intervention like balloon rhinoplasty, where they open up your nasal passages by inflating a "balloon" until, snap crackle and pop, you can breathe again; or you can start a little slower and less invasively with over-the-counter nose strips, just like the ones you see on your favorite NFL linebacker every fall Sunday. They pull open the nasal passages gently, allowing more air to pass into and out of your lungs and disengaging your face chain saw in the process.

Pro Tip: Didja Do the 'Doo?

A 2005 study showed that playing the didgeridoo, a long wind instrument native to Australia, every day for four months significantly reduced participants' sleep apnea. Playing the didge, as it is affectionately called, trains you in what is called circular breathing, which requires intense control over your breath apparatus. This appears to translate into more control during the night, when your unconscious self is in charge. In addition to sleep gains, playing the didge has also been shown to increase the number of invitations you receive to naked drum circle dance parties, which of course is why most of us want to do the 'doo.

▉ HYDRATION

Waking up and going to pee is a problem. For one, to make sure you have your faculties about you to get up and use the restroom, instead of your bed, your body releases small amounts of stress hormone that elevate your alertness just enough to bring you out of sleep. People who are sensitive to stress or who are naturally poor sleepers—*ahem*—can have trouble falling back asleep. To that end, being mindful of your fluid intake prior to sleepytime is important. I generally recommend that you stop intake of fluids a minimum of sixty minutes before bed. That is usually the least time it takes you to pass excess fluid. The exception here is if you have been drinking alcohol. Go ahead and continue drinking water right up to bedtime if that is the case. As for drinking water in the middle of the night, don't overdo it. More often than not a little bit of water will satisfy your thirst until you can drink that big ol' hydration cocktail first thing the next morning.

Prescription

Here is your down-and-dirty sleepytime checklist:

1. Don't stress about how much sleep you are about to get. If you don't get much, you can make up for it the next day, or later in the week. Sleep is not a daily task, it's a weekly task.
2. Prepare your environment by eliminating heat, light, and electronics, and bringing in plants in place of your pets.
3. Prepare yourself by battening down the hatches, getting yourself into a comfortable position, breathing through your nose, and throttling down the fluid consumption.

It's that simple—except when it isn't, and you either can't fall asleep or can't stay asleep. If you're anything like me, you're gonna be troubleshooting those issues a lot. That's why I developed an arsenal of tips and tactics to help me, including these two bad boys:

MELATONIN SUPPLEMENTS

If you can't fall asleep, it could be because your body isn't producing enough melatonin. Perhaps you spent a little too much time watching your show, or your bathroom lights are really bright, and your body didn't get the darkness signal it needed to produce melatonin. Using the minimum effective dose, usually 0.5 milligrams of melatonin, can really help ease you into sleep. Research indicates that more melatonin isn't necessarily better, however, so abide by the rule of minimum effective dose. It's also a good commonsense rule to give yourself breaks (minimum one day off per week, and one week off every six) so your supplemental melatonin use doesn't become habituated.

EMERGENCY SLEEP COCKTAIL

If you are in a phase where you're having trouble staying asleep, prepare this emergency sleep cocktail before bed, and keep it on your nightstand:

Emergency Sleep Cocktail

¼ teaspoon cream of tartar (dry spice)	½ teaspoon turmeric
¼ teaspoon sea salt	Dash of black pepper

Mix ingredients in 300ml filtered water. Drink.

The sodium and trace minerals in the sea salt support your adrenal system. The potassium in the cream of tartar relaxes your muscles. And the turmeric, along with the black pepper to assist with absorption, helps reduce inflammation. If I don't end up waking up in the middle of the night and needing to knock it back, I will either drink this concoction with some water as a substitute for my morning hydration cocktail or put it in the fridge for the following night, secure in the knowledge that I am well armed to tackle my sleep-cycle goals.

Now Do It

This is what I hope for you tomorrow: a day when you shoot out of bed two minutes before the alarm goes off, ready to face the world. When your joints don't crack, your head doesn't ache, and your stomach doesn't gurgle. When the light through the window feels like it was put there to warm you to perfect equilibrium with the world and kick-start you into the best day of your life. A day that you own completely, that you have been working hard to visualize, optimize, and create.

Yet no matter how well you have owned *this* day, if you don't sleep, you will start to lose the hard-earned ground that you've won. Like an athlete who trains hard and recovers poorly, your gains risk becoming losses if you don't cement them with sleep. You have to do it. Just don't let this call to arms stress you out. Ease into the process of figuring it out if you need to. Change happens slowly. Take your time, relax, and let sleep happen.

What I will not abide, my dudes and dudettes, is the notion that you "don't have time" to sleep. Unless you are Chuck Norris on an important mission, heed these words of advice clearly: DO LESS, DO IT BETTER! A life well lived has balance, and a day well lived has plenty of sleep. You don't have to listen to me, though; you can take it from Winston Churchill—you know, the guy who helped save Western civilization—when he was asked about his success in life: "Never sit down when you can lie down."

THREE POINTERS

+ We have made a mistake by thinking of sleep only in terms of hours per night. Instead, think about sleep as cycles per week. Understand that any form of polyphasic sleep, which includes napping, is a natural antidote to the anxiety of getting night-time sleep, and a supplement to your daily recovery.
+ To play out any great act, you have to set the stage. When it comes to sleep, this means eliminating the blue lights, keeping distractions to a minimum, making your room cool and dark like you're a cave bear, and adding some plants to push some oxygen into your life.
+ How you sleep will determine how you sleep. Generally aim for sleeping on your side, in a secure position. If you are waking up in the night, try to manage your bedtime hydration, including minerals and electrolytes.

BRING IT HOME

No man ever steps in the same river twice. For it's not the same river, and he is not the same person.

—HERACLITUS

Knowing what to do and why to do it are a big part of owning the day. Before you implement what you have learned, you are inevitably going to face a force called resistance. It will hit you from the outside and from within, so you need to acquire the tools to overcome it. You need to learn how to forgive yourself for past failings, how to motivate yourself to keep going, how to visualize your success, how to give yourself a pat on the back, and how to let your tribe know about your journey so they can support you in the struggle and celebrate you in success. Do it for them as much as you do it for yourself.

Getting Owned

It's hard to try something new. I get it. It's even harder to stick with it. Eighty percent of people give up on all their New Year's resolutions by February. Those ten new faces you saw at the gym January 2? Eight of them will be gone by Valentine's Day. Of course these are statistics drawn from people who have the time to fill out a survey. People who are crushing it don't fill out any fucking surveys! But it isn't just individuals who struggle to persevere and follow through with diets and gym memberships. Most small businesses fail. Most books don't make it to "The End," and, according to OG podcaster Jordan Harbinger, host of *The Art of Charm*, 95 percent of podcasts don't make it to their thirteenth episode.

Why is this?

Usually it isn't because the ideas are bad (though sometimes, the ideas are really bad), it's because we weren't able to win the mental battle necessary to get us there. We got discouraged when we ran into unforeseen obstacles. We got derailed when we didn't get the results we were expecting. Or worse, we listened to the flood of voices giving us a million good reasons why we should stop.

Sometimes the voices come from outside, from advertisers or people in lab coats telling you that it's not your fault. That you couldn't change if you tried. They are wrong. The science of epigenetics has shown that even many genetic characteristics may be changed by the choices we make. Chronic conditions are being reversed by ordinary people making extraordinary choices, like the ones described in this book.

Sometimes the voices come from inside our own heads, telling us we're not good enough, or we don't deserve it, or it's too late and we should have started earlier. As silly as it may sound, I heard those voices when I turned thirty years old. I'd founded Onnit earlier that year, and all it had done up to that point was lose money. I thought I must have zigged when I should have zagged, and now it was too late for me to ever live the life I was meant to live. Then I chose to stop feeling sorry for myself and do something about it. I borrowed money from my last two friends with any kind of bank balance, just to keep the lights on long enough for Alpha Brain—the last bullet in the gun—to be delivered, my first big success.

The author Steven Pressfield has heard those same voices, too. He even gave them a name. He called them, collectively, Resistance. Resistance is that force that will oppose you every time you attempt to ascend, to improve, to achieve. Pressfield heard it all the way up until he was about forty years old and decided that he was finally going to fulfill his lifelong vocation and become a professional writer. He wrote four screenplays that were made into movies over the next ten years, and published his first book when he was fifty-two years old. It was called *The Legend of Bagger Vance*, and it went on to become a massive bestseller as well as a feature film five years later. His second book, *Gates of Fire*, was a piece of historical fiction about the three hundred Spartan men who made a stand at a place in Greece called the Hot Gates. They faced an army of 100,000 Persian fighters. They didn't retreat. They didn't surrender. They died fighting to the last man, because they were Spartans.

How did they defeat Resistance? Silence those voices that told them they could never win, that there was no point, that it was hopeless? They had an ethos. *Never give up, never surrender.* Easier said than done. Ask anyone what the hardest thing is about doing something new or different or unheard of, and they'll tell you it's sticking with it. Well, the Spartans stuck with it. They always did. Not just for themselves, but for their loved ones. The best chance they had to keep their beloved safe was to let every enemy know that if they crossed the boundary into Sparta, they better be ready for a war to the last man. That simple, singular ethos was what helped the

Spartans send their message not just to the world, but down through history.

That is the beauty of singular focus, and the reason we are focusing on a single day. You are going to get results, the day you start. The *moment* you start. Forty minutes after you wake up, you are going to feel different than you have ever felt. That difference will compound like interest in the bank, and then the real transformation will begin.

Owning It

Resistance is a cunning adversary, make no mistake. It is also a necessary force. What kind of game would we be playing if there were no monsters? How could we adapt to stress if there was no stress? How could we seek enlightenment if we were already enlightened? There is no light without dark, after all. No hot without cold. No silver lining without the black cloud. But just because resistance is necessary, that doesn't mean that we shouldn't do everything in our power to kick its ass. Our goal is to own our life, not get owned by it.

That's why we're going to help you build an ethos in this chapter that will give you the encouragement you need to silence the voices and overcome the resistance. But building an ethos isn't the only technique you're going to need. You will need to visualize your success. You will need to employ positive self-talk, and rid yourself of self-ridicule. You will need the support of your tribe. But the first step you will need to take may be the hardest of all. It is, for me. It's forgiveness.

Forgive Yourself (All You Can Do Is Your Best)

There is a good chance you have tried diets and transformational programs before and failed. Guess what, so has everyone. But you are not the same person you were then, and this is not the same program. You are the person who learned from those experiences, who appreciates owning life even more than you did then.

For that knowledge to turn into wisdom, though, you have to forgive yourself for all your past failings. You did your best then, and your best now is different. There is a scene deep into the first season of one of my favorite shows on television, *Billions*, when genius fund manager Bobby Axelrod is talking to his brilliant psychotherapist about why he uncharacteristically blew a trade that cost his fund a billion dollars. After hours of banter, he realizes that it was his guilt surrounding the manipulation of his friend for his own financial gain that caused him to subconsciously seek retribution . . . on himself. He needed to pay the price to level out his internal scales of justice.

This isn't just something from fiction, though. I've seen it a hundred times. It is the motivation behind many forms of self-destruction. Whether in love, or in business, or in health, if we don't feel like we deserve a positive outcome, or even worse, like we deserve to be punished, we will manifest that outcome with the subconscious choices we make.

If we don't forgive ourselves, all that knowledge from our past failures will instead petrify into useless information, and we will continue to believe deep down that we deserve to get beaten down by life. We will find ourselves, again and again, on the short side of the trade. But if we truly forgive ourselves completely, we will know that we deserve better, and we will create the kind of positive reality that allows billion-dollar empires to blossom from blue-collar roots.

The reason this whole thing has to start with forgiveness is that your choices will never be perfect. Maybe you got frustrated in the car this morning, or sat too long in one position at work this afternoon, or ignored your kids when you got home tonight. That's okay. Your day is never going to be perfect. If there is anything about your day or your life that you need to own, it's that. You think I do everything I wrote about in this book every single day? I don't. But that doesn't mean I don't wake up and do my best the next day. Perfection is bullshit. It's just a ruse that our internal self-critic perpetrates on us to make us feel like shit.

What's worse, if we allow the inner critic to punish us every time we fail to meet the standards of perfection, we'll stop trying altogether. We'll decide that it is better to pretend that it's someone else's fault, hiding behind excuses and rationalizations. If we know that when we fail, we will forgive ourselves, then we get to play from inspiration rather than fear. We'll be able to look our mistakes right in the eye, take the medicine, and move on. It's what any good coach does for his players. It's why Pete Carroll, head coach of the NFL's Seattle Seahawks and formerly of the collegiate powerhouse USC Trojans, has won so many titles. You need to be your own good coach. You have to teach yourself to learn from failure, not be defined by it. You threw an interception? Fine, learn from your mistake, get back in there, and keep throwing.

Just do your best. That's all you can ask of yourself. If your best doesn't get the results you were hoping for, forgive yourself, because your best isn't determined by the outcome, after the fact, with perfect clarity. It's decided moment by moment, according to the effort you put toward the intention you have set for yourself. They say that the ends don't justify the means. Well, they don't invalidate them either. Do your best, remove the self-punishment for trying and failing, and let the rest sort itself out.

Build Your Ethos

The Spartans had a very simple ethos: *Never give up, never surrender.* Pete Carroll built one for his entire organization:

Always compete.
Protect the team.
Leave no doubt.
Play in the absence of fear.

Stay in the moment.
Support individuality.
Be an excellent communicator.
Have fun, show lots of love.

To own this day and own your life, you need to create an ethos of your own. Something that takes all the complex knowledge you've acquired from your failures and successes over the years, and turns it into a code. One that is instantly memorable and unbreakable, and that becomes like a second operating system, an app that allows you to eliminate the time and energy you spend bargaining with yourself. In that sense, creating an ethos is a shortcut to mental override. Instead of taxing your willpower, you're leaning on a simple message that reminds you: *This is just what I'm going to do.*

The key with an ethos is to make it something you can build on. You want small wins. What you *don't* want to do is say something like "I will never have sugar again." Then, a week later, when your friend brings you a chocolate chip cookie, your ethos is smeared across your upper lip like a dietary dirty sanchez. Start with simple things, like *When I promise people I am going to do something, I do it.* That's a pretty good start. *I will always forgive myself if I'm doing my best.* That's another good start. *I will choose one day and own it.* That's a great one!

Visualize

Every single peak performer I work with visualizes his or her success. I've always thought that it was a silly question when people ask an entrepreneur, "Did you ever imagine that Onnit could be this big?" Of course he did. To create it, you have to see it first. It's not just entrepreneurs. The speaker visualizes what she is going to say and the audience's reaction to it. The fighter visualizes what is going to happen in the cage. If you've ever watched *The Ultimate Fighter,* nearly every time they show a contestant doing sparring rounds in preparation for a fight, at the end of the final training round their coach makes them walk around the octagon with their hands raised in triumph, visualizing their victory. This is not some old fighter's superstition these guys are engaged in, like not talking to a pitcher in the middle of a no-hitter. Visualization is a legitimate powerful force.

In his book *You Are the Placebo*, Dr. Joe Dispenza discusses dozens upon dozens of cases where the placebo effect made a dramatic change in someone's life. His point is that instead of letting it happen by accident, getting fooled by some sugar pill or a sham surgery, we should harness the placebo effect to our advantage. Visualization is a prime example of that intentional placebo at work, one we've already seen in this book with those study participants who visualized themselves lifting heavy weights and getting stronger as a result. The same principle applies with owning the day. Visualizing yourself doing it will have a positive impact.

Employ Positive Self-Talk

I've always known that I'm hard on myself. But I didn't realize just how brutal I was until one evening when I was driving home from work, replaying the day in my head. I had solved a pretty complicated series of problems at the office that day in a surprising and inspired way. Out of nowhere, I said to myself, "Good job, Aubrey. You did good today." It hit me like a blast from a bomb. My whole body lit up, I was flooded with warmth, and my eyes welled up. I don't know if I had ever told myself something like that before. In thirty-four years, I had never given myself permission to be proud of myself. I certainly told myself how much I had sucked, or failed, or what a POS I was a thousand times. But never pride, never "Good job, buddy." I could acknowledge when I did something well, but I never said it to myself. I never *told myself* "Good job." Finally, after thirty years, I got what I had never realized I was always looking for . . . and I got it from myself. Just a little pat on the back.

Since then my podcast has tripled, my company has doubled, and my life has been colored with a lot more joy. It's funny how a turning point can happen after something so trivial. In my coaching course "Go for Your Win," I have everyone choose a single phrase they can tell themselves whenever times get tough. They need it (we all do, frankly) because in the absence of success or in the presence of obstacles, forgiveness will only take you halfway. Positive self-talk is what picks up the baton for the final leg and brings you across the finish line of your day, of your mission, of your life.

Get Support from Your Tribe

No one is an island. And while all the individual, personal work I've talked about in this chapter is essential to conquering resistance and owning the day, it's not yet enough, because we are tribal creatures, and we need the support of our tribe to truly thrive.

Psychologists agree that there are four keys to compelling positive action: (1) know what to do and how to do it; (2) believe it will work; (3) see the value; and (4) get support from your community/tribe/family. This entire book has been about turning those first three keys in the locked door of your optimized existence. We've given you prescriptions detailing all the steps you need to take to own the day. We have hundreds of clinical studies backing up the science behind the strategy. And we have helped show you what can happen if you follow the strategy by owning it, or if you fail the strategy by getting owned. Now we need to make sure you turn that final key and open the door to your best life.

Tell everyone about owning the day. Tell them when it is going to happen; make a big deal about it. As much as the digital environment has driven us into isolation from physical connection, we can also use it to support us. Announce it on your socials and hold yourself accountable. Have it be something that people are curious about. Tell them where the challenges were, what the big successes were.

If you're not sure where to start, right now there are already thousands of members in the Own the Day Facebook community ready to hear your stories, help support your mission, and answer your questions. Maybe you have a genetic condition, one leg, or live on a planet with a different gravitational environment. The majority of the principles in this book should be applicable to you, whoever you are, but everyone is different, so we're not taking anything for granted. I'll be stopping by there frequently too, as will the best coaches we have at Onnit, to help you overcome that resistance and turn all your knowledge into wisdom.

Prescription

Part of the problem with our current condition is that there is a ton of conflicting information. When people are confused about what they should do and how they should do it, they don't do anything at all. This book has been written to end the confusion. It takes you step by step through every single part of the day. It has broken down the prescriptions, the actions, and the mind-set necessary. Maybe the breadth of everything is so great, it feels overwhelming. That is when it becomes even more important to focus on the process, because you're not going to be able to put this book down and just randomly go out and own the day. It's going to take some personal reflection, some preparation, and some planning. Here are some practices to employ before you get started.

HO'OPONOPONO

The Hawaiian *kahunas* (shamans) have a practice for radical forgiveness they call Ho'oponopono, the purpose of which is to get you to a completely clean slate, a state of mind called the zero state (also the title of a book by Joe Vitale). It is a simple dialogue you have with yourself or a loved one, which requires you to say four things. We're going to focus it on yourself for now, but keep this in your medicine bag when you need to resolve a conflict with anyone else.

1. **"I love you."** Love is the appropriate bond that can unify all aspects of yourself. To express this love sets the foundation for all the communication to follow.
2. **"I'm sorry."** This is to clear you of any guilt you may carry for the times you've done yourself wrong—from negative self-talk to forcing your body to cope with way too much cheap tequila.
3. **"Forgive me."** The humble act of asking for forgiveness, when sincere, is not often opposed. Grant yourself the forgiveness you seek.
4. **"Thank you."** This is an expression of gratitude to your body and your mind, not only for the forgiveness but for everything it has given you. It's gotten you this far, after all, right?

Say it to yourself: I love you, I'm sorry, forgive me, thank you.

Now imagine all the things you judge yourself for. Think about everything you beat yourself up about. Keep saying it for each one of those things. Keep meaning it. Like a fighter landing the jab over and over again. Eventually you will vanquish the judge and reach radical forgiveness. Then you will have to do it again. The hero is simply someone who does battle with his demons every day.

I love you, I'm sorry, forgive me, thank you.

▓ DOWNLOAD THE ETHOS BRAIN APP

Don't just build your ethos. Write it down. Assimilate it into your brain and nervous system, like a second spine. Stress-test it and put pressure on it until the lump of carbon turns to a diamond. Knead it until the words become hard as bone. Your ethos, whatever it is, may start a little bit softer and more pliable when it is young; that is only natural. So when you fail early on, don't get discouraged and throw it away. Put in the work to strengthen it, instead, because when it is fully grown into your second spine, it is the thing that will keep you upright when everything else is trying to keep you down.

SEE YOUR FUTURE

I want you to imagine yourself a year from now. You know that in a year you are going to be different, whether you do nothing or something. And the choices you make between now and then will determine that difference. But for today, I want you to imagine owning all those other days. Visualize that you wake up with purpose and clarity. You push yourself against resistance. You take control of your diet and supplementation. You turn dead time into alive time. You work effectively and aren't afraid to power down the engines to rest. You train your body into a durable, capable machine. You connect with yourself, your friends, and the universe. You turn sex into an adventure of pleasure. You go to sleep with a mission, and actually . . . sleep. Imagine what a year of living like that has done for you. Walk in the shoes of that new person. See yourself through that person's eyes. Look in the mirror at that body. Maybe the circles under your eyes are gone, and that stubborn weight has lifted—mentally and physically. See what has happened in your career, and in your family. That person is you, on the other side of Resistance. If you see it clearly enough, it will be done.

CREATE YOUR MANTRA

Let's go, champ! This expression blasted across the public consciousness when heavyweight fighter Shannon Briggs dropped it on the *Joe Rogan Experience* podcast. He talked about a dark time in his life, when he felt he was at a crossroads. He developed the expression to help push him through the challenges, to buoy him during down times, and as a kind of magic spell against the wizardry of resistance. It became his mantra—a potent form of positive self-talk, holstered and ready for the first sign of turbulence. The expression I learned to tell myself, the expression that became my mantra, is "Go, hero, go." Maybe my favorite mantra, however, comes from editor in chief of *Entrepreneur* magazine, Jason Feifer. From the time he started working for a regional magazine, he would tell himself the same thing every day: "I'm not fucking around." Monday: Not fucking around. Tuesday: Not fucking around. Wednesday: You get the idea. This is really what this book has been about. Whether it is work or play or fitness or fucking around—to own your day, you are not fucking around.

Find your own mantra, and use it daily, you will not regret it . . . unless it's something like "The bomb is in the building!" That you might regret if you say it at the airport.

▌ TELL THE WORLD

When you have everything ready to own the day, mark the day on your calendar and tell your whole world. Go to the "Prescription" section in each chapter, and write down exactly what you are going to do. Focus on each little thing. If something isn't possible, don't worry. This is not binary, this is cumulative. If you have questions, log in to the Own the Day Facebook group to get answers and gather support. Then just focus on the process. Before you know it, you won't just be owning the day, you'll be owning your entire life.

Now Do It

The people of our world are hurting. Not just the poor and the impoverished, *all* people. People we know and love. We have lost control of the operating system, and we are getting owned by life. But it doesn't have to be that way.

There is a reason that in all great stories the strongest motivating force for the hero is a threat not to his own life but to the lives of the ones he loves. The girl, the child, the innocents; their safety means more to him than his own well-being. We are programmed to love others, even to sacrifice ourselves for the good of the tribe. Use that powerful force to drive you toward success, but recognize that it will always start with you. You can never fully love and support others until you love and support yourself. The quest to heal a hurting world begins with the man in the mirror. MJ had it right: "If you want to make the world a better place, take a look at yourself and make a change." Twirl and crotch-grab.

The reason is twofold. For one, to be of service, you have to be fit for service. A leaky cup can't effectively serve water. There's a reason they tell you to put your own oxygen mask on first before assisting others in case of emergency on an airplane. You need to be strong and vital to be of any use to other people.

The second reason is that by owning the day and taking control of your life, you can be the living proof to others of what is possible. You can lead by example. Why is it that when someone first does a new trick on a skateboard or a motocross bike that was previously believed to "never be possible," then all of a sudden a year later three more people can do the same trick? It's because when you do it, other people believe they can do it too.

All around you, right now, you have people looking at you. Some are in your family. Maybe you have kids. You certainly have friends or coworkers, and maybe even some strangers on social media. They are all looking for some sign that somebody knows what the hell is going on out there and that something better is possible. You can be that sign, that someone, that something better. You can be the one they point to. You aren't just owning the day for yourself, you are owning the day for everyone you know. For everyone you love!

I believe in you. One day, if we cross paths, I will shake your hand or give you a hug. I will be looking at a hero. Not at a perfect man or woman, but a regular person, just like myself, doing your best. Without you, this book wouldn't exist. Without you, I wouldn't have had the strength to beat my own resistance. So it is I who owe you a debt of gratitude. You have helped me become the hero of my own story, as hopefully I have helped you. Go hero, go.

THREE POINTERS

+ You need to give yourself every advantage when pushing up against resistance. The first and most important thing you can do is forgive yourself for any imperfections, any expectations you haven't lived up to. All you can do is your best, determined moment by moment. Perfection is a myth. If you forgive yourself, you will begin to feel that you deserve to change for the better, and so you will.

+ Creating an ethos is a shortcut to mastering mental override. It prevents you from the anguish of deliberation over your choices and starts to define the person you want to be. Create your ethos and support yourself with positive self-talk.

+ We are social creatures, designed to live in community with others. It is no surprise that accountability and support from our tribe is essential to creating any form of lasting change. Pick the day you want to own, begin the process, and let everyone you love know about it. Ask for their support, hold yourself accountable to your word, and you won't just own that day, you will be setting yourself on the path to owning your life.

ACKNOWLEDGMENTS

To author a book is to captain a ship. A book of this magnitude would have never left harbor if not for the generous contributions of a great many people. I'd like to start with Ryan Holiday and my book agent, Byrd Leavell, for convincing me that I should write this book in the first place. I had no idea what I was getting myself into, so thank you for holding back just enough information to get me to say yes! Next, of course, is Nils Parker, not only for helping to shape my ideas and prose into a compelling narrative but for being a mentor in the craft of writing. I have grown immensely in the time we have spent working together and I am forever grateful. Here are some of the other, no less important contributors I would like to acknowledge:

Karen Rinaldi and the Harper Wave team, thank you for taking a chance on a first-time author, and thank you for being total pros every step of the way. You don't always hear great stories about author-publisher relations, but I have no idea what people are talking about. I love you guys, and I hope this is just the beginning for us.

Stefanie McBride, thank you for being a friend, designing the cover, and making sure all the graphics were Gucci.

Ben Greenfield, I have learned an immense amount from you; thank you for taking the time to share your knowledge and help me architect the perfect day. You are a unique human being, and I'm grateful for our friendship.

Dr. Vince Kreipke, thank you for coming in and helping to clean up all the research and citations. I guess all those degrees are good for something after all!

Kyle Kingsbury, you bad MF, thanks for owning every day, testing all these practices, and living the life of a fully optimized human being in body, mind, and spirit.

To the rest of the Onnit team, especially John Wolf, Shane Heins, Noah Villalobos, Sean Hyson, and Liv Langdon, thank you for your support and making important contributions along the way.

To the inspiring figures in this book, Bode Miller, Wim Hof, Joe Rogan, Duncan Keith, Donald Cerrone, and everyone else I mentioned by name, I would tell you to keep doing what you are doing, but knowing you as I do, I know that you cannot do otherwise. So thank you.

Jon Bier, the best consigliere in the game, and to all the podcast hosts, allies, and friends, thanks in advance for helping to get this book out in front of as many people as possible.

To my readers and to the community, thank you for being awesome, holding me accountable, and fighting the fight alongside me.

Last but not least, my fiancée, Whitney, and my tribe of chosen family, thank you for helping to remind me why I work so hard.

Oh, yeah, I love you, Mom!

NOTES: HERE COMES THE SCIENCE!

CHAPTER 1: WATER. LIGHT. MOVEMENT.

9   a pound of water lost: "Why Do I Lose Weight While I Sleep?," *HowStuff Works.com*, 2009, http://health.howstuffworks.com/wellness/diet-fitness/weight -loss/question227.htm.

9   twenty scalding-hot gallons: "Showers," *Home Water Works*, accessed September 6, 2016, http://www.home-water-works.org/indoor-use/showers.

10   one in seven people: Niall McCarthy, "Americans Are Tired Most of The Week," *Statista*, 2015, https://www.statista.com/chart/3534/americans-are-tired -most-of-the-week/.

10   between 50 and 70 million Americans: "Insufficient Sleep Is a Public Health Problem," *Centers for Disease Control and Prevention*, 2015, https://www.cdc .gov/features/dssleep/.

10   studies on both men and women: Matthew S. Ganio et al., "Mild Dehydration Impairs Cognitive Performance and Mood of Men," *British Journal of Nutrition* 106, no. 10 (2011): 1535–43, doi:10.1017/S0007114511002005; L. E. Armstrong et al., "Mild Dehydration Affects Mood in Healthy Young Women," *Journal of Nutrition* 142, no. 2 (2012): 382–88, doi:10.3945/jn.111.142000.

11   2 percent loss in water: P. M. Gopinathan, G. Pichan, and V. M. Sharma, "Role of Dehydration in Heat Stress-Induced Variations in Mental Performance," *Archives of Environmental Health* 43, no. 1 (1988): 15–17, doi:10.1080/00039896 .1988.9934367.

11   78 percent of Americans: Alyson B. Goodman et al., "Behaviors and Attitudes Associated with Low Drinking Water Intake among US Adults, Food Attitudes and Behaviors Survey, 2007," *Preventing Chronic Disease* 10 (2013): E51, doi:10.5888/pcd10.120248.

11   circadian balance: D. Mircsof and S. A. Brown, "The Influence of Light, Exercise, and Behavior upon Circadian Rhythms," in *Encyclopedia of Sleep* (Waltham, MA: Academic Press, 2013), 435–44.

13   Sixty percent of the average adult human body: Howard Perlman, "The Water in You," *U.S. Geological Survey*, 2016, https://water.usgs.gov/edu/property you.html.

13   Earth's surface: Howard Perlman, "How Much Water Is There On, In, and Above the Earth?," *U.S. Geological Survey*, 2016, https://water.usgs.gov/edu /earthhowmuch.html.

14   throw your hormone balance out of whack: Johanna R. Rochester, "Bisphenol A and Human Health: A Review of the Literature," *Reproductive Toxicology*, 2013, doi:10.1016/j.reprotox.2013.08.008.

16   reduction of salt in one's diet prevented cardiovascular death or disease: Alma J. Adler et al., "Reduced Dietary Salt for the Prevention of Cardiovascular Disease," *Cochrane Database of Systematic Reviews*, no. 7 (2014), doi:10.1002/14651858.CD009217.pub3.

16   studies on populations of 11,346 and 3,681 subjects: M. Alderman, H. Cohen, and S. Madhavan, "Dietary Sodium Intake and Mortality: The National Health and Nutrition Examination Survey (NHANES I)," *Lancet* 351, no. 9105 (1998): 781–85, doi:10.1016/S0140-6736(97)09092-2; Katarzyna Stolarz-Skrzypek et al., "Fatal and Nonfatal Outcomes, Incidence of Hypertension, and Blood Pressure Changes in Relation to Urinary Sodium Excretion," *JAMA: The Journal of the American Medical Association* 305, no. 17 (2011): 1777–85, doi:10.1001/jama.2011.574.

17   atypical circadian rhythm: Namni Goel et al., "Circadian Rhythm Profiles in Women with Night Eating Syndrome," *Journal of Biological Rhythms* 24, no. 1 (2009): 85–94, doi:10.1177/0748730408328914.

17   body temperature: Jim Waterhouse et al., "The Circadian Rhythm of Core Temperature: Origin and Some Implications for Exercise Performance," *Chronobiology International* 22, no. 2 (2005): 207–25, doi:10.1081/CBI-200053477.

17   metabolism: F. A. Scheer et al., "Adverse Metabolic and Cardiovascular Consequences of Circadian Misalignment," *Proceedings of the National Academy of Sciences* 106, no. 11 (2009): 4453–58, doi:10.1073/pnas.0808180106.

17   life of the cell: Aziz Sancar et al., "Circadian Clock Control of the Cellular Response to DNA Damage," *FEBS Letters* 584, no. 12 (2010): 2618–25, doi:10.1016/j.febslet.2010.03.017.

17   increased incidence of cancer: Christos Savvidis and Michael Koutsilieris, "Circadian Rhythm Disruption in Cancer Biology," *Molecular Medicine* 18, no. 1 (2012): 1249–60, doi:10.2119/molmed.2012.00077.

19   "indefatigable two-month surge": "Blackhawks' Duncan Keith Claims Conn Smythe Trophy as Playoffs MVP," *ESPN.com*, 2015, http://www.espn.com/chicago/nhl/story/_/id/13087247/2015-stanley-cup-finals-duncan-keith-chicago-blackhawks-awarded-conn-smythe-trophy.

20   improves cognitive performance: Y. K. Chang et al., "The Effects of Acute Exercise on Cognitive Performance: A Meta-Analysis," *Brain Research*, 2012, doi:10.1016/j.brainres.2012.02.068.

20   circadian rhythm: Mircsof and Brown, "Circadian Rhythms."

20   set that internal biological clock: Yu Tahara, Shinya Aoyama, and Shigenobu Shibata, "The Mammalian Circadian Clock and Its Entrainment by Stress and Exercise," *Journal of Physiological Sciences*, 2017, doi:10.1007/s12576-016-0450-7.

21   the HumanCharger25: Ben Greenfield, "The Ultimate Guide to Using Light to Biohack Your Circadian Rhythms, Sleep Better and Beat Jet Lag Forever," *BenGreenfieldFitness*,2015,https://bengreenfieldfitness.com/article/sleep-articles/what-is-the-human-charger/.

22   reducing symptoms and increasing cognitive performance: Heidi Jurvelin et al., "Transcranial Bright Light Treatment via the Ear Canals in Seasonal Affective Disorder: A Randomized, Double-Blind Dose-Response Study," *BMC Psychiatry* 14, no. 1 (2014): 288, doi:10.1186/s12888-014-0288-6.

26   improve lymph movement: W. Olszewski et al., "Flow and Composition of Leg Lymph in Normal Men during Venous Stasis, Muscular Activity and Local Hyperthermia," *Acta Physiologica Scandinavica* 99, no. 2 (1977): 149–55, doi:10.1111/j.1748-1716.1977.tb10365.x.

26   study on fighter pilots: Paul W. Esposito and Lisa M. Esposito, "The Reemergence of the Trampoline as a Recreational Activity and Competitive Sport," *Current Sports Medicine Reports*, 2009, doi:10.1249/JSR.0b013e3181b8f60a.

CHAPTER 2: DEEP BREATH, DEEP FREEZE

31   "If you plan to get stressed": Mark Shwarts, "Robert Sapolsky Discusses Physiological Effects of Stress," *Stanford News*, 2007, http://news.stanford.edu/news/2007/march7/sapolskysr-030707.html.

32   we keep getting sicker: "Power of Prevention," *Centers for Disease Control and Prevention*, 2009, https://www.cdc.gov/chronicdisease/pdf/2009-power-of-prevention.pdf.

32   plummeting in comparison to their first-world peers: Steven H. Woolf and Laudan Aron, eds., *U.S. Health in International Perspective* (Washington, DC: National Academies Press, 2013), doi:10.17226/13497.

32   high levels of stress and poor health scores: "Health and Stress," *American Psychological Association*, 2010, http://www.apa.org/news/press/releases/stress/2010/health-stress.aspx.

32   suppresses the immune system: Mohd Razali Salleh, "Life Event, Stress and Illness," *Malaysian Journal of Medical Sciences*, 2008, doi:10.1097/MPG.0b013e31818b.

32   a major correlative to depression: George M. Slavich and Michael R. Irwin, "From Stress to Inflammation and Major Depressive Disorder: A Social Signal Transduction Theory of Depression," *Psychological Bulletin* 140, no. 3 (2014): 774–815, doi:10.1037/a0035302.

33   upward of 75 percent of all doctor visits: Jeffrey L. Boone and Jeffrey P. Anthony, "Evaluating the Impact of Stress on Systemic Disease: The MOST Protocol in Primary Care," *Journal of the American Osteopathic Association* 103, no. 5 (2003): 239–46, http://www.ncbi.nlm.nih.gov/pubmed/12776765.

33   less than 3 percent of doctor visits include counseling about stress: Aditi Nerurkar et al., "When Physicians Counsel about Stress: Results of a National Study,"

JAMA Internal Medicine 173, no. 1 (January 14, 2013): 76–77, doi:10.1001/2013
.jamainternmed.480.

33   76 percent of physicians: Holly Avey et al., "Health Care Providers' Training,
Perceptions, and Practices Regarding Stress and Health Outcomes," *Journal of
the National Medical Association* 95, no. 9 (2003): 833, 836–45, http://www.pub
medcentral.nih.gov/articlerender.fcgi?artid=2594476&tool=pmcentrez&render
type=abstract.

33   alter the immune system's inflammatory response to pathogens: M. Kox et
al., "Voluntary Activation of the Sympathetic Nervous System and Attenuation of
the Innate Immune Response in Humans," *Proceedings of the National Academy
of Sciences* 111, no. 20 (2014): 7379–84, doi:10.1073/pnas.1322174111.

36   reduced perceived stress: Vivek Kumar Sharma et al., "Effect of Fast and
Slow Pranayama on Perceived Stress and Cardiovascular Parameters in Young
Health-Care Students," *International Journal of Yoga* 6, no. 2 (2013): 104–10,
doi:10.4103/0973-6131.113400.

37   enhances relaxation: Judith A. Lothian, "Lamaze Breathing: What Every
Pregnant Woman Needs to Know," *Journal of Perinatal Education* 20, no. 2 (January 1, 2011): 118–20, doi:10.1891/1058-1243.20.2.118.

37   decreases perception of pain: Volker Busch et al., "The Effect of Deep and
Slow Breathing on Pain Perception, Autonomic Activity, and Mood Processing—
An Experimental Study," *Pain Medicine* 13, no. 2 (February 1, 2012): 215–28,
doi:10.1111/j.1526-4637.2011.01243.x.

38   "Think of hormesis": Mark Sisson, "Hormesis: How Certain Kinds of Stress
Can Actually Be Good for You," *Mark's Daily Apple*, 2012, http://www.marks
dailyapple.com/hormesis-how-certain-kinds-of-stress-can-actually-be-good-for
-you/.

38   many research-based advantages of cold exposure: Rhonda Patrick, "Cold
Shocking the Body," *Foundmyfitness.com*, 2015, https://www.foundmyfitness
.com/reports/cold-stress.pdf.

38   fewer respiratory tract infections: T. M. Kolettis and M. T. Kolettis, "Winter Swimming: Healthy or Hazardous? Evidence and Hypotheses," *Medical Hypotheses* 61, no. 5–6 (2003): 654–56, doi:10.1016/S0306-9877(03)00270-6.

38   potential treatment for depression: Nikolai A. Shevchuk, "Adapted Cold
Shower as a Potential Treatment for Depression," *Medical Hypotheses* 70, no. 5
(2008): 995–1001, doi:10.1016/j.mehy.2007.04.052.

38   making it to the age of a hundred: G. Haskó et al., "Exogenous and Endogenous Catecholamines Inhibit the Production of Macrophage Inflammatory Protein
(MIP) 1 Alpha via a Beta Adrenoceptor Mediated Mechanism," *British Journal of
Pharmacology* 125, no. 6 (1998): 1297–1303, doi:10.1038/sj.bjp.0702179.

40   300 percent more norepinephrine: P. Srámek et al., "Human Physiological
Responses to Immersion into Water of Different Temperatures," *European Journal of Applied Physiology* 81, no. 5 (2000): 436–42, doi:10.1007/s004210050065.

40   reliably produces more adrenaline and norepinephrine: Kurt Espersen et al., "The Human Spleen as an Erythrocyte Reservoir in Diving-Related Interventions," *Journal of Applied Physiology* 92, no. 5 (2002): 2071–79, doi:10.1152/jap plphysiol.00055.2001.

40   habituated to their presence: Carnegie Mellon University, "How Stress Influences Disease: Study Reveals Inflammation as the Culprit," *Science Daily*, 2012, https://www.sciencedaily.com/releases/2012/04/120402162546.htm.

40   the body becomes less responsive: Ibid.

42   reducing all-cause mortality: Tanjaniina Laukkanen et al., "Association between Sauna Bathing and Fatal Cardiovascular and All-Cause Mortality Events," *JAMA Internal Medicine* 175, no. 4 (2015): 542–48, doi:10.1001/jamain ternmed.2014.8187.

42   train your cardiovascular system: M. L. Hannuksela and S. Ellahham, "Benefits and Risks of Sauna Bathing," *American Journal of Medicine* 110, no. 2 (February 1, 2001): 118–26, http://www.ncbi.nlm.nih.gov/pubmed/11165553.

43   lead, cadmium, arsenic, and mercury: Margaret E. Sears, Kathleen J. Kerr, and Riina I. Bray, "Arsenic, Cadmium, Lead, and Mercury in Sweat: A Systematic Review," *Journal of Environmental and Public Health* 2012 (2012): 1–10, doi:10.1155/2012/184745.

43   detoxification: Gerald Ross and Marie Sternquist, "Methamphetamine Exposure and Chronic Illness in Police Officers: Significant Improvement with Sauna-Based Detoxification Therapy," *Toxicology and Industrial Health* 28, no. 8 (2012): 758–68, doi:10.1177/0748233711425070.

45   norepinephrine release: J. Leppäluoto et al., "Effects of Long-Term Whole-Body Cold Exposures on Plasma Concentrations of ACTH, Beta-Endorphin, Cortisol, Catecholamines and Cytokines in Healthy Females," *Scandinavian Journal of Clinical and Laboratory Investigation* 68, no. 2 (2008): 145–53, doi:10.1080/00365510701516350.

45   shoot for two minutes: Ibid.

CHAPTER 3: MORE FAT, LESS SUGAR, OR DON'T EAT

53   more likely to grant parole: S. Danziger, J. Levav, and L. Avnaim-Pesso, "Extraneous Factors in Judicial Decisions," *Proceedings of the National Academy of Sciences* 108, no. 17 (2011): 6889–92, doi:10.1073/pnas.1018033108.

54   Obesity, diabetes, heart disease, and even cancer: Matthias B. Schulze et al., "Sugar-Sweetened Beverages, Weight Gain, and Incidence of Type 2 Diabetes in Young and Middle-Aged Women," *JAMA* 292, no. 8 (2004): 927–34, doi:10.1001/jama.292.8.927; Quanhe Yang et al., "Added Sugar Intake and Cardiovascular Diseases Mortality Among US Adults," *JAMA Internal Medicine* 174, no. 4 (2014): 516–24, doi:10.1001/jamainternmed.2013.13563; Roberd M. Bostick et al., "Sugar, Meat, and Fat Intake, and Non-Dietary Risk Factors for Colon Cancer Incidence in Iowa Women (United States)," *Cancer Causes and Control* 5, no. 1 (1994): 38–52, doi:10.1007/BF01830725.

54   Thirty million Americans have diabetes: "National Diabetes Statistics Report," *Centers for Disease Control and Prevention*, 2017, https://www.cdc.gov /diabetes/pdfs/data/statistics/national-diabetes-statistics-report.pdf.

54   Cardiovascular disease is our leading cause of death: "Heart Disease Facts Sheet," *Center for Disease Control and Prevention*, 2017, https://www.cdc.gov /dhdsp/data_statistics/fact_sheets/fs_heart_disease.htm.

54   one out of every five children clinically obese: "Childhood Obesity Facts," *Center for Disease Control and Prevention*, 2017, https://www.cdc.gov/healthy schools/obesity/facts.htm.

54   don't ever worry about their weight: Joy Wilke, "Nearly Half in U.S. Remain Worried About Their Weight," *Gallup News*, 2014, http://news.gallup.com /poll/174089/nearly-half-remain-worried-weight.aspx.

54   The same is true for sugar: Nicole M. Avena, Pedro Rada, and Bartley G. Hoebel, "Evidence for Sugar Addiction: Behavioral and Neurochemical Effects of Intermittent, Excessive Sugar Intake," *Neuroscience and Biobehavioral Reviews*, 2008, doi:10.1016/j.neubiorev.2007.04.019.

56   degrade the skin and contribute to premature aging: Masamitsu Ichihashi et al., "Glycation Stress and Photo-Aging in Skin," *Anti-Aging Medicine* 8, no. 3 (2011): 23–29, doi:10.3793/jaam.8.23; H. Corstjens et al., "Glycation Associated Skin Autofluorescence and Skin Elasticity Are Related to Chronological Age and Body Mass Index of Healthy Subjects," *Experimental Gerontology* 43, no. 7 (2008): 663–67, doi:10.1016/j.exger.2008.01.012.

56   bans on television advertising: Marisa Tsai, "8 Countries Taking Action against Junk Food Marketing," *Alternet*, 2016, http://www.alternet.org/food/8 -countries-taking-action-against-junk-food-marketing.

57   self-regulate advertising to kids: "Children's Food and Beverage Advertising Initiative," *Better Business Bureau*, 2017.

57   cartoons and Cocoa Puffs are still as friendly: John McQuaid, "Despite Voluntary Restrictions, Junk Food Ads Aimed at Kids Are Still a Problem," *Forbes*, May 11, 2015, https://www.forbes.com/sites/johnmcquaid/2015/05/11/despite-voluntary -restrictions-junk-food-ads-aimed-at-kids-are-still-a-problem/#70ad485f3450.

57   converts this sugar into fuel in the form of glycogen: Robert K. Conlee, Russell M. Lawler, and Patrick E. Ross, "Effects of Glucose or Fructose Feeding on Glycogen Repletion in Muscle and Liver after Exercise or Fasting," *Annals of Nutrition and Metabolism* 31, no. 2 (1987): 126–32, doi:10.1159/000177259.

58   converts it to fat: David Faeh et al., "Effect of Fructose Overfeeding and Fish Oil Administration on Hepatic de Novo Lipogenesis and Insulin Sensitivity in Healthy Men," *Diabetes* 54, no. 7 (2005): 1907–13, doi:10.2337/diabetes .54.7.1907.

59   Today that number is 36 percent: "Adult Obesity Facts," *Centers for Disease Control and Prevention*, 2017, https://www.cdc.gov/obesity/data/adult.html.

60   no evidence that saturated fat increases the risk of heart disease: Patty W.

Siri-Tarino et al., "Meta-Analysis of Prospective Cohort Studies Evaluating the Association of Saturated Fat with Cardiovascular Disease 1–5," *American Journal of Clinical Nutrition* 91, no. 3 (2010): 535–46, doi:10.3945/ajcn.2009.27725.1.

60   had not lessened the risk of heart disease, stroke, or cardiovascular disease: Barbara V. Howard et al., "Low-Fat Dietary Pattern and Risk of Cardiovascular Disease: The Women's Health Initiative Randomized Controlled Dietary Modification Trial," *JAMA* 295, no. 6 (February 8, 2006): 655–66, doi:10.1001/jama.295.6.655.

60   "The positive ecological correlations": Uffe Ravnskov, "The Questionable Role of Saturated and Polyunsaturated Fatty Acids in Cardiovascular Disease," *Journal of Clinical Epidemiology* 51, no. 6 (1998): 443–60, doi:10.1016/S0895-4356(98)00018-3.

60   "We found that the people": "Why Coconut Oil Won't Kill You, but Listening to the American Heart Association Might!," *Sustainable Dish*, 2017, https://sustainabledish.com/coconut-oil-wont-listening-american-heart-association-might/.

61   helps you lose more weight than a low-fat diet: Nassib Bezerra Bueno et al., "Very-Low-Carbohydrate Ketogenic Diet v. Low-Fat Diet for Long-Term Weight Loss: A Meta-Analysis of Randomised Controlled Trials," *British Journal of Nutrition* 110, no. 7 (2013): 1178–87, doi:10.1017/S0007114513000548.

61   unfairly villainized companion, cholesterol: Maria L. Fernandez, "Rethinking Dietary Cholesterol," *Current Opinion in Clinical Nutrition and Metabolic Care* 15, no. 2 (2012): 117–21, doi:10.1097/MCO.0b013e32834d2259.

61   protecting against certain types of cancer and depression: J. D. Neaton et al., "Serum Cholesterol Level and Mortality Findings for Men Screened in the Multiple Risk Factor Intervention Trial," *Archives of Internal Medicine* 152, no. 7 (1992): 1490–1500, http://www.ncbi.nlm.nih.gov/pubmed/1627030; Jay R. Kaplan et al., "Assessing the Observed Relationship between Low Cholesterol and Violence-Related Mortality," *Annals of the New York Academy of Sciences*, 836:57–80, 1997, doi:10.1111/j.1749-6632.1997.tb52355.x.

61   Think of cholesterol as cargo: Kris Gunnars, "Diet, Cholesterol and Lipoproteins Explained in Human Terms," *Medical News Today*, 2017, https://www.medicalnewstoday.com/articles/318712.php.

62   no correlation was found between egg consumption and heart disease or stroke: Ying Rong et al., "Egg Consumption and Risk of Coronary Heart Disease and Stroke: Dose-Response Meta-Analysis of Prospective Cohort Studies," *BMJ (Clinical Research Ed.)* 346 (2013): e8539, doi:10.1136/bmj.e8539.

62   a lot of evidence points to sugar: Kimber L. Stanhope et al., "Consumption of Fructose and High Fructose Corn Syrup Increase Postprandial Triglycerides, LDL-Cholesterol, and Apolipoprotein-B in Young Men and Women," *Journal of Clinical Endocrinology and Metabolism* 96, no. 10 (2011): E1596-605, doi:10.1210/jc.2011-1251.

62   increase the size of the boats: Christopher N. Blesso et al., "Egg Intake

Improves Carotenoid Status by Increasing Plasma HDL Cholesterol in Adults with Metabolic Syndrome," *Food Funct.* 4, no. 2 (2013): 213–21, doi:10.1039/C2FO30154G.

62   shifting the ratio of "good" to "bad" lipoproteins: Christopher N. Blesso et al., "Whole Egg Consumption Improves Lipoprotein Profiles and Insulin Sensitivity to a Greater Extent than Yolk-Free Egg Substitute in Individuals with Metabolic Syndrome," *Metabolism: Clinical and Experimental* 62, no. 3 (2013): 400–410, doi:10.1016/j.metabol.2012.08.014.

62   increased the percentage of the larger particles: Darlene M. Dreon et al., "Low-Density Lipoprotein Subclass Patterns and Lipoprotein Response to a Reduced-Fat Diet in Men," *FASEB J.* 8, no. 1 (1994): 121–26, http://www.ncbi.nlm.nih.gov/pubmed/8299884.

62   54 percent of doctors: Mannuel Hörl, "Fat: The New Health Paradigm," *Credit Suisse*, 2015, https://www.credit-suisse.com/us/en/articles/articles/news-and-expertise/2015/09/en/fat-the-new-health-paradigm.html.

62   just not true: P. Schnohr et al., "Egg Consumption and High-Density-Lipoprotein Cholesterol," *Journal of Internal Medicine* 235, no. 3 (March 1994): 249–51, http://www.ncbi.nlm.nih.gov/pubmed/8120521.

62   did not specify an upper daily limit for dietary cholesterol: Peter Whoriskey et al., "Government Revises Dietary Guidelines for Americans: Go Ahead and Have Some Eggs," *Washington Post*, 2016, https://www.washingtonpost.com/news/wonk/wp/2016/01/07/government-revises-dietary-guidelines-for-americans-go-ahead-and-have-some-eggs/?utm_term=.09425bcb8246.

62   the body adjusts accordingly: Peter J. H. Jones et al., "Dietary Cholesterol Feeding Suppresses Human Cholesterol Synthesis Measured by Deuterium Incorporation and Urinary Mevalonic Acid Levels," *Arteriosclerosis, Thrombosis, and Vascular Biology* 16, no. 10 (1996): 1222–28, doi:10.1161/01.ATV.16.10.1222.

63   Fried oils: A. Perez-Herrera et al., "The Postprandial Inflammatory Response after Ingestion of Heated Oils in Obese Persons Is Reduced by the Presence of Phenol Compounds," *Molecular Nutrition and Food Research* 56, no. 3 (2012): 510–14, doi:10.1002/mnfr.201100533.

63   trans fats: David J. Baer et al., "Dietary Fatty Acids Affect Plasma Markers of Inflammation in Healthy Men Fed Controlled Diets: A Randomized Crossover Study," *American Journal of Clinical Nutrition* 79, no. 6 (2004): 969–73.

63   enhances the function and composition of microbiota: P. Veiga et al., "Changes of the Human Gut Microbiome Induced by a Fermented Milk Product," *Sci Rep* 4 (2014): 6328, doi:10.1038/srep06328.

63   improve lactose intolerance: T. He et al., "Effects of Yogurt and Bifidobacteria Supplementation on the Colonic Microbiota in Lactose-Intolerant Subjects," *Journal of Applied Microbiology* 104, no. 2 (2008): 595–604, doi:10.1111/j.1365-2672.2007.03579.x.

63   pathogenic microorganisms: Elise Alvaro et al., "Composition and Metabolism of the Intestinal Microbiota in Consumers and Non-Consumers of Yo-

gurt," *British Journal of Nutrition* 97, no. 1 (January 2007): 126–33, doi:10.1017/S0007114507243065.

66 not the most important meal of the day: Aristofanis Gikas, John K. Triantafillidis, and Pigi Perdikaki, "Breakfast Skipping and Its Association with Other Unhealthy Food Habits among Greek High School Adolescents," *Annals of Gastroenterology* 16, no. 4 (2003): 321–27.

66 medically supervised fasts: W. K. Stewart and L. W. Fleming, "Features of a Successful Therapeutic Fast of 382 Days' Duration," *Postgraduate Medical Journal* 49, no. 569 (1973): 203–9, doi:10.1136/pgmj.49.569.203.

68 increases your metabolic rate: Christian Zauner et al., "Resting Energy Expenditure in Short-Term Starvation Is Increased as a Result of an Increase in Serum Norepinephrine," *American Journal of Clinical Nutrition* 71, no. 6 (2000): 1511–15.

68 waist circumference reduction of 4 to 7 percent: A. R. Barnosky et al., "Intermittent Fasting vs Daily Calorie Restriction for Type 2 Diabetes Prevention: A Review of Human Findings," *Transl Res* 164, no. 4 (2014): 302–11, doi:10.1016/j.trsl.2014.05.013.

68 less muscle loss: K. A. Varady, "Intermittent versus Daily Calorie Restriction: Which Diet Regimen Is More Effective for Weight Loss?," *Obesity Reviews* 12, no. 7 (2011): e593-60, doi:10.1111/j.1467-789X.2011.00873.x.

68 growth hormone levels can increase: Mark L. Hartman et al., "Augmented Growth Hormone (GH) Secretory Burst Frequency and Amplitude Mediate Enhanced GH Secretion during a Two-Day Fast in Normal Men," *Journal of Clinical Endocrinology and Metabolism* 74, no. 4 (1992): 757–65, doi:10.1210/jcem.74.4.1548337.

69 cellular repair processes: Mehrdad Alirezaei et al., "Short-Term Fasting Induces Profound Neuronal Autophagy," *Autophagy* 6, no. 6 (2010): 702–10, doi:10.4161/auto.6.6.12376.

69 reduces oxidative stress and inflammation: Mark P. Mattson and Ruiqian Wan, "Beneficial Effects of Intermittent Fasting and Caloric Restriction on the Cardiovascular and Cerebrovascular Systems," *Journal of Nutritional Biochemistry* 16, no. 3 (2005): 129–37, doi:10.1016/j.jnutbio.2004.12.007.

69 leading causes of disease: Rinne De Bont and Nik van Larebeke, "Endogenous DNA Damage in Humans: A Review of Quantitative Data," *Mutagenesis*, 2004, doi:10.1093/mutage/geh025.

69 lowest levels of digestive enzymes and gastric acid: John G. Moore and Franz Halberg, "Circadian Rhythm of Gastric Acid Secretion in Men with Active Duodenal Ulcer," *Digestive Diseases and Sciences* 31, no. 11 (1986): 1185–91, doi:10.1007/BF01296516.

75 452 scientists who died at the peak of their prowess: Pierre Azoulay, Christian Fons-Rosen, and Joshua S. Graff Zivin, "Does Science Advance One Funeral at a Time?," National Bureau of Economic Research Working Paper 21788, December 2015, doi:10.3386/w21788.

CHAPTER 4: ESSENTIAL SUPPLEMENTS

80   "second brain": Ann M. O'Hara and Fergus Shanahan, "The Gut Flora as a Forgotten Organ," *EMBO Reports* 7, no. 7 (2006): 688–93, doi:10.1038/sj.embor.7400731.

80   Thirty-two percent of kids: Brady Hamilton et al., "Births: Provisional Data for 2016," NVSS *Vital Statistics Rapid Release*, 2017, https://www.cdc.gov/nchs/data/vsrr/report002.pdf.

80   kick-start infant immunity: Joann Romano-Keeler and Jörn-Hendrik Weitkamp, "Maternal Influences on Fetal Microbial Colonization and Immune Development," *Pediatric Research* 77 (2015): 189–95, doi:10.1038/pr.2014.163.

80   diabetes, hypertension, sudden cardiac death, headaches, asthma: J. H. F. de Baaij, J. G. J. Hoenderop, and R. J. M. Bindels, "Magnesium in Man: Implications for Health and Disease," *Physiological Reviews* 95, no. 1 (2015): 1–46, doi:10.1152/physrev.00012.2014.

80   irritability: Namju Lee, "A Review of Magnesium, Iron, and Zinc Supplementation Effects on Athletic Performance," *KJPE* 56, no. 1 (n.d.): 797–806.

80   weakness, and muscle twitches: Uwe Gröber, Joachim Schmidt, and Klaus Kisters, "Magnesium in Prevention and Therapy," *Nutrients*, 2015, doi:10.3390/nu7095388.

81   over a billion people are deficient in vitamin D: Opinder Sahota, "Understanding Vitamin D Deficiency," *Age and Ageing*, 2014, doi:10.1093/ageing/afu104.

81   depression, fibromyalgia, Alzheimer's disease: Jonathan A. Shaffer et al., "Vitamin D Supplementation for Depressive Symptoms: A Systematic Review and Meta-Analysis of Randomized Controlled Trials," *Psychosomatic Medicine* 76, no. 3 (2014): 190–96, doi:10.1097/PSY.0000000000000044; Carlos A. S. Jesus, David Feder, and Mario F. P. Peres, "The Role of Vitamin D in Pathophysiology and Treatment of Fibromyalgia," *Current Pain and Headache Reports* 17, no. 8 (2013): 355, doi:10.1007/s11916-013-0355-6; Thomas J. Littlejohns et al., "Vitamin D and the Risk of Dementia and Alzheimer Disease," *Neurology* 83, no. 10 (2014): 920–28, doi:10.1212/WNL.0000000000000755.

81   immune response and hormone function: Barbara Prietl et al., "Vitamin D and Immune Function," *Nutrients*, 2013, doi:10.3390/nu5072502; Li Yan Chun, Guilin Qiao, Milan Uskokovic, Wei Xiang, Wei Zheng, and Juan Kong, "Vitamin D: A Negative Endocrine Regulator of the Renin-Angiotensin System and Blood Pressure," *Journal of Steroid Biochemistry and Molecular Biology* 89–90:387–92, 2004, doi:10.1016/j.jsbmb.2004.03.004.

85   more likely to be sick: Thomas A. Barringer et al., "Effect of a Multivitamin and Mineral Supplement on Infection and Quality of Life: A Randomized, Double-Blind, Placebo-Controlled Trial," *Annals of Internal Medicine* 138, no. 5 (2003): 365–71, doi:10.7326/0003-4819-138-5-200303040-00005.

85   violent: S. J. Schoenthaler and I. D. Bier, "The Effect of Vitamin-Mineral Supplementation on Juvenile Delinquency among American Schoolchildren: A

Randomized, Double-Blind Placebo-Controlled Trial," *J Altern Complement Med* 6, no. 1 (2000): 7–17, doi:10.1089/act.2000.6.7.

86   facilitating healthy bone mass: Thomas O. Carpenter et al., "A Randomized Controlled Study of Effects of Dietary Magnesium Oxide Supplementation on Bone Mineral Content in Healthy Girls," *Journal of Clinical Endocrinology and Metabolism* 91, no. 12 (2006): 4866–72, doi:10.1210/jc.2006-1391.

86   the performance of athletes: L. R. Brilla and T. F. Haley, "Effect of Magnesium Supplementation on Strength Training in Humans," *Journal of the American College of Nutrition* 11, no. 3 (1992): 326–29, doi:10.1080/07315724.1992 .10718233.

86   supporting men and women during exercise: Lindsy S. Kass and Filipe Poeira, "The Effect of Acute vs Chronic Magnesium Supplementation on Exercise and Recovery on Resistance Exercise, Blood Pressure and Total Peripheral Resistance on Normotensive Adults," *Journal of the International Society of Sports Nutrition* 12, no. 1 (2015): 19, doi:10.1186/s12970-015-0081-z.

86   diminishing insulin resistance: Frank Mooren et al., "Oral Magnesium Supplementation Reduces Insulin Resistance in Non-Diabetic Subjects— A Double-Blind, Placebo-Controlled, Randomized Trial," *Journal of Diabetes, Obesity and Metabolism* 13, no. 3 (2011): 281–84, doi:10.1111/j.1463-1326.2010.01332.x.

86   reduce normal systemic inflammation: Philip C. Calder, "N-3 Polyunsaturated Fatty Acids, Inflammation, and Inflammatory Diseases," *American Journal of Clinical Nutrition* 83, no. 6 Suppl (2006): 1505S–19S, doi:16841861.

87   the same metabolic effects at lower doses: Stine M. Ulven et al., "Metabolic Effects of Krill Oil Are Essentially Similar to Those of Fish Oil but at Lower Dose of EPA and DHA, in Healthy Volunteers," *Lipids* 46, no. 1 (2011): 37–46, doi:10.1007/s11745-010-3490-4.

87   menstrual cycle: Fotini Sampalis et al., "Evaluation of the Effects of Neptune Krill Oil™ on the Management of Premenstrual Syndrome and Dysmenorrhea," *Alternative Medicine Review* 8, no. 2 (2003): 171–79.

87   body fat mass: A. Salehpour et al., "A 12-Week Double-Blind Randomized Clinical Trial of Vitamin D(3) Supplementation on Body Fat Mass in Healthy Overweight and Obese Women," *Nutrition Journal* 11, no. 1 (2012): 78, doi:10.1186/1475-2891-11-78.

87   maintain muscle mass and reduce fractures: Yoshihiro Sato et al., "Low-Dose Vitamin D Prevents Muscular Atrophy and Reduces Falls and Hip Fractures in Women after Stroke: A Randomized Controlled Trial," *Cerebrovascular Diseases* 20, no. 3 (2005): 187–92, doi:10.1159/000087203.

87   correct mood-related issues: Sue Penckofer et al., "Vitamin D and Depression: Where Is All the Sunshine?," *Issues in Mental Health Nursing* 31, no. 6 (May 7, 2010): 385–93, doi:10.3109/01612840903437657.

88   *S. Boulardii* is the shit: Lynne V. McFarland, "Systematic Review and Meta-Analysis of Saccharomyces Boulardii in Adult Patients," *World Journal of Gastroenterology*, 2010, doi:10.3748/wjg.v16.i18.2202.

89　significant improvements in obesity with probiotic supplementation: Maria Sáez-Lara et al., "Effects of Probiotics and Synbiotics on Obesity, Insulin Resistance Syndrome, Type 2 Diabetes and Non-Alcoholic Fatty Liver Disease: A Review of Human Clinical Trials," *International Journal of Molecular Sciences* 17, no. 6 (2016): 928, doi:10.3390/ijms17060928.

89　psychobiotics: Peter Andrey Smith, "Can the Bacteria in Your Gut Explain Your Mood?," *New York Times*, 2015, https://www.nytimes.com/2015/06/28/magazine/can-the-bacteria-in-your-gut-explain-your-mood.html?_r=0.

90　benefited from methylfolate supplementation: P. S. Godfrey et al., "Enhancement of Recovery from Psychiatric Illness by Methylfolate," *Lancet* 336, no. 8712 (August 18, 1990): 392–95, doi:10.1016/0140-6736(90)91942-4.

CHAPTER 5: DRIVE TIME, ALIVE TIME

99　over 8 million drivers exhibited extreme versions of road rage: Tamara Johnson, "Nearly 80 Percent of Drivers Express Significant Anger, Aggression or Road Rage," *AAA Newsroom*, 2016, http://newsroom.aaa.com/2016/07/nearly-80-percent-of-drivers-express-significant-anger-aggression-or-road-rage/.

105　43 percent less likely to need any form of hospital care: James E. Stahl et al., "Relaxation Response and Resiliency Training and Its Effect on Healthcare Resource Utilization," *PLoS ONE* 10, no. 10 (2015): e0172874, doi:10.1371/journal.pone.0140212.

105　"robust" effectiveness of mindfulness-based therapy: Stefan G. Hofmann et al., "The Effect of Mindfulness-Based Therapy on Anxiety and Depression: A Meta-Analytic Review," *Journal of Consulting and Clinical Psychology* 78, no. 2 (2010): 169–83, doi:10.1037/a0018555.

108　blood pressure ends up lower: Hisao Mori et al., "How Does Deep Breathing Affect Office Blood Pressure and Pulse Rate?," *Hypertens Res* 28, no. 6 (2005): 499–504, doi:10.1291/hypres.28.499.

CHAPTER 6: THE POWER PLANTS

114　prevent altitude sickness: M. F. Shackelton et al., "The Effect of Homeopathic Coca on High Altitude Mountain Sickness: Mt. Everest Base Camp," *Complementary Health Practice Review* 6, no. 1 (2000): 45–55, doi:10.1177/153321010000600107.

114　boost aerobic energy: R. Favier et al., "Coca Chewing for Exercise: Hormonal and Metabolic Responses of Nonhabitual Chewers," *Journal of Applied Physiology*, 1996, http://onlinelibrary.wiley.com/o/cochrane/clcentral/articles/213/CN-00134213/frame.html.

115　close to 900,000 people are addicted: Statistics in this paragraph from "What Is the Scope of Cocaine Use in the United States?," *NIDA*, 2016, https://www.drugabuse.gov/publications/research-reports/cocaine/what-scope-cocaine-use-in-united-states.

116　more than 20,000 overdose deaths: "Opioid Addiction 2016 Facts and Figures," *American Society of Addictive Medicine*, 2016, https://www.asam.org/docs/default-source/advocacy/opioid-addiction-disease-facts-figures.pdf.

116   steal an average of thirteen years: "Tobacco Facts and Figures," *BeTobacco Free.gov*, 2017, https://betobaccofree.hhs.gov/about-tobacco/facts-figures/index.html.

116   41,000 people die every year: "Fast Facts," *Centers for Disease Control and Prevention*, 2017, https://www.cdc.gov/tobacco/data_statistics/fact_sheets/fast_facts/index.htm.

118   90 percent of adults: Melanie A. Heckman, Jorge Weil, and Elvira Gonzalez de Mejia, "Caffeine (1, 3, 7-Trimethylxanthine) in Foods: A Comprehensive Review on Consumption, Functionality, Safety, and Regulatory Matters," *Journal of Food Science* 75, no. 3 (2010): R77–R87, doi:10.1111/j.1750-3841.2010.01561.x.

118   delay the time it takes for muscles to reach exhaustion: A. Nehlig and G. Debry, "Caffeine and Sports Activity: A Review," *International Journal of Sports Medicine* 15, no. 5 (1994): 215–23, doi:10.1055/s-2007-1021049.

118   increasing physical performance: Mike Doherty and Paul M. Smith, "Effects of Caffeine Ingestion on Exercise Testing: A Meta-Analysis," *International Journal of Sport Nutrition and Exercise Metabolism* 14, no. 6 (2004): 626–46, doi:10.1519/JSC.0b013e3181aeb0cf.

119   fight bad breath: Miki Ui et al., "Effect of Tea Catechins for Halitosis and Their Application to Chewing Gum," *Nippon Shokuhin Kogyo Gakkaishi* 38, no. 12 (1991): 1098–1102, doi:10.3136/nskkk1962.38.1098.

119   anxiety: K. Kimura et al., "L-Theanine Reduces Psychological and Physiological Stress Responses," *Biol Psychol* 74, no. 1 (2007): 39–45, doi:10.1016/j.biopsycho.2006.06.006.

119   unique advantages for brain function: Simon P. Kelly et al., "L-Theanine and Caffeine in Combination Affect Human Cognition as Evidenced by Oscillatory Alpha-Band Activity and Attention Task Performance," *Journal of Nutrition* 138, no. 8 (2008): 1572S–1577S, doi:138/8S-I/1572S [pii].

119   alpha frequency brainwaves: Anna C. Nobre, Anling Rao, and Gail N. Owen, "L-Theanine, a Natural Constituent in Tea, and Its Effect on Mental State," *Asia Pacific Journal of Clinical Nutrition* 17, no. 1 Suppl. (2008): 167–68, doi:10.6133/APJCN.2008.17.S1.40.

122   decreased risk of depression: Longfei Wang et al., "Coffee and Caffeine Consumption and Depression: A Meta-Analysis of Observational Studies," *Australian and New Zealand Journal of Psychiatry* 50, no. 3 (2016): 228–42, doi:10.1177/0004867415603131.

122   13 percent lower chance of depression: Giuseppe Grosso et al., "Coffee, Tea, Caffeine and Risk of Depression: A Systematic Review and Dose-Response Meta-Analysis of Observational Studies," *Molecular Nutrition & Food Research* 60, no. 1 (2016): 223–34, doi:10.1002/mnfr.201500620.

122   45 percent less likely to commit suicide: Michel Lucas et al., "Coffee, Caffeine, and Risk of Completed Suicide: Results from Three Prospective Cohorts of American Adults," *World Journal of Biological Psychiatry* 15, no. 5 (2014): 377–86, doi:10.3109/15622975.2013.795243.

122 helps protect the liver: Susanna C. Larsson and Alicja Wolk, "Coffee Consumption and Risk of Liver Cancer: A Meta-Analysis," *Gastroenterology* 132, no. 5 (2007): 1740–45, doi:10.1053/j.gastro.2007.03.044.

122 support gut health: Muriel Jaquet et al., "Impact of Coffee Consumption on the Gut Microbiota: A Human Volunteer Study," *International Journal of Food Microbiology* 130, no. 2 (March 31, 2009): 117–21, doi:10.1016/j.ijfoodmicro.2009.01.011.

123 one of the slowest foods to digest: G. Stacher et al., "Fat Preload Delays Gastric Emptying: Reversal by Cisapride," *British Journal of Clinical Pharmacology* 30, no. 6 (1990): 839–45, doi:10.1111/j.1365-2125.1990.tb05449.x.

124 improved cognitive function: Mark A. Reger et al., "Effects of β-Hydroxybutyrate on Cognition in Memory-Impaired Adults," *Neurobiology of Aging* 25, no. 3 (2004): 311–14, doi:10.1016/S0197-4580(03)00087-3.

124 weight management: Marie Pierre St.-Onge and Aubrey Bosarge, "Weight-Loss Diet That Includes Consumption of Medium-Chain Triacylglycerol Oil Leads to a Greater Rate of Weight and Fat Mass Loss than Does Olive Oil," *American Journal of Clinical Nutrition* 87, no. 3 (2008): 621–26, doi:87/3/621 [pii].

124 5 percent more energy: A. G. Dulloo et al., "Twenty-Four-Hour Energy Expenditure and Urinary Catecholamines of Humans Consuming Low-to-Moderate Amounts of Medium-Chain Triglycerides: A Dose-Response Study in a Human Respiratory Chamber," *European Journal of Clinical Nutrition* 50, no. 3 (1996): 152–58, http://www.ncbi.nlm.nih.gov/pubmed/8654328.

125 full-fledged medical disorder: Trent Stockton, "Caffeine Withdrawal Recognized As A Disorder," *Johns Hopkins Medicine*, 2004, http://www.hopkinsmedicine.org/press_releases/2004/09_29_04.html.

126 generally considered safe: "Advisory Report," *Health.gov*, 2015, https://health.gov/dietaryguidelines/2015-scientific-report/.

126 susceptible to caffeine's effects: "Teen Girl Dies of 'Caffeine Toxicity' after Downing 2 Energy Drinks," *Today*, 2012, https://www.today.com/health/teen-girl-dies-caffeine-toxicity-after-downing-2-energy-drinks-506441.

126 take a week off: D. Robertson et al., "Tolerance to the Humoral and Hemodynamic Effects of Caffeine in Man," *Journal of Clinical Investigation* 67, no. 4 (1981): 1111–17, doi:10.1172/JCI110124.

126 estimated billion people smoke: Marie Ng et al., "Smoking Prevalence and Cigarette Consumption in 187 Countries, 1980-2012," *JAMA* 311, no. 2 (2014): 183–92, doi:10.1001/jama.2013.284692.

127 zone: "The Biocybernaut Process," 2016, http://www.biocybernaut.com/projects/.

127 alpha frequency brainwave state: Edward F. Domino et al., "Tobacco Smoking Produces Widespread Dominant Brain Wave Alpha Frequency Increases," *International Journal of Psychophysiology* 74, no. 3 (2009): 192–98, doi:10.1016/j.ijpsycho.2009.08.011.

127 alertness: Natalia S. Lawrence, Thomas J. Ross, and Elliot A. Stein, "Cognitive Mechanisms of Nicotine on Visual Attention," *Neuron* 36, no. 3 (2002): 539–48, doi:10.1016/S0896-6273(02)01004-8.

127 improved fine motor skills, attention, accuracy, response time, short-term memory, and working memory: Stephen J. Heishman, Bethea A. Kleykamp, and Edward G. Singleton, "Meta-Analysis of the Acute Effects of Nicotine and Smoking on Human Performance," *Psychopharmacology*, 2010, doi:10.1007/s00213-010-1848-1.

127 cognitive impairment: N. A. Goriounova and H. D. Mansvelder, "Short- and Long-Term Consequences of Nicotine Exposure during Adolescence for Prefrontal Cortex Neuronal Network Function," *Cold Spring Harb Perspect Med* 2, no. 12 (2012): a012120, doi:10.1101/cshperspect.a012120.

127 Even responsible nicotine use may cause: Jacob Heller, David Zieve, and Brenda Conway, "Nicotine Poisoning," *MedlinePlus*, 2017, https://medlineplus.gov/ency/article/002510.htm.

128 increases levels of three of the most pleasurable chemicals: David J. K. Balfour, "The Neurobiology of Tobacco Dependence: A Preclinical Perspective on the Role of the Dopamine Projections to the Nucleus," *Nicotine and Tobacco Research*, 2004, doi:10.1080/14622200412331324965.

128 trigger the release of these chemicals: Michael Rabinoff et al., "Pharmacological and Chemical Effects of Cigarette Additives," *American Journal of Public Health* 97, no. 11 (2007): 1981–91, doi:10.2105/AJPH.2005.078014.

128 100 of which are psychoactive: Ibid.

128 35 million people: "Nicotine (Tobacco Addiction and Abuse)," accessed February 23, 2017, http://www.medicinenet.com/nicotine/article.htm.

129 less attractive to potential partners: Eveline Vincke, "The Young Male Cigarette and Alcohol Syndrome: Smoking and Drinking as a Short-Term Mating Strategy," *Evolutionary Psychology* 14, no. 1 (2016), doi:10.1177/1474704916631615.

129 end up earning less money: Judith J. Prochaska et al., "Likelihood of Unemployed Smokers vs Nonsmokers Attaining Reemployment in a One-Year Observational Study," *JAMA Internal Medicine* 176, no. 5 (2016): 662–70, doi:10.1001/jamainternmed.2016.0772.

129 "as a way of using nicotine": Royal College of Physicians, "Promote E-Cigarettes Widely as Substitute for Smoking Says New RCP Report," *Nicotine without Smoke: Tobacco Harm Reduction*, 2016, https://www.rcplondon.ac.uk/news/promote-e-cigarettes-widely-substitute-smoking-says-new-rcp-report.

129 $117 billion in annual revenue: Jennifer Maloney and Saabira Chaudhuri, "Against All Odds, the U.S. Tobacco Industry Is Rolling in Money," *Wall Street Journal*, April 23, 2017, https://www.wsj.com/articles/u-s-tobacco-industry-rebounds-from-its-near-death-experience-1492968698.

129 little difference in overall health and life expectancy: Coral E. Gartner et al., "Assessment of Swedish Snus for Tobacco Harm Reduction: An Epidemiolog-

ical Modelling Study," *Lancet* 369, no. 9578 (2007): 2010–14, doi:10.1016/S0140 -6736(07)60677-1.

130 may impair cellular function: Lindsey Konkel, "Concerns Explode over New Health Risks of Vaping," *Science News for Students*, 2017, https://www.science newsforstudents.org/article/concerns-explode-over-new-health-risks-vaping.

130 unlikely to exceed 5 percent of the harm from smoking tobacco: Royal College of Physicians, *Nicotine without Smoke*.

130 drops your risk for a lot of the cancers associated with cigarette smoking to virtually nil: Cindy M. Chang et al., "Systematic Review of Cigar Smoking and All Cause and Smoking Related Mortality," *BMC Public Health* 15, no. 1 (2015): 390, doi:10.1186/s12889-015-1617-5.

132 shown marginal benefit: Bai Song Wang et al., "Efficacy and Safety of Natural Acetylcholinesterase Inhibitor Huperzine A in the Treatment of Alzheimer's Disease: An Updated Meta-Analysis," *Journal of Neural Transmission* 116, no. 4 (2009): 457–65, doi:10.1007/s00702-009-0189-x.

132 memory and learning performance: Q. Q. Sun et al., "Huperzine-A Capsules Enhance Memory and Learning Performance in 34 Pairs of Matched Adolescent Students," *Zhongguo Yao Li Xue Bao = Acta Pharmacologica Sinica*, 1999.

CHAPTER 7: DOIN' WORK

138 Facebook alone: Mark Fahey, "Facebook Turns 12—Trillions in Time Wasted," *CNBC*, 2016, https://www.cnbc.com/2016/02/04/facebook-turns-12-- trillions-in-time-wasted.html.

139 80 percent of people are dissatisfied with their jobs: Alyson Shontell, "80% Hate Their Jobs—But Should You Choose a Passion or a Paycheck?," *Business Insider*, 2010.

139 40 percent who say their job is "very or extremely stressful": Steve Tobak, "Work Stress? You're Not Alone, CDC Says," *Cnet*, 2008, https://www.cnet.com /news/work-stress-youre-not-alone-cdc-says/.

139 57 percent of their paid vacation days: A. Pawlowski, "Why Is America the 'No-Vacation Nation'?," *CNNtravel*, 2011, http://www.cnn.com/2011 /TRAVEL/05/23/vacation.in.america/index.html.

140 10,000 workers per year drop dead: Zaria Gorvett, "Can You Work Yourself to Death?," *BBC.com*, 2016, http://www.bbc.com/capital/story/20160912-is -there-such-thing-as-death-from-overwork.

140 peak income correlated to happiness is $83,000: Doug Short, "$83,000 Is The New $75,000 Happiness Benchmark For Annual Income," *Business Insider*, 2014, http://www.businessinsider.com/happiness-benchmark-for-annual-income-2014-7.

145 distracting: Brigitta Danuser et al., "Performance in a Complex Task and Breathing under Odor Exposure," *Human Factors* 45, no. 4 (2003): 549–62, doi:10.1518/hfes.45.4.549.27093.

145 anger and disgust: O. Alaoui-Ismaïli et al., "Basic Emotions Evoked by Odor-

ants: Comparison between Autonomic Responses and Self-Evaluation," *Physiology and Behavior* 62, no. 4 (1997): 713–20, doi:10.1016/S0031-9384(97)90016-0.

145   In Japan: Leigh Stringer, *The Healthy Workplace* (AMACOM, 2016).

146   reduce anxiety and stress, blood pressure, nausea, even depression: S. D. Ehrlich, "Aromatherapy," *University of Maryland Medical Center*, 2011, http://www.umm.edu/health/medical/ altmed/treatment/aromatherapy.

146   "the 'smell' receptors": Rachel Gillett, "Productivity Hack of The Week: Use Aromatherapy to Improve Your Work," *Fast Company*, 2014, https://www.fastcompany.com/3036242/productivity-hack-of-the-week-use-aromatherapy-to-improve-.

147   even if you exercise regularly: Peter T. Katzmarzyk and I-Min Lee, "Sedentary Behaviour and Life Expectancy in the USA: A Cause-Deleted Life Table Analysis," *BMJ Open* 2, no. 4 (2012): e000828, doi:10.1136/bmjopen-2012-000828.

148   250 workplace ergonomics case studies: "Examples of Costs and Benefits of Ergonomics," (n.d.), https://www.pshfes.org/Resources/Documents/Ergonomics_cost_benefit_case_study_collection.pdf.

150   mirror neurons: Marco Iacoboni, "Imitation, Empathy, and Mirror Neurons," *Annual Review of Psychology* 60, no. 1 (2009): 653–70, doi:10.1146/annurev.psych.60.110707.163604.

153   sixty-four seconds to return: Thomas W. Jackson, Ray Dawson, and Darren Wilson, "Understanding Email Interaction Increases Organizational Productivity," *Communications of the ACM* 46, no. 8 (2003): 80–84, doi:10.1145/859670.859673.

156   fancy software apps: Frances Caballo, "10 Apps to Help You Stay Focused on Your Writing," *Jane Friedman*, 2014, https://www.janefriedman.com/10-apps-help-stay-focused-writing/.

CHAPTER 8: EAT A WEIRD LUNCH

163   75 percent of the world's food: Mark L. Heiman and Frank L. Greenway, "A Healthy Gastrointestinal Microbiome Is Dependent on Dietary Diversity," *Molecular Metabolism*, 2016, doi:10.1016/j.molmet.2016.02.005.

166   elicited significant increases in muscle protein synthesis: T. Brock Symons et al., "Moderating the Portion Size of a Protein-Rich Meal Improves Anabolic Efficiency in Young and Elderly," *Journal of the American Dietetic Association* 109, no. 9 (2009): 1582–86, doi:10.1016/j.jada.2009.06.369.

167   metabolic benefits: Martin O. Weickert and Andreas F. H. Pfeiffer, "Metabolic Effects of Dietary Fiber Consumption and Prevention of Diabetes," *Journal of Nutrition* 138, no. 3 (2008): 439–42, doi:10.3390/nu2121266.

167   helps speed the complete passage of food and waste: James W. Anderson et al., "Health Benefits of Dietary Fiber," *Nutrition Reviews*, 2009, doi:10.1111/j.1753-4887.2009.00189.x.

169   slows down the absorption of the sugar in the gut: D. J. Jenkins et al., "Dietary Fibres, Fibre Analogues, and Glucose Tolerance: Importance of Viscosity," *BMJ* 1, no. 6124 (1978): 1392–94, doi:10.1136/bmj.1.6124.1392.

169 60 percent increase in childhood obesity: David S. Ludwig, Karen E. Peterson, and Steven L. Gortmaker, "Relation between Consumption of Sugar-Sweetened Drinks and Childhood Obesity: A Prospective, Observational Analysis," *Lancet* 357, no. 9255 (2001): 505–8, doi:10.1016/S0140-6736(00)04041-1.

169 increasing the signal for satiety: Rania Abou Samra, "Fats and Satiety," in *Fat Detection: Taste, Texture, and Post Ingestive Effects*, ed. Jean-Pierre Montmayeur and Johannes Le Coutre (Boca Raton: CRC Press/Taylor & Francis, 2010), doi:10.1201/9781420067767.

169 as early as the first bite: Astrid J. P. G. Smeets and Margriet S. Westerterp-Plantenga, "Satiety and Substrate Mobilization after Oral Fat Stimulation," *British Journal of Nutrition* 95, no. 4 (2006): 795–801, doi:10.1079/BJN20051725.

170 high cholesterol can be protective: A. W. Weverling-Rijnsburger et al., "Total Cholesterol and Risk of Mortality in the Oldest Old," *Lancet* 350, no. 9085 (1997): 1119–23, doi:10.1016/S0140-6736(97)04430-9.

170 the higher the cholesterol, the lower your risk of heart disease: Irwin J. Schatz, Kamal Masaki, Katsuhiko Yano, Randi Chen, Beatriz L. Rodriguez, and J. David Curb, "Cholesterol and All-Cause Mortality in Elderly People from the Honolulu Heart Program: A Cohort Study," *Lancet* 358, no. 9279 (2001): 351–55, doi:10.1016/S0140-6736(01)05553-2.

170 cancer and suicide: J. D. Neaton et al., "Serum Cholesterol Level and Mortality Findings for Men Screened in the Multiple Risk Factor Intervention Trial," *Archives of Internal Medicine* 152, no. 7 (1992): 1490–1500; and Jay R. Kaplan et al., "Assessing the Observed Relationship between Low Cholesterol and Violence-Related Mortality," *Annals of the New York Academy of Sciences*, 836:57–80, 1997, doi:10.1111/j.1749-6632.1997.tb52355.x.

170 starting point for the production of many important hormones: J. Mark Berg, J. L. Tymoczko, and L. Stryer, "Biochemistry," in *Biochemistry*, 5th ed., 1120 (New York: W. H. Freeman, 2002), doi:10.1007/s13398-014-0173-7.2.

170 female: R. Goldstat et al., "Transdermal Testosterone Therapy Improves Well-Being, Mood, and Sexual Function in Premenopausal Women," *Menopause* 10, no. 5 (2003): 390–98, doi:10.1097/01.GME.0000060256.03945.20.

170 mood, body composition, libido, and energy: R. S. Swerdloff and C. Wang, "Three-Year Follow-up of Androgen Treatment in Hypogonadal Men: Preliminary Report with Testosterone Gel," *Aging Male* 6, no. 3 (2003): 207–11, http://ovidsp.ovid.com/ovidweb.cgi?T=JS&PAGE=reference&D=med4&NEWS=N&AN=14628501.

171 CLA: Leah D. Whigham, Abigail C. Watras, and Dale A. Schoeller, "Efficacy of Conjugated Linoleic Acid for Reducing Fat Mass: A Meta-Analysis in Humans," *American Journal of Clinical Nutrition* 85, no. 5 (2007): 1203–11, doi:17490954.

171 50 percent more antioxidants: Marcin Baranski et al., "Higher Antioxidant and Lower Cadmium Concentrations and Lower Incidence of Pesticide Residues in Organically Grown Crops: A Systematic Literature Review and Meta-

Analyses," *British Journal of Nutrition* 112, no. 5 (2014): 794–811, doi:10.1017/S0007114514001366.

172 more robust and more diverse group of microbiota: Mark L. Heiman and Frank L. Greenway, "A Healthy Gastrointestinal Microbiome Is Dependent on Dietary Diversity," *Molecular Metabolism*, 2016, doi:10.1016/j.molmet.2016.02.005.

172 potential health benefits: Catherine A. Lozupone et al., "Diversity, Stability and Resilience of the Human Gut Microbiota," *Nature* 489, no. 7415 (2012): 220–30, doi:10.1038/nature11550.

172 outnumber the rest of the body's cells ten to one: Ron Sender, Shai Fuchs, and Ron Milo, "Revised Estimates for the Number of Human and Bacteria Cells in the Body," *PLOS Biology*, August 19, 2016, http://journals.plos.org/plosbiology/article?id=10.1371/journal.pbio.1002533.

173 inulin: "Dandelion Greens, Raw Nutrition Facts and Calories," *Self NutritionData*, 2014, http://nutritiondata.self.com/facts/vegetables-and-vegetable-products/2441/2.

173 helping reduce constipation: Daniéla Oliveira Magro et al., "Effect of Yogurt Containing Polydextrose, *Lactobacillus Acidophilus* NCFM and *Bifidobacterium Lactis* HN019: A Randomized, Double-Blind, Controlled Study in Chronic Constipation," *Nutrition Journal* 13, no. 1 (2014): 75, doi:10.1186/1475-2891-13-75.

173 retrogradation: S. G. Haralampu, "Resistant Starch—a Review of the Physical Properties and Biological Impact of RS3," *Carbohydrate Polymers* 41, no. 3 (March 2000): 285–92, doi:10.1016/S0144-8617(99)00147-2.

173 artichokes: P. Ramnani et al., "Prebiotic Effect of Fruit and Vegetable Shots Containing Jerusalem Artichoke Inulin: A Human Intervention Study," *British Journal of Nutrition* 104, no. 2 (2010): 233–40, doi:10.1017/S000711451000036X.

173 blueberries: Stefano Vendrame et al., "Six-Week Consumption of a Wild Blueberry Powder Drink Increases Bifidobacteria in the Human Gut," *Journal of Agricultural and Food Chemistry* 59, no. 24 (2011): 12815–20, doi:10.1021/jf2028686.

173 almonds and pistachios: Maria Ukhanova et al., "Effects of Almond and Pistachio Consumption on Gut Microbiota Composition in a Randomised Crossover Human Feeding Study," *British Journal of Nutrition* 111, no. 12 (2014): 2146–52, doi:10.1017/S0007114514000385.

174 in our typical diet the ratio is more like 1:16: A. P. Simopoulos, "Evolutionary Aspects of Diet, the Omega-6/Omega-3 Ratio and Genetic Variation: Nutritional Implications for Chronic Diseases," *Biomedicine and Pharmacotherapy* 60, no. 9 (2006): 502–7, doi:10.1016/j.biopha.2006.07.080.

174 grass-fed beef: Cynthia A. Daley et al., "A Review of Fatty Acid Profiles and Antioxidant Content in Grass-Fed and Grain-Fed Beef," *Nutrition Journal* 9, no. 1 (2010): 10, doi:10.1186/1475-2891-9-10.

175 reduce oxidative stress: Satish Balasaheb Nimse and Dilipkumar Pal, "Free

Radicals, Natural Antioxidants, and Their Reaction Mechanisms," *RSC Adv.* 5, no. 35 (2015): 27986–6, doi:10.1039/C4RA13315C.

175   part of the inflammation process: Kenneth L. Rock and Hajime Kono, "The Inflammatory Response to Cell Death," *Annual Review of Pathology* 3 (2008): 99–126, doi:10.1146/annurev.pathmechdis.3.121806.151456.

175   reduce something called C-reactive protein: Xenofon Tzounis et al., "Pre-biotic Evaluation of Cocoa-Derived Flavanols in Healthy Humans by Using a Randomized, Controlled, Double-Blind, Crossover Intervention Study," *American Journal of Clinical Nutrition* 93, no. 1 (2011): 62–72, doi:10.3945/ajcn.110.000075.

175   reduce inflammation: Julie S. Jurenka, "Anti-Inflammatory Properties of Curcumin, a Major Constituent of Curcuma Longa: A Review of Preclinical and Clinical Research," *Alternative Medicine Review*, 2009.

175   help reduce the burden of age-related brain conditions: Suzhen Dong et al., "Curcumin Enhances Neurogenesis and Cognition in Aged Rats: Implications for Transcriptional Interactions Related to Growth and Synaptic Plasticity," *PLoS ONE* 7, no. 2 (2012): e31211, doi:10.1371/journal.pone.0031211.

175   skyrocket up to 2,000 percent: Guido Shoba et al., "Influence of Piperine on the Pharmacokinetics of Curcumin in Animals and Human Volunteers," *Planta Medica* 64, no. 4 (1998): 353–56, doi:10.1055/s-2006-957450.

176   reduced the number of colds by 63 percent: P. Josling, "Preventing the Common Cold with a Garlic Supplement: A Double-Blind, Placebo-Controlled Survey," *Advances in Therapy* 18, no. 4 (2001): 189–93, doi:10.1007/BF02850113.

176   reduce the number of days someone feels sick with cold of flu by 61 percent: Meri P. Nantz et al., "Supplementation with Aged Garlic Extract Improves Both NK and Γδ-T Cell Function and Reduces the Severity of Cold and Flu Symptoms: A Randomized, Double-Blind, Placebo-Controlled Nutrition Intervention," *Clinical Nutrition (Edinburgh, Scotland)* 31, no. 3 (June 2012): 337–44, doi:10.1016/j.clnu.2011.11.019.

176   900 percent fewer: "Cauliflower, Raw Nutrition Facts and Calories," *Self NutritionData*, 2014, http://nutritiondata.self.com/facts/vegetables-and-vegetable-products/2390/2.

178   causing massive systemic inflammation: Dariush Mozaffarian et al., "Dietary Intake of Trans Fatty Acids and Systemic Inflammation in Women," *American Journal of Clinical Nutrition* 79, no. 4 (2004): 606–12, http://www.pubmedcentral.nih.gov/articlerender.fcgi?artid=1282449&tool=pmcentrez&rendertype=abstract.

178   pro-inflammatory state: Li Gang Yang et al., "Low N-6/n-3 PUFA Ratio Improves Lipid Metabolism, Inflammation, Oxidative Stress and Endothelial Function in Rats Using Plant Oils as N-3 Fatty Acid Source," *Lipids* 51, no. 1 (January 2016): 49–59, doi:10.1007/s11745-015-4091-z.

178   more likely to die from heart disease: M. W. Gillman et al., "Margarine

Intake and Subsequent Coronary Heart Disease in Men," *Epidemiology* 8, no. 2 (1997): 144–49, doi:10.1128/AAC.03728-14.

179 burn it or fry it on high heat: R. A. Scanlan, "Formation and Occurrence of Nitrosamines in Food," *Cancer Research* 43, no. 5 Suppl. (1983): 2435–40.

179 carcinogen called nitrosamines: J. L. Brown, "N-Nitrosamines," *Occupational Medicine* 14, no. 4 (1999): 839–48, http://www.ncbi.nlm.nih.gov/pubmed/10495488.

180 four times more likely on nonorganic crops: Marcin Baranski et al., "Higher Antioxidant and Lower Cadmium Concentrations and Lower Incidence of Pesticide Residues in Organically Grown Crops."

180 cadmium: "Factsheet: Cadmium," *Center for Disease Control and Prevention*, 2016, https://www.cdc.gov/biomonitoring/Cadmium_FactSheet.html.

180 50–90 percent increased risk of ADHD: Maryse F. Bouchard et al., "Attention-Deficit/Hyperactivity Disorder and Urinary Metabolites of Organophosphate Pesticides," *Pediatrics* 125, no. 6 (June 2010): e1270-7, doi:10.1542/peds.2009-3058.

180 the development of Parkinson's later in life: Amanpreet S. Dhillon et al., "Pesticide/environmental Exposures and Parkinson's Disease in East Texas," *Journal of Agromedicine* 13, no. 1 (2008): 37–48, doi:10.1080/10599240801986215.

181 increased hyperactivity in children: David W. Schab and Nhi-Ha T. Trinh, "Do Artificial Food Colors Promote Hyperactivity in Children with Hyperactive Syndromes? A Meta-Analysis of Double-Blind Placebo-Controlled Trials," *Journal of Developmental and Behavioral Pediatrics* 25, no. 6 (December 2004): 423–34, http://www.ncbi.nlm.nih.gov/pubmed/15613992.

181 behavioral changes including irritability, restlessness, depression, and difficulty sleeping: K. S. Rowe and K. J. Rowe, "Synthetic Food Coloring and Behavior: A Dose Response Effect in a Double-Blind, Placebo-Controlled, Repeated-Measures Study," *Journal of Pediatrics* 125, no. 5 Pt. 1 (November 1994): 691–98, http://www.ncbi.nlm.nih.gov/pubmed/7965420.

181 increased hyperactivity: Ibid.

181 extremely high in mercury: M. M. Storelli and G. O. Marcotrigiano, "Fish for Human Consumption: Risk of Contamination by Mercury," *Food Additives and Contaminants* 17, no. 12 (December 2000): 1007–11, doi:10.1080/02652030050207792.

181 decrease in fine motor skills, dexterity, memory, and attention: Edna M. Yokoo et al., "Low Level Methylmercury Exposure Affects Neuropsychological Function in Adults," *Environmental Health* 2 (December 4, 2003): 8, doi:10.1186/1476-069X-2-8.

181 depression, anxiety, and even Alzheimer's and Parkinson's: Farhana Zahir et al., "Low Dose Mercury Toxicity and Human Health," *Environmental Toxicology and Pharmacology* 20, no. 2 (September 2005): 351–60, doi:10.1016/j.etap.2005.03.007.

182 dental work: Y. Omura et al., "Significant Mercury Deposits in Internal

Organs Following the Removal of Dental Amalgam, and Development of Pre-Can-cer on the Gingiva and the Sides of the Tongue and Their Represented Organs as a Result of Inadvertent Exposure to Strong Curing Light," *Acupuncture and Electro-Therapeutics Research* 21, no. 2 (n.d.): 133–60, http://www.ncbi.nlm.nih.gov /pubmed/8914687.

182 help the body chelate . . . heavy metal accumulation: Y. Omura and S. L. Beck-man, "Role of Mercury (Hg) in Resistant Infections & Effective Treatment of Chlamydia Trachomatis and Herpes Family Viral Infections (and Potential Treat-ment for Cancer) by Removing Localized Hg Deposits with Chinese Parsley and Delivering Effective Antibiotics," *Acupuncture & Electro-Therapeutics Research* 20, no. 3–4 (1995): 195–229, http://www.ncbi.nlm.nih.gov/pubmed/8686573.

182 prevent the accumulation of metals: Veena Sharma, Leena Kansal, and Arti Sharma, "Prophylactic Efficacy of Coriandrum Sativum (Coriander) on Testis of Lead-Exposed Mice," *Biological Trace Element Research* 136, no. 3 (September 2010): 337–54, doi:10.1007/s12011-009-8553-0.

182 prevents full absorption of key minerals: Ulrich Schlemmer et al., "Phytate in Foods and Significance for Humans: Food Sources, Intake, Processing, Bioavail-ability, Protective Role and Analysis," *Molecular Nutrition and Food Research* 53 Suppl 2 (September 2009): S330-75, doi:10.1002/mnfr.200900099.

183 particularly calcium: R. P. Heaney and C. M. Weaver, "Oxalate: Effect on Calcium Absorbability," *American Journal of Clinical Nutrition* 50, no. 4 (Octo-ber 1989): 830–32, http://www.ncbi.nlm.nih.gov/pubmed/2801588.

183 disable and degrade phytic acid: C. Centeno et al., "Effect of Several Ger-mination Conditions on Total P, Phytate P, Phytase, and Acid Phosphatase Ac-tivities and Inositol Phosphate Esters in Rye and Barley," *Journal of Agricultural and Food Chemistry* 49, no. 7 (July 2001): 3208–15, http://www.ncbi.nlm.nih.gov /pubmed/11453753.

183 lysine: K. P. Parameswaran and S. Sadasivam, "Changes in the Carbohy-drates and Nitrogenous Components during Germination of Proso Millet, *Pani-cum Miliaceum*," *Plant Foods for Human Nutrition* 45, no. 2 (February 1994): 97–102, http://www.ncbi.nlm.nih.gov/pubmed/8153070.

183 promotes phytate breakdown: Anna Reale et al., "Phytate Degradation by Lactic Acid Bacteria and Yeasts during the Wholemeal Dough Fermentation: A 31P NMR Study," *Journal of Agricultural and Food Chemistry* 52, no. 20 (Octo-ber 6, 2004): 6300–6305, doi:10.1021/jf049551p.

183 significantly reduces the amount of oxalate: Weiwen Chai and Michael Liebman, "Effect of Different Cooking Methods on Vegetable Oxalate Content," *Journal of Agricultural and Food Chemistry* 53, no. 8 (April 20, 2005): 3027–30, doi:10.1021/jf048128d.

183 symptoms: Naiyana Gujral, Hugh J. Freeman, and Alan B. R. Thomson, "Celiac Disease: Prevalence, Diagnosis, Pathogenesis and Treatment," *World Jour-nal of Gastroenterology* 18, no. 42 (November 14, 2012): 6036–59, doi:10.3748 /wjg.v18.i42.6036.

184 in the 0.5–13 percent range: J. Molina-Infante et al., "Systematic Review: Noncoeliac Gluten Sensitivity," *Alimentary Pharmacology and Therapeutics* 41, no. 9 (May 2015): 807–20, doi:10.1111/apt.13155.

184 less than 15 percent: Annalisa Capannolo et al., "Non-Celiac Gluten Sensitivity among Patients Perceiving Gluten-Related Symptoms," *Digestion* 92, no. 1 (2015): 8–13, doi:10.1159/000430090.

193 continues to develop even through our twenties: C. Lebel and C. Beaulieu, "Longitudinal Development of Human Brain Wiring Continues from Childhood into Adulthood," *Journal of Neuroscience* 31, no. 30 (July 27, 2011): 10937–47, doi:10.1523/JNEUROSCI.5302-10.2011.

194 it gets stronger largely through exercise: Liuyang Cai et al., "Brain Plasticity and Motor Practice in Cognitive Aging," *Frontiers in Aging Neuroscience* 6, no. 31 (March 10, 2014), doi:10.3389/fnagi.2014.00031.

CHAPTER 9: THE BINAURAL POWER NAP

201 outperform high doses of caffeine: Sara C. Mednick et al., "Comparing the Benefits of Caffeine, Naps and Placebo on Verbal, Motor and Perceptual Memory," *Behavioural Brain Research* 193, no. 1 (November 2008): 79–86, doi:10.1016/j.bbr.2008.04.028.

201 improve logical reasoning: M. H. Bonnet, "The Effect of Varying Prophylactic Naps on Performance, Alertness and Mood throughout a 52-Hour Continuous Operation," *Sleep* 14, no. 4 (August 1991): 307–15, http://www.ncbi.nlm.nih.gov/pubmed/1947593.

201 reaction time: Simon S. Smith et al., "Napping and Nightshift Work: Effects of a Short Nap on Psychomotor Vigilance and Subjective Sleepiness in Health Workers," *Sleep and Biological Rhythms* 5, no. 2 (April 2007): 117–25, doi:10.1111/j.1479-8425.2007.00261.x.

201 immune function: Brice Faraut et al., "Benefits of Napping and an Extended Duration of Recovery Sleep on Alertness and Immune Cells after Acute Sleep Restriction," *Brain, Behavior, and Immunity* 25, no. 1 (January 2011): 16–24, doi:10.1016/j.bbi.2010.08.001.

201 doubled levels of alertness: Mark Rosekind et al., "Crew Factors in Flight Operations IX: Effects of Planned Cockpit Rest on Crew Performance and Alertness in Long-Haul Operations," *NASA Technical Memorandum 108839*, 1994.

201 The nap—yes, the nap!—won: James Horne et al., "Sleep Extension versus Nap or Coffee, within the Context of 'Sleep Debt'," *Journal of Sleep Research* 17, no. 4 (December 2008): 432–36, doi:10.1111/j.1365-2869.2008.00680.x.

201 frustration and impulsiveness: Jennifer R. Goldschmied et al., "Napping to Modulate Frustration and Impulsivity: A Pilot Study," *Personality and Individual Differences* 86 (2015): 164–67, doi:10.1016/j.paid.2015.06.013.

202 it's a signal: Kenneth P. Wright, Christopher A. Lowry, and Monique K. LeBourgeois, "Circadian and Wakefulness-Sleep Modulation of Cognition in Humans," *Frontiers in Molecular Neuroscience* 5 (2012): 50, doi:10.3389/fnmol.2012.00050.

203 improvements for everything from cognitive performance to enhanced relaxation: Leila Chaieb et al., "Auditory Beat Stimulation and Its Effects on Cognition and Mood States," *Frontiers in Psychiatry* 6 (May 12, 2015), doi:10.3389/fpsyt.2015.00070.

CHAPTER 10: TRAINING

210 80 percent of Americans: Ryan Jaslow, "CDC: 80 Percent of American Adults Don't Get Recommended Exercise," *CBS*, 2013.

210 Over 100 million suffer: Institute of Medicine, *Relieving Pain in America: A Blueprint for Transforming Prevention, Care, Education, and Research* (Washington, DC: National Academies Press, 2011), doi:10.17226/13172.

210 20,000 of whom die every year: "Opioid Addiction: 2016 Facts and Figures," *American Society of Addictive Medicine*, 2016, https://www.asam.org/docs/default-source/advocacy/opioid-addiction-disease-facts-figures.pdf.

211 restore good energy levels: Lillebeth Larun et al., "Exercise Therapy for Chronic Fatigue Syndrome," *Cochrane Database of Systematic Reviews* 12 (2016): CD003200, doi:10.1002/14651858.CD003200.pub6.

211 improve your mood: Jacob D. Meyer et al., "Influence of Exercise Intensity for Improving Depressed Mood in Depression: A Dose-Response Study," *Behavior Therapy* 47, no. 4 (July 2016): 527–37, doi:10.1016/j.beth.2016.04.003.

211 improve your sleep quality: Paul D. Loprinzi and Bradley J. Cardinal, "Association between Objectively-Measured Physical Activity and Sleep, NHANES 2005–2006," *Mental Health and Physical Activity* 4, no. 2 (December 2011): 65–69, doi:10.1016/j.mhpa.2011.08.001.

211 in pain: Louise J. Geneen et al., "Physical Activity and Exercise for Chronic Pain in Adults: An Overview of Cochrane Reviews," *Cochrane Database of Systematic Reviews* 1 (2017): CD011279, doi:10.1002/14651858.CD011279.pub2.

211 perform better in bed: Erin R. McNamara, Jean Alfred-Thomas, and Stephen J. Freedland, "1500 Exercise Correlates to Higher Sexual Function Scores in a Cohort of Healthy Men," *Journal of Urology* 183, no. 4 (April 2010): e578, doi:10.1016/j.juro.2010.02.1237.

215 Aerobic capacity increased 13.8 percent: Nick Beltz et al., "Effects of Kettlebell Training on Aerobic Capacity, Muscular Strength, Balance, Flexibility, and Body Composition," *Journal of Fitness Research* 2, no. 2 (2013).

219 a part of their daily morning regimen: Brett McKay and Kate McKay, "Train Like an Ancient Hindu Warrior: The Steel Mace Workout," *Art of Manliness*, 2013, http://www.artofmanliness.com/2013/04/23/train-like-an-ancient-hindu-warrior-the-steel-mace-workout/.

220 Club swinging grew in popularity: Brett McKay and Kate McKay, "An Introduction to Indian Club Training," *The Art of Manliness*, 2012, http://www.artofmanliness.com/2012/03/18/an-introduction-to-indian-club-training/.

224 a multifaceted origin story: Conor Heffernan, "A Brief History of the Bar-

bell," *Physical Culture Study*, 2017, https://physicalculturestudy.com/2017/02/28 /history-of-the-barbell/.

229 sustained muscular effort: Elizabeth Quinn, "Measure and Improve Muscular Endurance," *Verywell*, 2017, https://www.verywell.com/what-is-muscular-en durance-3120360.

250 "recommendations for an active lifestyle": Alia J. Crum and Ellen J. Langer, "Mind-Set Matters: Exercise and the Placebo Effect," *Psychological Science* 18, no. 2 (February 6, 2007): 165–71, doi:10.1111/j.1467-9280.2007.01867.x.

250 increased actual bicep strength by 13.5 percent in just a few weeks: Phillip Cohen, "Mental Gymnastics Increase Bicep Strength," *New Scientist*, 2001, https://www .newscientist.com/article/dn1591-mental-gymnastics-increase-bicep-strength/.

CHAPTER 11: RESET AND RECONNECT

254 30 percent greater risk of dying: Julianne Holt-Lunstad et al., "Loneliness and Social Isolation as Risk Factors for Mortality," *Perspectives on Psychological Science* 10, no. 2 (March 11, 2015): 227–37, doi:10.1177/1745691614568352.

255 50 percent higher likelihood of survival: Julianne Holt-Lunstad, Timothy B. Smith, and J. Bradley Layton, "Social Relationships and Mortality Risk: A Meta-Analytic Review," *PLoS Medicine* 7, no. 7 (July 27, 2010): e1000316, doi:10.1371/journal.pmed.1000316.

259 nearly half of unemployed working-age men are addicted to opiate painkillers: Alan B. Krueger, "Where Have All the Workers Gone? An Inquiry into the Decline of the U.S. Labor Force Participation Rate," *Brookings Papers on Economic Activity*, 2017, https://www.brookings.edu/wp-content/uploads/2017/09/1_kru eger.pdf.

259 64 percent reduction in chronic pain: Penny F. Whiting et al., "Cannabinoids for Medical Use: A Systematic Review and Meta-Analysis," *JAMA* 313, no. 24 (June 23, 2015): 2456–73, doi:10.1001/jama.2015.6358.

259 pain reduction and pain scale assessment: Eva Martín-Sánchez et al., "Systematic Review and Meta-Analysis of Cannabis Treatment for Chronic Pain," *Pain Medicine* 10, no. 8 (November 1, 2009): 1353–68, doi:10.1111/j.1526 -4637.2009.00703.x.

260 50 percent of users report enhanced creativity when using cannabis: Bob Green, David Kavanagh, and Ross Young, "Being Stoned: A Review of Self-Reported Cannabis Effects," *Drug and Alcohol Review* 22, no. 4 (December 2003): 453–60, doi:10.1080/09595230310001613976.

262 literally 12 percent closer when music is playing: John Paul Titlow, "How Music Changes Your Behavior at Home," *Fast Company*, 2016, https://www.fast company.com/3056554/how-music-changes-our-behavior-at-home.

263 your biological markers actually start to reverse: Laura M. Hsu, Jaewoo Chung, and Ellen J. Langer, "The Influence of Age-Related Cues on Health and Longevity," *Perspectives on Psychological Science* 5, no. 6 (November 7, 2010): 632–48, doi:10.1177/1745691610388762.

264 mutually produce the connection hormone oxytocin: Robert M. Sapolsky, *Behave: The Biology of Humans at Our Best and Worst* (New York: Penguin Random House, 2017).

264 reduce blood pressure and resting heart rate: K. Allen et al., "Cardiovascular Reactivity and the Presence of Pets, Friends, and Spouses: The Truth About Cats and Dogs," *Psychosomatic Medicine* 64, no. 5 (2002): 727–39. doi:10.1097/01 .PSY.0000024236.11538.41.

264 greater empathy, higher self-esteem, and increased participation in social and physical activities: K. Hodgson et al., "Pets' Impact on Your Patients' Health: Leveraging Benefits and Mitigating Risk," *Journal of the American Board of Family Medicine* 28, no. 4 (July 1, 2015): 526–34, doi:10.3122/jabfm.2015.04.140254.

CHAPTER 12: EAT DINNER LIKE A KING
270 "Food is such a large burden": Lizzie Widdicombe, "The End of Food," *New Yorker*, 2014, https://www.newyorker.com/magazine/2014/05/12/the-end-of -food.

273 81 percent of those diagnosed with lactose intolerance reported reduced symptoms of indigestion: Ted Beals, "Pilot Survey of Cow Share Consumer/Owners Lactose Intolerance Section," *A Campaign for Real Milk*, 2014, http://www .realmilk.com/health/lactose-intolerance-survey/.

273 consumption of raw milk has a significant benefit in the reduction of allergies and asthma: Mark Holbreich et al., "Amish Children Living in Northern Indiana Have a Very Low Prevalence of Allergic Sensitization," *Journal of Allergy and Clinical Immunology* 129, no. 6 (June 2012): 1671–73, doi:10.1016/j .jaci.2012.03.016; Georg Loss et al., "The Protective Effect of Farm Milk Consumption on Childhood Asthma and Atopy: The GABRIELA Study," *Journal of Allergy and Clinical Immunology* 128, no. 4 (October 2011): 766–73, e4. doi:10.1016/j.jaci.2011.07.048; M. Waser et al., "Inverse Association of Farm Milk Consumption with Asthma and Allergy in Rural and Suburban Populations across Europe," *Clinical and Experimental Allergy: Journal of the British Society for Allergy and Clinical Immunology* 37, no. 5 (May 2007): 661–70, doi:10.1111/j.1365 -2222.2006.02640.x.

273 93 percent of infants showed less allergic reaction to goats' milk: *Nutritional and Dietary Interests of Goat Milk: Proceedings of the Symposium Goat's Milk, an Asset for Health, November 7, 1996* (Niort, France: INRA, 1997).

274 more effective than blueberries or açaí: Stephen J. Crozier et al., "Cacao Seeds Are a 'Super Fruit': A Comparative Analysis of Various Fruit Powders and Products," *Chemistry Central Journal* 5, no. 1 (2010): 5, doi:10.1186/1752 -153X-5-5.

274 caffeine and theobromine that boost mood and cognition: Hendrik J. Smit, Elizabeth A. Gaffan, and Peter J. Rogers, "Methylxanthines Are the Psycho-Pharmacologically Active Constituents of Chocolate," *Psychopharmacology* 176, no. 3–4 (November 5, 2004): 412–19, doi:10.1007/s00213-004-1898-3.

274 boosts nitric oxide production: Tankred Schewe, Yvonne Steffen, and

Helmut Sies, "How Do Dietary Flavanols Improve Vascular Function? A Position Paper," *Archives of Biochemistry and Biophysics* 476, no. 2 (August 15, 2008): 102–6, doi:10.1016/j.abb.2008.03.004.

274   heart-healthy food: Luc Djoussé et al., "Chocolate Consumption Is Inversely Associated with Prevalent Coronary Heart Disease: The National Heart, Lung, and Blood Institute Family Heart Study," *Clinical Nutrition (Edinburgh)* 30, no. 2 (April 2011): 182–87, doi:10.1016/j.clnu.2010.08.005.

275   the famous nocebo effect: Winfried Häuser, Ernil Hansen, and Paul Enck, "Nocebo Phenomena in Medicine: Their Relevance in Everyday Clinical Practice," *Deutsches Ärzteblatt International* 109, no. 26 (2012): 459–65, doi:10.3238/arztebl.2012.0459.

276   would make them run slower, and it did: Christopher J. Beedie, Damian A. Coleman, and Abigail J. Foad, "Positive and Negative Placebo Effects Resulting from the Deceptive Administration of an Ergogenic Aid," *International Journal of Sport Nutrition and Exercise Metabolism* 17, no. 3 (June 2007): 259–69, doi:10.1123/ijsnem.17.3.259.

276   changed their bodies' responses to it: Alia J. Crum et al., "Mind over Milkshakes: Mind-sets, Not Just Nutrients, Determine Ghrelin Response," *Health Psychology: Official Journal of the Division of Health Psychology, American Psychological Association* 30, no. 4 (July 2011): 424–29, doi:10.1037/a0023467.

276   can be vast: Kitty C. M. Verhoeckx et al., "Food Processing and Allergenicity," *Food and Chemical Toxicology* 80 (June 2015): 223–40, doi:10.1016/j.fct.2015.03.005.

277   how far the mind can go when it comes to controlling the body: Daniel Goleman, "Probing the Enigma of Multiple Personality," *New York Times*, 1988, http://www.nytimes.com/1988/06/28/science/probing-the-enigma-of-multiple-personality.html?pagewanted=all.

279   115 percent more likely to be obese: Sook Ling Leong et al., "Faster Self-Reported Speed of Eating Is Related to Higher Body Mass Index in a Nationwide Survey of Middle-Aged Women," *Journal of the American Dietetic Association* 111, no. 8 (August 2011): 1192–97, doi:10.1016/j.jada.2011.05.012.

279   gained the most body weight since age twenty: Rei Otsuka et al., "Eating Fast Leads to Obesity: Findings Based on Self-Administered Questionnaires among Middle-Aged Japanese Men and Women," *Journal of Epidemiology* 16, no. 3 (May 2006): 117–24, http://www.ncbi.nlm.nih.gov/pubmed/16710080.

279   overweight people chew less than normal-weight people: Yong Zhu and James H. Hollis, "Relationship between Chewing Behavior and Body Weight Status in Fully Dentate Healthy Adults," *International Journal of Food Sciences and Nutrition* 66, no. 2 (March 2015): 135–39, doi:10.3109/09637486.2014.979317.

279   15 percent less: Yong Zhu and James H. Hollis, "Increasing the Number of Chews before Swallowing Reduces Meal Size in Normal-Weight, Overweight, and Obese Adults," *Journal of the Academy of Nutrition and Dietetics* 114, no. 6 (June 2014): 926–31, doi:10.1016/j.jand.2013.08.020.

279 slows down your digestion: D. N. Bateman, "Effects of Meal Tempera-ture and Volume on the Emptying of Liquid from the Human Stomach," *Journal of Physiology* 331 (October 1982): 461–67, http://www.ncbi.nlm.nih.gov/pubmed/7153912.

280 "longer, healthier, and more vital life": Jon Barron, "Digestive Enzymes for a Modern Diet," *Baseline of Health Foundation*, 2014, https://jonbarron.org/digestive-health/digestive-enzymes-healthy-diet#footnote12_2oobogi.

281 up to 50 percent: Keng-Liang Wu et al., "Effects of Ginger on Gastric Empty-ing and Motility in Healthy Humans," *European Journal of Gastroenterology and Hepatology* 20, no. 5 (May 2008): 436–40, doi:10.1097/MEG.0b013e3282f4b224.

281 blood vessels dilate: S. Moncada and E. A. Higgs, "Nitric Oxide and the Vascular Endothelium," *Handbook of Experimental Pharmacology*, no. 176, pt. 1 (2006): 213–54, http://www.ncbi.nlm.nih.gov/pubmed/16999221.

281 blood flow and circulation: Kenyatta Cosby et al., "Nitrite Reduction to Nitric Oxide by Deoxyhemoglobin Vasodilates the Human Circulation," *Nature Medicine* 9, no. 12 (December 2, 2003): 1498–1505, doi:10.1038/nm954.

282 easily converted: Klaus D. Kröncke, Karin Fehsel, and Victoria Kolb-Bachofen, "Nitric Oxide: Cytotoxicity versus Cytoprotection—How, Why, When, and Where?," *Nitric Oxide* 1, no. 2 (April 1997): 107–20, doi:10.1006/niox.1997.0118.

283 fat and fiber: I. M. Welch et al., "Duodenal and Ileal Lipid Suppresses Postprandial Blood Glucose and Insulin Responses in Man: Possible Implica-tions for the Dietary Management of Diabetes Mellitus," *Clinical Science* (Lon-don: 1979) 72, no. 2 (1987): 209–16, doi:10.1042/cs0720209; James M. Lattimer and Mark D. Haub, "Effects of Dietary Fiber and Its Components on Meta-bolic Health," *Nutrients* 2, no. 12 (December 15, 2010): 1266–89, doi:10.3390/nu2121266.

283 how you get fat: D. Faeh et al., "Effect of Fructose Overfeeding and Fish Oil Administration on Hepatic De Novo Lipogenesis and Insulin Sensitivity in Healthy Men," *Diabetes* 54, no. 7 (July 1, 2005): 1907–13, doi:10.2337/diabetes.54.7.1907.

284 diminished impact on blood sugar levels: R. K. Conlee, R. M. Lawler, and P. E. Ross, "Effects of Glucose or Fructose Feeding on Glycogen Repletion in Muscle and Liver after Exercise or Fasting," *Annals of Nutrition and Metabolism* 31, no. 2 (1987): 126–32, http://www.ncbi.nlm.nih.gov/pubmed/3592616.

285 dramatically reduced the impact on blood glucose of high-carbohydrate foods: L. M. Morgan et al., "The Effect of Unabsorbable Carbohydrate on Gut Hormones. Modification of Post-Prandial GIP Secretion by Guar," *Diabetologia* 17, no. 2 (August 1979): 85–89, http://www.ncbi.nlm.nih.gov/pubmed/488570.

285 increased satiety: J. F. Bergmann et al., "Correlation between Echographic Gastric Emptying and Appetite: Influence of Psyllium," *Gut* 33, no. 8 (August 1992): 1042–43, http://www.ncbi.nlm.nih.gov/pubmed/1398229.

285 bowel-clearing: J. W. McRorie et al., "Psyllium Is Superior to Docusate

Sodium for Treatment of Chronic Constipation," *Alimentary Pharmacology and Therapeutics* 12, no. 5 (May 1998): 491–97, http://www.ncbi.nlm.nih.gov /pubmed/9663731.

285 blood sugar management: A. M. White and C. S. Johnston, "Vinegar Ingestion at Bedtime Moderates Waking Glucose Concentrations in Adults with Well-Controlled Type 2 Diabetes," *Diabetes Care* 30, no. 11 (November 1, 2007): 2814–15, doi:10.2337/dc07-1062.

285 mild weight loss: Tomoo Kondo et al., "Vinegar Intake Reduces Body Weight, Body Fat Mass, and Serum Triglyceride Levels in Obese Japanese Subjects," *Bioscience, Biotechnology, and Biochemistry* 73, no. 8 (August 2009): 1837–43, http://www.ncbi.nlm.nih.gov/pubmed/19661687.

286 blood sugar reducer: Paul A. Davis and Wallace Yokoyama, "Cinnamon Intake Lowers Fasting Blood Glucose: Meta-Analysis," *Journal of Medicinal Food* 14, no. 9 (September 2011): 884–89, doi:10.1089/jmf.2010.0180.

286 had lower blood sugar levels and less of a peak in blood sugar: Andrew N. Reynolds et al., "Advice to Walk after Meals Is More Effective for Lowering Postprandial Glycaemia in Type 2 Diabetes Mellitus Than Advice That Does Not Specify Timing: A Randomised Crossover Study," *Diabetologia* 59, no. 12 (December 17, 2016): 2572–78, doi:10.1007/s00125-016-4085-2.

287 assists with step 2, the reduction of acetaldehyde: H. Weiner and K. Takahashi, "Effects of Magnesium and Calcium on Mitochondrial and Cytosolic Liver Aldehyde Dehydrogenases," *Pharmacology, Biochemistry, and Behavior* 18 Suppl. 1 (1983): 109–12, http://www.ncbi.nlm.nih.gov/pubmed/6634825.

287 essential for the body's production of chemicals that neutralize acetaldehyde: D. A. Richert and W. W. Westerfeld, "Acetaldehyde Oxidation in Molybdenum Deficiency," *Journal of Biological Chemistry* 227, no. 1 (1957): 533–36; K. V. Rajagopalan, "Molybdenum: An Essential Trace Element in Human Nutrition," *Annual Review of Nutrition* 8 (1988): 401–27, doi:10.1146/annurev .nu.08.070188.002153.

287 reduce regular aches and pains: Margaret Moss, "Effects of Molybdenum on Pain and General Health: A Pilot Study," *Journal of Nutritional and Environmental Medicine* 5, no. 1 (1995): 55–61, doi:10.3109/13590849509008762.

288 dismantles all forms of toxicity, including our nemesis acetaldehyde: Helen Anni, Pavlo Pristatsky, and Yedy Israel, "Binding of Acetaldehyde to a Glutathione Metabolite: Mass Spectrometric Characterization of an Acetaldehyde-Cysteinyl- glycine Conjugate," *Alcoholism, Clinical and Experimental Research* 27, no. 10 (October 2003): 1613–21, doi:10.1097/01.ALC.0000089958.65095.84.

288 good for testosterone: Amy R. Lane, Joseph W. Duke, and Anthony C. Hackney, "Influence of Dietary Carbohydrate Intake on the Free Testosterone: Cortisol Ratio Responses to Short-Term Intensive Exercise Training," *European Journal of Applied Physiology* 108, no. 6 (April 20, 2010): 1125–31, doi:10.1007 /s00421-009-1220-5.

289 helps you sleep: Ahmad Afaghi, Helen O'Connor, and Chin Moi Chow,

"High-Glycemic-Index Carbohydrate Meals Shorten Sleep Onset," *American Journal of Clinical Nutrition* 85, no. 2 (February 2007): 426–30, http://www.ncbi.nlm.nih.gov/pubmed/17284739.

CHAPTER 13: MORE, BETTER SEX

304 having less sex than ever before: Jean M. Twenge, Ryne A. Sherman, and Brooke E. Wells, "Sexual Inactivity during Young Adulthood Is More Common among U.S. Millennials and iGen: Age, Period, and Cohort Effects on Having No Sexual Partners after Age 18," *Archives of Sexual Behavior* 46, no. 2 (February 1, 2017): 433–40, doi:10.1007/s10508-016-0798-z.

304 only once or twice per week: Jean M. Twenge, Ryne A. Sherman, and Brooke E. Wells, "Declines in Sexual Frequency among American Adults, 1989–2014," *Archives of Sexual Behavior*, March 6, 2017, doi:10.1007/s10508-017-0953-1.

307 testosterone has dipped in the USA and worldwide: Thomas G. Travison et al., "A Population-Level Decline in Serum Testosterone Levels in American Men," *Journal of Clinical Endocrinology and Metabolism* 92, no. 1 (January 2007): 196–202, doi:10.1210/jc.2006-1375; Tom R. Trinick et al., "International Web Survey Shows High Prevalence of Symptomatic Testosterone Deficiency in Men," *Aging Male* 14, no. 1 (March 9, 2011): 10–15, doi:10.3109/13685538.2010.511325.

307 twice as likely to experience erectile dysfunction: Juha Koskimäki et al., "Regular Intercourse Protects against Erectile Dysfunction: Tampere Aging Male Urologic Study," *American Journal of Medicine* 121, no. 7 (July 2008): 592–96, doi:10.1016/j.amjmed.2008.02.042.

308 mental health: Stuart Brody and Petr Weiss, "Simultaneous Penile–Vaginal Intercourse Orgasm Is Associated with Satisfaction (Sexual, Life, Partnership, and Mental Health)," *Journal of Sexual Medicine* 8, no. 3 (March 2011): 734–41, doi:10.1111/j.1743-6109.2010.02149.x.

308 immune function: Carl J. Charnetski and Francis X. Brennan, "Sexual Frequency and Salivary Immunoglobulin A (IgA)," *Psychological Reports* 94, no. 3, pt. 1 (June 2004): 839–44, doi:10.2466/pr0.94.3.839-844.

308 depression, wound healing, aging, prostate health, and pain tolerance: Brian Alexander, "Not Just Good, Good for You," *NBC News*, 2013, http://www.nbcnews.com/id/5263250/ns/health-sexual_health/t/not-just-good-good-you/#.WcfvStN96qS.

310 even depression: Charlotte Wessel Skovlund et al., "Association of Hormonal Contraception with Depression," *JAMA Psychiatry* 73, no. 11 (November 1, 2016): 1154–62, doi:10.1001/jamapsychiatry.2016.2387.

310 repelled by those who were different: Melinda Wenner, "Birth Control Pills Affect Women's Taste in Men," *Scientific American*, 2008, https://www.scientificamerican.com/article/birth-control-pills-affect-womens-taste/.

311 saturated fat and cholesterol: David R. Hooper et al., "Endocrinological Roles for Testosterone in Resistance Exercise Responses and Adaptations," *Sports Medicine* 47, no. 9 (September 21, 2017): 1709–20, doi:10.1007/s40279-017-0698-y.

311   testosterone levels to drop with a low-fat diet and bounce back on a high-fat diet: Christina Wang et al., "Low-Fat High-Fiber Diet Decreased Serum and Urine Androgens in Men," *Journal of Clinical Endocrinology and Metabolism* 90, no. 6 (June 2005): 3550–59, doi:10.1210/jc.2004-1530.

311   bumps up testosterone levels 15 percent or more: A. R. Granata et al., "Relationship between Sleep-Related Erections and Testosterone Levels in Men," *Journal of Andrology* 18, no. 5 (1997): 522–27, http://www.ncbi.nlm.nih.gov /pubmed/9349750.

311   curbed testosterone production: Rafael Luboshitzky et al., "Disruption of the Nocturnal Testosterone Rhythm by Sleep Fragmentation in Normal Men," *Journal of Clinical Endocrinology and Metabolism* 86, no. 3 (March 2001): 1134–39, doi:10.1210/jcem.86.3.7296.

311   testosterone increases with heavy lifting: K. Häkkinen et al., "Neuromuscular and Hormonal Adaptations in Athletes to Strength Training in Two Years," *Journal of Applied Physiology* 65, no. 6 (December 1988): 2406–12, http://www .ncbi.nlm.nih.gov/pubmed/3215840.

311   larger muscles contribute to higher testosterone: S. Hansen et al., "The Effect of Short-Term Strength Training on Human Skeletal Muscle: The Importance of Physiologically Elevated Hormone Levels," *Scandinavian Journal of Medicine and Science in Sports* 11, no. 6 (December 2001): 347–54, doi:10.1034/j.1600 -0838.2001.110606.x.

312   rhesus monkey access to an orgasm button: "1953: Dr. John Lilly Used Electric Stimulation to 'Map' Brain Locations That Control Body Functions," *Alliance for Human Research Protection*, http://ahrp.org/1953-dr-john-lilly-used-electric -stimulation-to-map-brain-locations-that-control-body-functions/.

313   described more like a "brother" or "father": C. Wedekind et al., "MHC-Dependent Mate Preferences in Humans," *Proceedings of the Royal Society B: Biological Sciences* 260, no. 1359 (June 22, 1995): 245–49, doi:10.1098 /rspb.1995.0087.

316   *lower levels* of many negative characteristics, including depression, anxiety, post-traumatic stress disorder (PTSD), and paranoia: Pamela H. Connolly, "Psychological Functioning of Bondage/Domination/Sado-Masochism (BDSM) Practitioners," *Journal of Psychology and Human Sexuality* 18, no. 1 (July 24, 2006): 79–120. doi:10.1300/J056v18n01_05.

316   Basically, they were chill AF: Joe Magliano, "The Surprising Psychology of BDSM," *Psychology Today*, 2015, https://www.psychologytoday.com/blog/the -wide-wide-world-psychology/201502/the-surprising-psychology-bdsm.

316   less neurotic and rejection sensitive: Andreas A. J. Wismeijer and Marcel A. L. M. van Assen. "Psychological Characteristics of BDSM Practitioners." *Journal of Sexual Medicine* 10, no. 8 (August 2013): 1943–52, doi:10.1111/jsm.12192.

317   increase the hardness of erections: Grace Dorey et al., "Randomised Controlled Trial of Pelvic Floor Muscle Exercises and Manometric Biofeedback for Erectile Dysfunction," *British Journal of General Practice* 54, no. 508 (2004): 819–25.

319 fresh air and sunlight have been shown to increase nitric oxide: Catharine Paddock, "Sun Exposure Benefits May Outweigh Risks, Say Scientists," *Medical News Today*, 2013, https://www.medicalnewstoday.com/articles/260247.php.

319 laughing or watching funny movies: Bill Seiler, "School of Medicine Study Shows Laughter Helps Blood Vessels Function Better," *University of Maryland Medical Center*, 2005, http://www.umm.edu/news-and-events /news-releases/2005/school-of-medicine-study-shows-laughter-helps-blood-ves sels-function-better.

CHAPTER 14: TURN OFF, TUNE IN

326 between fifty and seventy-five times a day: Craig Wigginton, "Global Mobile Consumer Survey: US Edition," *Deloitte*, 2016, https://www2.deloitte.com/us /en/pages/technology-media-and-telecommunications/articles/global-mobile -consumer-survey-us-edition.html.

327 correlation between self-described addictive phone and internet use and anxiety + depression scores: Tayana Panova and Alejandro Lleras, "Avoidance or Boredom: Negative Mental Health Outcomes Associated with Use of Information and Communication Technologies Depend on Users' Motivations," *Computers in Human Behavior* 58 (May 2016): 249–58, doi:10.1016/j.chb.2015.12.062.

327 releases dopamine powerful enough to override even financial incentives: D. I. Tamir and J. P. Mitchell, "Disclosing Information about the Self Is Intrinsically Rewarding," *Proceedings of the National Academy of Sciences* 109, no. 21 (May 22, 2012): 8038–43, doi:10.1073/pnas.1202129109.

327 the longer one spends on email in an hour, the higher stress levels are: Gloria Mark et al., "Email Duration, Batching and Self-Interruption: Patterns of Email Use on Productivity and Stress," in *Proceedings of the 2016 CHI Conference on Human Factors in Computing Systems—CHI '16* (New York: ACM Press, 2016), 1717–28, doi:10.1145/2858036.2858262.

328 the act of checking can increase stress: Thomas Jackson, "Email Stress," *Professor Jackson's Research*, 2012, http://www.profjackson.com/email_stress.html.

331 the number of things we can hold at once in our conscious: Clara Moskowitz, "Mind's Limit Found: 4 Things at Once," *Live Science*, 2008, https://www .livescience.com/2493-mind-limit-4.html.

332 report feeling happier and less negative: K. A. Baikie and Kay Wilhelm, "Emotional and Physical Health Benefits of Expressive Writing," *Advances in Psychiatric Treatment* 11, no. 5 (September 1, 2005): 338–46, doi:10.1192 /apt.11.5.338.

334 associated with a twenty-two-minute reduction in life expectancy: J. Lennert Veerman et al., "Television Viewing Time and Reduced Life Expectancy: A Life Table Analysis," *British Journal of Sports Medicine* 46, no. 13 (October 24, 2012): 927–30, doi:10.1136/bjsports-2011-085662.

335 ten to twelve favorite books: Aubrey Marcus, "Top 10 Reads," *Aubreymar cus.com*, 2017, https://www.aubreymarcus.com/blogs/aubrey-marcus/tagged/top -10-reads.

336   with rates as high as 99 percent: K. Kretsos and G.B. Kasting, "Dermal Capillary Clearance: Physiology and Modeling." *Skin Pharmacology and Physiology* 18, no. 2 (March 10, 2005): 55–74. doi:10.1159/000083706.

337   increase your chances of infection: Jenny L. Martino and Sten H. Vermund, "Vaginal Douching: Evidence for Risks or Benefits to Women's Health," *Epidemiologic Reviews*, 2002, doi:10.1093/epirev/mxf004.

337   they also emit chemicals: Wendee Nicole, "A Question for Women's Health: Chemicals in Feminine Hygiene Products and Personal Lubricants," *Environmental Health Perspectives* 122, no. 3 (March 1, 2014): A70–75, doi:10.1289/ehp.122-A70.

337   listed by the World Health Organization as a carcinogen: World Health Organization, "Styrene," in *Air Quality Guidelines*, 2nd ed. (Copenhagen, 2000), http://www.euro.who.int/__data/assets/pdf_file/0018/123066/AQG2ndEd_5_12Styrene.pdf?ua=1.

337   chloroform: Agency for Toxic Substances and Disease Registry, "Chloroform," *Toxic Substance Portal*, 2011, https://www.atsdr.cdc.gov/substances/toxsubstance.asp?toxid=16.

CHAPTER 15: SLEEP

345   report sleep difficulties: Russell Rosenburge et al., "Annual Sleep in America Poll Exploring Connections with Communications Technology Use and Sleep," *Sleep.org*, 2011, https://sleepfoundation.org/media-center/press-release/annual-sleep-america-poll-exploring-connections-communications-technology-use-.

346   combat obesity: Shahrad Taheri et al., "Short Sleep Duration Is Associated with Reduced Leptin, Elevated Ghrelin, and Increased Body Mass Index," *PLoS Medicine* 1, no. 3 (December 7, 2004): e62, doi:10.1371/journal.pmed.0010062.

346   improves the immune system: Luciana Besedovsky, Tanja Lange, and Jan Born, "Sleep and Immune Function," *Pflügers Archiv* 463, no. 1 (January 10, 2012): 121–37, doi:10.1007/s00424-011-1044-0.

346   improves all markers of physical performance: Jonathon P. R. Scott, Lars R. McNaughton, and Remco C. J. Polman, "Effects of Sleep Deprivation and Exercise on Cognitive, Motor Performance and Mood," *Physiology and Behavior* 87, no. 2 (February 2006): 396–408, doi:10.1016/j.physbeh.2005.11.009.

346   you can't outsmart sleep: Ed Glauser, "Increase Longevity with Seven Hours of Sleep," *Psychology Today*, 2012, https://www.psychologytoday.com/blog/golden-slumbers/201210/increase-longevity-seven-hours-sleep.

348   polyphasic sleep: "Alternative Sleep Schedule Overviews," *Polyphasic Society*, 2016, https://www.polyphasicsociety.com/polyphasic-sleep/overviews/.

352   counteracts the natural release of melatonin: Mariana G. Figueiro et al., "The Impact of Light from Computer Monitors on Melatonin Levels in College Students," *Neuro Endocrinology Letters* 32, no. 2 (2011): 158–63, http://www.ncbi.nlm.nih.gov/pubmed/21552190.

352   correlation between sleep disturbances and exposure to EMF frequencies:

Martin Röösli et al., "Symptoms of Ill Health Ascribed to Electromagnetic Field Exposure—a Questionnaire Survey," *International Journal of Hygiene and Environmental Health* 207, no. 2 (February 2004): 141–50, doi:10.1078/1438-4639-00269.

353   smartphone: Klodiana Lanaj, Russell E. Johnson, and Christopher M. Barnes, "Beginning the Workday yet Already Depleted? Consequences of Late-Night Smartphone Use and Sleep," *Organizational Behavior and Human Decision Processes* 124, no. 1 (May 2014): 11–23, doi:10.1016/j.obhdp.2014.01.001.

355   estimated 22 million people in the United States: "Sleep Apnea Information for Clinicians," *American Sleep Apnea Association*, 2017, https://www.sleepap nea.org/learn/sleep-apnea-information-clinicians/.

356   significantly reduced participants' sleep apnea: M. A. Puhan et al., "Didgeridoo Playing as Alternative Treatment for Obstructive Sleep Apnoea Syndrome: Randomised Controlled Trial," *BMJ* 332 (February 4, 2006): 266–70, doi:10.1136/bmj.38705.470590.55.

358   0.5 milligrams of melatonin: Lisa M. Hack et al., "The Effects of Low-Dose 0.5-Mg Melatonin on the Free-Running Circadian Rhythms of Blind Subjects," *Journal of Biological Rhythms* 18, no. 5 (October 2003): 420–29, doi:10.1177/0748730403256796.

358   isn't necessarily better: K. Marrin et al., "A Meta-Analytic Approach to Quantify the Dose–Response Relationship between Melatonin and Core Temperature," *European Journal of Applied Physiology* 113 (September 16, 2013): 2323–29, doi:10.1007/s00421-013-2668-x.

CHAPTER 16: BRING IT HOME

362   give up on all their New Year's resolutions by February: Joseph Luciani, "Why 80 Percent of New Year's Resolutions Fail," *U.S. News & World Report*, 2015, https://health.usnews.com/health-news/blogs/eat-run/articles/2015-12-29/why-80-percent-of-new-years-resolutions-fail.

366   Pete Carroll built one for his entire organization: Tatiyana Sussex, "Leadership and Coaching Philosophies from Superbowl-bound Pete Carroll," *Liquid Planner Blog*, January 31, 2014, https://www.liquidplanner.com/blog/leadership-and-coaching-philosophies-from-superbowl-bound-pete-carroll/.

INDEX

Hancock, Graham, 260
happiness
  deathbed regrets, 266–67
  Emerson on, 143
  of employees, 141, 142
  income level and, 140
  work and, 144
Harbinger, Jordan, 362
Hardcore History (podcast), 109
Harvard mind-set study, 249–50
HCL supplements, 280
headaches, 10, 11, 80, 125, 150, 183,
  260
health and longevity, 1
  acute stress and, 32, 37, 49
  American mortality rates, 32
  blue zones, 174
  chronic stress and, 32
  digestive enzymes and, 280
  exercise and, 210
  good inflammation and, 38–39
  IF and, 68–69, 76
  loneliness and, 254
  pet ownership, benefits of, 264
  sex and, 308
  sickness in America, 32
  sitting at work and, 147
  sleep and, 346
  strong social relationships and, 255
  sugar and, 54, 56, 59, 60, 62, 76
  See also specific conditions, diseases
Healthy Workplace, The, 145
heartburn, 279–80
heart disease
  dietary fat and, 59, 60, 61–62, 178
  increase in, 59
  margarine or butter substitutes,
  178
  obesity and, 16
  sugar linked to, 54, 56, 59, 60, 62
heavy metals, 181–82
hedonic tolerance, 309, 311–12
Heffernan, Margaret, 325
hemp seeds, 166
Heraclitus, 361
Herrigel, Eugen, *Zen in the Art of
  Archery*, 103

History on Fire (podcast), 109
Hof, Wim, 30, 33, 34, 42
  Lamaze and, 36–37
  method (breathing exercise), 35–36
Hogan, Hulk, 77
Holker, Allison, 5
hormesis, 37–38, 49
  appropriate dose and, 46, 47
  cold and, 38, 40, 43–47
  exercise and, 211
  heat and, 42–43
  vaginal birth and, 80
Howes, Lewis, 109
Huerta, Roger, 214–15
Huffington, Arianna, 344
HumanCharger25, 21–22
hunger and satiety, 53, 169, 170, 285
Huperzia serrata (club moss), 132–34,
  136
Huxley, Aldous, 127
  Island, 299
hydration. *See* dehydration; water
hyperthemic conditioning, 42–43

I Am Not Your Guru (film), 26
immune system
  anthocyanins as booster, 175
  chronic stress and, 32
  gut biomes and, 80, 122
  Hof altering inflammatory response,
  33
  mini trampoline for, 26
  vaginal birth and, 80
  vitamin D and, 81
inflammation, 38–40
  antinutrients and, 177
  chronic, 39
  chronic stress and, 32, 40
  cold or flu and, 39
  cold to modulate, 38
  C-reactive protein and, 175
  curcuminoids to reduce, 175
  good vs. bad, 39–40
  Hof and altering immune response
  to, 33, 39–40
  how it feels, 87
  krill oil to reduce, 86, 95

ABOUT THE AUTHOR

Aubrey Marcus is the founder and CEO of Onnit, one of the fastest-growing human performance companies in America. His philosophy has attracted hundreds of thousands of customers and millions of fans, among them dozens of elite performers. Marcus is also the host of the celebrated *Aubrey Marcus Podcast*. He resides in Austin, Texas.